Labour Law in Cyprus

Labour Law in Cyprus

Achilles Emilianides & Christina Ioannou

This book was originally published as a monograph in the International Encyclopaedia of Laws/Labour Law and Industrial Relations.

General Editors: Roger Blanpain, Frank Hendrickx

Wolters Kluwer

Published by:
Kluwer Law International B.V.
PO Box 316
2400 AH Alphen aan den Rijn
The Netherlands
Website: www.wklawbusiness.com

Sold and distributed in North, Central and South America by:
Wolters Kluwer Legal & Regulatory U.S.
7201 McKinney Circle
Frederick, MD 21704
United States of America
Email: customer.service@wolterskluwer.com

Sold and distributed in all other countries by:
Turpin Distribution Services Ltd.
Stratton Business Park
Pegasus Drive, Biggleswade
Bedfordshire SG18 8TQ
United Kingdom
Email: kluwerlaw@turpin-distribution.com

ISBN 978-90-411-8660-7

e-Book: ISBN 978-90-411-8661-4
web-PDF: ISBN 978-90-411-8662-1

This title is available on www.kluwerlawonline.com

The Authors

Achilles Emilianides is a Professor, Head of the Department of Law at the University of Nicosia, and a practising advocate. He holds a PhD in Law and an LLM in History, Philosophy and Sociology of Law from the Aristotle University of Thessaloniki and an LLM in European Law and Integration from Leicester University. He has handled several high profile cases and has been involved in legal consultancy and funded research. During the Cypriot Presidency of the Council of the European Union in 2012 he acted as the Chairman of two working groups of the European Council. Major publications include: *Media Law in Cyprus* (Kluwer, 2015), *Private International Law in Cyprus* (Kluwer, 2015), *Religion and Law in Cyprus* (2nd edn, Kluwer, 2014), *Cypriot Succession Law* (2nd edn, Hippasus, 2014), *Annotated Legal Documents on Islam in Cyprus* (Brill, 2014), *Constitutional Law in Cyprus* (Kluwer 2013), *Family and Succession Law in Cyprus* (Kluwer 2012), *The New European Private International Law of Contracts* (2009, in Greek), *Cypriot Law of Public Procurement* (2007, in Greek), *Professional Law of Advocates* (2007, in Greek), *Parliamentary History of Cyprus 1964–1976* (2007, in Greek), *Beyond the Cyprus Constitution* (2006, in Greek), *The Cypriot Law of Marriage and Divorce* (2006, in Greek), *Bibliography of Cyprus Law* (2005), *The Parliamentary Co-existence of Greeks and Turks in Cyprus* (2003, in Greek).

The Authors

Christina Ioannou is an Associate Professor of European Politics and Labour Law in the Department of European Studies and International Relations and the Department of Law of the University of Nicosia. She holds a PhD and MA from the University of Manchester and a BSc from the University of Warwick. She is the coordinator of the MA programme in European Public Law and Politics. She acts as a consultant on labour and employment law issues with the Law Firm A. & E. C. Emilianides, C. Katsaros and Associates LLC. She is a member of the board of directors of the Centre of Scientific Dialogue and Research. Her areas of specialization include labour law, European integration, Europeanization and social policy. She has participated in a number of EU funded projects, as well as a number of conferences, colloquia and discussion networks. Her latest publications include articles in international peer reviewed journals, book chapters and the edited volume *Cyprus in the New Era* (2014, in Greek).

Table of Contents

Preface

This study consists of an extensive analysis of the Cypriot legislation, case law and theory concerning labour and employment law. It is the first time that a comprehensive monograph about labour law and employment has been published in the English language. While each chapter retains its autonomy, the reader might benefit significantly from reading the general introduction first, which provides the basis for understanding the historical background and social data.

This project is a joint effort, and accordingly we share responsibility for the entirety of the monograph. We are indebted to numerous persons who have provided assistance in collecting data and engaging in discussions with us. The teaching of labour and employment law at the University of Nicosia, both at the LLB and the LLM level, has been a source of inspiration in the writing of this book. The *International Encyclopaedia of Laws* and editor Roger Blanpain were kind enough to include this monograph in their *Encyclopaedia*. Without them and the publisher, Kluwer Law International, this volume would have never been written. We would like to thank our family and friends for their support during all these years.

This monograph is jointly dedicated to Zeta and Carolina, who share the same birthday, albeit sixty years apart.

Christina Ioannou & Achilles C. Emilianides

List of Abbreviations

AETR	European Agreement concerning the Work of Crews of Vehicles Engaged in International Road Transport
AKEL	Progressive Party of Working People
BOT	Build–Operate–Transfer
CJEU	Court of Justice of the European Union
COLA	Cost of Living Allowance
CYTA	Cyprus Telecommunications Authority
DEOK	Democratic Labour Federation of Cyprus
DISY	Democratic Rally
EAC	Electricity Authority of Cyprus
EAE	Association of European Airlines
EC	European Community
ECA	European Cockpit Association
ECB	European Central Bank
ECHR	European Convention of Human Rights
ECtHR	European Court of Human Rights
EEA	European Economic Area
EEC	European Economic Community
EOKA	National Organization of Cypriot Fighters
ERA	European Regions Airline Association
ETF	European Transport Workers' Federation
ETYK	Cyprus Union of Bank Employees
EU	European Union
EWC	European Works Councils
GDP	Gross Domestic Product
GMI	Guaranteed Minimum Income
IACA	International Air Carrier Association

List of Abbreviations

IDT	Industrial Dispute Tribunal
ILO	International Labour Organization
IMF	International monetary Fund
IRC	Industrial Relations Code
JLC	Joint Labour Committee
JSC	Joint Staff Committee
KEBE	Cyprus Chamber of Commerce and Industry
KEST	Cyprus Bank Employers' Association
MoU	Memorandum of Understanding
OEB	Employers and Industrialists Federation
OELMEK	Organization of Greek Secondary Education Teachers
OSEOK	Cyprus Federation of the Association of Building Constructors
PASYDY	Pancyprian Trade Union of Public Servants
PASYXE	Pancyprian Association of Hoteliers
PEO	Pancyprian Federation of Labour
POAS	Pancyprian Federation of Independent Trade Unions
POED	Pancyprian Organization of Greek Teachers
POVEK	Pancyprian Professional Small Shopkeepers' Federation
PTUC	Pancyprian Trade Union Committee
SEK	Cyprus Workers' Federation
SNB	Special Negotiating Body
TEU	Treaty on European Union
TFEU	Treaty on the Functioning of the European Union
TRNC	Turkish Republic of Northern Cyprus
UN	United Nations

List of Abbreviations

IDT	Industrial Dispute Tribunal
ILO	International Labour Organization
IMF	International monetary Fund
IRC	Industrial Relations Code
JLC	Joint Labour Committee
JSC	Joint Staff Committee
KEBE	Cyprus Chamber of Commerce and Industry
KEST	Cyprus Bank Employers' Association
MoU	Memorandum of Understanding
OEB	Employers and Industrialists Federation
OELMEK	Organization of Greek Secondary Education Teachers
OSEOK	Cyprus Federation of the Association of Building Constructors
PASYDY	Pancyprian Trade Union of Public Servants
PASYXE	Pancyprian Association of Hoteliers
PEO	Pancyprian Federation of Labour
POAS	Pancyprian Federation of Independent Trade Unions
POED	Pancyprian Organization of Greek Teachers
POVEK	Pancyprian Professional Small Shopkeepers' Federation
PTUC	Pancyprian Trade Union Committee
SEK	Cyprus Workers' Federation
SNB	Special Negotiating Body
TEU	Treaty on European Union
TFEU	Treaty on the Functioning of the European Union
TRNC	Turkish Republic of Northern Cyprus
UN	United Nations

List of Abbreviations

AETR	European Agreement concerning the Work of Crews of Vehicles Engaged in International Road Transport
AKEL	Progressive Party of Working People
BOT	Build–Operate–Transfer
CJEU	Court of Justice of the European Union
COLA	Cost of Living Allowance
CYTA	Cyprus Telecommunications Authority
DEOK	Democratic Labour Federation of Cyprus
DISY	Democratic Rally
EAC	Electricity Authority of Cyprus
EAE	Association of European Airlines
EC	European Community
ECA	European Cockpit Association
ECB	European Central Bank
ECHR	European Convention of Human Rights
ECtHR	European Court of Human Rights
EEA	European Economic Area
EEC	European Economic Community
EOKA	National Organization of Cypriot Fighters
ERA	European Regions Airline Association
ETF	European Transport Workers' Federation
ETYK	Cyprus Union of Bank Employees
EU	European Union
EWC	European Works Councils
GDP	Gross Domestic Product
GMI	Guaranteed Minimum Income
IACA	International Air Carrier Association

6. The House of Representatives would consist of 50 Representatives; 70 per cent of the members of the House of Representatives were to be elected separately by the members of the Greek Community, while 30 per cent were to be elected separately by the members of the Turkish Community. The President of the House of Representatives would be a Greek Cypriot, elected from among the Greek Cypriot Representatives, while the Vice-President would be a Turkish Cypriot, elected from among the Turkish Cypriot Representatives. Any amendments to the electoral law, the passing of laws concerning municipalities and laws imposing taxes or duties, would require a separate majority among Greek and Turkish Cypriot representatives, present and voting. In addition, the amendment of non-fundamental constitutional provisions would require a two-thirds majority of the representatives of each Community, voting separately. The Constitution also provided for two communal chambers: a Greek communal chamber and a Turkish communal chamber, which should have legislative power in educational, cultural, religious and other matters of purely communal nature.

7. It was further provided that judicial power was to be exercised by the Supreme Constitutional Court, the Supreme Court and their subordinate courts. The Supreme Constitutional Court should be composed of a non-Cypriot citizen as its President, and two members, a Greek Cypriot and a Turkish Cypriot, all appointed jointly by the President and Vice-President of the Republic. The Supreme Court would consist of two Greek Cypriot judges and one Turkish Cypriot judge, while the President of the Court would also be a non-Cypriot. The bi-communal element was evident in the judiciary. The composition of the security forces was also based on increased proportions: an army of 2,000 men should consist of 60 per cent Greek Cypriots and 40 per cent Turkish Cypriots, while the Public Service, Police, Gendarmerie would be composed on the basis of a 7:3 ratio.

8. Essentially the structure provided by the Constitution aimed at ensuring that each Community would enjoy partial administrative autonomy, while at the same time the numerically smaller Turkish Community would effectively participate in the exercise and functions of government in such a way as to avoid the supremacy of the larger Community. De Smith noted that the 1960 Constitution is a tragic and occasionally an almost ludicrous document and that it is possibly the most rigid, detailed and complicated Constitution in the world, weighed down by checks and balances, procedural and substantive safeguards, guarantees and prohibitions which set daunting obstacles to the people who are called on to abide to it.[6]

9. The Zurich Agreement failed to establish cooperation between the Greek and Turkish Communities on the island[7] and proved to be unworkable in practice.[8] In

6. A. S. De Smith, *The New Commonwealth and its Constitutions* (London: Stevens & Sons, 1964): 296.
7. See A. Emilianides, *The Parliamentary Co-existence of Greeks and Turks in Cyprus* (Nicosia: Epiphaniou, 2003, in Greek).
8. See C. Tornaritis, *Peculiarities of the Constitution of Cyprus and Effect on the Normal Function of the State* (Nicosia, 1980, in Greek); T.W. Adams, 'The First Republic of Cyprus: Review of an Unworkable Constitution', *Western Political Quarterly* 19 (1966): 475–490.

1963 there was an outbreak of violence in the island, which led to a constitutional breakdown.[9] In 1964 a United Nations (UN) Peacekeeping operation was stationed on the island and has remained there ever since.[10] In July 1974, Turkey invaded Cyprus and occupied the northern part of the island.[11] As a result of the Turkish invasion, the Greeks and other Christians of the region were displaced to the southern part of the island, whereas the Turks of the southern part of the island were forced to move to the north. The area occupied by Turkey amounts to 36.4 per cent of the territory of the Republic of Cyprus. Some 43,000 Turkish troops continue to be based on the island, while settlers from Turkey were brought to Cyprus in an effort to change its demographic character.[12]

10. Resolution 3212/74 of the General Assembly of the UN demanded that all foreign armed forces leave at once from the Republic of Cyprus and that any foreign intervention in the Republic's affairs should cease immediately. This Resolution was endorsed by Resolution 365/74 of the Security Council. As a result the Republic of Cyprus has been prevented from exercising its powers over its occupied territory since 1974. Negotiations for the solution of the Cyprus problem have so far failed to produce results.[13] In 1983, the Turkish-occupied area declared itself the 'Turkish Republic of Northern Cyprus' (TRNC); this entity is recognized only by Turkey. The fact that the government of the Republic of Cyprus is the only internationally recognized government has also been confirmed by various decisions of international courts, such as the European Court of Justice (ECJ)[14] and the European Court of Human Rights (ECtHR).[15] The so-called TRNC was held to be a subordinate administration to Turkey.

11. As a result of the Cyprus problem and the abnormal constitutional situation prevailing in the island, a significant number of constitutional provisions which refer to the Turkish Cypriot community have not been in force for over forty years,

9. See S. Kyriakides, *Cyprus: Constitutionalism and Crisis Government* (Philadelphia: University of Pennsylvania Press, 1968).
10. See A. Emilianides, 'The United Nations Forces Function, Its International Conflicts and Civil Strifes', in *Melanges Bridel* (Lausanne: Imprimeries Réunies, 1968): 147–168.
11. Security Council Resolution 360/1974. See I. Brownlie, 'The Prohibition of the Use of Armed Force for the Solution of International Differences with Particular Reference to the Affairs of the Republic of Cyprus' in *International Law Conference on Cyprus* (Nicosia: Cyprus Bar Council, 1979): 198–213, D. Constantopoulos, *The Turkish Invasion of Cyprus from the Aspect of International Law* (Thessaloniki, 1978).
12. See C. Tornaritis, *The Turkish Invasion of Cyprus and Legal Problems Arising therefrom* (Nicosia, 1975).
13. See, *inter alia*, A. Emilianides *et al.*, *The Annan Plan: Five Critical Essays* (Ypsilon/Egean 2003, in Greek); C. Palley, *An International Relations Debacle* (Hart 2005); A. Syrigos, *The Annan Plan: The Legacies of the Past and the Prospects of the Future* (Patakis 2005, in Greek); A. Emilianides, M. Kontos, G. Kentas, *A Marked Deck: The Confidential Documents of the Negotiations between Christofias and Talat* (Power Publishing 2010, in Greek).
14. Case C-432/92, *R* v. *Minister of Agriculture, Fisheries and Food*, ex p. *S. P. Anastasiou (Pissouri) Ltd and Others* [1994] ECR I-3087.
15. *Loizidou* v. *Turkey*, ECHR Judgment of 23 March 1995 and 18 December 1996; *Cyprus* v. *Turkey*, ECtHR Judgment of 10 May 2001.

even though they are considered to be fundamental and thus not subject to modification. A doctrine of necessity has been accepted by the Supreme Court of Cyprus, so that the House of Representatives may enact laws, even contrary to those provisions of the Constitution which are temporarily not in force because of the Cyprus problem.[16] This has resulted in a fundamental differentiation between the written form of the 1960 Constitution and the living Constitution as applied in Cypriot case law and practice since 1964.

12. On 1 May 2004, the Republic of Cyprus, including the occupied territory, joined the European Union (EU).[17] However, the application of the *acquis communautaire* in the occupied areas has been suspended. In the landmark *Orams* case the ECJ held that the suspension of the application of the *acquis* in the occupied areas should be interpreted restrictively and must be limited to what was absolutely necessary to attain its objectives. The suspension is therefore limited to the application of the *acquis* in the northern area of the Republic of Cyprus, which is currently not under the effective control of the Republic; the suspension, however, does not apply with respect to judgments of courts sitting in the government-controlled area, the recognition of which is sought, even if such judgments concern land situated in the occupied areas.[18] Furthermore, the provisions of Cypriot law and the *acquis* do not apply in the British sovereign base areas, which despite being geographically part of Cyprus, do not form part of the Republic of Cyprus.[19] All references in this study are to the law as applied in the Republic of Cyprus.

16. On the doctrine see A. Emilianides, 'Accession of the Republic of Cyprus to the EU, the Constitution and the Cypriot Doctrine of Necessity', *Cyprus Yearbook of International Relations* [2007]: 65–82, Idem, *Beyond the Constitution of Cyprus* (Thessaloniki: Sakkoulas, 2006, in Greek), C. Tornaritis, *The Principle of Necessity and the Cypriot Legal System* (Nicosia, 1978, in Greek), P. Polyviou, *The Case of Ibrahim, the Doctrine of Necessity and the Republic of Cyprus*, Nicosia: Chryssafinis and Polyviou, 2015, C. Kombos, *The Doctrine of Necessity in Constitutional Law* (Athens: Sakkoulas, 2015), L. Papaphilippou, *The Doctrine of Necessity and the Constitutional Order of Cyprus* (Nicosia, 1995, in Greek).
17. See S. Laulhé-Shaelou, *The EU and Cyprus: Principles and Strategies of Full Integration* (Leiden: Brill, 2010), A. Markides, 'The Cyprus Problem as a Legal Problem within Europe', *Revue Européenne de Droit Public* 12 (2000): 1195–1214, A. Syrigos, 'Cyprus and the EU: Sovereign State, Negotiations and Objections from an International Law Point of View', in A. Theophanous, N. Peristianis, A. Ioannou (eds.), *Cyprus and the European Union* (Nicosia: Intercollege Press, 1999): 91– 106.
18. C-420/07, *Orams* v. *Apostolides* [2009] ECR I-3571.
19. See A. Emilianides, *Constitutional Law in Cyprus* (The Hague: Kluwer, 2013), S. Theodoulou, *Bases militaires en droit international: le cas de Chypre* (Manheim: Bibliopolis, 2006), A. Pellet, 'The British Sovereign Areas', *The Cyprus Yearbook of International Law* [2012]: 57–72. See also S. Laulhe Shaelou, 'Focus on Territorial Exclusion and SuiGenerisTerritories in the EU: The British Bases in Cyprus. A Special Case', *The Cyprus Yearbook of International Law* [2012]: 73–110, C. Theodoulou, *The Legal Status of the British Military Base Areas in the Territory of the Republic of Cyprus* (Nicosia, 1995, in Greek), L. Papaphilippou, *The Legal Status of the British Base Areas in Cyprus: Nature and Extent of the Sovereignty of the British Authorities* (Nicosia, 1993, in Greek).

III. Vital Statistics

A. Population

13. According to the official census of 1960, the population of Cyprus was 573,666, out of whom 441,656 (77 per cent) were of Greek origin and adhered to the Orthodox Christian religion, while 104,492 (18.3 per cent) were of Turkish origin and adhered to the Islamic religion. The ratio between Greek and Turkish Cypriots had not been materially affected prior to the Turkish invasion of 1974. Since the Turkish invasion, providing precise figures with respect to the population of Cyprus has presented certain difficulties, due to the abnormal situation prevailing on the island. According to the 2011 official census the population of Cyprus (Turkish Cypriots residing in the occupied areas excluded) was 840,407, out of whom 667,398 (79.41 per cent) were Cypriots, 106,270 (12.64 per cent) were European citizens and 64,113 (7.62 per cent) were third country nationals (the majority being Asian or Russian nationals).[20]

14. The actual number of Turkish Cypriots residing in Cyprus is difficult to estimate with precision, as the numbers of settlers from Turkey currently residing in Cyprus cannot be determined with accuracy. It is estimated, however, that more than 100,000 settlers from mainland Turkey are currently residing in the occupied areas. These settlers are not included in any estimation of the current population of Cyprus, as it was considered that any potential legalization of the Turkish settlers would illegally modify the demographic structure of the island and threaten the stability and security of the Republic.[21] This view has also been adopted by the Council of Europe.[22] While the Statistical Service of the Republic of Cyprus estimated in 2006 that the number of Turkish Cypriots currently residing in the areas not controlled by the Republic reached approximately 89,000, the actual number may be closer to 130,000 as estimated by Turkish Cypriot sources.[23] Turkish Cypriot representatives increase the number to 220,000.[24]

B. Employment

15. The blow inflicted on the economy by the Turkish invasion of 1974 was devastating. Considering, however, that the occupied part of the country at that time accounted for almost 70 per cent of Gross Domestic Product (GDP), recovery was

20. The remaining 0.33 per cent were unidentified.
21. L. Loucaides, 'Expulsion of Settlers from Occupied Territories: The Case of Turkish Settlers'. in *idem*, *Essays on the Developing Law of Human Rights* (Dordrecht: Martinus Nijhoff, 1995): 108–138, A. De Zayas, 'The Annan Plan and the Implantation of Turkish Settlers in Northern Cyprus', *The Cyprus Yearbook of International Relations* [2006]: 163–178.
22. Council of Europe, 2 May 2003, Doc. 9799, *Colonisation by Turkish Settlers of the Occupied Part of Cyprus* (Rapporteur Mr Laakso).
23. See also M. Hatay, *Is the Turkish Cypriot Population Shrinking?* (Oslo: PRIO, 2007).
24. 'They raise the number of Turkish Cypriots to 220,000', *Phileleftheros*, 6 November 2015 (in Greek).

IV. Distinction between Private and Public Sectors

21. Cypriot law distinguishes between employees of the private and the public (or semi-public)[30] sector. The employment relationships of public servants are governed by the principles of administrative law,[31] rather than labour law, unless where the labour law legislation explicitly applies also to permanent employees of the public service or the semi-public sector. It should be noted, however, that non-permanent employees of the public sector are not considered as public servants and accordingly their employment relationship is not governed by public law, but by private law and in particular labour law legislation.[32] Thus, the status of non-permanent employees of the public sector is the same as the status of private sector employees; it is only permanent public sector employees who enjoy a special constitutional status.

22. A question arose recently whether employees of the wider public sector, and in particular semi-public sector, enjoy the same status as that of permanent employees of the strictly defined public sector. Expressing his opinion with regard to the 2014 privatization law, the Attorney-General of the Republic opined that the employees of the semi-public sector should not be considered as enjoying an equivalent permanent status as public sector employees. This was based on the definition of 'public service' in the Public Service Law 1/1990 which defines public service as referring only to public sector in the strict sense, i.e. excluding semi-public organizations.

23. However, Law 1/1990 is a specialized law whose aim is precisely to regulate the status of employees of the public sector in the strict sense and it could accordingly not be expected to regulate employees of the semi-public sector who are regulated by other specialized legislation. On the other hand, Article 122 of the Constitution, which is the relevant constitutional provision, provides that the term 'public service' also includes the semi-public sector, i.e. employment in legal persons of public law. The public law status of employees of the semi-public sector thus arises directly from the Constitution and no distinction should accordingly be drawn between permanent public law employees of the public and the semi-public sectors. It is therefore submitted that both the Constitution and the existing case law

30. The semi-public sector includes a great number of organizations, such as the Cyprus Telecommunications Authority, the Electricity Authority of Cyprus, local authorities, independent collective organs, public universities etc. For a detailed list see V. Georgiou, *Public Administration in Cyprus* (Nicosia: En Typois, 2012, in Greek).
31. See in general A. Emilianides, *Constitutional Law in Cyprus* (The Hague: Kluwer, 2013), N. Charalambous, *The Action and Control of Public Administration*, 3rd edn (Nicosia, 2013, in Greek), A. Angelides, S. Angelides, *Administrative Procedural Law* (Nicosia: Cyprus Bar Association, 2011, in Greek), C. Melides, 'Administrative Law', in Andreas Neocleous & Co LLC, *Introduction to Cyprus Law*, 3rd edn (Limassol, 2010): 87–117, Z. Nedjati, *Cyprus Administrative Law* (Nicosia, 1970), A. Angelides, 'Administrative Law: Article 146 of the Constitution', *Cyprus Law Review* 12 (1985): 1926–1935; *Cyprus Law Review* 13 (1986): 2111–2128 (in Greek), S. Angelides, 'Administrative Law in the Republic of Cyprus' *Cyprus and European Law Review* 8 (2008): 213–280 (in Greek).
32. *Avraam* v. *The Republic* [2008] 3 CLR.

of the Supreme Court support the conclusion that permanent employees of the semi-public sector should be deemed to enjoy the same status as permanent employees of the public sector.[33]

24. According to Article 125 of the Constitution, the Public Service Commission has the exclusive competence to appoint, promote, transfer, retire and exercise disciplinary control over public officers. The Public Service Commission was to be composed, by virtue of Article 124 of the Constitution, of ten members, seven Greek Cypriots and three Turkish Cypriots. If the issue concerned whether a vacant post should be filled by a Greek, or a Turkish Cypriot, a minimum number of votes from either Community were needed for a decision to be reached. However, the Public Service Commission provided in the Constitution has ceased to function due to the abnormal situation prevailing since 1963 and has been replaced by a new Public Service Commission established by law.[34]

25. The new Public Service Commission was initially established by the Public Service Law 33/67 and is currently governed by the provisions of the Public Service Law 1/90. It is comprised of five members – one of which acts as President of the Public Service Commission – who are appointed by the President of the Republic for a six-year period; they cannot be dismissed from office, except for the same reason and in the same manner as judges of the Supreme Court. The Public Service Commission has competence over public servants, but not over employees of the wider public service or public corporations; the matters concerning the latter fall under the competence of the board of the respective corporation. It has been held that the law regarding the new Public Service Commission must be as similar as possible to the constitutional provisions.[35]

26. It has been repeatedly held that the House of Representatives cannot involve itself directly or indirectly in the appointment or termination of appointment of public service personnel. The Supreme Court has held that the House of Representatives may, in accordance with the Constitution, prohibit by legislation the engagement of temporary employees by the Republic, even if expenditure by means of the Budget of the Republic has been approved for this purpose;[36] however, a provision whereby the procedure for the approval of the engagement of casual employees is subject to the approval of the House of Representatives is unconstitutional, since this would entail the House of Representatives interfering with the exercise of the administrative powers of the Council of Ministers in relation to the general

33. *Cyprus Tourism Organization* v. *Hadjidemetriou* [1987] 3 CLR 780, *Messaritou* v. *Cyprus Broadcasting Corporation* [1972] 3 CLR 100. See also the obiter comments in *President of the Republic* v. *House of Representatives* [2011] 3 CLR 777.

34. *The Republic* v. *Kyriacou* [1987] 3 CLR 1189, *Hadjianastassiou* v. *The Republic* [1982] 3 CLR 1173, *Coupepides* v. *TheRepublic* [1980] 3 CLR 256. See also A. Emilianides, *Beyond the Constitution of Cyprus* (Sakkoulas: Thessaloniki, 2006, in Greek).

35. *The Republic* v. *Kyriacou* [1987] 3 CLR 1189.

36. [1985] 3 CLR 1724, [1991] 3 CLR 746 (in Greek).

direction and control of the government of the Republic under Article 54(a) of the Constitution.[37]

27. Similarly, it has been held that the House of Representatives may not enact legislation to provide for the permanent appointment to the public service of employees serving on a temporary basis, even if such a law is enacted with the concurrence of the Council of Ministers or the President of the Republic. This is due to the fact that the appointment of members of the public service is a matter outside of the legislative sphere and within the exclusive competence of the Public Service Commission. Appointment by legislation would not only violate the principle of separation of powers, but would also be inconsistent with the principle of equality, since it would not grant to all individuals the necessary qualifications an equal right to compete for appointment to the said positions in the public service. The Supreme Court has therefore repeatedly held that vacancies should be properly advertised, affording everyone having the qualifications the opportunity to apply for appointment; personalised legislation aiming at transforming temporary employees into permanent ones cannot be tolerated.[38]

28. It used to be that only citizens of the Republic could be appointed as members of the Public Service of the Republic in accordance with Article 123 of the Constitution. The accession of the Republic of Cyprus to the EU has somewhat changed the absolutism of this requirement. Section 31 of the Public Service Law 1/1990, as modified by Section 3(a) of Law 128(I)/2003, provides that only citizens of the Republic may be appointed as members of the Public Service of the Republic; however, if the position does not imply direct or indirect participation in the exercise of public power and the preservation of the general interests of the state, members of the EU or the European Economic Area (EEA), or Switzerland, may be appointed. Section 31(f) further provides that the Council of Ministers may, in exceptional circumstances, and for the public interests, permit a person who is not a citizen of the Republic to apply for appointment to the Public Service.

V. Underlying Social Values and Their Effect on Social Policy

29. In a study of small European states, Katzenstein puts forward the idea that small states tend to regulate their social systems more actively than larger ones. This is the result of an effort to offset the negative effects brought upon them as a result of their small size, which makes them susceptible to external shocks, owing to their weak and fragile international position.[39] This argument seems very fitting for the small state of Cyprus, as indeed, through the country's industrial relations structure, a great degree of control is exerted over labour policy issues. In the case of Cyprus,

37. [1985] 3 CLR 1724.
38. *Republic* v. *Yiallourou* [1995] 3 CLR 363 (in Greek), *Menelaou* v. *Republic* [1996] 3 CLR 370 (in Greek), *Elia* v. *Republic* [1999] 3 CLR 884 (in Greek).
39. P. Katzenstein, *Small States in World Markets: Industrial Policy in Europe* (Ithaca: Cornell University Press, 1985).

however, apart from having to compensate for its small size and vulnerability, the country is also faced with some distinct problems which, as already indicated, relate to its political situation. It could be suggested then, that owing to these factors, Cyprus may be even more predisposed than other small European states, to protect its citizens through domestic policies.

30. The key to understanding the 'Cypriot corporatist model'[40] is by examining its reliance on cooperation between a set of organized interests and the state. It is, in effect, a tripartite structure of cooperation between the trade unions, the employers' associations and the Government of the Republic (through the Ministry of Labour, Welfare and Social Insurance) – the three social partners that constitute the 'model'. A tradition of smooth cooperation between the social partners exists in the industrial arrangement of the country. The 'corporatist culture' of the island has been the main variable in securing a climate of cooperation between the social partners over time.

31. Over the years, the system had succeeded in bringing industrial peace in the island. The success of the system of industrial relations in Cyprus rests upon the willingness of the social partners to cooperate and on voluntariness rather than legislative imposition. Collective agreements, though not legally binding, have rarely been violated over the years. Following the Turkish invasion of 1974 and the catastrophe which occurred to the fabric of Cypriot society, the social partners showed a capacity to cooperate with one another in order to alleviate the problems created. They agreed to suspend the COLA system, which had been a major achievement of years of struggles by the working force. In other words, during the period from 1974 until 1978 (when COLA was re-introduced) wages stopped rising. This reduced the overall cost to the economy, helping it to recover sooner. This suspension of the COLA system is considered to be a great sacrifice on the part of trade unions during a crisis point. In other words, the experience has been incorporated into a vision of the essentially cooperative nature of the Cypriot model.

32. It can thus be argued that the need for physical survival, as a result of the invasion, in a way affected the system's success, as it created conditions where organized interests had to come together and cooperate very closely, letting go of any demands that would jeopardize the structure. It can thus be suggested that the political problem of the island has played a very significant role in determining the smooth functioning of the 'Cypriot corporatist model', both in the period immediately following the invasion, and also in later years, as this crisis played a catalytic role in bringing the social partners closer together in industrial cooperation. It thus created, to an extent, a tradition of closer cooperation, which has been described as the 'corporatist culture' of the island.

40. C. Ioannou, 'The Development of the Cypriot Corporatist Model, the Emergence of a Corporatist Culture and its Impact on the Process of Europeanization' (2009) 10 *Cyprus and European Law Review*: 700–736.

remarkable. The decline in the volume of production experienced during 1974 was quickly reversed and, by 1977, it even surpassed its pre-1974 levels. Business confidence returned, followed by a sharp upturn in investments. By 1979 conditions of full employment had been restored. The rate of unemployment, which approached 30 per cent of the economically active population during the second half of 1974, had been virtually eliminated (1.8 per cent), and the displaced persons were relocated temporarily, pending return to their homes.

16. In the post-1974 period, Cyprus has been transformed from a net exporter of agricultural products and minerals to a services-oriented economy, with tourism and provision of services being the main pillars of this economic growth. The country has for years been attractive as a base for offshore companies, owing mainly to its highly developed infrastructure, as well as to the tax incentives offered to these companies. International trade is today of considerable importance to the economy of Cyprus. On the production side, the lack of raw materials, energy resources and heavy industry for the production of capital goods, necessitates the import of such inputs. On the demand side, due to the small size of the domestic market, exports are vital in supplementing the aggregate demand for Cypriot agricultural and manufactured products, as well as for services. The main economic/trading partners of Cyprus are its EU counterparts, other non-EU countries of Central and Eastern Europe, as well as neighbouring Middle Eastern countries.

17. Since its accession to the EU in 2004, Cyprus has undergone significant economic and structural reforms, which have transformed its economic landscape; tariffs and quantitative restrictions have been eliminated for all manufactured goods and agricultural products originating in EU countries. Trade and interest rates have also been liberalised, while price controls and investment restrictions have, as a principle, been lifted. Private financing has been introduced for the construction and operation of infrastructural projects, while the state monopoly in the telecommunications sector has been abolished. EU Law provisions concerning competition and public procurement now form part of Cypriot internal law, with superior force. As of 1 January 2008, Cyprus has adopted the euro as a national currency.

18. From 2008 onwards, however, there has been a deterioration of the financial position of the country, which has unavoidably affected the main characteristics of the Cypriot welfare state.[25] Following a financial collapse in early 2013,[26] Cyprus adopted a Eurogroup agreement for the recapitalization of the Cypriot banking sector which essentially imposed the resolution of the country's second-largest bank and the bail-in of depositors of the country's largest bank as conditions for Cyprus receiving a EUR 10 billion bailout loan.[27] A Memorandum of Understanding (MoU)

---

25. A. Shekeris, C. Ioannou and C. Panagiotopoulos, 'Welfare Adaptation in a Divided State: The Cypriot Welfare System' in K. Schubert, S. Hegelich and U. Bazant (eds.), *The Handbook of European Welfare System* (Routledge, New York/London, 2009): 83.
26. C. Ioannou, A. Emilianides, 'How the Cypriot Crisis came to be: The Real Causes and Responsibility' *Foreign Affairs: The Hellenic Edition*, 12 (2013): 41-51 (in Greek).
27. C. Ioannou and A. Emilianides, 'The Haircut of Cypriot Deposits and the Protection of Fundamental Rights', (2013) *Cyprus Human Rights Law Review* 2: 141–166, C. Ioannou and A. Emilianides,

was signed with the Troika[28] in order to secure the loan for the Cypriot economy; the agreement introduced a series of austerity measures in the island. The objectives of the MoU included fiscal consolidation by means of increasing the efficiency and reducing spending in the country's public sector, as well as improving revenue collection. Structural adjustments included public spending cuts and tax increases, reform of the system of distribution of public benefits, as well as a privatization scheme for profitable semi-governmental organizations.

19. In 2012, even prior to the ratification of the MoU, Cyprus implemented a progressively scaled reduction in emoluments of public and broader public sector employees that ranged from 0 per cent for the lowest wage bracket (below EUR 1,000) up to 12.5 per cent for the highest wage bracket (above EUR 4,000). An additional flat-rate reduction of 3 per cent on all wages of public and broader public sector employees and pensioners was implemented in 2014. Additional expenditure measures included the extension of the suspended practice of Cost of Living Allowance (COLA) for the public and broader public sector, as well as the extension of the freeze of increments and general wage increases on gross earnings and pensions until the end of the programme in 2016. Steps were also taken to reduce the number of public sector employees by at least 4,500 over the period of 2012–2016 through the implementation of a hiring freeze of new personnel on first-entry posts in the broader public sector until the end of 2016, the introduction of a four-year plan aimed at the abolition of at least 1,880 permanent posts (a reduction of 3.8 per cent), and the adoption of a ratio of recruitment for new positions to retirements of 1:4, as well as a hiring freeze of new hourly paid employees.[29]

20. The MoU specifically called for labour market reforms as a way of mitigating the impact of the crisis on employment, limiting the occurrence of long-term and youth unemployment, facilitating occupational mobility and contributing to the improvement of the future resilience of the Cypriot economy. The yearly average unemployment rate increased from 7.9 per cent to 11.8 per cent between 2011 and 2012, as opposed to an unemployment rate of only 3.7 per cent in 2008. The increase in unemployment revealed the structural problems of the economy which intensified during the financial crisis. Following a steady increase of the unemployment rate, with unemployment reaching an all-time high of 16.9 per cent in October 2013, while remaining over 16 per cent during 2014, it would seem that, contrary to estimates predicting a rise of unemployment over 20 per cent, the unemployment rate steadily decreased to below 15 per cent by the end of 2015.

'Cyprus and EU following the Haircut of Deposits' in C. Ioannou, D. Sotiropoulos and A. Emilianides (eds), Cyprus in a new Era: Geostrategy, Economy, Foreign Policy (Nicosia: Foreign Affairs: Hellenic Edition and Hippasus, 2014): 124–153.

28. The tripartite committee composed of the European Commission, the European Central Bank (ECB) and the International Monetary Fund (IMF).

29. O. Christou, C. Ioannou and A. Shekeris, 'The Cypriot Welfare State in a Time of Crisis', in K. Schubert *et al.* (ed.), *Challenges to European Welfare Systems* (Berlin: Springer, 2015), O. Christou and C. Ioannou, 'The Cypriot Welfare State in the Memorandum Era', in S. Valyrakis *et al.*, *From Crisis to Development: In Search of New Developmental Models for Greece and the European South* (Athens: Papazisis, 2015): 119–130 (in Greek).

IV. Distinction between Private and Public Sectors

21. Cypriot law distinguishes between employees of the private and the public (or semi-public)[30] sector. The employment relationships of public servants are governed by the principles of administrative law,[31] rather than labour law, unless where the labour law legislation explicitly applies also to permanent employees of the public service or the semi-public sector. It should be noted, however, that non-permanent employees of the public sector are not considered as public servants and accordingly their employment relationship is not governed by public law, but by private law and in particular labour law legislation.[32] Thus, the status of non-permanent employees of the public sector is the same as the status of private sector employees; it is only permanent public sector employees who enjoy a special constitutional status.

22. A question arose recently whether employees of the wider public sector, and in particular semi-public sector, enjoy the same status as that of permanent employees of the strictly defined public sector. Expressing his opinion with regard to the 2014 privatization law, the Attorney-General of the Republic opined that the employees of the semi-public sector should not be considered as enjoying an equivalent permanent status as public sector employees. This was based on the definition of 'public service' in the Public Service Law 1/1990 which defines public service as referring only to public sector in the strict sense, i.e. excluding semi-public organizations.

23. However, Law 1/1990 is a specialized law whose aim is precisely to regulate the status of employees of the public sector in the strict sense and it could accordingly not be expected to regulate employees of the semi-public sector who are regulated by other specialized legislation. On the other hand, Article 122 of the Constitution, which is the relevant constitutional provision, provides that the term 'public service' also includes the semi-public sector, i.e. employment in legal persons of public law. The public law status of employees of the semi-public sector thus arises directly from the Constitution and no distinction should accordingly be drawn between permanent public law employees of the public and the semi-public sectors. It is therefore submitted that both the Constitution and the existing case law

30. The semi-public sector includes a great number of organizations, such as the Cyprus Telecommunications Authority, the Electricity Authority of Cyprus, local authorities, independent collective organs, public universities etc. For a detailed list see V. Georgiou, *Public Administration in Cyprus* (Nicosia: En Typois, 2012, in Greek).
31. See in general A. Emilianides, *Constitutional Law in Cyprus* (The Hague: Kluwer, 2013), N. Charalambous, *The Action and Control of Public Administration*, 3rd edn (Nicosia, 2013, in Greek), A. Angelides, S. Angelides, *Administrative Procedural Law* (Nicosia: Cyprus Bar Association, 2011, in Greek), C. Melides, 'Administrative Law', in Andreas Neocleous & Co LLC, *Introduction to Cyprus Law*, 3rd edn (Limassol, 2010): 87–117, Z. Nedjati, *Cyprus Administrative Law* (Nicosia, 1970), A. Angelides, 'Administrative Law: Article 146 of the Constitution', *Cyprus Law Review* 12 (1985): 1926–1935; *Cyprus Law Review* 13 (1986): 2111–2128 (in Greek), S. Angelides, 'Administrative Law in the Republic of Cyprus' *Cyprus and European Law Review* 8 (2008): 213–280 (in Greek).
32. *Avraam* v. *The Republic* [2008] 3 CLR.

of the Supreme Court support the conclusion that permanent employees of the semi-public sector should be deemed to enjoy the same status as permanent employees of the public sector.[33]

24. According to Article 125 of the Constitution, the Public Service Commission has the exclusive competence to appoint, promote, transfer, retire and exercise disciplinary control over public officers. The Public Service Commission was to be composed, by virtue of Article 124 of the Constitution, of ten members, seven Greek Cypriots and three Turkish Cypriots. If the issue concerned whether a vacant post should be filled by a Greek, or a Turkish Cypriot, a minimum number of votes from either Community were needed for a decision to be reached. However, the Public Service Commission provided in the Constitution has ceased to function due to the abnormal situation prevailing since 1963 and has been replaced by a new Public Service Commission established by law.[34]

25. The new Public Service Commission was initially established by the Public Service Law 33/67 and is currently governed by the provisions of the Public Service Law 1/90. It is comprised of five members – one of which acts as President of the Public Service Commission – who are appointed by the President of the Republic for a six-year period; they cannot be dismissed from office, except for the same reason and in the same manner as judges of the Supreme Court. The Public Service Commission has competence over public servants, but not over employees of the wider public service or public corporations; the matters concerning the latter fall under the competence of the board of the respective corporation. It has been held that the law regarding the new Public Service Commission must be as similar as possible to the constitutional provisions.[35]

26. It has been repeatedly held that the House of Representatives cannot involve itself directly or indirectly in the appointment or termination of appointment of public service personnel. The Supreme Court has held that the House of Representatives may, in accordance with the Constitution, prohibit by legislation the engagement of temporary employees by the Republic, even if expenditure by means of the Budget of the Republic has been approved for this purpose;[36] however, a provision whereby the procedure for the approval of the engagement of casual employees is subject to the approval of the House of Representatives is unconstitutional, since this would entail the House of Representatives interfering with the exercise of the administrative powers of the Council of Ministers in relation to the general

33. *Cyprus Tourism Organization* v. *Hadjidemetriou* [1987] 3 CLR 780, *Messaritou* v. *Cyprus Broadcasting Corporation* [1972] 3 CLR 100. See also the obiter comments in *President of the Republic* v. *House of Representatives* [2011] 3 CLR 777.

34. *The Republic* v. *Kyriacou* [1987] 3 CLR 1189, *Hadjianastassiou* v. *The Republic* [1982] 3 CLR 1173, *Coupepides* v. *TheRepublic* [1980] 3 CLR 256. See also A. Emilianides, *Beyond the Constitution of Cyprus* (Sakkoulas: Thessaloniki, 2006, in Greek).

35. *The Republic* v. *Kyriacou* [1987] 3 CLR 1189.

36. [1985] 3 CLR 1724, [1991] 3 CLR 746 (in Greek).

direction and control of the government of the Republic under Article 54(a) of the Constitution.[37]

27. Similarly, it has been held that the House of Representatives may not enact legislation to provide for the permanent appointment to the public service of employees serving on a temporary basis, even if such a law is enacted with the concurrence of the Council of Ministers or the President of the Republic. This is due to the fact that the appointment of members of the public service is a matter outside of the legislative sphere and within the exclusive competence of the Public Service Commission. Appointment by legislation would not only violate the principle of separation of powers, but would also be inconsistent with the principle of equality, since it would not grant to all individuals the necessary qualifications an equal right to compete for appointment to the said positions in the public service. The Supreme Court has therefore repeatedly held that vacancies should be properly advertised, affording everyone having the qualifications the opportunity to apply for appointment; personalised legislation aiming at transforming temporary employees into permanent ones cannot be tolerated.[38]

28. It used to be that only citizens of the Republic could be appointed as members of the Public Service of the Republic in accordance with Article 123 of the Constitution. The accession of the Republic of Cyprus to the EU has somewhat changed the absolutism of this requirement. Section 31 of the Public Service Law 1/1990, as modified by Section 3(a) of Law 128(I)/2003, provides that only citizens of the Republic may be appointed as members of the Public Service of the Republic; however, if the position does not imply direct or indirect participation in the exercise of public power and the preservation of the general interests of the state, members of the EU or the European Economic Area (EEA), or Switzerland, may be appointed. Section 31(f) further provides that the Council of Ministers may, in exceptional circumstances, and for the public interests, permit a person who is not a citizen of the Republic to apply for appointment to the Public Service.

V. Underlying Social Values and Their Effect on Social Policy

29. In a study of small European states, Katzenstein puts forward the idea that small states tend to regulate their social systems more actively than larger ones. This is the result of an effort to offset the negative effects brought upon them as a result of their small size, which makes them susceptible to external shocks, owing to their weak and fragile international position.[39] This argument seems very fitting for the small state of Cyprus, as indeed, through the country's industrial relations structure, a great degree of control is exerted over labour policy issues. In the case of Cyprus,

37. [1985] 3 CLR 1724.
38. *Republic* v. *Yiallourou* [1995] 3 CLR 363 (in Greek), *Menelaou* v. *Republic* [1996] 3 CLR 370 (in Greek), *Elia* v. *Republic* [1999] 3 CLR 884 (in Greek).
39. P. Katzenstein, *Small States in World Markets: Industrial Policy in Europe* (Ithaca: Cornell University Press, 1985).

however, apart from having to compensate for its small size and vulnerability, the country is also faced with some distinct problems which, as already indicated, relate to its political situation. It could be suggested then, that owing to these factors, Cyprus may be even more predisposed than other small European states, to protect its citizens through domestic policies.

30. The key to understanding the 'Cypriot corporatist model'[40] is by examining its reliance on cooperation between a set of organized interests and the state. It is, in effect, a tripartite structure of cooperation between the trade unions, the employers' associations and the Government of the Republic (through the Ministry of Labour, Welfare and Social Insurance) – the three social partners that constitute the 'model'. A tradition of smooth cooperation between the social partners exists in the industrial arrangement of the country. The 'corporatist culture' of the island has been the main variable in securing a climate of cooperation between the social partners over time.

31. Over the years, the system had succeeded in bringing industrial peace in the island. The success of the system of industrial relations in Cyprus rests upon the willingness of the social partners to cooperate and on voluntariness rather than legislative imposition. Collective agreements, though not legally binding, have rarely been violated over the years. Following the Turkish invasion of 1974 and the catastrophe which occurred to the fabric of Cypriot society, the social partners showed a capacity to cooperate with one another in order to alleviate the problems created. They agreed to suspend the COLA system, which had been a major achievement of years of struggles by the working force. In other words, during the period from 1974 until 1978 (when COLA was re-introduced) wages stopped rising. This reduced the overall cost to the economy, helping it to recover sooner. This suspension of the COLA system is considered to be a great sacrifice on the part of trade unions during a crisis point. In other words, the experience has been incorporated into a vision of the essentially cooperative nature of the Cypriot model.

32. It can thus be argued that the need for physical survival, as a result of the invasion, in a way affected the system's success, as it created conditions where organized interests had to come together and cooperate very closely, letting go of any demands that would jeopardize the structure. It can thus be suggested that the political problem of the island has played a very significant role in determining the smooth functioning of the 'Cypriot corporatist model', both in the period immediately following the invasion, and also in later years, as this crisis played a catalytic role in bringing the social partners closer together in industrial cooperation. It thus created, to an extent, a tradition of closer cooperation, which has been described as the 'corporatist culture' of the island.

40. C. Ioannou, 'The Development of the Cypriot Corporatist Model, the Emergence of a Corporatist Culture and its Impact on the Process of Europeanization' (2009) 10 *Cyprus and European Law Review*: 700–736.

33. Following the Turkish invasion of 1974, the Republic began issuing individual visas to migrant workers for employment purposes, which were short term and restricted to specific sectors. Demand for labour in Cyprus in specific sectors, such as the tourism industry, led to the granting of visas and work permits on the condition that the worker would be attached to a particular employer without the freedom to change employer, unless the original employer consented to such a change; in any event the duration of the stay of the worker in Cyprus ought to be of a temporary and limited nature.[41] Employing migrants who do not have a work permit or who do not reside lawfully in the Republic of Cyprus is a criminal offence, with the penalty of imprisonment normally being imposed on wrongdoers.

34. The accession of Cyprus to the EU in 2004 was seen as the culmination of a long history of attempts to find a viable solution to the political division of the island. The rationale behind the country's application for EU membership was primarily political. A clear connection was made between the Cyprus problem and the approach of the country to the EU, to the extent that the two became almost synonymous. As a result, the harmonization process, in relation to the transposition of the various directives of the *acquis communautaire* regarding social policy, was mostly conflict free as it was thought likely to promote the long-anticipated solution to the Cyprus problem. This was the dominant perception among the Cypriot political elite as well as the wider public, who linked harmonization, and thus accession to the EU, to the solution of the country's political problem. Thus while the process was largely politicized on a high politics field, it was largely 'apolitical' on the lower politics field.[42] The wider objectives of the Cypriot adjustment process were to achieve reunification of the island by 'playing' on the 'higher' politics field and, at the same time, to convince the other members – through a smooth adjustment path – that the country is a 'good European'.[43]

35. This rather 'enthusiastic' process of Europeanization reached its apogee on 1 May 2004, when the country acceded to the EU. Since accession there has been increasing Euroscepticism as well as disappointment among Cypriot public opinion regarding the expected benefits arising from EU membership and its effects on Cypriot social policy. Euroscepticism reached its climax during the ongoing financial crisis and especially following the decisions of the Eurogroup in March 2013.[44] Increase in unemployment and a cheaper labour force due to migration of workers has led to changes in the landscape and effective application of the Cypriot model.

41. For a criticism of the system of free movement of workers in Cyprus see N. Trimikliniotis (ed.), *Free Movement of Workers in Cyprus and the EU* (Oslo: Prio, 2010), *idem*, 'Exceptions, Soft Borders and Free Movement for Workers', in P. Minderhoud (ed.), *Rethinking the Free Movement of Workers: The European Challenges ahead* (Nimegen: Wolf Legal Publishers, 2009): 135–154.
42. See in detail C. Ioannou, 'The Europeanisation of Cypriot Social Policy: An "Apolitical" Europeanisation Process' (2008–2009), *Journal of Modern Hellenism*: 97–128.
43. C. Ioannou and G. Kentas, 'Social and Societal Aspects of EU Membership', in J. Ker-Lindsay, H. Faustmann and F. Mullen (eds.), *An Island in Europe: The EU and the Transformation of Cyprus* (London: I.B. Tauris, 2011): 89–111.
44. N. Zannetos, 'Increase of Euro-Scepticism in Cyprus', 6 September 2013, available at http://www.sigmalive.com/news/local/63739/afksanetai-o-euroskeptikismos-stin-kypro.

Many employers have viewed the economic crisis as an opportunity to restrict the rights of employees previously agreed by collective agreements and to violate their obligations towards their employees; fear of unemployment has led many employees to accept various forms of violations of their rights. The maintenance of industrial peace in a period of economic crisis remains a major challenge for the future of the Cypriot voluntary model.

§2. Definitions and Notions

I. Distinction between Labour Law and Other Branches of Law

36. Cyprus is characterized as a mixed legal system,[45] albeit a unique mixed legal system where common law mostly dominates in the field of private law, whereas continental law dominates in the field of public law.[46] Labour law is generally classified as part of private law[47] and is accordingly common law oriented. Employment relationships in Cyprus are governed by ordinary contract law principles and are supplemented by statutory rights and obligations where appropriate.[48] Thus, labour law is closely associated with contract law. However, there are also aspects of labour law which are governed by public law, such as the constitutional safeguards for the right to strike and the freedom of workers to organize, whereas the government through the Ministry of Labour, Welfare and Social Insurance actively participates in the mediation procedures for resolving disputes between employers and trade unions.[49] The incorporation of EU law, particularly legislation related to non-discrimination, is also relevant to human rights considerations, through *drittwirkung* and the application of the positive obligations of the state under the Constitution and the ECHR.[50]

45. A. Emilianides, 'Cyprus: Everything Changes and Nothing Remains Still', in S. Farran *et al.*, *A Study of Mixed Legal Systems: Endangered, Entrenched or Blended* (Aldershot: Ashgate, 2014): 215–240, S. Symeonides, 'The Mixed Legal System of the Republic of Cyprus' (2003) 78 *Tulane Law Review*: 441, N Hatzimichail, 'Cyprus as a Mixed Legal System' (2013) 3 *Journal of Civil Law Studies*: 38.
46. A. Emilianides, 'Cyprus: Everything Changes and Nothing Remains Still', above, N. Hadjimichail, 'Reconstructing Mixity: Sources of Law and Legal Method in Cyprus' in V. Palmer *et al.*, *Mixed Legal Systems: East and West* (Aldershot: Ashgate, 2015): 75.
47. In A. Emilianides, 'An Introduction to the Bibliography of Cypriot Law' (2013) 3 *Cyprus Law Tribune*; the 'Employment law' references are sub-categorized under the general heading of 'Private Law'.
48. See in general N. Ktenas, 'Employment' in Andreas Neocleous & Co, *Introduction to Cyprus Law* (3rd edn, Limassol, 2010): 991–1016, T. Papamiltiades, 'Labour Law' in *Corpus de Jure Cyprii*, v. II (Nicosia: Cyprus Bar Council, 1988): 265–308.
49. A. Emilianides and X. Xenofontos, 'Mediation in Cyprus', in C. Esplugues *et al.* (eds.), *Civil and Commercial Mediation in Europe: National Mediation Rules and Procedures* (Intersentia, Cambridge 2012): 87–95.
50. For *dirittwirkung* in the Cypriot legal order see e.g. See S. Papasavvas, 'There is Drittwirkung of Human Rights in the Cypriot Legal Order: Comments and Thoughts on the Judgment of the Supreme Court in Civil Appeal 9931 Yiallouros v. Nicolaou', *Dikaiomata tou Anthropou* 15 (2002): 837–861 (in Greek).

37. This peculiar nature of labour law disputes might lead to suggestions that it should be treated as a branch of law with dual nature, i.e. both public and private,[51] especially in light of the importance of social law for the wider social policy aspects of the state. Labour law remains a central part of the development of Cypriot social policy[52] and is therefore interlinked with welfare law;[53] the state's welfare policies and its policies in order to lower unemployment rates are intertwined, especially in times of economic crisis, as they both form part of Cypriot social policy.[54] This is also the rationale of the inclusion of labour, welfare and social insurance issues under the competence of the same ministry, i.e. the Ministry of Labour, Welfare and Social Insurance. However, the relationship should not be overestimated; whereas, the objectives of both labour law and welfare and social insurance law might be similar, the structure of labour law legislation is altogether different from welfare and social insurance legislation. Both welfare and social insurance legislation are strictly categorized under public law and decisions relating to welfare, financial assistance and social insurance are administrative acts which are governed by administrative law; on the other hand, labour law disputes are classified under private law and are mainly governed by private law principles. In light of the peculiarities of labour law, specialized courts, specifically the Industrial Disputes Tribunals (IDT), were introduced for the adjudication of labour law disputes.

II. Defining Employee and Employer under Labour Law

38. Under section 2 of the Termination of Employment Law 24/1967 an 'employee' is defined as any person who works for another person either under a contract of employment or in circumstances from which the existence of a relation of employee and employer may be concluded; and the expression 'employer' shall be construed accordingly and include the Republic. This is the general definition of the terms of employer and employee under Cypriot labour law. Therefore, a person may be regarded as an employee even if he does not work under a contract of service, as long as he works for another person in circumstances under which the existence of an employment relationship may be concluded. An employer is conversely defined as the person for whom the employee works, either under a contract of

51. See T. Papamiltiades, 'Labour Law' in *Corpus de Jure Cyprii*, v. II (Nicosia: Cyprus Bar Council, 1988): 265, 270. Also for a wider discussion also D. Stranis, *Public Law in Labour Law of 21*st *Century* (Thessaloniki: Sakkoulas, 2010, in Greek).
52. See e.g. C. Ioannou and G. Kentas, 'The Social Dimension of Cyprus' Accession in the EU' in *International and European Politics* (Athens: Papazisis, 2012, v. 25, in Greek): 140–148 (in Greek), C. Ioannou and G. Kentas, 'Social and Societal Aspects of EU Membership', in J. Ker-Lindsay *et al.* (eds.), *An Island in Europe: The EU and Transformation of Cyprus* (London: IB Tauris, 2011): 89.
53. See generally G. Amitsis, *Social Security Law in Cyprus* (The Hague: Kluwer, 2014).
54. O. Christou O, C. Ioannou and A. Shekeris, 'The Cypriot Welfare State in a Time of Crisis', in K. Schubert *et al.* (ed.), *Challenges to European Welfare Systems* (Berlin: Springer, 2015), O. Christou and C. Ioannou, 'The Cypriot Welfare State in the Memorandum Era', in S. Valyrakis *et al.*, *From Crisis to Development: In Search of New Developmental Models for Greece and the European South* (Athens: Papazisis, 2015): 119–130 (in Greek).

service or in circumstances from which the existence of an employment relationship may be concluded.[55]

39. The term 'employee' under section 2 of Law 24/67 includes persons employed by legal persons of public law or organizations of public law without legal personality and the term 'employer' is construed so as to include also the Republic of Cyprus when it acts as employer. A proviso of section 2 of Law 24/67, however, provides that the term employee shall include any person who is a shareholder in a private company and is employed in such company, but not under a contract of employment or circumstances from which the employer-employee relationship may be derived. Paragraph 1A of the Fourth Schedule of the Law provides that the employees referred to in the proviso of section 2 of Law 24/67 are entitled to compensation equal to a percentage of 1 per cent of their weekly salary, calculated by 52 and by the years of service. The law thus distinguishes between employees and the presumed employees who are essentially the directors of the company.[56]

40. A contract of service should be distinguished from a contract for the provision of services. It is accepted that the fundamental test to be applied is whether the person who has engaged himself to perform the services performs them as a person in business on his own account, or in the employment of another person. If he carries them on his own account, then it is a contract for the provision of services, whereas if he carries them in the employment of another person it is a contract of employment. The degree of control exercised by the employer over his employee remains an important factor; it is no longer, however, the sole determining factor.

41. The court should examine whether the person performing the services provides his own equipment, whether he hires his own assistants, the degree of financial risk he takes, the degree of responsibility for investment and management and the opportunity for profit from sound management in the performance of the tasks at hand.[57] The parties' expressed intention might be a relevant factor in deciding what is the true nature of the contract; it is not, however, a conclusive factor, as regard should be had to the arrangement as a whole, the terms of the contract and in particular to the rights and obligations of the parties. The role of the court is therefore to establish the true relationship of the parties, irrespective of the manner in which they have themselves labelled their relationship.[58]

---

55. See also M. Antoniou, *The Law of Termination of Employment in Cyprus* (Nicosia: OEB, 2000, in Greek): 53–75.
56. *Redundancy Fund* v. *Theodorou* [2004] 1 CLR 349 (in Greek).
57. *Proiki* v. *Michaelidou* [2002] 1 CLR 736 (in Greek), *Cleanthis Christofides Ltd* v. *Fund for Redundant Employees and another* [1978] 1 CLR 208, citing with approval *Global Plant Ltd* v. *Secretary of State for Health and Social Security* [1971] 3 All ER 385, *Market Investigations Ltd* v. *Minister of Social Security* [1968] 3 All ER 732. See also *Evripides Sykopetritis Ltd* v. *Athinaki* [2005] 1 CLR 844 (in Greek).
58. *Proiki* v. *Michaelidou* [2002] 1 CLR 736 (in Greek), *Cleanthis Christofides Ltd* v. *Fund for Redundant Employees and another* [1978] 1 CLR 208, citing with approval *Ferguson* v. *John Dawson &*

42. In *Christophides* the relationship between the employer and the employee was terminated on grounds of redundancy, following the reorganization of the employer's company. A new agency contract for the provision of services was signed between the parties, under which the agent (former employee) would be paid commission, would not be allowed to connect himself with any competing insurance business and his right to any additional business, other than insurance business, would be subject to the company's consent. When he applied to the Redundancy Fund for redundancy payment, the Fund refused, alleging that the employment relationship had never been terminated, a construction which was affirmed at first instance.

43. The Supreme Court, however, disagreed; it was held that the employer–employee relationship has always been understood as one of master and servant and that the purpose of the law would be defeated if agents and independent contractors were to be included within the definition of an 'employee'. The Supreme Court disagreed with the approach of the trial court that a person would be defined as an employee if his living was totally or largely dependent upon the continuation of the relationship for the provision of services. It was thus held that the relationship was not that of an employer–employee.[59]

44. In *Angelides* the Supreme Court held that the Appellant was not an 'employee' within the definition of the law so as to be entitled to compensation; it was considered that the claimant was the founder, main shareholder and a director of the company and determined his terms of employment and salary together with the other members of the board of directors. Moreover, in his capacity as managing director of the company, he was not controlled by anyone with respect to his employment and the manner in which he carried out his work and his only obligation was to inform the other directors about his actions. It was therefore concluded that it was the appellant who controlled the company and not vice versa.[60]

45. Similar was the conclusion of the Supreme Court in *Prousi* where the appellant was one of the two original shareholders and directors of the employer, holding 50 per cent of the shares; whereas, he eventually transferred his shares to his children, he continued to have the right to administer them at his discretion. The employment of the appellant was terminated on grounds of the impending dissolution of the company upon petition by the appellant and his children; the decision to dismiss the appellant was taken by the appellant and the other original shareholder. his application for redundancy allowance from the Fund was dismissed as the employer–employee relationship had not been established. The Supreme Court noted that the payment of salary is not the only criterion for establishing an employment relationship; it has to be further established that the employer exercises some

---

Partners (Contractors) Ltd [1976] 3 All ER 817, *Ready Mixed Concrete (South East) Ltd* v. *Minister of Pensions and National Insurance* [1968] 1 All ER 433, *Addiscombe Garden Estates Ltd* v. *Crabbe* [1957] 3 All ER 563. See also *Papalazarou Bros Ltd* v. *Republic* [1995] 4 CLR 560 (in Greek).

59. *Cleanthis Christofides Ltd* v. *Fund for Redundant Employees and another* [1978] 1 CLR 208.

60. *Angelides* v. *Kypri Hatzimarkou and Son Ltd and another* [2000] 1 CLR 465 (in Greek).

amount of control over the employee, which, under the circumstances, was not the case.[61]

46. In *Avacom* it was held that there existed an employment relationship since the employee was under the control of the company and acted under the company's instructions and received a salary. The Court held that the employment relationship existed despite the fact that the contract itself provided that the employee was a self-employed person, or that he could exercise his own judgment on how to organize his work, or that under certain circumstances he could be paid a commission in addition to the salary.[62]

47. Guidance might be drawn from the CJEU case law, as the term is found in several EU legislative acts which apply in Cyprus. The Court of Justice has defined the notion of a 'worker' by for the purposes of the Treaty. It was held that the term must be defined in accordance with objective criteria which distinguish the employment relationship by reference to the rights and duties of the persons concerned; the essential feature of an employment relationship is that a person performs services of some economic value for and under the direction of another person in return for which he receives remuneration. The sphere in which the services are provided and the nature of the legal relationship between employee and employer were held to be immaterial.[63] The term might thus include employees, irrespective of their salary, or whether they are full-time or part-time.

48. An interpretation on the basis of which the application of an employment relationship would be subject to the criterion of what the legislation of the host state declares to be a minimum wage, would frustrate the uniform Community interpretation of the term; part-time activities may also fall under the scope of an employment relationship, so long as they are conducted in the genuine and effective pursuit of economic activity and not purely marginal or ancillary. In the field of application, the concept of an employment relationship should not be interpreted restrictively.[64] In *Scenavai* the Court of Justice held that employment contracts differ from other contracts by virtue of certain particularities; they establish a lasting bond which brings the worker, to some extent, within the organizational framework of the business of the undertaking or employer and they are linked to the place where the activities are pursued, a fact which determines the application of mandatory rules and collective agreements which safeguard the rights of the employee.[65]

---

61. *Prousi* v. *Redundant Employees Fund* [1988] 1 CLR 363, *Krasias* v. *Director of Social Security and another* [1996] 4 CLR 3134 (in Greek).
62. *Avacom Computed Services Ltd* v. *Republic*, Case 58/98, dated 20 June 1999.
63. Case 66/85, *Lawrie Blum* v. *Land Baden Württemberg* [1986] ECR 2121.
64. Case 53/81, *Levin* v. *Staatsecretaris van Justitie* [1982] ECR 1035, Case 196/87, *Steymann* v. *Staatsecretaris van Justitie [1988] ECR 6159, Bettray* v. *Staatsecretaris* van Justitie [1989] ECR 1621. The above judgments concerned the interpretation of the Treaty.
65. Case 266/85, *Shenavai* v. *Kreischer* [1987] ECR 239.

49. In *Neocli* the Supreme Court held that the termination of employment law applies only with respect to the employment of persons in Cyprus; thus, employment of an employee abroad did not amount to 'employment' for the purposes of compensation for termination of employment on grounds of redundancy or for any other purpose. It was accordingly held that the IDT's judgment to calculate in the compensation for redundancy the period, during which the employee was employed by a Cypriot company abroad, was erroneous.[66] It is submitted that the above judgment should be read narrowly; the termination of employment law should also apply to the employment of persons outside of Cyprus, if the applicable law for such employment relationship is Cypriot law, in accordance with the rules of private international law.

§3. Historical Background

I. Prior to Independence

50. A detailed historical introduction is considered significant to properly appreciate labour law and industrial relations in Cyprus, as the current legal framework is the outcome of history and societal struggles.[67] The history of industrial relations in Cyprus can be dated back as early as 1910, when workers made their first attempts to join in some form of group. These attempts were not systematic or organized, yet they succeeded in setting up some social and political alliances, which were registered as clubs. These clubs were however short-lived, as following the failure of the 1931 October uprising – where the people of Cyprus sought *enosis* (union) with Greece – all clubs were dissolved by order of the colonial governor.[68]

51. The island's economy at the time was chiefly a peasant economy and no real need for any sort of labour movement was deemed necessary. As the 1931 Colonial Report on the Census of Cyprus stated, no labouring class, in the generally accepted sense of the term, existed.[69] In fact, out of a total population of 347,959 persons – recorded at the time in the Report – only 5,462[70] were reported as 'employed by others'. The main reason why this figure was so small is because most of the gainfully employed population, at the time, worked on its own account, but also because the 'factory system' was, at that period, virtually unknown in the country, and hence factories were few in number and small in size.[71]

---

66. *Neocli* v. *Redundancy Fund* [1992] 1 CLR 44 (in Greek).
67. See also C. Ioannou, The 'Apolitical' Europeanisation of Cypriot Social Policy: When Harmonisation becomes a 'National Goal' (PhD Thesis, University of Manchester, 2007): 111ff.
68. A. Avraamides, 'A Brief History of Labour Relations in Cyprus: The Colonial Period – Labour Relations in Cyprus 1931–1956', in J. H. Slocum (ed.), *The Development of Labour Relations in Cyprus* (Nicosia: Proodos, 1972): 7.
69. Government of Cyprus, *Colonial Report on Cyprus* (Nicosia: Government Printing Office, 1931).
70. This figure excluded the mineworkers, who totalled about 3,197 of the total population.
71. A. Avraamides, 'A Brief History of Labour Relations in Cyprus: The Colonial Period – Labour Relations in Cyprus 1931–1956', in John H. Slocum (ed.), *The Development of Labour Relations in Cyprus* (Nicosia: Proodos, 1972): 8.

52. Unfortunately, no figures for the wages paid at the time are available. What is known is that these were agreed privately, and no commonly fixed standard rates existed. Working hours were largely unregulated, with the exceptions of the mines and government public works, where the hours of work were about eight a day.[72] But in the agricultural sector, where most of the working population was to be found, the 'sunrise to sunset' working hours were recognized. Benefits to the workers were also rather minimal. No injury compensation for workers existed – with the exception of the mines – nor was there any kind of legislation providing for medical benefits or sickness insurance.

53. The first wave of change came in 1932 when the Trade Union Law was introduced. Even though no official records exist to verify the state of industrial relations during the period preceding World War II, it can be safely deduced that, in the absence of any substantial coordination, it is hardly possible that much could have been achieved for workers in employment. Hours of work did in fact remain largely unregulated, and there were only minor improvements in the 1930s in the benefits received: Accident pay covered government employees and free medical care was only granted to workers injured in the course of their work (and even then, no provision for compensation was made). Sick pay, or sick leave, was yet unknown at the time. As far as the private sector was concerned, nothing of the sort existed.

54. Thus, industrial relations – in the sense of cooperation among employers and trade unions – were as yet to develop. Agreements between employers and trade unions were not only infrequent, but they also covered exceptionally few areas of industrial life. More specifically, they covered wages, hours of work and notice of dismissal, even though again, with relation to the latter, nothing of significance had, by the late 1930s, been achieved. This remained the state of affairs until 1939 and the outbreak of World War II, while the same situation continued in the immediate postwar period, as unemployment and economic depression ensued.

55. An important landmark was reached in 1941: the colonial government passed a law by which it established the Department of Labour. This Department assumed responsibilities for the enactment of sufficient labour legislation and for looking after labour matters in general. In fact, the legislation introduced by this Department in 1941 embodied laws which included provisions for trade disputes, minimum wages, regulation of shop hours and the hours of employment of shop assistants, as well as regulation of the working hours of hotel employees. It also included provisions for compensation payments to those killed or incapacitated in the course of their employment, prohibition of employment for children under 12 years of age, as well as regulations for better inspection of factories and workshops, which helped towards the improvement of the sanitary and safety conditions of industrial premises. Moreover, certain provisions were made for trade unions, conferring upon them various rights, immunities and privileges, while a comprehensive legal framework was introduced, providing for their constitutional growth. Trade unions thus gained recognition under this law.

72. No organizations for public employees existed at the time.

56. The early war period (1939–1941) was marked by economic hardship, as unemployment plagued the island. The later part of the period (1942–1945), however, saw full employment in the island, owing mainly to some large-scale military works that were undertaken by the British colonial government. Under these developments, not only were workers made more eager to join a trade union – so as to be able to put forward their claims to their employers in a more coordinated fashion – but trade unions were also placed in a better position to press for these demands. Chief among their requests were those for shorter working hours and higher wages. So despite the rifts in the ranks of the trade unions, significant regulations were introduced in the hours of work, as the demand for the eight-hour day became the main issue of trade disputes, and changes were also brought about in the conditions of employment.

57. As far as wages are concerned, these rose steadily throughout the period – even though there is an absence of official records that can confirm whether these increases were in line with the rising cost of living. The early 1940s saw massive strikes by the workers, who demanded the introduction of a system that would link price increases to wages (as wage rises did not match price increases). These struggles involved the whole of the workforce, which was mobilized in this direction. Despite the fact that the COLA scheme[73] was not officially applied until 1950–1951, the period of the early 1940s marked a significant beginning. As regards benefits for the workers, nothing of value can be reported in the immediate postwar period, as this was not yet an area of primary importance to the trade unions.

58. In the decade following the end of the war, the trade union movement grew considerably. This was to an extent sponsored by the increased significance that trade unions attracted in the field of industrial relations, through the establishment of the Labour Advisory Board in 1948. This marked the beginning of the Cypriot tripartite model. The period was marked by further important developments in the industrial field. These were mainly the twin result of both the relative success of the trade unions in securing some of their demands, as well as the economic advancement of the country. The industrialization of the island was indeed beginning to become a reality and more regulations in the area of industrial relations were, as a result, deemed necessary. To this end, the Labour Advisory Board was set up in 1948, as outlined earlier, with the purpose of studying the conditions of labour and drafting proposed legislation. The legislation introduced in the postwar period embodied significant changes.

59. The new legislation contained provisions for minimum wages for shop and office employees, as well as for female packers, graders and sorters of agricultural produce in the Paphos District. The laws also fixed the closing hours of shops, barbers, hairdressers and restaurant employees, reduced the working hours of hotel employees and regulated the wages and working conditions of port workers. Nonetheless, in many unauthorized trades, such as agriculture and domestic service,

73. By the COLA scheme, wages increase automatically with an increase in the price of a pre-agreed package of goods.

working hours remained long. A law introducing further compensation payments to workers injured in the course of their work was also introduced at the time. The previous arrangement that existed was extended under this law, to cover more working groups, as well as workers affected by certain occupational diseases, such as those employed in hospitals and sanatoria. Compensation payments were also extended to cover cases in which the injury resulted in the death or permanent incapacity of the worker. A lot of these arrangements focused on the public sector, rather than the private sector. What is striking about this period is the existence of a very highly regulated labour sector alongside a virtually unregulated one.

60. Trade unions were able to achieve a lot of their demands at the time. These chiefly included improvements in wages and COLA rates, working hours and other benefits for the workers. The latter included, for instance, annual leave with pay, an area in which considerable progress was made. Trade unions also demanded the introduction of a Social Insurance Scheme to be organized by the government. This was achieved in 1956, when the government passed the Social Insurance Law, which contained provisions for the creation of the Social Insurance Fund, thus ensuring benefits for sickness, unemployment, widowhood, orphanhood, marriage, maternity, old age and death. These were the main developments in the ten years following the end of World War II. The progress and expansion of the trade union movement at this time, meant that they were in a better position to put forward their claims.

61. By 1960, when Cyprus gained its independence, significant advances had been made in the industrial field.[74] It must be noted, however, that despite these advances, nothing of substance was achieved in the years preceding independence, as far as institutional bargaining arrangements are concerned. In fact, no clear procedures existed, either for negotiations and collective bargaining practices, or for conflict resolution in cases of labour disputes. The first concrete step towards achievements in this direction was that made in 1948, with the establishment of the Labour Advisory Board, which marked the beginning of tripartite cooperation and social dialogue. From 1955 to 1959 the Greek Cypriots fought their struggle of liberation against the British. This period was marked by a standstill in industrial life, and so the achievements in the field of industrial relations, made in the previous years, reached a halt. Emergency orders and regulations were imposed, and unprecedented powers were conferred upon the colonial governor to regulate many forms of industrial activity.

II. Independence

62. After Independence, there was a gradual resurgence of industrial activity. The Constitution directly recognized the people's right to freedom of peaceful assembly and freedom of association with others, including forming or joining a trade union, and, with some exceptions, the right to strike. This was considered as

74. J. H. Slocum, *The Development of Labour Relations in Cyprus* (Nicosia: Proodos, 1972): 36.

a substantial development that would transform the framework of industrial relations. The government introduced two five-year plans, so as to revive industrial development. The first plan covered the period 1962–1966, while the second one the period 1967–1971. Both plans included objectives for achieving conditions of full employment, improving social benefits, increasing productivity, providing freedom of association, industrial peace, protection against arbitrary dismissal and safety at work.

63. In all these areas, significant achievements were made under the First Five-Year Plan.[75] Chief among these was the extension of the Social Insurance Scheme to cover all employees and self-employed. This was also complemented by an increase in social insurance benefits. Further to these, provisions also included more protection of the right of employees and employers to join freely in organizations, as well as the establishment of safety committees in many industries to inspect safety at work, along with revised and tightened regulations. Industrial peace was also promoted, and the Ministry of Labour and Social Insurance assumed an active role in settling disputes through mediation.[76]

64. Another important development in this period was the 'Basic Agreement of Standard Rules for the Negotiation of Agreements and for Settlement of Disputes and/or Grievances', which was signed in 1962 between the four trade union federations, the Cyprus Employers' Consultative Association and the then Minister of Labour and Social Insurance.[77] This agreement, which was based on International Labour Organization (ILO) Recommendations, secured the right to organize and the right to strike, and also provided for a procedural framework for negotiation of agreements and for settlement of disputes or grievances (ILO Recommendation No. 130). The procedures laid out in the Basic Agreement had to be adhered to, and only in the absence of any agreement – following the exhaustion of these procedures – would a strike or lock-out be carried out.

65. The achievements of the First Five-Year Plan were carried on to the Second Five-Year Plan, and further developments were recorded in that period as well.[78] The most important accomplishment was in relation to the Ministry of Labour's efforts to establish training schemes, which would promote productive and efficient employment. Under the Industrial Training Section of the Ministry of Labour, established in 1969, training was provided to those in the building industry, to jockeys, and retraining was provided to redundant former British base employees. But the most specialized training centres of the Ministry were introduced mainly in the engineering, as well as in the hotel and catering sectors. What is of main importance here is that this was also a period during which trade unions were successful

75. Republic of Cyprus, *Cyprus: The First Five-Year Plan* (in Greek) (Nicosia: Press and Information Office, 1962).
76. J. H. Slocum, *The Development of Labour Relations in Cyprus* (Nicosia: Proodos, 1972): 45.
77. Republic of Cyprus, *The Basic Agreement of Standard Rules for the Negotiation of Agreements and for Settlement of Disputes and/or Grievances* (in Greek) (Nicosia: Press and Information Office, 1962).
78. C. Christodoulou, *A Study of Labour Law in Cyprus* (PhD Thesis, University of Wales, 1992): 42.

in promoting a number of their claims. Most important among their achievements was the establishment of the 40-hour week in almost all sectors of economic life. As we have already seen, the Social Insurance Scheme was also improved under the First and Second Five-Year Plans, and this was also partly due to trade union claims.

66. All these training institutes established in the late 1960s and early 1970s functioned under tripartite boards, with nominated members from the trade unions and the employers' associations. These tripartite arrangements progressively spread to control more areas of industrial relations life; tripartite advisory committees were introduced at all levels and ensured a genuine approach of cooperation.[79] It can be argued that all these significant institutional developments of the time were largely inspired and facilitated, both by the colonial legacy, as well as by attempts to industrially advance the infant Republic. The progress that was achieved, in the industrial relations field, in the post-independence period, was seriously interrupted, however, in 1974 with the Turkish invasion of Cyprus. With the thousands of dead and missing people, and the hundreds of thousands of refugees, the economy suffered great damage.

67. Under the conditions created by the Turkish invasion and occupation, it was deemed appropriate to adopt an expansionary fiscal and monetary policy. This was intended to provide immediate help to the displaced and affected persons, and to reverse the economic recession, create employment opportunities, and in general to reactivate the economy. The trade union movement suspended the submission of any claims, despite the fact that unemployment rocketed sky high and the standard of living of the working population seriously suffered. Following some 'sacrifices' on the part of the trade unions – specifically their consent to the government to suspend the COLA system, mentioned above – and some extensive economic struggles on the part of the Cypriot government, pre-invasion macroeconomic and employment levels were to a great extent restored in the period 1978–1979; in fact the period after the Turkish invasion until the late 1970s has been characterized as an 'economic miracle'.[80]

68. By 1980–1981, wage increases were granted for the first time after some years, owing to the reintroduction of the COLA system in 1978. Industrial relations were thus gradually re-established in the late 1970s, and an important development occurred in 1977. This was the introduction of the Industrial Relations Code (IRC), which still exists today and regulates the process of collective bargaining and dispute resolution. Once the targets of rapid reactivation of the economy and the creation of conditions of full employment had been achieved, the government's policy priorities changed. Whereas, in the late 1970s and early 1980s, emphasis was placed on combating inflationary pressures and relieving the imbalances on the island's balance of payments, throughout the 1980s, the main targets set by the government

79. Slocum, *op. cit.*, 47.
80. D. Christodoulou, *Inside the Cyprus Miracle: Labours of an Embattled Mini-Economy* (University of Minneapolis: Modern Greek Studies, 1992).

were technological upgrading, restructuring and reinforcing competitiveness in all sectors of the economy.

III. The Harmonization and Post-EU Accession Period (1998–Present)

69. The rational expectation with regard to the harmonization process of a small country like Cyprus would be that, owing to the small size of its national administration, it would be faced with many practical problems in its adjustment path. An important practical problem that emerged in the process of transposition of the *acquis* was that most of the existing legislation needed to be amended or replaced and the number of drafters with expertise in EU law did not meet the volume of drafting required. The European Union section of the Law Office of the Republic of Cyprus addressed this problem by training a group of young and well qualified drafters. Nevertheless, this was arguably not adequate.[81]

70. What came to add to this problem was the fact that the government also felt the need to get the social partners involved in the process of drafting and introducing new legislation in the field of labour law. So, in the end, the technical committees were made up of young and inexperienced drafters and social partners (trade union officials and employers' representatives) with no expertise in EU law. These inexpert actors were key figures in the process of adjustment, as the technical committees had the task of drafting the bills, prior to presenting them to the competent department of the Ministry of Labour and Social Insurance, which then prepared a draft law in cooperation with the Law Office of the Republic. Once the draft law was prepared, it was resubmitted to the technical committees as a working document for discussion. At this stage, the technical committees also had the task of preparing a report expressing the views of the parties involved. What clearly emerges from this is that key actors in the process of harmonization either lacked the experience or the expertise to be involved in this procedure.

71. The government felt from the beginning of the process that the social partners should be involved in the adjustment. It was believed that their good record of cooperation over the years would render the process smooth and conflict free.[82] The 'tradition' of maintaining a rather peaceful climate of cooperation between the social partners over the years, and the already established mechanisms for debating policy issues between these parties, did in fact have a positive impact on the process of harmonization in this field. It should also be noted is that Cyprus is a country where political dealings rely heavily on informality. The key elite figures usually tend to know each other, and thus informal channels of communication tend to emerge between them, which speed up the formal process of cooperation.

81. C. Stefanou, 'Introduction', in C. Stefanou (ed.), *Cyprus and the EU: The Road to Accession* (Aldershot: Ashgate, 2005): 5.
82. N. Ioannou, 'Social Policy and Employment', in C. Stefanou (ed.), *Cyprus and the EU: The Road to Accession* (Aldershot: Ashgate, 2005): 206.

72. However, both the speed with which EU directives were transposed in the Cypriot legal system, as well as the limited expertise of the drafters in EU law, led to problems in the actual implementation of EU law. It could be argued that the processes of construction, diffusion, and institutionalization of formal and informal rules, procedures, policy paradigms, styles, ways of doing things, and shared beliefs and norms, identified by Radaelli, have not yet been 'incorporated in the logic of domestic (national and subnational) discourse, identities, political structures, and public policies'[83] in Cyprus. More than a decade of application of EU law, however, has led to a more thorough appreciation of interaction with EU legislation, despite the inherent problems involved in a small country. It could be thus considered that EU legislation, together with the implementation of the ILO conventions, has transformed Cypriot labour law.

§4. Role of Government Institutions in the Shaping and Administration of Labour and Industrial Relations Policy

I. Degree of Government Intervention

73. The Constitution does not specify a particular economic system. However, the Cypriot economy is in general based on the free market system, with the private sector being the backbone of economic activity. The government's role is limited to safeguarding a transparent framework for the operation of market mechanisms, the exercise of indicative planning and the provision of public utilities. As the system of collective agreements relies mostly on its voluntary character, the role of the Ministry is to supervise and to control the procedure and to provide assistance and mediation for resolution of industrial disputes. The structure of government intervention is in general consistent with the ILO Convention 150/1978 which was ratified by Law 64/80, as it provides for a tripartite system of negotiations with regard to industrial relations. The Ministry also monitors the application of statutory requirements regarding individual employment contracts by assigning responsibilities to inspectors whose role is to safeguard compliance with the various legislative instruments. This is consistent with the ILO Labour Inspection Convention 81/1947, which was ratified by Law 31(III)/1999.

II. Incomes Policy

74. The Republic of Cyprus committed to reform the social protection system and income policy under the MoU signed with the Troika. At the request of the Ministry of Labour, Welfare and Social Insurance and the Ministry of Finance, a technical assistance mission by the IMF visited Nicosia during 3–17 June 2013. The purpose of the mission was to develop a proposal for reforming the social protection system in the context of increasing unemployment and decreasing household

83. See C. Radaelli, 'The Europeanization of Public Policy', in K. Featherstone and C. Radaelli (eds,), *The Politics of Europeanization* (Oxford: Oxford University Press, 2003): 27.

incomes. The main aim of the new policy adopted by the Ministry of Labour, Welfare and Social Insurance was to improve the targeting of social benefits so as to generate the fiscal space needed to reallocate social protection spending to programmes that more effectively protect vulnerable households; ensuring work incentives to avoid welfare dependency was also considered as a priority.

75. The unemployment benefit system was considered effective even prior to reform, as it provided for a six-month protection to unemployed persons, with low-income families and families with children receiving increased protection. Reform focused, however, on the centralization of social benefits which were previously provided by different government ministries and agencies, with limited coordination of implementation. The fragmentation of the system resulted in different benefits with overlapping objectives being provided by different ministries, as well as duplication of administrative structures. The allocation of public spending resulted in coverage gaps since insufficient amounts were allocated to programs targeted at the increasing numbers of families adversely affected by the economic downturn; generous, but untargeted benefits were provided, so that households with similar needs might well receive very different levels of benefits.

76. Following the reform, the Ministry of Labour, Welfare and Social Insurance undertook the role of coordinating the welfare policy of the Republic and introduced a universal scheme targeted at protecting lower income families; the introduction of this guaranteed minimum income (GMI) scheme, coupled with an integrated beneficiary database and strict controls on whether beneficiaries fulfil the criteria provided by legislation, amounted to a virtual transformation of the previous system, minimized abuse and targeted the incomes policy of the Republic within the budgetary framework available. Furthermore, the Ministry introduced obligations on behalf of the beneficiaries of welfare dependency, as well as several schemes to combat unemployment.

III. Competence of Ministries in Labour Questions

77. The Department of Labour of the Ministry of Labour, Welfare and Social Insurance is responsible for the promotion and implementation of government policy in the field of employment. The government's main policy aim in this respect is to maintain conditions of full and productive employment and promote conditions for the rational utilization of the labour force. The Department's objectives are to encourage participation in employment and safeguard the proper application of legislation relating to conditions of employment, protection of special categories of workers, health and safety at work and non-discrimination. In general, the Ministry of Labour, Welfare and Social Insurance has a role in virtually all activities of the labour sector, either by monitoring the application of statutory legislation, mediating between employers and trade unions in industrial disputes, engaging in tripartite negotiations and setting up priorities to restrict unemployment and to improve the welfare of workers.

§5. SOURCES OF LABOUR LAW

I. Constitution

A. The Framework

78. The Constitution of Cyprus is a written and lengthy document, consisting of 199 articles and three annexes.[84] Article 179, paragraph 1 provides that the Constitution shall be the supreme law of the Republic, while Article 179, paragraph 2 provides that no law or decision of the House of Representatives, or of any of the Communal Chambers, and no act or decision of any organ, authority or person in the Republic exercising executive power or any administrative function shall in any way be repugnant to, or inconsistent with, any of the provisions of the Constitution. The Constitution of Cyprus is thus the supreme law of the Republic and any ordinary laws, or international law instruments must not be inconsistent with the Constitution. A detailed list of the constitutionally safeguarded fundamental rights is included in Part II of the Constitution of Cyprus (Articles 6 the volume of drafting required did not meet 35) under the heading 'Fundamental Rights and Liberties'.[85]

79. Legislation which is contrary to the provisions of the Constitution safeguarding individual human rights may be declared unconstitutional by the trial court. It has been held that the fundamental rights and liberties safeguarded by the Constitution have to be narrowly construed and in case of doubt, should always be interpreted in favour of the individual protected, rather than in favour of the state.[86] It is further noted that the Constitution safeguards minimum rights; the legislator may always opt to afford wider protection of a right or establish a new right; however, in the latter cases such right shall not enjoy a constitutional level of protection, but shall only be protected by ordinary legislation. Authorities of the Republic, legislative, executive and judicial, are duty bound, in accordance with Article 35 of the Constitution, to secure within the limits of their respective competence, the effective application of the provisions of Part II of the Constitution.[87]

80. Article 33 of the Constitution explicitly provides that the fundamental rights and liberties guaranteed by the Constitution shall not be subject to any other limitations or restrictions other than those provided in Part II of the Constitution. Such limitations may further only be introduced by legislation enacted by the House of

84. See in detail, A. Emilianides, *Constitutional Law in Cyprus* (The Hague: Kluwer, 2013).

85. See in general, C. Tornaritis, *The State Law of the Republic of Cyprus* (Cyprus Research Centre: Nicosia, 1982, in Greek), *idem*, *The Legal Aspects of Human Rights* (Nicosia, 1977, in Greek), *idem*, *The Human Rights as Recognized and Protected by Law, With Special Reference to the Law of Cyprus* (Nicosia, 1967), P. Evangelides, *The Republic of Cyprus and its Constitution, with Special Regard to the Constitutional Rights* (Bamburg: Difo – Druck GmbH, 1996), A. Loizou, *Constitution of the Republic of Cyprus* (Nicosia, 2001, in Greek), C. Paraskeva, *Cypriot Constitutional Law: Fundamental Rights and Freedoms* (Athens: Nomiki Vivliothiki, 2015, in Greek).

86. *Fina (Cyprus) Ltd* v. *Republic* (1962) 3 RSCC 26.

87. *Police* v. *Georghiades* [1983] 2 CLR 33.

Representatives or legislation deemed to be part of Cypriot law under Article 188 of the Constitution,[88] or, since the accession of the Republic of Cyprus to the EU, legislation which forms part of EU law. It is further stipulated in Article 33 §2 that limitations or restrictions to the fundamental rights safeguarded by the Constitution should be interpreted strictly and should not be applied for any purpose other than those for which they have been prescribed. Interference with constitutional rights should never be given wider effect that what clearly and beyond doubt is warranted by their context.

81. Part II of the Constitution guarantees to the individual certain social and economic rights which provide for a set of conditions that have to be met while structuring the economic system.[89] The main constitutional articles relevant to labour law are Article 9 concerning the right to a decent existence and social security, Article 10 prohibiting forced or compulsory labour, Article 21 safeguarding the right to trade unionism, Article 25 guaranteeing the right to work, Article 26 providing for the right to contract, including the right to enter into collective agreements, Article 27 which protects the right to strike and Article 28 which safeguards the right to equality and non-discrimination. Articles 21, 26, 27 and 28 of the Constitution shall be considered in the appropriate sections of this monograph; the remaining articles are briefly discussed below.

B. Prohibition of Compulsory Labour

82. It is further provided, in section 2 of Article 10, that no person shall be required to perform forced or compulsory labour; the term 'forced or compulsory labour' shall not include: (a) any work required to be done in the ordinary course of detention or during conditional release from such detention; (b) any service of a military character if imposed or, in case of conscientious objectors, subject to their recognition by a law, service exacted instead of compulsory military service; or (c) any service exacted in case of an emergency or calamity threatening the life or well-being of the inhabitants.

83. Contrary to Article 4 of the ECHR, Article 10 of the Constitution does not provide for an exception for 'any work or service which forms part of normal civic obligations'. It could thus reasonably be argued that in view of such omission, the imposition of 'work or service which forms part of normal civic obligations' might well fall under the notion of prohibited forced or compulsory labour. It should be noted that the Republic of Cyprus has further ratified the ILO Forced Labour Convention 29/1930 and the Abolition of Forced Labour Convention 105/1957.

88. *Police* v. *Hondrou and Another* (1962) 3 RSCC 82.
89. See C. Tornaritis, 'The Social and Economic Rights under the Law of the Republic of Cyprus', *Mélanges Bridel* (Lausanne, 1968): 533 the volume of drafting required did not meet 556.

C. *Right to Social Security and Decent Existence*

84. Article 9 of the Constitution stipulates that every person has the right to a decent existence and to social security. A law shall provide for the protection of the workers, assistance to the poor and for a system of social insurance. The Constitution does not attempt to define the notion of a 'decent existence'; however, it is submitted that the state has an obligation to 'create and maintain such conditions of living, of work and of health as to enable every person to enjoy a standard of living adequate for the health and well-being of himself and his family'.[90] The Republic further has a constitutional duty to enact legislation in order to provide for the protection of workers, assistance to the poor and for a system of social insurance. The right to social security is aimed at protecting the individual in the event of unemployment, illness, old age or other similar conditions. Article 9 of the Constitution could be interpreted as a constitutional demand for the existence of some form of welfare state.

85. However, the right to a decent existence does not imply that there is a free licence for anyone to act as he deems fit, irrespective of the general interests of society, for the purpose of allegedly ensuring a decent existence. Any interpretation to the contrary would lead to absurd results, since it would negate the prerogative of the state to regulate, within reason and in order to safeguard the general welfare, social and economic life. In light of the above, the Supreme Constitutional Court dismissed the argument that section 16 of the Shop Assistants Law, Cap. 185, which regulated the exercise of the profession of a shopkeeper, was inconsistent with Article 9 of the Constitution.[91]

D. *Right to Work*

86. Article 25 of the Constitution safeguards the right of every person to practise any profession or to carry on any occupation, trade or business. The exercise of this right may be subject to such formalities, conditions or restrictions as are prescribed by law and relate exclusively to the qualifications usually required for the exercise of any profession or are necessary only in the interests of the security of the Republic or the constitutional order or the public safety or the public order or the public health or the public morals or for the protection of the rights and liberties guaranteed by the Constitution to any person or in the public interest. Legislation should not provide for formalities, conditions or restrictions, if they are contrary to the interests of either Community.

87. As an exception a law may provide, if it is in the public interest, that certain enterprises of the nature of an essential public service, or relating to the exploitation of sources of energy or other natural resources, shall be carried out exclusively by

90. C. Tornaritis, *The Human Rights as Recognized and Protected by the Law of the Republic of Cyprus* (Nicosia, 1974): 15.
91. *Police* v. *Milliotis* [1961] 1 RSCC 113.

the Republic or a municipal corporation or by a public corporate body created for the purpose by such law and administered under the control of the Republic, and having a capital which may be derived from public and/or private funds; provided that where such enterprise has been carried out by any person, other than a municipal corporation or a public corporate body, the installations used for such enterprise shall, at the request of such person, be acquired on payment of a just price, by the Republic or such municipal corporation or such public corporate body, as the case may be.

88. The right guaranteed by Article 25 of the Constitution is thus not unrestricted, but it might be subject to qualifications in accordance with the law. Furthermore, Article 25 guards only against direct and not indirect interference with the right safeguarded thereunder.[92] It was accordingly held that reasonable restrictions imposed on the right to practise the profession or trade of a driver or of an owner of a public vehicle are not unconstitutional, since they are necessary for the public safety, for the protection of the rights and liberties guarantees by the Constitution to any person and in the public interest.[93] On the other hand, it was held that section 3 of the Bakeries (Night Work) Law, Cap. 177, which prohibited night work in bakeries was not necessary for the protection of public health and accordingly ran contrary to Article 25 of the Constitution.[94]

89. In *Shistris* it was held that nothing in Article 25 limits the right of the state to subject the exercise of a trade or profession to any number of licences for the public interest; so long as the conditions imposed are reasonable the law will be upheld.[95] Control of the profession or trade which may be considered as necessary for the exercise of such right is therefore not excluded by Article 25; a test of reasonableness should guide the Courts in deciding whether a restriction to the exercise of the rights safeguarded by Article 25 should be considered as legitimate.[96] In *Voyias* it was held that the imposition of a licence fee does not infringe the right of the Applicant to practice his profession, since it is only imposed with a view to exact revenue for the Municipality and for assessing the tax and not a regulatory process of the activities constituting a profession. Moreover, in *Kyriakides* it was confirmed that conditions or restrictions laid down to regulate the qualifications required for the exercise of a profession (such as an architect, engineer, doctor or advocate), are not in principle inconsistent with the provisions of Article 25.[97]

90. In the case *of Lapertas Fisheries* the Supreme Court held that section 3 §1 of the Stock Exchange Law of Cyprus (Amendment) Law 42(I)/2000, which imposed on a company the obligation to proceed to an initial public offering, irrespective of considerations about the damaging or even destructive effect of such an obligation to the financial interests of the company or its members, was inconsistent

92. *Loizou* v. *Poullis* [1969] 1 CLR 17, at 24.
93. *Police* v. *Liveras* [1962] 3 RSCC 65.
94. *Nicosia Police* v. *Georghiou* [1962] 4 RSCC 36.
95. *Shistris* v. *Cyprus Tourism Organization* [1983] 2 CLR 72.
96. *President of the Republic* v. *House of Representatives* [1992] 3 CLR 165 (in Greek).
97. *The Board for Registration of Architects and Civil Engineers* v. *Kyriakides* [1966] 3 CLR 640.

with Article 25 of the Constitution. The Court held that the impugned legislation completely disregarded the financial interests of the company and its right to exercise a trade or profession and deprived them of the opportunity to act in a manner that they themselves consider as beneficial for their own interests. The obligation was so extensive that it effectively negated the right safeguarded by Article 25 of the Constitution.[98] A similar conclusion was reached in *Pitsillides*; it was held that obligating an investment fund to invest 80 per cent of their funds within a timescale of 12 months, irrespective of whether such investments would be considered as financially sound by the management of the investment fund, was inconsistent with Article 25 of the Constitution.[99]

II. European Union Law

91. The Court of Justice of the EU (CJEU) has long considered that the Treaty on European Union (TEU) is different from other treaties in that it has established a new legal order for the benefit of which the Member States have permanently limited their sovereign rights.[100] The CJEU has therefore considered that the supremacy and primacy of EU law extends even against the provisions of the national constitutions of the Member States of the Union.[101] Following the accession of the Republic of Cyprus to the EU, the Constitution was amended with the Fifth Constitutional Amendment of 2006, 127(I)/2006, which aimed at facilitating the exercise of the rights and obligations of the Republic of Cyprus as an EU Member State.

92. The newly added paragraph 4 of Article 169 of the Constitution provides that the Republic may exercise any option and discretion provided for in the Treaty establishing the EC or the TEU and to any Treaties substituting or modifying them. Modified Article 179, paragraph 2 of the Constitution provides that no law or decision of the House of Representatives, or of any of the Communal Chambers, and no act or decision of any organ, authority or person in the Republic exercising executive power or any administrative function shall in any way be repugnant to, or inconsistent with, any obligation imposed upon the Republic as a result of its participation as a Member State of the EU.

93. Furthermore, the newly inserted Article 1A of the Constitution provides that no constitutional provision is considered to invalidate any laws, acts or measures which are deemed necessary due to the obligations of the Republic of Cyprus as a Member State of the EU, or may impede the legal effect and application of Regulations, Directives or other EU, or EC legal instruments of a binding nature in the

98. [2002] 2 CLR 335 (in Greek).
99. *Pitsillides* v. *Cyprus Securities and Exchange Commission* [2004] 3 CLR 7 (in Greek). See also *Cyprus Securities and Exchange Commission* v. *Laser Investments Ltd* [2007] 3 CLR 224 (in Greek).
100. Case 26/62, *Van Gend en Loos* [1963] ECR I; Case 6/64, *Costa* v. *ENEL* [1964] ECR 585.
101. Case 11/70, *InternationaleHandelsgesellschaft* [1970] ECR 1125.

Republic.[102] As a result, EU law now has an intra-constitutional effect, in the sense that it is considered to be an integral part of the Constitution, and no constitutional provision may invalidate any provision of a binding nature of EU law.

94. It should be noted that it is the Constitution itself which provides for the facilitation of Community law within the Cypriot legal order and its specific primacy. EU law is therefore accorded a constitutional status by the Constitution itself, in the sense that no other provision of the Constitution may be invoked so as to declare the provisions of EU law unconstitutional. Such effect is purely intra-constitutional as far as the Cypriot legal order is concerned. In addition to the EU's primary law, there are a number of directives which are directly of interest to Cypriot employment law; there is little doubt that Cypriot employment law is a field substantially influenced and transformed by the harmonization process in the EU.[103]

III. International Treaties

95. Article 169, paragraph 1 of the Constitution provides that every international agreement with a foreign state or with any international organization relating to commercial matters, economic cooperation (including payments and credit) and *modus vivendi,* shall be concluded under a decision of the Council of Ministers. Any other treaty, convention or international agreement shall be negotiated and signed under a decision of the Council of Ministers, in accordance with Article 169, paragraph 2, and it shall only be operative and binding on the Republic of Cyprus when approved by a law made by the House of Representatives whereupon it shall be concluded.

96. The above are subject to the veto right of the President or the Vice-President of the Republic, provided for in Articles 50 and 57, paragraph 13, if the decision of the Council of Ministers relates to foreign affairs, defence or security. An international treaty, convention or agreement that has been concluded in accordance with the procedure described above shall have as from its publication in the Official Gazette of the Republic superior force to any municipal law, on condition that such a treaty, convention or agreement is also applied by the other party thereto, in accordance with Article 169, paragraph 3 of the Constitution.

---

102. See also C. Lycourgos, 'Cyprus Public Law as Affected by Accession to the European Union', in C. Kombos, *Studies in European Public Law* 101ff. (Sakkoulas, 2010), 101ff; *idem*, 'The Application of EU Law in Cyprus: Selected Aspects', *The Cyprus Yearbook of International Law* 43 (2012); S. Laulhe-Shaelou, 'Back to Reality: The Implications of EU Membership in the Constitutional Legal Order of Cyprus', in A. Lazowski (ed.), *Brave New World. Application of EU Law in the New Member* States: 471–502 (TMC Asser Press 2010), C. Kombos, *The Impact of EU Law on Cypriot Public Law* (Thessaloniki: Sakkoulas, 2015).

103. For a detailed assessment see C. Ioannou, *The Eager Europeanisation of Cypriot Social Policy: When Accession becomes a National Goal* (PhD thesis, Manchester, 2007). See also M. Antoniou, *Social Policy and Occupation: Harmonization of the Cypriot Legislation with the Acquis Communautaire* (Nicosia: OEB, 2002, in Greek).

97. In view of the above, the Constitution provides for a dualistic approach with respect to the relationship between national and international law. An international treaty, convention or agreement will therefore not become part of the Cypriot legal order unless and until it has been ratified by the Council of Ministers, approved by law by the House of Representatives and published in the Official Gazette of the Republic. It is only through publication in the Official Gazette that the international law instrument may be invoked before the Cypriot courts and be applied in the Cypriot legal order.

98. Such an international law instrument has superior force over any ordinary domestic legislation, not in the sense of an obligation to repeal any inconsistent domestic law, but in the sense of having superiority and precedence in its application. International law, once incorporated in the national legal order and published in the Official Gazette, is superior to any other municipal law, irrespective of whether such law is prior or subsequent to the international law instrument. An international law instrument may not be implicitly repealed through the enactment of conflicting subsequent municipal legislation.[104] Hierarchically, international law instruments are therefore placed above any municipal legislation, with the exception of the Constitution. The Constitution, as the supreme law of the Republic, does not fall within the definition of municipal law of Article 169, paragraph 3 of the Constitution.

99. Consequently, an international law instrument, either treaty, convention or agreement, is inferior to the Constitution, and the constitutional provisions prevail in case of any inconsistency between them and the provisions of the international law instrument.[105] It should be further noted that while an international law instrument has to be ratified and published in the Official Gazette in order to become part of the Cypriot legal order, its interpretation is governed by the principles and interpretation of international law and particularly those contained in the Vienna Convention on Treaties. The rules and principles of interpretation of ordinary statutes do not apply with respect to the interpretation of international law instruments.

100. Article 169, paragraph 3 of the Constitution introduces the condition of reciprocity, namely the condition that the international law instruments, either treaties, conventions or agreements, have to be applied also by the other party thereto, in order to enjoy superior force over municipal legislation. It has been held, however, that the nature, objective and function of certain international treaties and conventions is such so as to exclude the condition of reciprocity. These are multilateral conventions, the object of which is not to create any subjective or reciprocal rights

---

104. *Malachtou* v. *Armefti and Another* [1987] 1 CLR 207. See also C. Tornaritis, 'The Introduction of International Law into the Legal System of Cyprus', 3 *Cyprus Law Tribune* 460 (1990); *idem*, *The Treaty Making Power, especially under the Law of the Republic of Cyprus* (Nicosia 1973).

105. *Malachtou* v. *Armefti and Another* [1987] 1 CLR 207; *Ship Owners Union and Another* v. *The Registrar of Trade Unions and Others* [1988] 3 CLR 457.

for the contracting parties themselves, but rather to promote certain principles of law, moral and legal values, and which a contracting party signs and ratifies only for the realization of this objective. Examples of such international conventions are those which protect human rights, or those whose aim is the improvement and formulation of common rules and the achievement of social justice.

101. For an international law instrument to be applicable, it must be self-executing, in the sense that its provisions must be of such nature so that they may be applied by the organs of the state and be enforced by the courts, or that they may create rights for the individuals, govern or affect directly relations of the internal life between the individuals, and between the individuals and the state or the public authorities.[106] The Republic of Cyprus has signed and ratified a number of ILO conventions which fall under the latter category and are self-executing.[107] The International Covenant on Civil and Political Rights and the International Covenant on Economic, Social and Cultural Rights of 16 December 1966 were ratified by the Republic of Cyprus with Law 14/1969.[108]

IV. The European Convention on Human Rights

102. Part II of the Constitution of Cyprus which guarantees the fundamental rights and liberties is modelled on the European Convention on Human Rights (ECHR). However, the provisions of the ECHR have been extended and enlarged in some respects with a number of social and economic rights added in order to meet the basic requirements of a modern society.[109] The ECHR itself was ratified and was incorporated in the internal legal order by the European Convention for the Protection of Human Rights (Ratification) Law 39/1962.[110] On the basis of Article 169, paragraph 3 of the Constitution, the ECHR and its Protocols have superior force to any municipal law; however, the constitutional provisions shall prevail in case of any inconsistency between them.[111]

---

106. *Malachtou* v. *Armefti* [1987] 1 CLR 207.
107. *Cypriot Shipowners Union and another* v. *The Registrar of Trade Unions and others* [1988] 3 CLR 457, affirmed on appeal on the interpretative approach *Registrar of Companies and others* v. *Cypriot Shipowners Union* [1991] 3 CLR 93 (in Greek). By the end of 2015, the Republic of Cyprus had ratified 50 ILO Conventions in force. For a complete list see http://www.ilo.org/dyn/normlex/en/f?p=NORMLEXPUB:11200:0::NO::P11200_COUNTRY_ID:103070.
108. M. Triantafyllides, 'A Comparison of the Provisions for Civil and Political Rights in the Cyprus Constitution with Relevant Internationally Adopted Provisions', 6 *Cyprus Law Tribune* 3 (1967): 1. *Cyprus Law Tribune* 5 (1968); O. Ozgur, 'Implementation of International Human Rights Norms in the Republic of Cyprus: Some Problem Areas' in *10th Commonwealth Law Conference* (1993): 261–269.
109. Acknowledged in several judgments of the Supreme Court of Cyprus, such as *Attorney-General* v. *Ibrahim* [1964] CLR 195, 225; *Attorney-General* v. *Afamis* 1 RSCC 121: 125–126.
110. C. Tornaritis, *Council of Europe and the Republic of Cyprus* 42 (1978); A. Loizou, 'Cyprus' in R. Blackburn, J. Polakiewicz, *Fundamental Rights in Europe: The European Convention on Human Rights and its Member States, 1950–2000* (Oxford University Press 2001): 219.
111. T. Hadjanastassiou, 'The European Convention on Human Rights applicable in Cyprus', 3 *Cyprus Law Tribune* (1976): 97.

103. To the extent, however, that it has been incorporated in constitutional provisions and to the degree that its provisions have not been altered during incorporation, the ECHR enjoys limited constitutional status.[112] Cypriot courts frequently invoke the case law of the ECtHR, not only with respect to the interpretation of the ECHR, but also with respect to the interpretation of the corresponding constitutional articles. Therefore, the courts will try, wherever possible, to interpret the relevant constitutional provisions in a manner which is consistent with the interpretation adopted by the ECtHR.[113] The most important provision of the ECHR relevant to Labour Law is Article 11 safeguarding the right of trade unionism; Article 14 safeguarding the right to non-discrimination is also relevant.

V. Ordinary Legislation

104. Article 61 of the Constitution provides that the legislative power of the Republic shall be exercised by the House of Representatives in all matters except those expressly reserved to the Communal Chambers under this Constitution. Following the self-dissolution of the Greek Communal Chamber, and following the withdrawal of Turkish Cypriots from all organs of the Republic after the events of 1963–1964, the whole of the legislative power of the Republic has been transferred to the House of Representatives. The legislative power of the House of Representatives includes the power to both enact general legislation which sets out rules of general application, and legislation which concerns specific cases; it is, however, subject to the application of the principle of separation of powers, in the sense that the legislative power of the House of Representatives may not interfere with the powers of the executive or of the judiciary.[114]

105. It should be noted that the Laws of Cyprus in force immediately prior to Independence were compiled by Criton Tornaritis and were published in six volumes in 1959, separated into 354 Chapters (Caps).[115] These laws are referred to by their respective Cap. of the 1959 edition. Many of these laws continue to be in force, sometimes with minor or no amendments, and they are referred to by their respective Cap. of the 1959 edition. By virtue of Article 188 of the Constitution, the laws which were in force during the British rule of Cyprus remained in force to the extent that they were not subsequently repealed or modified by an act of the House of Representatives, and to the extent that they are not contrary to or inconsistent with the Constitution.

---

112. See A. Emilianides, *Beyond the Constitution of Cyprus* (Sakkoulas 2006, in Greek).
113. See further A. Loizou, *Cyprus and the European Convention on Human Rights* (Sakkoulas 2003, in Greek), C. Tornaritis, 'The Operation of the European Convention for the Protection of Human Rights in the Republic of Cyprus', 3 *Cyprus Law Review* (1983): 455; C. Clerides, 'The Operation of the European Convention on Human Rights in the Civil Courts of Cyprus', 39–40 *Cyprus Law Review* (1992): 6029 (in Greek).
114. A. Emilianides, *Constitutional Law in Cyprus* (Kluwer 2013).
115. *The Statute Laws of Cyprus in force on 1 April 1959*, v. I-VI, London, 1959.

VI. Administrative Regulations and Orders

106. When enacting primary legislation, the House of Representatives may authorize the various organs of the administration to issue administrative regulations or orders in the form of secondary legislation. Such administrative regulatory acts set rules of a legislative nature, which are general and impersonal, and which could apply to cases irrespective of whether they actually exist or may exist in the future.[116] The authority to enact regulatory acts is usually delegated by the House of Representatives to the Council of Ministers. However, the House of Representatives may delegate such power to any other administrative organ; in the case of labour law the delegation of powers is typically to the Minister of Labour, Welfare and Social Insurance. If the primary legislation has not explicitly specified the administrative organ to which it has delegated the authority to issue administrative regulations, the Council of Ministers shall have the authority to make any order or regulation in order to carry into effect of the primary legislation, in accordance with Article 54 (g) of the Constitution.[117]

107. The power of the administration to issue administrative regulations or orders is not autonomous; it is always dependent upon the primary legislation which should explicitly authorize the administration to enact secondary legislation in the form of administrative regulations. It is normal for the House of Representatives to determine the issues which ought to be regulated with administrative regulatory acts instead of primary legislation. The House of Representatives may well consider that it does not have sufficient time or expertise to regulate a specific issue; or it might well consider that the administration is better equipped to regulate specific aspects in accordance with some general guidelines provided by the legislator. It is often the case that the primary legislation provides certain guidelines or main rules that authorize the administration to regulate the matter in more detail. It should be noted that restriction of constitutional rights may normally occur only by legislation enacted by the House of Representatives and not by secondary legislation. The secondary legislation may, however, provide in more detail the manner in which the restrictions set by the primary law are to be applied.[118]

VII. Jurisprudence

108. The principles of common law and equity apply as a source of Cypriot employment law.[119] Previous judgments of the Supreme Court are binding for lower courts. Thus, case law is of great significance with regard to the interpretation of

116. N. Charalambous, *The Action and Control of the Public Administration* (2nd edn, 2004, in Greek): 236ff.
117. *Theodorides* v. *Central Bank of Cyprus* [1989] 3 CLR 1457; *Holy Archbishopric of Cyprus* v. *Republic* [1990] 3 CLR 1175 (in Greek).
118. *Spyrou* v.The *Republic* [1973] 3 CLR 627.
119. L. Loucaides, 'The Dependence of Cypriot Law from Common Law', in *Topics of Cypriot Law* (1982, in Greek): 36–77; G. Pikis, T*he English Common Law: The Rules of Equity and their Application in Cyprus* (1981, in Greek).

legal provisions.[120] The Supreme Court itself may depart from its earlier decisions whenever it concludes that a previous decision is founded on an indisputably wrong principle of law, or on a principle leading to manifest injustice, or on a principle which cannot be reconciled to changed legal or social circumstances. It is thus noted that previous case law is only binding so far as a subsequent law with different content has not been enacted. The legal rule which must be applied is the *ratio decidendi*, or the legal principle on which the previous decision was founded. The *ratio* of the case is distinguishable from *obiter dicta*, which are statements on principles of law made in the course of a decision, but on which the decision does not depend.

109. Having a substantially codified legal system, Cyprus applies common law principles where there is no Cypriot legislation in force and insofar as existing Cypriot legislation is not contradicted.[121] With respect to constitutional and administrative law, however, the Supreme Court regularly cites judgments of continental law courts, such as the Greek *Symvoulio tis Epikrateias* and the French *Conseil d'État*.[122] It could therefore be argued that Cypriot constitutional justice forms an idiosyncratic osmosis between continental and common law.[123] Cypriot administrative law in particular is similar to Greek, French and German continental administrative law, and not to English administrative law. As a result, Greek and French authorities and jurisprudence have guided the evolution of Cypriot administrative law. It should also be noted that recourses against public authorities which exercise administrative or executive functions are administrative law recourses.

VIII. Collective Agreements: The Industrial Relations Code

110. Article 26(2) of the Constitution provides that a law may provide for collective labour contracts of obligatory fulfilment by employees and workers, with adequate protection of the rights of any person, whether or not represented at the conclusion of such contract. However, no such law has ever been enacted by the Republic. Collective agreements are an important source of labour law; however, the general rule is that collective agreements between trade unions and employers are not legally binding to them.[124] Thus, their success rests on the willingness of the

120. C. Artemides, 'The Principle of Commitment of Courts to Case-Law in English Common Law', in *Aspects of Cypriot Law* v. I (Asselia 1981, in Greek): 219–231; S. Nikitas, 'The Principle of Judicial Precedent in English Common Law', in *Corpus de Jure Cyprii* v.I (Legal Studies Council 1987, in Greek): 119–133.

121. Symeonides, *The Mixed Legal System*: 441–455.

122. From 1960 to 1963, while the President of the Supreme Constitutional Court was the German Ernst Forsthoff, the Supreme Court regularly cited German jurisprudence with respect to constitutional law cases.

123. See S. Papasavvas, *La Justice Constitutionelle à Chypre* (Presses Universitaires d'Aix-Marseilles, 1998); *idem*, *The Osmosis of Continental Public Law and Common Law in Cyprus*, 28 *To Syntagma* (2002): 693 (in Greek).

124. C. Tornaritis, 'Collective Employment Agreement' [1972] 1-2 *Cyprus Law Tribune*: 14–17. However, C. Christodoulou, *Handbook of Cypriot Labour Law* (Nicosia: Epifaniou, 2009, in Greek): 133–138, argues that the provisions of the IRC are legally binding.

social partners to abide by them, and the voluntary cooperation of the workers and the employers.

111. One of the most defining characteristics of the 'Cypriot corporatist model' is its reliance on collective bargaining agreements, which involve negotiations between the parties concerned. The 'Basic Agreement' constituted the first social contract signed between the social partners in 1962, shortly after independence. This secured the right to organize, negotiate, sign collective agreements, and the right to strike, and also provided for a procedural framework dealing with industrial disputes. In 1977 this Agreement was replaced by the IRC. The latter adopted the main conventions of the ILO.

112. The IRC is essentially a soft law document, a gentlemen's agreement that regulates the collective bargaining process, and presents a conflict resolution mechanism when employers' and employees' representatives fail to reach a mutually acceptable outcome. In the preamble to the IRC, the then Minister of Labour and Social Insurance, stated that its smooth application presupposes a spirit of responsibility for the faithful observance of the IRC by both employers and employee organizations.[125] A violation of the IRC does not involve any legal sanctions. Nevertheless, deviations from the IRC have been relatively rare, as it has always assumed a great degree of respect by all parties concerned. It has been held that the IDT has judicial knowledge of the IRC; the IDT is composed by two lay members who have knowledge of industrial relations from the view of both the employer and the employee; accordingly, matters of good industrial relations practice need not be proved before the IDT since the lay members are taken to know them and bring their specialist knowledge and experience in the workings of the tribunal.[126]

113. Collective agreements which have not been incorporated in legislation do not, as a principle, create rights and obligations under public law.[127] Accordingly, a collective agreement may not amend the rights of the employee under public law, unless it has become part of the practice of the administrative organ.[128] However, their terms may be incorporated in individual employment contracts and so become binding on the parties thereto.[129] Moreover, a collective employment agreement may not prevail over an individual employment agreement, unless the terms of the

125. Markos Spanos, 'Preamble to the Industrial Relations Code', in Republic of Cyprus, Ministry of Labour and Social Insurance, *Industrial Relations Code* (Nicosia: Press and Information Office, 1977): 4.
126. *United Hotels Ltd* v. *Stavrou and others* [2003] 1 CLR 515 (in Greek).
127. *Kontemeniotis* v. *CyBC* [1982] 3 CLR 1027, *Papadopoulosand others* v. *CyBC* [1996] 3 CLR 1 (in Greek), *Evangelou and others* v. *CyBC* [1985] 3 CLR 1410, *Angelides* v. *CYTA*, Case 46/2011, dated 1/9/2014 (in Greek), *Mesaritis and others* v. *TEPAK*, Cases 1322-1333/2011, dated 11 June 2015 (in Greek).
128. *DerParthogh* v. *CyBC* [1984] 3 CLR 635.
129. *Lanitis Bros Co Ltd* v. *Ioannides and others* [1979] 1 CLR 815.

collective agreement have been incorporated, expressly or impliedly, in the individual employment agreement.[130]

114. In *Hatzikonstanti* the employee was also a minor shareholder in the company of the employer; a shareholders' agreement had been signed which, inter alia, provided that the employee would be employed until his compulsory retirement insofar as he did not violate the terms of employment. The Cyprus Hotel Association had signed a collective agreement with the trade unions providing that hotels would temporarily suspend their business during winter and consequently that the employment of most employees would also be suspended during the same period; such employees would receive only a small part of their salaries, while at the same time receiving an unemployment stipend from the Social Insurance Fund. The employer, as a hotel, had signed the collective agreement and was bound by its terms.

115. When the employment of the employee was suspended in accordance with the terms of the collective agreement he filed an application before the IDT, claiming that the terms of his employment had been violated; the IDT held that the employer had a right to terminate the employment in good faith, since the terms of the collective agreement prevailed over the terms of the shareholders agreement. The Supreme Court reversed this decision. It was held that the terms of the collective agreement could not prevail over the terms of an individual employment agreement; the terms of the shareholders agreement which formed part of the individual employment agreement of the employee, could not unilaterally change because a collective agreement had been signed.[131]

§6. International Private Labour Law

116. Following the accession of the Republic of Cyprus to the EU, Law 15(III)/2006 implemented the Rome Convention into Cypriot law.[132] The Rome Convention has since been converted into Rome I which applied exclusively in contractual relations concluded after 17 December 2009.[133] Thus, the common law rules no longer apply insofar as contractual relations falling within the scope of the Rome Convention, and subsequently Rome I, are concerned. Article 8 of the Rome I Regulation sets out specific rules governing individual employment contracts. The aim of Article 8 is to provide for rules that are more favourable to the interests of

130. *Hatzikonstanti* v. *Golden Coast Ltd*, Civ. Appeal 314/08, dated 24 January 2012 (in Greek), *Loizou* v. *Stylson Engineering Co Ltd* [1998] 1 CLR 2077 (in Greek).

131. *Hatzikonstanti* v. *Golden Coast Ltd*, Civ. Appeal 314/08, dated 24 January 2012 (in Greek).

132. Although it should be noted that the Rome Convention had already been implemented before accession by Law 31(III)/2002.

133. See A. Emilianides, *The New European Private International Law of Contracts* (Thessaloniki: Sakkoulas, 2009, in Greek), Plender and Wilderspin, *The European Private International Law of Obligations* (3rd edn, London: Sweet & Maxwell, 2009), A. Belohlavek, *Rome Convention/Rome I Regulation* (Prague: Juris, 2010), v. I-II.

employees who are presumed to be the weaker party in employment contracts.[134] Collective employment contracts are not included in the scope of Article 8; collective employment contracts are concluded between the employer and trade unions which are considered as having significant bargaining power, contrary to what is normally the case when the employer enters into a contract with an individual employee.

117. The Regulation does not define the notion of an individual employment contract, nor does it distinguish such a contract from a collective employment contract or from similar contracts, such as a contract to supply services, a work contract or an agency contract; the legislative definition of the term would be useful, in light of the varying definitions found in the various Member States.[135] The notion of an individual employment contract should in any event be interpreted on the basis of autonomous criteria of Community law and not on the basis of national law or on the basis of the law of the forum.[136] The employment contract should therefore include an element of permanence and exercise of control; the facts of the case, the terms of the contract and the will of the parties are elements to be taken into account in order to decide whether an employment relationship exists, as even de facto employment relationships might be caught within the scope of Article 8 of the Rome I Regulation.

118. Article 8 of the Rome I Regulation stipulates that the law chosen by the parties in accordance with Article 3 may not have the result of depriving the employee of the protection afforded to him by provisions that cannot be derogated from by agreement under the law that, in the absence of choice, would have been applicable to the individual employment contract. This is an important qualification which implies that the provisions that cannot be derogated from by agreement under the law that would have been applicable to the contract in the absence of choice should be applied in parallel to the provisions of the law chosen by the parties. Deciding, however, which law is more favourable to the employee in a given case is not always a simple task; the court should compare between the conflicting provisions of the two laws (the chosen one and the one which would apply in absence of choice) in order to determine *in concreto* which provisions are more favourable to the employee and how such provisions may be reconciled.[137]

---

134. This corresponds with recital 23 of the Regulation which provides that in contracts concluded with parties regarded as being weaker, those parties should be protected by conflict-of-law rules that are more favourable to their interests than the general rules.
135. See G. Cavalier and R. Upex, 'The Concept of Employment Contract in European Union Private Law' (2006) 55 *International and Comparative Law Quarterly*: 587–608. See also C. Morse, 'The EEC Convention on the Law Applicable to Contractual Obligations', in P.M. North (ed.), *Contract Conflicts. The EEC Convention on the Law Applicable to Contractual Obligations: A Comparative Study* (Amsterdam: North Holland Publishing, 1982): 143–184.
136. See Case 133/91, *Ivenel* v. *Schwab* [1982] ECR 1891, Case 25/79, *Sanicentral* v. *Collin* [1979] ECR 3423, at 3434. See also Case 75/63, *Unger*; [1964] ECR 177 where it was decided that the notion of an employee found in the Treaty ought to be interpreted on the basis of Community criteria.
137. See H. Morgenstern, *Les Conflits des Lois en Droit du Travail. Etude sur la Loi Applicable à la Relation du Travail Internationale* (Geneva, 1986): 81.

119. The law applicable in default of choice by the parties is the law of the country in which, or failing that from which, the employee habitually carries out his work in performance of the contract. The determination of the country in which, or from which, the employee habitually carries out his work in performance of the contract shall be determined on the basis of autonomous criteria of Community law; this is the place where the employee actually carries out the most important part of his obligations towards the employer. Thus, where the employee performs his work in more than one state, the place of performance shall be the place where, or from which, the employee discharges principally his obligations towards the employer.[138]

120. It is further provided that where the law applicable cannot be determined on the basis of the above principles, because the country in which or from which the employee habitually carries out his work in performance of the contract cannot be properly determined, the contract shall be governed by the law of the country where the place of business through which the employee was engaged is situated (Article 8 §3 of the Rome I Regulation). The country where the work is habitually carried out shall not be deemed to have changed if the employee is temporarily employed in another country;[139] the conclusion of a new contract of employment with the original employer or an employer belonging to the same group of companies as the original employer should not preclude the employee from being regarded as carrying out his work temporarily in another country.

121. Article 8 §4 of the Rome I Regulation provides for an escape clause, by safeguarding the application of the law of the country which appears from the circumstances as a whole to be more closely connected to the contract, when compared to the country in which or from which the employee habitually carries out his work, or the country where the place of business through which the employee was engaged is situated, depending on the case. The application of the escape clause does not refer to the law of the country which is more favourable to the interests of the employee, but rather to the law of the country which is more closely connected to the contract; this might potentially deprive the employee from the protection afforded by the law of the country in which or from which he habitually carries out his work, and accordingly the escape clause should be narrowly construed, so that its application is restricted only to clear cases, or to cases where its application shall not be contrary to the interests of the employee.

---

138. Case C-125/92, *Mulox* v. *Hendrick* [1993] ECR I-4075, Case C-383/95, *Rutten* v. *Cross Medical Ltd* [1997] ECR I-57, Case C-37/00, *Weber* v. *Universal Ogden Services Ltd* [2002] ECR I-2013 which related to the interpretation of the Brussels Convention. See also *Ferwerda* v. *Banque Nationale de Paris, Cour d'appel de Paris*, 8 October 1996.
139. Recital 36 of the Regulation clarifies that work carried out in another country should be regarded as temporary if the employee is expected to resume working in his country of origin after carrying out his tasks abroad.

Part I. The Individual Employment Relation

Chapter 1. Definition and Concepts

§1. The Different Categories of Employee

122. The most typical category of employment in Cyprus is an employment contract of indeterminate or indefinite duration. During the first 26 weeks of employment in such a contract, the employee is considered to be on probation and can, subject to specific provisions in the contract of employment or special grounds, be dismissed without notice and without cause. Other common categories of employment are fixed-term contracts and part-time employment. Employees are further classified by reference to their field of work and there are specific legislations governing categories of employees, such as hotel employees, catering employees, shop employees, seafarers, flying personnel, mobile workers, workers in quarries and mines and office employees.

§2. The Individual Labour Contract

I. Different Categories of Labour Contract

A. *Definite Period*

123. Fixed-term contracts last for a specific period only and, accordingly, do not normally grant rights to the employee once the specific period ends, other than those referred to in the individual employment agreement itself. A fixed-term worker is defined in section 2 of Law 98(I)/03, as a person having an employment contract or relationship entered into directly between an employer and a worker, where the end of the employment contract or relationship is determined by objective conditions, such as reaching a specific date, completing a specific task, or the occurrence of a specific event.

124. It is thereby provided in section 5(d) of the Termination of Employment Law 24/1967 that the employee has no right to compensation for dismissal, if the employment was terminated due to the end of the period specified in the fixed-term contract of employment. However, even prior to the introduction of Law 98(I)/2003, the proviso to section 5(d) provided that where the IDT considers that any fixed-term contract, or any series of fixed-term contracts, should, either alone, or in conjunction, be considered as a contract of indeterminate duration, then such contract, or series of contracts, shall be deemed not to be a fixed-term contract and, accordingly, it shall not be terminated at its end. The proviso in question was applicable, irrespective of the establishment of any bad faith on behalf of the employer.[140]

125. The Fixed-Term Contracts (Prohibition of Discrimination) Law 98(I)/2003 harmonized Cypriot law with Directive 1999/70/EC.[141] The purpose of Directive 1999/70/EC is to put into effect the framework agreement on fixed-term contracts concluded on 18 March 1999 between the general cross-industry organizations, thus improving the quality of fixed-term work by ensuring the application of the principle of non-discrimination and establishing a framework to prevent abuse arising from the use of successive fixed-term employment contracts or relationships. Law 98(I)/03 applies to fixed-term workers who have an employment contract or employment relationship as defined in law, collective agreements or practice; it does not apply to initial vocational training relationships and apprenticeship schemes, nor to employment contracts and relationships which have been concluded within the framework of a specific public or publicly supported training, integration and vocational retraining programme (section 4 of Law 98(I)/03).[142]

126. Law 98(I)/03 introduced the principle of non-discrimination in the treatment of fixed-term workers (section 5 of Law 98(I)/03). It is thereby provided that in respect of employment conditions,[143] fixed-term workers shall not be treated in a less favourable manner than comparable permanent workers solely because they have a fixed-term contract or relation,[144] unless different treatment is justified on objective grounds; where appropriate, the principle of *pro rata temporis* shall apply. The period of service qualifications relating to particular conditions of employment shall be the same for fixed-term workers as for permanent workers except where different length of service qualifications are justified on objective grounds. A 'comparable permanent worker' is defined in section 2 of Law 98(I)/03, as a worker with an employment contract or relationship of indefinite duration, in the same establishment, engaged in the same or similar work/occupation, due regard being given to qualifications/skills; when there is no comparable permanent worker in the same

140. *Servos* v. *The Attorney-General* [1977] 1 CLR 154 (in Greek).
141. Council Directive 1999/70/EC of 28 June 1999 concerning the framework agreement on fixed-term work concluded by ETUC, UNICE and CEEP.
142. As permitted by clause 2 of the Annex of Directive 1999/70/EC.
143. The concept of 'employment conditions' covers the compensation that the employer must pay to an employee on account of the unlawful insertion of a fixed-term clause into his employment contract; the compensation paid in this respect need not be the same as that paid for unlawful termination of a permanent employment contract. See Case C-361/12, *Carratu* v. *Poste Italiane SpA* EU, C-2013: 830.
144. Case C-38/13, *Nierodzik* v. *Samodzielny Publiczny Psychiatryczny Zaklad Opieki Zdrowotnej im dr. Stanislawa Deresza w Choroszczy* EU, C-2014: 152.

undertaking or establishment, the comparison should be made by reference to the existing legislation, collective agreements or practice.[145]

127. To prevent abuse arising from the use of successive fixed-term employment contracts or relationships,[146] section 7 of Law 98(I)/03 provides that if an employee has been employed by a fixed-term contract for a cumulative period of 30 months – either by renewal of the contract or otherwise – then the contract shall be considered for all purposes as a contract of indefinite duration and any contractual provision to the contrary limiting the duration of the contract shall not apply; this provision shall apply irrespective of the sequence of the successive fixed-term contracts of employment.[147] Fixed-term contracts may be considered as successive even if they are separated by reasonable short intervals between them, since otherwise the employer would be in a position to abuse the system by renewing the contracts with brief delays;[148] if they are separated, however, by a period of two or three months, this might be considered as a break which could potentially deprive them of their character as 'successive'.[149] Law 98(I)/03 does not seem to be applicable to workers who entered into a first or single fixed-term employment contract, even if such a contract in fact covers fixed and permanent needs of the employer.[150]

128. The contract shall not be considered as a contract of indefinite duration if the employer can prove that the employment by a fixed-term contract may be justified on objective grounds;[151] objective grounds apply in particular when: (i) the needs of the undertaking with regard to the carrying out of work are temporary,[152] (ii) the employee substitutes for another employee, (iii) the particularities of the work carried out justify the fixed-term duration of the contract, (iv) the fixed-term

145. See Case C-273/10, *Medina* v. *Fordo de Garantia Salarial et Universidad de Alicante* [2011] ECR I-32, Case C-556/11, *Martinez* v. *Junta de Castilla y Leon* EU, C-2012: 67, Case C-177/14, *Regojo Dans* v. *Consejo de Estado* EU, C-2015: 450.

146. Case C-519/08, *Koukou* v. *Elliniko Dimosio* [2009] ECR I-65, Cases C-22/13, 61-63/13, 418/13, *Mascollo and others* v. *Ministero dell' Istruzione, dell' Universita e della Ricerca* EU, C-2014: 2401.

147. A number of recent decisions of the IDT have declared that a fixed-term employee became an employee of indefinite duration. See *Syrimi* v. *Attorney-General*, App. 338/2012, decision of 30 June 2015 (first instance judgment, in Greek), *Briel* v. *EDEX-Educational Excellence Corporation Ltd*, App. 264/2013, decision of 30 September 2015 (first instance judgment, in Greek).

148. Case C-212/04, *Adeneler and others* v. *Ellinikos Organismos Galaktos* [2006] ECR I-6057.

149. See Case C-364/07, *Vassilakis and others* v. *Dimos Kerkyraion* [2008] ECR I-90, Case C-362-363/13, 407/13, *Fiamingo and others* v. *Rete Ferroviaria Italiana SpA* EU:C:2014:2044. See also *Deutsche Lufthansa AG* v. *Kumpan* [2011] ECR I-1309.

150. See Cases C-378-380/07, *Angelidaki and others* v. *Organismos Nomarchiakis Autodioikisis Rethymnis* [2009] ECR I-3071, Cases C-162-164/08, *Lagoudakis* v. *Kentro Aniktis Prostasias Ilikiomenon Dimou Rethymnis* [2009] ECR I-195, Case C-20/10, *Damiano* v. *Poste Italiane SpA* [2011] ECR I.

151. The temporary nature of the employment relationship of certain public servants does not, in itself, constitute an objective ground. See Cases C-444/09 and 456/09, *Gavieiro and Torres* v. *Conselleria de Educacion e Ordenacion Universitaria de la Xunta de Galicia* [2010] ECR I-14031.

152. Case C-290/12, *Rocca* v. *Poste Italiane SpA* EU, C-2013: 235, Case C-190/13, *Samohano* v. *Universitat Pompeu Fabra* EU, C-2014: 146.

employee is employed on probation, (v) the fixed-term employment is made in compliance with a judicial decision or (vi) the employment refers to the contracts of Volunteer Sub-Officers of a Five Year Term, or of Volunteer Sub-Officers (section 7(2) of Law 98(I)/03).

129. It has been held that the concept of 'objective grounds' requires the existence of specific factors relating to the activity in question and the conditions under which it is carried out; objective reasons cannot be justified by the mere fact that they are provided for by domestic legislation.[153] The assessment whether the renewal of fixed-term employment contracts is justified by such an objective reason, should take account of all the circumstances of the case, including the number and cumulative duration of the fixed-term employment contracts or relationships concluded in the past with the same employer.[154] The mere fact that the fixed-term worker completed the periods of service on the basis of fixed-term employment does not constitution an objective ground.[155]

130. The employer has the obligation to inform fixed-term workers about vacancies which become available in the undertaking or establishment to ensure that they have the same opportunity to secure permanent positions; such information may be provided by way of a general announcement at a suitable place in the undertaking or establishment. Employers should further facilitate access by fixed-term workers to appropriate training opportunities to enhance their skills, career development and occupational mobility (section 8 of Law 98(I)/03). The employer should provide appropriate information to existing workers' representative bodies about fixed-term work in the undertaking; furthermore, fixed-term workers shall be taken into consideration in calculating the threshold for the constitution of workers' representative bodies (section 9 of Law 98(I)/03).

131. Any employer who violates any provision of Law 98(I)/03 shall be guilty of a criminal offence punishable by a fine not exceeding €3,400. The Minister of Labour, Welfare and Social Insurance may appoint inspectors for monitoring the proper application of Law 98(I)/03; the inspectors have the power to enter any premises and proceed to any inspections, inquests, examinations or controls they consider necessary and request any person to provide information and facilitate them at the exercise of their duties. Any act which impedes the exercise of the functions of the inspectors amounts to a criminal offence punishable by imprisonment of up to three months and/or a fine not exceeding €5,100 (section 12 of Law 98(I)/03).

132. The IDT has jurisdiction over any dispute of a civil nature with regard to the application of Law 98(I)/03 (section 10 of Law 98(I)/03). In *Avraam*, an employee who was employed under successive fixed-term contracts applied before

---

153. Case C-212/04, *Adeneler and others* v. *Ellinikos Organismos Galaktos* [2006] ECR I-6057, *Den Cerro Alonso* v. *Osakidetza – Servicio Vasco de Salud* [2007] ECR I-7109.
154. Case C-586/10, *Kücük* v. *Land Nordhein-Westfalen* EU, C-2012: 39.
155. Cases C-302-305/11, *Valenza and others* v. *Autorita Garante della Concorrenza del Mercato* EU, C-2012: 646.

the Supreme Court under Article 146 of the Constitution against the termination of her employment, alleging that she had become an employee under a contract for indefinite duration by virtue of Law 98(I)/2003. The Full Bench of the Supreme Court held that the IDT has exclusive jurisdiction to adjudicate disputes arising out of the interpretation of Law 98(I)/2003, since the said legislation referred to contracts of employment under private law and not to contracts of employment under public law; under Article 146 of the Constitution, the Supreme Court had original jurisdiction only with respect to recourses of employees of the public sector who are employed under contracts of public law.[156] Therefore, an employee of the public or semi-public sector who is employed under a contract of employment of private law cannot file a recourse under administrative law, but can only apply before the IDT.[157]

133. The employee in *Panayides* was initially employed as a temporary employee of the Republic of Cyprus under a fixed-term contract; his employment was renewed by successive fixed-term employment contracts and thus he became a temporary employee under contracts for indefinite duration by virtue of Law 98(I)/2003. The employee alleged that by becoming an employee of indefinite duration, he should enjoy all pension and other benefits of permanent public servants who held a similar position. The IDT rejected his claim, holding that the purpose of Law 98(I)/03 was not to compare between permanent public servants and temporary employees under contracts of indefinite duration, but between the latter category of employees and employees under fixed-term contracts. The employee appealed. The Supreme Court affirmed the judgment of the IDT.[158] It was held that the objective of Directive 98(I)/03 was to abolish the abuse of fixed-term contracts and the discrimination between employees under successive fixed-term contracts on the one hand and employees under indefinite contracts on the other.[159]

134. It was further held that the employee essentially sought to become a permanent member of the public service, without ever having been employed as a public servant by the competent organ by virtue of the Public Service Law 1/1990; however, the notion of a public servant is entirely different from the notion of an employee under a contract of indefinite duration. In this respect the Supreme Court distinguished *Santana and Andaloucia*;[160] in this case the CJEU held that Directive 1999/70/EC applies to contracts and relationships concluded with the public authorities and other public sector bodies, precluding any difference in treatment between career civil servants and interim civil servants of a Member State, based

156. *Avraam* v. *Republic* [2008] 3 CLR 49 (in Greek).
157. *Burston* v. *University of Cyprus*, Case 874/2012, dated 4 June 2015 (in Greek), *Venizelou* v. *Republic*, Administrative Appeal 67/2010, dated 21 May 2015 (in Greek).
158. *Panayides* v. *Attorney-General*, Civil Appeal 132/09, dated 19 July 2012 (in Greek).
159. Case C-53/04, *Marrosu and Sardino* v. *Azienda Ospedaliera Ospedale San Martino di Genova e Cliniche Universitarie Convenzionate* [2006] ECR I-7213, Case C-180/04, *Vassallo* v. *Azienda Ospedaliera Ospedale San Martino di Genova e Cliniche Universitarie Convenzionate* [2006] ECR I-7251.
160. Case C-177/10, *Santana* v. *Consejeria de Justicia y Administracion Publica de la Junta de Andaloucia* [2011] ECR I-7907.

solely on the grounds that the latter are employed for a fixed-term period, unless different treatment is justified on objective grounds. It was further held that even if it was to be argued that the case was subject to the provisions of Directive 1999/70/EC, there were objective grounds which justified the difference in treatment, namely the manner in which temporary employees are employed, which is entirely different from the manner in which public servants are appointed.[161]

B. Indefinite and Probationary Period

135. The most important safeguard of employees under contracts of employment of indefinite duration under Cypriot law is their protection from unfair dismissal under the provisions of the Termination of Employment Law 24/67. In cases of unjust dismissal, an employee should be given sufficient notice and shall have a right to compensation, whereas in certain exceptional cases the employer might be required to re-hire the employee. The employee shall have a right to compensation only if he has been employed for a continuous period of at least 26 weeks, a period which can be extended by written agreement of the parties to 104 weeks at a maximum; the period during which the employee does not enjoy a right to compensation is in general regarded as a trial period, or probationary period, during which the employer has the power to dismiss the employee without sanctions.

C. Part-time

136. Part-time contracts of employment are regulated by the Part-Time Employees (Prohibition of Discrimination) Law 76(I)/2002, as amended by Laws 14(I)/2007 and 55(I)/2007, which transpose Directive 97/81/EC into the Cypriot legal order.[162] Cyprus has also ratified ILO Convention 175/1994 on Part-Time Work with Law 6(III)/1997. The purpose of Directive 97/81/EC is to implement the Framework Agreement on part-time work concluded on 6 June 1997 between the general cross-industry organizations, by providing for the removal of discrimination against part-time workers, improving the quality of part-time work and facilitating the development of part-time work on a voluntary basis. Law 76(I)/02 applies to all part-time workers who have an employment contract or employment relationship, with the exception of part-time workers who are employed on a casual basis[163] and full-time workers who suffer from partial and temporary unemployment leading to the reduction of their normal working hours for economic, technical or restructuring reasons (section 4 of Law 76(I)/02).

137. A 'part-time worker' is defined by virtue of section 2 of Law 76(I)/02 as an employee whose normal hours of work, calculated on a weekly basis or on average

161. *Panayides* v. *Attorney-General*, Civil Appeal 132/09, dated 19 July 2012 (in Greek).
162. Council Directive 97/81/EC of 15 December 1997 concerning the Framework Agreement on part-time work concluded by UNICE, CEEP and the ETUC.
163. The exception is permitted by Clause 2 of the Annex of Directive 97/81/EC.

over a period of employment of up to one year, are less than the normal hours of work of a comparable full-time worker; i.e. a full-time worker in the same establishment having the same type of employment contract or relationship, who is engaged in the same or a similar work/occupation, due regard being given to other considerations which may include seniority and qualification/skills. Where there is no comparable full-time worker in the same establishment, the comparison shall be made by reference to the applicable domestic legislation, collective agreement or practice (section 5 of Law 76(I)/02).

138. The principle of non-discrimination between part-time and comparable full-time workers is safeguarded by virtue of section 6 of Law 76(I)/02, which provides that in respect of employment conditions, part-time workers shall not be treated in a less favourable manner than comparable full-time workers solely because they work part-time unless different treatment is justified on objective grounds; where appropriate, the principle of *pro rata temporis* shall apply.[164] Where justified by objective reasons, the Minister of Labour, Welfare and Social Insurance may, where appropriate, subject the access to particular conditions of employment to a period of service, time worked or earnings qualifications; qualifications relating to access by part-time workers to particular conditions of employment should be reviewed periodically regarding the principle of non-discrimination.

139. Part -time workers are generally entitled to equivalent terms and conditions of service and protection as comparable full-time workers, particularly with regard to: salary and benefits (calculated *pro rata temporis*),[165] social insurance contributions, termination of employment, protection of maternity, annual leave with pay and public holidays, sick leave and parental leave; however, this does not preclude rules which make the length of weekly working time and the organization of working time of part-time workers dependent on quantitative needs in terms of work.[166] Part-time employees are also entitled to receive the same treatment and protection in relation to collective bargaining, organization and employee representation, health and safety at work and protection from discrimination (section 7 of Law 76(I)/02).

140. Moreover, the employer should, to the extent possible, examine requests by full-time employees to become part-time employees and vice versa, inform employees for vacancies, facilitate access to part-time employment and provide the necessary information to trade unionists about part-time employees (section 9 of Law 76(I)/02). The conversion of a full-time to a part-time employee, or vice versa, should in principle be voluntary, and refusal by the employee should not give rise

164. See Case C-527/13, *Fernandez* v. *Instituto Nacional de la Seguridad Social and Tesoreria General de la Seguridad Social* EU, C-2015: 215, *Instituto nazionale della previdenza sociale* v. *Bruno and others* [2010] ECR I-5119.
165. Case C-476/12, *Österreichischer Gewerkschaftsbund* v. *Verband Österreichischer Banken und Bankiers* EU, C-2014: 2332.
166. Case C-313/02, *Wippel* v. *Peek & Cloppenburg GmbH & Co KG* [2004] ECR I-9483.

to termination of employment (section 8 of Law 76(I)/02); however, whereas conversion from full-time work to part-time work should not take place without the consent of the employee, it is possible for the employer to order the conversion of a part-time employment relationship to full-time, without the consent of the worker concerned. It was held that a situation whereby a worker has his full-time employment relationship converted into a part-time employment relationship contrary to his wishes cannot be regarded as comparable, because the reduction of working time does not involve the same consequences as an increase, in particular with regard to the worker's remuneration.[167]

141. Any employer who violates the provisions of Law 76(I)/02 is subject to a fine not exceeding €3,400 (section 12 of Law 76(I)/02). The Minister of Labour, Welfare and Social Insurance may appoint inspectors for monitoring the proper application of Law 76(I)/02; the inspectors have the power to enter any premises and proceed to any inspections, inquests, examinations or controls they consider necessary and request any person to provide information and facilitate them at the exercise of their duties. Any act which impedes the exercise of the functions of the inspectors amounts to a criminal offence punishable by imprisonment of up to three months and/or fine not exceeding €5,100 (section 13 of Law 76(I)/02). The IDT has jurisdiction over any dispute of a civil nature with regard to the application of Law 76(I)/02 (section 11 of Law 76(I)/02).

II. Form and Content

142. A contract of employment is a contract and, as such, the conditions for its conclusion are governed by the provisions of the Contract Law, Cap. 149, to the extent that there are no conflicting provisions in other specific legislation. Accordingly, a contract of employment may be either express or implied if the circumstances prove that the employee is actually employed by the employer despite the lack of an express agreement.[168] No formality is required for the conclusion of employment contracts; thus, they may be concluded orally and without witnesses, or requirements for a specific form. However, by virtue of the Provision of Information to the Employee by the Employer on the Conditions Applicable to the Contract or Employment Relationship Law 100(I)/2000, the employer should inform the employee about the material provisions of the employment contract in writing within one month from the commencement of the employment. As far as the content of the individual employment contract is concerned, all statutory rights and obligations are generally implied into employment contracts and the parties may not waive mandatory statutory provisions by agreement. They may, however, agree to terms or conditions of employment which are more favourable for the employee than those provided by statute, or by existing collective agreements.

---

167. Case C-221/13, *Mascellani* v. *Ministero della Guistizia* EU, C-2014: 2286.
168. *A. Iasonos Ltd* v. *Christou and others* [1994] 1 CLR 703 (in Greek).

III. Ability to Conclude a Labour Contract

A. *Minors*

143. A minor, namely a person under 18 years of age, has limited capacity to enter into contracts (section 11 of the Contract Law, Cap. 149). Minors' contracts are voidable at the option of the minor, irrespective of whether the other party to the contract was aware of a minor's age. However, there are exceptions to the rule that a minor lacks capacity to enter into a contract and one of those exceptions refers to contracts which are for the minor's benefit, including contracts of employment, apprenticeship, service and education; such contracts are therefore considered as valid and enforceable.

144. The employment of children under 15 years of age is generally prohibited under section 5 of the Protection of Young People at Work Law 48(I)/2001 which transposed Directive 94/33/EC.[169] However, a child who has attained the age of 14 and who has successfully completed the first cycle of secondary education (gymnasium), or has been lawfully discharged from the obligation to attend such education, may be admitted to a combined occupational and vocational programme aiming at teaching the child a profession or trade; this can only occur if the Minister of Labour, Welfare and Social Insurance grants a special permit for the child to attend the particular programme. A child admitted to such a programme should enjoy a period of at least one month of leave during school vacations.[170]

145. The Minister may further grant a permit, following consultation with the Welfare Services and the Department of Inspection of Work, to enable the child to exercise cultural, artistic, sport or advertising activities, if it is decided that this would be in the child's welfare.[171] Any activity of this kind should not be harmful to the safety, mental or bodily health, or bodily, mental, moral or social development of children and should not prevent the child's attendance at school, participation in vocational guidance or training programmes approved by the competent authority or capacity to benefit from the instruction received (section 7 of Law 48(I)/01). The permit should be given for each child separately and for a time not exceeding in total, either continuous or intermittently, three months a year for each child. During activities the children should be accompanied by their parent or guardian, or an authorized person. Under no circumstances may any child be occupied with itinerant trade activities (section 12 of Law 48(I)/01).

B. *Pensioners*

146. The private sector does not have a mandatory retirement age; this may be set, however, by individual or collective agreements. Accordingly a contract of

---

169. Council Directive 94/33/EC of 22 June 1994 on the protection of young people at work.
170. This exception is permitted under Article 4 of Directive 94/33/EC.
171. See also the Protection of Young People at Work Regulations 78/2012.

employment may be concluded even by persons who are over 65 years of age, which is the statutory pensionable age for both men and women. Liability for the payment of contributions ceases on the day the insured person reaches the pensionable age (65 years).[172] An insured person, however, who reaches the pensionable age and does not satisfy the contribution conditions for the old age pension may continue to pay contributions until these conditions are satisfied. Under no circumstances are contributions payable after the age of 68. A person may lawfully conclude a contract of employment, even if he receives the old age pension and even if he is over 68 years of age. An employee working beyond retirement age, however, may not receive compensation for unlawful termination of employment (section 4 of Law 24/67).

C. *Sound Mind*

147. As is standard to the conclusion of all contracts, a natural person has capacity to contract if he is not of unsound mind and has not been deprived of the capacity to contract by virtue of any law of the Republic (section 11 of the Contract Law, Cap. 149);[173] a contract made with a person of unsound mind is valid, but if the other party was aware that he was contracting with a person who could not understand the nature of the contract by reason of the unsoundness of his mind, then the contract is voidable at the option of the person who is of unsound mind. A person may be considered as a person of unsound mind, even without the existence of a prior court judgment to this effect, so long as the person has no free will, because he is incapable to appreciate the consequences of his actions due to old age, or disease.[174]

148. If a person has a lucid interval he shall be considered as having a sound mind, but only for as long as the lucid interval lasts; a lucid interval understandably shall be extremely difficult to prove.[175] Persons who have been adjudged as psychiatrically ill in accordance with the provisions of the Psychiatric Hospitalization Law 77(I)/1997,[176] or who have been declared as incapable in accordance with the provisions of the Administration of the Estate of Incapable Persons Law 23(I)/1996[177]

---

172. The old age pension is payable to all insured persons, employed, self-employed, or voluntary insured, provided they meet the prescribed insurance criteria. A person may be entitled to the old age pension in some cases on completion of the age of 63 years (and in the case of miners at the age of 58).
173. Y. Constantinides, 'Contract Law, Cap. 149', *Aspects of Cypriot Law*, v. I (Nicosia: Asselia, 1981): 235ff., A. Malliotis, 'Contracts', in Andreas Neocleous & Co LLC, *Introduction to Cyprus Law* (3rd edn, Limassol, 2010): 756–757.
174. *Re Fuld* [1968] P 675, *Waring* v. *Waring* (1848) 6 Moo PC 530.
175. See *Attorney-General* v. *Parnther* (1792) 3 Bro CC 441, *In the Estate of Walker* (1912) 28 TLR 466.
176. I.e. persons who are psychiatrically ill and suffer from a psychiatric disorder.
177. I.e. persons who, due to a mental disorder, drug addiction, alcoholism, or due to either mental or other bodily injury, are unable to exercise their judgement or will and are not in a position to administer their property or conduct their own affairs.

should properly be considered as a person of unsound mind. Coercion, undue influence, fraud, misrepresentation or mistake all constitute grounds for declaring a contract of employment as voidable for lack of genuine consent (sections 14–22 of Cap. 149).

D. Aliens

149. Any agreement whose object or consideration is prohibited by law shall be void pursuant to section 23 of the Contact Law. Cap. 149 provides that the consideration or object shall be unlawful if it is forbidden by law, or is of such a nature that, if permitted, it would defeat the provisions of the law, or of it is fraudulent, or if it involves or implies injury to the person or property of another, or if it immoral or opposed to public policy. An agreement which is made in violation of the law is therefore void.[178] The employment of an alien without permission by the immigration authorities is prohibited by the Aliens and Immigration Law, Cap. 105; the prohibition aims at safeguarding the public interest of the Republic, from the unauthorized entry and employment of aliens. There are various reasons why the Republic requires aliens to acquire a work permit in order to be employed in Cyprus which refer to economic, demographic and social grounds, as well as the fact that there are limited jobs available and an overflow of alien workers might lead to increased unemployment.

150. It has been held that the contract of employment of an alien who does not have a work permit in the Republic is illegal and accordingly void. Furthermore, employing an alien without a lawful permit is considered as a serious criminal offence, irrespective of whether the alien entered the Republic illegally to begin with, or whether he entered the Republic legally and his stay in Cyprus subsequently became illegal.[179] The employment of an alien who resides legally in the Republic, but who does not have a lawful work permit, is also a criminal offence, although not of the same gravity.[180] In *White* the employee filed an action against his employers claiming damages for the termination of his employment and accrued salaries; his claim was rejected on the ground that he did not have a work permit and that accordingly the contract of employment was unlawful and void *ab initio*.[181]

178. See in general P. Polyviou, *Contract Law*, v. II (Chrysafinis and Polyviou, 2014, in Greek): 595, *Glamor Development Ltd* v. *Christodoulou* [1984] 1 CLR 444, *Alam* v. *Toumazides* [1998] 1 CLR 968 (in Greek).

179. *Tabrizi* v. *Police* [2004] 1 CLR 421 (in Greek), *Ioannou* v. *Police* [2010] 2 CLR 243 (in Greek).

180. *Quinlong and others* v. *Police* [2006] 2 CLR 501 (in Greek), *Attorney-General* v. *Nicolaou* [2006] 2 CLR 488 (in Greek).

181. *White* v. *Association of Athletic Union of Kition and another* [2007] 1 CLR 742 (in Greek). In *Panayiotis Kountourides Ltd* v. *Awadalla and others* [2008] 1 CLR 852 (in Greek) it was determined as a matter of fact that the employees had the necessary permits and that accordingly the contract was lawful.

Chapter 2. Rights and Duties of the Parties during Employment

§1. Duties of the Employee

151. Employees have the obligation to carry out their duties in a reasonably satisfactory manner; by virtue of section 5(a) of the Termination of Employment Law 24/1967, any employee who fails to do so is not entitled to compensation in case of dismissal by his/her employer; this does not include however cases of temporary incapacity to work owing to illness, injury, pregnancy or a disease. In order to carry out their obligations the employee should not act negligently and should accordingly act in the manner expected by a reasonable competent employee (section 51 of the Civil Wrongs Law, Cap. 148). They should further, in accordance with the Safety and Health Law 89(I)/1996, take reasonable care for the safety and health of both themselves and other persons who might be affected by their acts, or omissions during work and use the protective equipment or plant given to them by the employer and in general cooperate with the employer in order to carry out any obligation or duty imposed under the existing legislation on health and safety.[182]

152. Employees should further fulfil their obligations under any of the terms of their individual employee agreements. Moreover, they have the obligation to adhere to certain codes of conduct and may thus also be dismissed by their employer without notice in case he commits gross misconduct, serious offence while executing his duties, a criminal offence while executing his duties, without the consent of the employer, immoral behaviour in the course of his duties, or for repeatedly or seriously violating or ignoring rules at work. An employee should cooperate with his employer and show fidelity towards him. The employee must accordingly obey all lawful and reasonable orders and instructions of his employer.[183]

153. Failure to obey reasonable orders, disrespect or indifference to the manner in which the employer expects the work to be carried out, offends against the prestige and dignity of the employer, continuous absence from work, might all, depending on the circumstances, amount to behaviour which may breach the foundations of the employer–mployee relationship.[184] Good discipline and responsible behaviour at all levels are implied conditions in most contracts of employment; behaviour which undermines the business of the employer and its reputation, as well as the public's confidence may not be tolerated.[185] A duty of confidentiality and trust are also implied conditions of the employment relationship.[186] An employee who intends to terminate his employment has to give a minimum period of notice to his employer, depending on the duration of his employment by virtue of section 10 of Law 24/67.

---

182. See also the Safety Commission at Work Regulations 134/1997 and the Management of Safety and Health Issues at Work Regulations 172/2002.
183. *KEM (Taxi) Ltd* v. *Anastassis Tryphonos* [1969] 1 CLR 52.
184. *Demstar Information Group Ltd* v. *Anastasiades* [2008] 1 CLR 1146 (in Greek), *Makris* v. *Makrisbros Ltd* [1980] 1 CLR 238.
185. *KEM (Taxi) Ltd* v. *Anastassis Tryphonos* [1969] 1 CLR 52.
186. *L. Papaphilippou & Co* v. *Louca*, Civ. Appeal 59/2010, judgment of 20 June 2014 (in Greek).

§2. Duties of the Employer

I. General Duties

154. The employer is generally required to respect any terms of the individual employment relationship signed with the employee, to provide him with work and to pay his salary or wages without delay. An employer intending to terminate the employment of an employee who has completed at least 26 weeks of continuous employment with that employer, is obliged to give the employee a minimum period of notice, depending on the length of his service, in accordance with section 9(1) of Law 24/67; the notice must be in writing. Furthermore, the employer should notify the employee in writing and as timely as possible, in the event of any action that will result in the transfer or posting of the employee to another employer, whether permanently or temporarily, even where the transfer or posting will not result in a change of duties or the place of work (section 15A of Law 24/67).

II. Provision of Information

155. The Provision of Information to the Employee by the Employer on the Conditions Applicable to the Contract or Employment Relationship Law 100(I)/2000, as amended by Law 121(I)/2007, has incorporated Directive 91/533/EEC in the Cypriot legal order.[187] Law 100(I)/00 applies to every employee having an employment contract or relation; it does not apply, however, to employees whose total duration of employment does not exceed one month or eight hours per week, or whose employment is of casual and/or specific nature, provided that the non-application of the Law is justified on objective grounds (section 3(2) of Law 100(I)/00).[188] Law 100(I)/00 further applies to expatriate employees who are working abroad under an employment contract or relationship concluded in Cyprus or governed by Cypriot law or practice and whose duration is of at least one month.

156. By virtue of section 4 of Law 100(I)/00, the employer must notify the employee in writing of the material conditions of employment;[189] these cover at least: (i) the identities of the parties, (ii) the place of work and the registered place of business or home address of the employer, (iii) the title, specialization, grade and category, and object of work, (iv) the date of commencement of the employment contract or relationship and its expected duration in the case of fixed-term work, (v) the length of the period of paid annual leave to which the employee is entitled and the manner and time of granting such leave, (vi) the length of the period of notice to be observed by the employer and the employee in case of termination of the employment contract or relationship, (vii) all the components of the employee's

187. Council Directive 91/533/EEC of 14 October 1991 on an employer's obligation to inform employees of the conditions applicable to the contract or employment relationship.

188. The exception is consistent with Article 1 of Directive 91/533/EEC.

189. See also C-253/96-256/96, *Kampelmann and others* v. *Landschaftsverband Westfalen-Lippe* [1997] ECR I-6907.

remuneration and the frequency of its payment, viii) the length of the employees' normal working day or week, (ix) reference to any collective agreement applicable to the terms and/or conditions of the employees' employment.

157. None of the abovementioned conditions of employment can be less favourable to the employee concerned than those provided for by the respective legislation; failure to mention the essential elements of the agreement with sufficient precision in a written document does not imply that the terms are inapplicable.[190] In case of expatriate employees the notice must be given to the employee prior to his departure and should in addition include the duration of the employment abroad, the currency to be used for the payment of the employee's remuneration, all possible benefits, in cash or in kind, attendant on the expatriation and any conditions governing the employee's repatriation (section 7 of Law 100(I)/00).

158. The notice is given by either a written contract of employment, or a letter of engagement or any other document signed by the employer and containing at least all the information referred to above (section 5 of Law 100(I)/00). The information must be given to the employee not later than one month after the commencement of employment (section 6(1) of Law 100(I)/00).[191] Section 6(2) of Law 100(I)/00 further provides that if the employment contract or relation for whatever reason lasts for less than a month, the information must be given to the employee at the end of this period; the latter provision does not make sense as Law 100(I)/00 does not apply to employees whose duration of employment does not exceed one month. If there is a change in the conditions of employment, the employer must inform the employee in writing, within one month at the latest, after the date of the change (section 6(3) of Law 100(I)/00); however, failure to provide it does not lead to the invalidity of the employment contract or relation (section 6(4) of Law 100(I)/00).

159. The competent court for settling any dispute of a civil nature is the IDT (section 11 of Law 100(I)/00). The Minister of Labour, Welfare and Social Insurance further has the power to appoint inspectors who have the responsibility to monitor the application of Law 100(I)/00 and to examine complaints and provide information and counselling to both employers and employees; the inspectors have the power to enter any premises and proceed to any inspections, inquests, examinations or controls they consider necessary and request any person to provide information and facilitate them at the exercise of their duties. Any act which impedes the exercise of the functions of the inspectors amounts to a criminal offence punishable by imprisonment of up to three months and/or fine not exceeding €5,100 (section 10 of Law 100(I)/00).

160. The employer has in all cases the burden of proof that he gave notice to the employee (section 9 of Law 100(I)/00) and if he violates the law without good cause, is guilty of a criminal offense and is subject to a fine not exceeding €854; the

190. C-350/99, *Wolfgang Lange* v. *Georg Schunemann GmbH* [2001] ECR I-1061.
191. Instead of two months provided in Article 3 of Directive 91/533/EEC.

burden of proof of good cause also lies on the employer also (section 12 of Law 100(I)/00). In *Menelaou* the employer had not notified in writing the employee on the main terms of his employment contract, in violation of Law 100(I)/2006. The Supreme Court held that such an omission on the part of the employer did not invalidate the employment contract, but simply meant that the IDT should determine the terms of employment by oral evidence.[192]

III. Consultation with Employees

161. Certain categories of employers also have obligations in accordance with the provisions of Law 78(I)/2005 establishing a general framework for informing and consulting employees, incorporating Directive 2002/14/EC.[193] Law 78(I)/05 sets out the minimum requirements for the right to information and consultation of employees in undertakings employing at least 30 employees (section 3 of Law 78(I)/05);[194] the number of employees is calculated by reference to the average number of employees of the undertaking during the past two years, either with definite or indefinite duration, or part-time employees (section 4 of Law 78(I)/05).[195] However, contrary to the provisions of Directive 2002/14/EC,[196] there is no reference in Law 78(I)/05 to a similar obligation for establishments. Law 78(I)/05 does not apply to the crews of vessels plying the high seas.[197]

162. Information and consultation shall cover, in accordance with section 5 of Law 78(I)/05: (i) information on the recent and probable development of the undertaking's or the establishment's activities and economic situation, (ii) information and consultation on the situation, structure and probable development of employment within the undertaking or establishment and on any anticipatory measures envisaged, in particular where there is a threat to employment, (iii) information and consultation on decisions likely to lead to substantial changes in work organization or in contractual relations. The information shall be given at such time, in such fashion and with such content as are appropriate to enable, in particular, employees' representatives to conduct an adequate study and, where necessary, prepare for consultation.

192. *Menelaou* v. *Antonis Askanis Ltd* [2011] 1 CLR 312 (in Greek).
193. Directive 2002/14/EC of the European Parliament and of the Council of 11 March 2002 establishing a general framework for informing and consulting employees in the European Community.
194. An undertaking is defined as a public or private undertaking carrying out an economic activity, whether or not operating for gain, which is located within the territory of the Republic of Cyprus. The threshold is lower than the Directive which provides for undertakings employing 50 employees.
195. C-385/05, *Confédération générale du travail (GDT) and others* v. *Premier ministre and Ministre de l' Emploi, de la Cohésion sociale et du Logement* [2007] ECR I-611 held that national legislation is precluded from excluding a specific category of workers from the calculation of staff numbers.
196. Which defines an establishment as a unit or business where an economic activity is carried out on an ongoing basis with human and material resources; Article 3 (1)(b) of Directive 2002/14/EC provides for a threshold of employment of at least 20 employees.
197. As permitted by Article 3(3) of Directive 2002/14/EC.

163. Consultation shall take place: (a) while ensuring that the timing, method and content thereof are appropriate, (b) at the relevant level of management and representation, depending on the subject under discussion, (c) on the basis of information supplied by the employer and of the opinion which the employees' representatives are entitled to formulate, and (d) in such a way as to enable employees' representatives to meet the employer and obtain a response, and the reasons for that response, to any opinion they might formulate and with a view to reaching an agreement on decisions within the scope of the employer's powers. The employer has a duty to ensure that information and consultation is properly conducted prior to reaching any decisions which may affect the employees. The practical arrangements for informing and consulting employees may be further defined by collective agreements, which may establish additional requirements for the employer (section 6 of Law 78(I)/05).

164. The trade union or other employees' representatives shall enjoy adequate protection and guarantees to enable them to properly perform their duties under Law 78(I)/05 (section 8).[198] Both the employees' representatives and any experts assisting them have a duty of confidentiality for any information which has been provided to them in confidence, which shall continue to apply even after the expiry of their term of office (section 7 of Law 78(I)/05). They may, however, pass on confidential information to employees and to third parties bound by an obligation of confidentiality.[199] The employer is not obliged to communicate information or undertake consultation when the nature of that information or consultation is such that, according to objective criteria, it would seriously harm the functioning of the undertaking or would be prejudicial to it, or is considered as confidential by legislation, such as banking or advocate privilege, patents or matters of national security. The employer may be required to furnish such information only following a court order.[200]

165. The competent court for settling any dispute of a civil nature is the IDT (section 11 of Law 78(I)/05). The Minister of Labour, Welfare and Social Insurance further has the power to appoint inspectors who have the responsibility to monitor the application of Law 78(I)/05 (section 10 of Law 78(I)/05). Any violation of Law 78(I)/05 amounts to a criminal offence punishable by a fine not exceeding €3,400.

IV. Duty to Take Reasonable Care: Safe System of Work

166. Under common law the employer has a duty to take reasonable care of the physical safety of his employees and to protect them from harm suffered at work,

198. This does not mean that more extensive protection against dismissals is safeguarded for employees' representatives. C-405/08, *Ingeniørforeningen i Danmarkv Dansk Arbejdsgiverforening* [2010] I-985.
199. As permitted by Article 6, para.1 of Directive 2002/14/EC.
200. Thereby implementing Article 6, paras. 2 and 3 of Directive 2002/14/EC.

even by actions of other employees.[201] The employer may also be liable for psychiatric harm as a result of foreseeable occupational stress,[202] or from workplace bullying,[203] but his liability does not extend to safeguarding the employee's economic welfare; thus, it has been held that an employer has no duty to make arrangements for accident insurance for a person working abroad or to warn the employee of the need to be insured.[204] The employer's duty consists of the provision of competent staff, provision of adequate and safe plant and equipment and of providing a proper system and effective supervision of work, as well as maintaining a safe system of work.[205]

167. Liability to provide a safe system of work cannot be discharged by delegation to a competent employee and accordingly the employer will remain liable even if the employee was an experienced and competent one who could have devised a safe system of work on his own; however, in the latter case, the employee might have contributory negligence.[206] The employer thus owes a duty to the employees to select competent staff and to give them proper instructions and supervision.[207] The employer should further provide a safe system of work, as safe as reasonable skill and care would permit;[208] however, such duty will be discharged if the employer has taken reasonable steps to ensure that the premises are safe.[209]

168. The obligation to provide a safe system of work includes the duty to provide the employee with proper plant and equipment; this extends to any kind of defective plants or equipment with which the employee is required to work.[210] It further requires the employer to apply a safe organization of work, including the way in which the work is to be carried out, the sequence in which the work is to be carried out, the number of staff and working hours of each employee, the provision of precautions, warnings and notices in appropriate cases and the issue of special instructions, so as not to subject his employees to unnecessary risks; the duty includes the obligation to provide a safe place of work.[211]

169. The Supreme Court has interpreted unnecessary risks as referring to any risks which the employer can reasonably foresee and against which he can guard by

201. *Municipality of Limassol* v. *Charalambous* [1989] 1 CLR 423 (in Greek).
202. *Walker* v. *Northumberland County Council* [1995] IRLR 35, *Hatton* v. *Sutherland* [2002] EWCA Civ 76, *Barber* v. *Somerset* [2004] UKHL 13.
203. *Walters* v. *Commissioner of Police of the Metropolis* [2000] 1 WLR 1607.
204. *Reid* v. *Rush & Tompkins Group Pic* [1989] 3 All ER 228.
205. *Kakou* v. *Adriatica* [1980] 1 CLR 357.
206. *Alexandrou* v. *Kyriacou and Sons Ltd* [1997] 1 CLR 506 (in Greek), *Wilsons & Clyde Coal Co Ltd* v. *English* [1937] UKHL 2.
207. *General Cleaning Contractors* v. *Christmas* [1953] AC 180
208. Naismith v. London Film Productions Ltd [1939] 1 All ER 794, *London Graving Dock* v. *Horton* [1951] AC 737.
209. *Latimer* v. *AEC Ltd* [1953] 2 All ER 499.
210. *Manthopoulos Plastics Ltd* v. *Hatziiosif* [1983] 1 CLR 291, *Georghiou* v. *Planet Shipping* [1979] 1 CLR 188, *Coltman* v. *Bibby Tankers* [1988] AC 276.
211. *Manthopoulos Plastics Ltd* v. *Hatziiosif* [1983] 1 CLR 291, *United Bricks Works Ltd* v. *Evangelou* [1992] 1 CLR 123 (in Greek), *Speed* v. *Thomas Swift and Co Ltd* [1943] KB 557, *Pape* v. *Cumbria County Council* [1992] 1 CLR 132, *Smith* v. *Baker* [1891] AC 325.

any measures, and the convenience and expense of which are not entirely disproportionate to the risk involved; thus, the court will consider whether the risk was reasonably foreseeable, whether the degree of injury was likely to result and whether there were no precautions to guard against such risk, or whether existing precautions involved great and disproportionate expense. [212] The extent of reasonable care required by the employer is a question of fact to be determined in light of the circumstances of the case.[213]

V. Health and Safety Obligations

170. In addition to their common law obligations, health and safety legislation has introduced significant obligations for employers. The Safety and Health at Work Law 89(I)/96[214] has incorporated the provisions of Directive 89/391/EEC,[215] whereas specialized obligations of the employer are provided for in secondary legislation which has transposed EU law.[216] It should further be noted that there are several ILO conventions safeguarding the health and safety of employees, which have been signed by the Republic of Cyprus; these include the Occupational Health and Safety Convention 155/1981 (ratified by Law 242/1988), Convention 171/1990 concerning Night Work (ratified by Law 34(III)/1993) and the Promotional Framework for Occupational Safety and Health Convention 187/2009 (ratified by Law 1(III)/2009).

171. The employer has a general duty to ensure the safety, health and welfare of his employees in every aspect related to work pursuant to section 13 of Law 89(I)/96; the employer shall be discharged from liability where occurrences are due to unusual and unforeseeable circumstances, beyond the employer's control, or due to exceptional events, the consequences of which could not have been avoided despite the exercise of all due care.[217] Without prejudicing the general nature of the above obligation, the liability of the employer extends to: (i) provision and maintenance

212. *Athanassiou* v. *Attorney-General* [1969] 1 CLR 160, citing *Harris* v. *Bright's Asphalt Contractors Ltd, Allard & Saunders Ltd* [1953] 1 All ER 395, *Hicks* v. *British Transport Commission* [1958] 2 All ER 39. See also *Stratmarko Ltd* v. *Michael* [1989] 1 CLR 453 (in Greek).

213. *Charalambous* v. *Metalko Ltd* [1982] 1 CLR 636, citing *Qualcast Wolverhampton Ltd* v. *Haynes* [1959] 2 All ER 38.

214. See also *Evralia Trading Ltd* v. *Attorney-General* [2008] 2 CLR 162 (in Greek), *Attorney-General* v. *Z. Demetriou and Sons (Forklift) Ltd* [2006] 2 CLR 467 (in Greek), *Attorney-General* v. *Evrika Ltd* [2005] 2 CLR 23 (in Greek), *Attorney-General* v. *Pharmacas Quarries Ltd* [2004] 2 CLR 573 (in Greek), *Attorney-General* v. *C. Kythreotis-Concrete Ltd* [2004] 2 CLR 143 (in Greek), *Director of Department of Labour Inspection* v. *Chrysostomou* [2002] 2 CLR 575 (in Greek), *Attorney-General* v. *P. Pastellis Engineering Works Ltd and another* [2001] 2 CLR 90 (in Greek), *Georghios Toumazou and Sons Ltd* v. *Limassol District Officer of Work* [2000] 2 CLR 452 (in Greek).

215. Directive 89/391/EEC of 12 June 1989 on the introduction of measures to encourage improvements in the safety and health of workers at work.

216. For the harmonization process in the area of health and safety at work see in detail C. Ioannou, *The Eager Europeanisation of Cypriot Social Policy: When Accession becomes a National Goal* (PhD thesis, Manchester, 2007): Ch. 6. See also OEB, *Handbook of Officer of Labour Relations:Safety and Health at Work* (Nicosia, 2015, in Greek).

217. This is permitted under Article 5, para.4 of Directive 89/391/EEC.

of safe work plant, systems and methods, (ii) safeguarding the safety and lack of dangers for health relating to the use, storage and transfer of objects and substances, (iii) provision of information, instructions, training and supervision for the maintenance of safety and health of employees at work, (iv) provision and maintenance of any workplace under his control in a safe position, including means of entering and exiting, (v) provision and maintenance of a safe work environment, without dangers for health, vi) taking the necessary measures to protect safety and health at work of employees, including the activities for prevention of occupational hazards, training, information and organization and providing the necessary means and supervising their proper implementation and adjusting to changing circumstances and improving them and (vii) providing the safety representatives the necessary means and sufficient leave from work, without loss of wages, to fulfil their obligations and duties.[218]

172. The employer shall implement measures with the aim of avoiding and combating risks at source and evaluating risks which cannot be avoided, adapting the work to the individual and to technical progress, replacing the dangerous tasks and materials by non-dangerous or less dangerous, developing a coherent overall prevention policy, giving collective protective measures priority over individual protective measures and giving appropriate instructions to workers. The employer should further ensure that the equipment, machinery and instruments made available to the employees are proper for the work, or suitably adapted to safeguard the safety and health at work during their use.[219] Obligations also extend to protection of pregnant female employees from occupational hazard and dangers.[220] They should further ascertain that the employee has sufficient knowledge and experience to carry out the work assigned to him, without danger for himself or other persons.

173. The employer has a duty to consult with his employees and safety representatives for the establishment and maintenance of an efficient cooperation for promoting and implementing measures which safeguard safety, health and welfare of employees.[221] He further has to ensure that the planning and introduction of new technologies are the subject of consultation with the workers and/or their safety representatives, as regards the consequences of the choice of equipment, the working conditions and the working environment for the safety and health of workers. When the employer allows another person to carry out activities in his undertaking or premises, or subcontracts part of his work, then he would need to ascertain that the

218. See also, *inter alia*, the Management of Safety and Health Issues at Work Regulations 172/2002, the Safety and Health at Work (First Aid) Regulations 198/2009, the Minimum Requirements for Safety and Health Signs at Work 212/2000, the Safety and Health at Work (Notification of Occupational Diseases) Regulations 530/2007, the Safety and Health at Work (Notification of Accidents and Dangerous Incidents) Regulations 531/2007, the Health and Safety at Work (Protection of Youth) Regulations 77/2012, the Minimum Requirements for Safety and Health at Work Regulations 174/2002
219. See also the Minimum Requirement for Safety and Health (Use of Personal Protective Equipment at Work) Regulations 444/2001.
220. See also the Protection of Motherhood (Safety and Health at Work) Regulations 255/2002.
221. See also the Safety Commission at Work Regulations 134/1997 and the Management of Safety and Health Issues at Work Regulations 172/2002.

other person is in a position to implement or maintain at least the same levels of safety and health at work.

VI. Posted Community Workers

174. EU law does not in general preclude Member States from applying their legislation, or collective labour agreements to any person who is employed, even temporarily within their territory, no matter in which country the employer is established.[222] However, the application of such rules must not go beyond what is necessary in order to attain the objective of protecting posted workers.[223] Directive 96/71/EC,[224] which was implemented in the Cypriot legal order by Law 137(I)02, introduced certain obligations for undertakings established in a Member State which, in the framework of the transnational provision of services, post workers to the territory of the Republic Cyprus. A posted worker is defined as a worker who normally works in the territory of a Member State and who is posted, for a limited period, to carry out his work in the territory of the Republic of Cyprus. Law 137(I)/02 does not apply to merchant navy undertakings as regards seagoing personnel.

175. Law 137(I)/02, similarly to the Directive, applies to the extent that the undertakings take one of the following transnational measures: (i) post workers to the territory of the Republic of Cyprus on their account and under their direction, under a contract concluded between the undertaking making the posting and the party for whom the services are intended, operating in the Republic of Cyprus; or (ii) post workers to an establishment or to an undertaking owned by the group in the territory of the Republic of Cyprus; or (iii) if a temporary employment undertaking or placement agency hires out a worker to a user undertaking established or operating in the territory of the Republic of Cyprus[225] (section 3 of Law 137(I)/02). These measures (i)–(iii) apply, provided there is an employment relationship between the (temporary) employment undertaking (or placement agency) and the worker during the period of posting.

176. Undertakings which fall under the ambit of Law 137(I)/02 and post workers in the Republic of Cyprus should guarantee to posted workers the terms and conditions of employment laid down by legislation and regulations, or by collective

222. Cases 62/81 and 63/81, *Société anonyme de droit français Seco and Société anonyme de droit français Desquenne & Giral* v. *Etablissement d'assurance contre la vieillesse et l'invalidité* [1982] ECR 223, and Case C-164/99, *Portugaia Construções* [2002] ECR I-787.

223. Cases C-369 and 376/96, *Arblade and Others* [1999] ECR I-8453, Case C-341/02, *Commission* v. *Germany* [2005] ECR I-2733.

224. Directive 96/71/EC of the European Parliament and of the Council of 16 December 1996 concerning the posting of workers in the framework of the provision of services.

225. Case C-586/13, *Martin Meat kft* v. *Geza Simonfray and another* EU:C:2015:405, Cases C-307-309/09, *Vicoplus SC PUH and others* v. *Minister van Sociale Zaken en Werkgelegenheid* [2011] ECR I-453.

agreements, but only to the extent that such collective agreements refer to the activities of building work relating to the construction, repair, upkeep, alteration or demolition of buildings as described in the Annex of Law 137(I)/02. The matters covered by such legislation, regulations, or collective agreements in the field of building work, are the following: (i) maximum work periods and minimum rest periods, (ii) minimum paid annual holidays, (iii) minimum rates of pay, (iv) conditions of hiring-out of workers, in particular the supply of workers by temporary employment undertakings, (v) health, safety and hygiene at work, (vi) protective measures with regard to the terms and conditions of employment of pregnant women or women who have recently given birth, of children and of young people and (vii) equality of treatment between men and women and other provisions on non-discrimination (section 4 of 137(I)/02).

177. In accordance with Article 3(1) of Directive 96/71/EC, the concept of minimum rates of pay is defined in accordance with national law.[226] This has been defined by virtue of section 4(2) of Law 137(I)/02 as the benefits determined by the legislation or collective agreements in force and which consist of wages, any additional stipends or benefits, including overtime pay; they do not include contributions to, and benefits from, supplementary occupational retirement schemes, or benefits paid in reimbursement of expenditure actually incurred on account of the worker's posting, such as expenditure on travel, board and lodging. It is provided, however, that as a matter of exemption, the minimum rates of pay and the minimum paid annual holidays requirement shall not apply if the period of posting does not exceed eight days and in case of initial assembly or first installation of goods where this is an integral part of a contract for the supply of goods and necessary for taking the goods supplied into use and carried out by the workers of the supplying undertaking; the above proviso does not apply to activities in the building area.[227] The length of the posting shall be calculated on the basis of a reference period of one year from the beginning of the posting; account shall be taken of any previous periods for which the post has been filled by a posted worker (section 6 of Law 137(I)/02).

178. The Ministry of Labour, Welfare and Social Insurance is the competent authority for supervising and monitoring the application of Law 137(I)/02 (section 2 and 9 of Law 137(I)/02). In this respect undertakings falling within the ambit of Law 137(I)/02 are required to provide the Ministry with a list of documents as specified in section 8 of Law in order to be able to post workers. The Ministry shall provide information regarding the terms and conditions of employment that the undertakings should guarantee to posted employees and co-operate with the public authorities of other Member States and reasoned requests from those authorities on

226. Case C-396/13, *Sähköalojen ammattiliittory* v. *Elektrobudowa Spółka Akcyjna* EU, C-2015: 86, Case C-522/12, *Tevfik Isbir* v. *DB Services GmbH* EU, C-2013: 711.

227. Law 137(I)/02 has not provided for further exemptions as would be possible in accordance with Article 3(5) of Directive 96/71/EC.

the transnational hiring of workers (section 8 of Law 137(I)/02). Any employer violating the provisions of Law 137(I)/02 is guilty of a criminal offence punishable with imprisonment of up to three months and/or a fine not exceeding €3,400.

179. The objective of section 4 of Law 137(I)/02 is to safeguard fair competition between national undertakings and undertakings which provide services transnationally, since it requires the latter to afford their workers, as regards a limited list of matters, the terms and conditions of employment safeguarded from national undertakings. Thus, a minimum protection is ensured for posted workers, which may well be higher than the protection offered in the Member State of origin.[228] Law 137(I)/02 does not prevent the application of terms and conditions of employment which are more favourable to posted workers (section 7 of Law 137(I)/02). However, undertakings established in a non-Member State must not receive more favourable treatment than undertakings established in a Member State.

180. The CJEU has held that the host Member State may not make the provision of services in its territory conditional on the observance of terms and conditions of employment which go beyond the mandatory rules for minimum protection established in Directive 96/71/EC; it was held that attempting, by means of collective action, to force a provider established in another Member State to enter into negotiations on the rates of pay for posted workers and to sign a collective agreement laying down more favourable conditions than those resulting from the relevant legislative provisions and on matters not referred to in Article 3 of Directive 96/71/EC, is precluded.[229]

VII. Transfer of Ownership

181. The contracts of employment of people working in undertakings that are transferred between owners are safeguarded by the provisions of the Safeguarding of Employees' Rights in the Event of Transfers of Undertakings, Businesses or Parts of Undertakings or Businesses Law 104(I)/2000,[230] which implemented the Transfers of Undertakings Directive 2001/23/EC.[231] Law 104(I)/00 applies to any transfer of an undertaking, business, or part of an undertaking or business to another employer as a result of a legal transfer or merger; a transfer is defined as any transfer of an economic entity which retains its identity as an organized grouping of resources which has the objective of pursuing an economic activity, whether or not

228. Case C-341/05, *Laval un Partneri Ltd* v. *Svenska Byggnadsarbetareförbundet* [2007] ECR I-11767.

229. Case C-341/05, *Laval un Partneri Ltd* v.*Svenska Byggnadsarbetareförbundet* [2007] ECR I-11767, C-438/05, Case C-438/05, *International Transport Workers' Federation and Finnish Seamen's Union* v. *Viking Line ABP* and another [2007] ECR I-10779.

230. As amended by Law 39(I)/2003.

231. Council Directive 2001/23/EC of 12 March 2001 on the approximation of the laws of the Member States relating to the safeguarding of employees' rights in the event of transfers of undertakings, businesses or parts of undertakings or businesses.

that activity is central or ancillary;[232] however, an administrative reorganization of public administrative authorities, or the transfer of administrative functions between public administrative authorities, does not amount to a transfer. Law 104(I)/00 applies to both profit and non-for-profit public and private undertakings. It does not apply to seagoing vessels (section 3 of Law 104(I)/00).

182. It has been held that the manner in which the transfer takes place is irrelevant; what is important is that the work positions remain unchanged and accordingly it is justified for the transferee to undertake the employment relationships of the transferor. The court should assess the totality of the circumstances in order to determine whether a transfer within the meaning of the law has taken place; factors such as the transfer of material or non-material things and their value, the employment or not of a substantial part of the employees by the transferee, the transfer or not of the clientele, the degree of similarity between the activities exercised prior and after the transfer and the duration of any suspension of activities, shall be taken into account depending on the nature of the enterprise to be transferred and its methods for production.[233]

183. It is thereby provided, by virtue of section 4 of Law 104(I)/00, that the transferor's rights and obligations, arising from a contract of employment or from an employment relationship existing on the date of a transfer, shall be transferred to the transferee; the transferor and the transferee may agree to be jointly and severally liable in respect of obligations which arose before the date of transfer and existing on the date of the transfer.[234] It should be noted, however, that Law 104(I)/00 cannot be relied upon in order to force an employee to continue his employment relationship with a transferee, in case the latter insists that his employment relationship with the transferor continues to exist;[235] the aim of Law 104(I)/00 is to safeguard the rights of the employees and not to determine whether a transfer has validly taken place.

184. Following the transfer, the transferee shall continue to observe the terms and conditions agreed in any collective agreement on the same terms applicable to the transferor under that agreement, until the date of termination or expiry of the collective agreement or the entry into force or application of another collective agreement; the period for observing such terms and conditions shall be no less than

232. Cases 232-233/04, *Nurten Güney-Görres and Another* v. *Securicor Aviation (Germany) Ltd and Another* [2005] ECR I-11237, Case C-458/05, *Jouini and others* v. *Princess Personal Service GmbH* [2007] ECR I-7301, Case C-466/07, *Klarenberg* v. *Ferrotron Technologies GmbH* [2009] ECR I-803, Case C-463/09, *CLECE SA* v. *Valor* [2011] ECR I-95, Case C-160/14, *Da Silva e Brito and Others* v. *Estado português* EU, C-2015: 565, Case C-509/14, *Administrador de Infraestructuras Ferroviarias*) v. *Pascual and Others* EU, C-2015: 781.

233. *Savvides* v. *SSP Catering Cyprus Ltd and Others*, Civ. Appeal 179/09, dated 20 September 2012 (in Greek).

234. Thereby implementing the second subparagraph of Article 3(1) of Directive 2001/23/EC; the Republic of Cyprus opted to adopt no measures for implementing Article 3(2) of the Directive.

235. Case C-297/03, *Sozialhilfeverband Rohrbach* v. *Arbeiterkammer Oberösterreich* and another [2005] ECR I-4305.

one year.[236] The transfer of rights described above shall not, however, apply in relation to employees' right to old-age, invalidity or survivors' benefits under supplementary company or intercompany pension schemes outside those provided under the Social Insurance legislation (section 4(3) of Law 104(I)/00).[237] It should further be noted that Law 104(I)/00 does not require the transferee to maintain contractual relationship with third parties so as not to risk the termination of employment of the transferred employees; the CJEU has accordingly held that the preservation of the lease of commercial premises entered into by the transferor with a third party is not required, even though the termination of the lease is likely to entail the termination of contracts of employment transferred to the transferee.[238]

185. Furthermore, the transfer of the undertaking or business shall not, by virtue of section 5 of Law 104(I)/00, constitute grounds for dismissal by the transferor or the transferee;[239] however, dismissals on grounds of economic, technical or organizational reasons entailing changes in the workforce may take place. If the contract of employment or the employment relationship is terminated because the transfer involves a substantial change in working conditions to the detriment of the employee, the employer shall be regarded as having been responsible for termination. It has been held that Law 104(I)/00 does not imply that the termination of a contract of employment may not take place, where that would have taken place irrespective of any transfer, as in the case of mandatory retirement, or the end of a fixed-term employment.[240] It should further be noted that the transfer of rights under section 4 and the protection from dismissals under section 5 do not apply where the transferor is the subject of bankruptcy proceedings or any analogous insolvency proceedings which have been instituted with a view to the liquidation of the assets of the transferor and are under the supervision of a competent authority (section 6 of Law 104(I)/00).

186. The status and function of the representatives of the employees affected by the transfer shall also be preserved, on the same terms and conditions as those existing before the date of the transfer, provided that the undertaking or business preserves its autonomy[241] and that the conditions necessary for the constitution of the employee's representation are fulfilled; if, however, the conditions necessary for the reappointment of the representatives of the employees, or for the reconstitution of the representation of the employees, are fulfilled under any legislation, regulations

236. Case C-328/13, *Österreichischer Gewerkschaftsbund* v. *Wirtschaftskammer Österreich* EU, C-2014: 2197. See, however, Case C-426/11, *Alemo* v. *Herron and others* EU, C-2013: 521.
237. However, employees no longer employed in the transferor's business at the time of the transfer maintain their rights on immediate or prospective entitlement to old age benefits, including survivors' benefits, under any supplementary company or intercompany schemes.
238. Case C-313/07, *Kirtruna SL* v. *Red Elite de Electrodomésticos SA* [2008] ECR I-7907.
239. This applies to all workers, as the Republic of Cyprus has opted not to exclude any categories of employees under Article 4(1), second subparagraph.
240. Case C-396/07, *Juuri* v. *Fazer Amica Oy* [2008] ECR I- 8883, Case C-386/09, *Briot* v. *Randstad Interim* [2010] ECR I-8471.
241. I.e. if the powers granted to those in charge of that entity remain, within the organizational structures of the transferee, essentially unchanged. See Case C-151/09, *Federación de Servicios Públicos de la UGT* v. *Ayuntamiento de La Línea de la Concepción* [2010] ECR I-7591.

or agreement, then such reconstitution or reappointment shall take place.[242] If the undertaking or business does not preserve its autonomy, the transferor and transferee should take all necessary measures to ensure that, the employees transferred who were represented before the transfer continue to be properly represented during the period necessary for the reconstitution or reappointment of the representation of employees. If the term of office of the representatives of the employees affected by the transfer expires as a result of the transfer, the representatives shall continue to enjoy the protection provided by laws, regulations and practice (section 7 of Law 104(I)/00).

187. The transferor and transferee are further required, pursuant to section 8 of Law 104(I)/00, to inform the employees affected by the transfer, or their representatives, of the date or proposed date of the transfer, the reasons for the transfer, the legal, economic and social implications of the transfer for the employees and of any measures envisaged in relation to the employees; the information should be given in good time before the transfer is carried out and before the employees are directly affected by the transfer as regards their conditions of work and employment.[243] Where the transferor or the transferee envisages measures in relation to his employees, he should further consult the representatives of the employees in good time on such measures with a view to reaching an agreement; the information and consultation should cover at least the measures envisaged in relation to the employees. An employer who violates the provisions relating to information and consultation is subject to a fine not exceeding €850. Any employer who abusively applies for insolvency proceedings in order to deprive his employees of their rights is subject to a fine not exceeding €1,700, whereas the employees have rights to apply for compensation (section 9 of Law 104(I)/00). The IDT is the competent court to adjudicate any disputes of a civil nature (section 8 of Law 104(I)/00).

188. In *Savvides* the employer administered the duty free shops of the Larnaca airport in accordance with a contract signed with the Republic of Cyprus. When another company assumed management and control of the Larnaca airport under a BOT (Build–Operate–Transfer) concession agreement with the Republic of Cyprus, the agreement of the employer with the Republic was terminated and all rights and obligations of the parties were transferred to the company managing the airport. The IDT held that the transfer fell under the provisions of Law 104(I)/2000. However, the Supreme Court disagreed; it was held that there was no contractual relationship between the transferee and the transferor; furthermore, the former duty-free shops were delivered empty to the transferee by the transferor, following the termination of the contract on the basis of which the employer administered such shops. In light of the circumstances, it was irrelevant that the new manager of the airport employed the majority of the employees of the employer and that they had also made an offer to the employee who declined such offer.

242. The Republic of Cyprus has opted not to take measures pursuant to Article 6(1) third subparagraph of Directive 2001/23/EC.

243. The obligations shall apply irrespective of whether the decision resulting in the transfer is taken by an undertaking controlling the employer.

Chapter 3. Working Time, Annual Vacations, Holidays

§1. Working Time

I. The Organization of Working Time Law

189. Working time is regulated by various pieces of legislation. The Organization of Working Time Law 63(I)/2002, as amended by Laws 131(I)/2003 and 15(I)/2007, contains general provisions for the hours of work, and covers all sectors of activity of the private and public sector, except the armed forces, the police force and the seafarers. The preamble of Law 63(I)/2002 states that its intention is to harmonize Cypriot law with Directive 93/104/EC;[244] however, it is sufficiently clear that Law 63(I)/02 currently incorporates in the Cypriot legal order the provisions of Directive 2003/88/EC, which repealed Directive 93/104/EC.[245] Law 63(I)/02 sets minimum health and safety requirements on issues regarding the organization of working time. The provisions of Law 63(I)/02 lay down the minimum rights of workers in relation to the organization of their working time and in no case do they affect more favourable conditions of employment provided for by law, collective agreement or otherwise.

190. 'Working time' is defined in section 2 of Law 63(I)/02 as any period during which a worker is at work, at the employer's disposal and carrying out his activities or duties, in accordance with the arrangements in force for the worker category to which he belongs. It has been held, however, that in circumstances in which workers do not have a fixed or habitual place of work, the time spent each day by those workers travelling between their homes and the premises of the first and last customers designated by their employer constitutes 'working time' and should accordingly be calculated as working time for the purposes of Law 63(I)/02.[246]

191. In relation to minimum daily rest, section 4 of Law 63(I)/02 provides for a period of a minimum daily rest of 11 consecutive hours per 24-hour period.[247] If the working time exceeds 6 hours a day, then the worker is entitled to a rest break by virtue of section 5 of Law 63(I)/02, i.e. a continuous period of at least 15 minutes during which the worker may leave his workstation; the breaks should not be taken immediately after the start or immediately before the end of the working day. As far as the technical details of the rest intervals are concerned (including their duration and the terms under which they are to be taken), if these are not regulated by

244. Council Directive 93/104/EC, of 23 November 1993 concerning certain aspects of the organization of working time, as amended by Directive 2000/34/EC of 22 June 2000.

245. Directive 2003/88/EC of the European Parliament and of the Council of 4 November 2003 concerning certain aspects of the organization of working time.

246. Case C-266/14, *Federación de Servicios Privados del sindicato Comisiones obreras (CC.OO.)* v. *Tyco Integrated Security SL and Tyco Integrated Fire & Security Corporation Servicios SA* EU, C-2015: 578.

247. Where the 24-hour period starts on 00.01 on any day and ends at 24.00 hours the same day.

collective agreements, they must be agreed by consultation between the employer and the representatives of the workers at the level of the undertaking concerned.[248]

192. The minimum weekly rest period is set at a minimum uninterrupted period of 24 consecutive hours per week in accordance with section 6 of Law 63(I)/02;[249] this is in addition to the 11-hour daily rest provided for in section 4 of Law 63(I)/02. If objective, technical or work organization conditions so justify, however, a minimum rest period of 24 hours, without adding the 11 hours of daily rest, may apply. It is further provided in section 6(3) of Law 63(I)/02 that if the employer so decides, an employee shall be entitled to either two rest periods of 24 consecutive hours each in any 14-day period, or one continuous rest period of a minimum of 48 hours every 14 days.

193. Maximum weekly work may not exceed 48 hours on average, including overtime, subject to any other laws or regulations providing for more favourable conditions for the employees (section 7 of Law 63(I)/02). The term of reference for calculating the average weekly working hours is a period of four months; periods of paid annual leave and sick leave are not calculated. It is, however, provided in section 7(4) of Law 63(I)/02 that the provisions on maximum weekly work do not apply if the employee consents for the provision of work, does not suffer any detriment by the employer if he does not accept to carry out the work and the employer keeps a record of all employees providing such work; the Minister of Labour, Welfare and Social Insurance may restrict or prohibit the possibility of work exceeding 48 hours for safeguarding the health and safety of the employees. It has been held that the compulsory transfer of a worker employed as a fire fighter to another service of the public sector on the operational ground that the worker has requested compliance with the maximum average weekly working time amounts to a violation of the Directive, even if no specific detriment is suffered by the worker by reason of the transfer.[250]

194. As far as night work is concerned, section 9 of Law 63(I)/02[251] provides that the working time of a night worker[252] shall not exceed on average eight hours in any 24-hour period, within a period of one month or in such other period as may be provided for in a collective agreement; the 24-hour period of weekly rest is not

248. These provisions implement Article 4 of Directive 2003/88/EC.
249. Where the week stars at 00:01 hours on a Monday and ends at 24:00 hours on the following Sunday.
250. C-243/09, *Günter Fuß* v. *Stadt Halle*, OJ C 346, 18 December 2010.
251. Implementing Article 2(4) of Directive 2003/88/EC.
252. A 'night worker' is defined by section 2 of Law 63(I)/02, which implements Article 2(4) of Directive 2003/88/EC in the Cypriot legal order, as any worker who, during night time works at least three hours of his daily working time as a normal course, or is likely during night time to work at least 726 hours of his/her annual working time, provided that no smaller number of hours is provided by collective agreements. The total daily working time of the worker shall be taken into account for the calculation of the above hours provided that it includes at least three hours during the period between 23:00 on any day and 06.00 hours on the following day, regardless of the time that his shift begins or ends, and that the worker performs his work in at least seven consecutive working hours.

taken into account for the calculation of this average. An employer who employs night workers on a regular basis must further inform the competent authority of that fact in writing (section 12 of Law 63(I)/02). In case a night work entails special hazards or heavy physical or mental strain for the worker, the latter should not work at night for more than eight hours in any 24-hour period during which they perform night work; work which involves special hazards or heavy physical or mental strain shall be agreed, if not determined by collective agreement, by consultation between the employer and representatives of workers or their representatives on health and safety matters, in accordance with a written assessment of risks which shall include any risks related to night work (section 9(3) of Law 63(I)/02).

195. The employer must ensure, in accordance with section 10 of Law 63(I)/02, that before any worker commences night work for the first time, and at regular intervals thereafter, he undergoes, free of charge and in compliance with medical confidentiality, the necessary medical examinations in order to ascertain whether he is suitably fit for the specific work. If the medical examination proves that a night worker has any health problems caused by night work he must be transferred, if possible, to a suitable day work. The employer should take all necessary measures to safeguard the protection of the health and safety of both night workers and shift workers (section 13 of Law 63(I)/02); if the employer intends to organize work according to a certain pattern, he must take into account the general principle of adapting work to the worker, with a view in particular to alleviating monotonous work and work at a pre-determined work rate, depending on the type of activity, and health and safety requirements, especially regarding breaks during working time (section 14 of Law 63(I)/02).

196. Various derogations consistent with Articles 17–20 of Directive 2003/88/EC may apply in the application of the provisions of Law 63(I)/02. Thus, in accordance with section 16 of Law 63(I)/02, the above rules do not apply to managing executives or other persons with autonomous decision-taking powers, family workers, or workers officiating at religious ceremonies in churches and religious communities. Derogations from provisions regarding minimum daily and weekly rest are also allowed in relation to: (a) shift work, each time the worker changes shift and cannot take daily or weekly rest periods between the end of one shift and the beginning of the next one, (b) any activities involving two or more separate periods of work in a day, particularly those of cleaning staff.

197. Medical practitioners under training are also excluded from a number of provisions of this law. Derogations from a number of provisions concerning daily and weekly rest, rest intervals and night work, also apply to mobile workers (section 17 of Law 63(I)/02). Derogations may also be made by means of collective agreements or agreements between employers and representatives of workers, on the condition that the workers concerned are afforded equivalent periods of compensatory rest or that, in exceptional cases in which it is not possible, for objective reasons, to grant such equivalent periods of compensatory rest, the workers concerned are afforded appropriate protection in several specific work activities.[253]

198. Any employer who violates the provisions of Law 63(I)/02 is subject to imprisonment of up to a year and/or a fine not exceeding €3,400 (section 19 of Law 63(I)/02). The competent court for settling any dispute of a civil nature is the IDT (section 18 of Law 63(I)/02). The Minister of Labour, Welfare and Social Insurance further has the power to appoint inspectors who have the responsibility to monitor the application of Law 63(I)/02 and to examine complaints and provide information and counselling to both employers and employees; the inspectors have the power to enter any premises and proceed to any inspections, inquests, examinations or controls they consider necessary and request any person to provide information and facilitate them at the exercise of their duties. Any act which impedes the exercise of the functions of the inspectors amounts to a criminal offence punishable by imprisonment of up to three months and/or fine not exceeding €5100 (section 20 of Law 63(I)/02).

199. The CJEU has repeatedly held that on-call duty performed by a doctor under a system where he is expected to be physically present at the place of work, but in the course of which he does no actual work, should necessarily be treated as wholly constituting 'working time' within the meaning of Directive 2003/88/EC.[254] Working time and rest periods are mutually exclusive; accordingly, Directive 2003/88/EC does not provide for any intermediate category between working time and rest periods; moreover, the intensity of the work performed by the employee and his output are not amongst the defining characteristics of 'working time'.[255] The fact that on-call duty includes periods of inactivity is thus completely irrelevant; the decisive factor is that the employee is required to be physically present at the place determined by the employer and to be available to the employer in order to be able to immediately provide the appropriate services in case of need.

200. In *Kogkorozi* the employees, who were firemen, claimed compensation for the time they remained on on-call duty. In accordance with their terms of employment, the employees would be employed for 38 hours a week and would further remain on call for 82 hours a week; they would be compensated by receiving a salary representing 65 hours a week. However, the employees claimed that they should be compensated for a total of 120 hours a week, representing both their actual time of work and their on-call duty; thus, they claimed that the time of their on-call duty should be treated and remunerated as actual working time. The IDT held that one of the two employees was entitled to the compensation claimed.

---

253. Which coincide to those stipulated in Article 7(3) of Directive 2003/88/EC.
254. Case C-437/05, *Vorel* v. *Nemocnice Cesky Krumlov* [2007] 1 ECR-331, Case C-151/02, *Landeshauptstadt Kiel* v. *Jaeger* [2003] I-8389, C-303/98, *Sindicato de Medicos de Asistencia Publica (Simap)* v. *Conselleria de Sanidad y Consumo de la Generalidad Valenciana* [2000] ECR I-7963.
255. C-101/04, *Dellas and others* v. *Premier ministre and Ministre des Affaires sociales, du Travail et de la Solidarité* [2005] ECR I-253, Case C-437/05, *Vorel* v. *Nemocnice Cesky Krumlov* [2007] 1 ECR-331.

201. The Supreme Court reversed this decision; it was held that the object of Law 63(I)/2002 and Directive 93/104/EC was to set out minimum requirements for health and safety insofar as the organization of working time is concerned and not to provide for compensation. The employees could have applied for declaring the provisions of their contract agreement as unlawful under the provisions of Law 63(I)/02, but not seek additional compensation.[256] CJEU case-law confirms that Directive 2003/88/EC does not apply to the remuneration of workers and that the Directive does not prevent a Member State from applying legislation on the remuneration of workers and relating to on-call duties performed by them at the workplace which makes a distinction between the treatment of periods in the course of which work is actually performed and those during which no actual work is performed.[257]

II. Shop Employees

202. Law 155(I)/2006 for the Regulation of the Operation of Shops and Conditions of Employment of Shop Employees, as amended by Laws 68(I)/2007, 6(I)/2011, 36(I)/15, 55(I)/15 and 70(I)/15, regulates issues that concern both the operation of shops, as well as the minimum standards of the employment terms of their employees. If an employer fails to comply with any of the provisions of Law 55(I)/06, he is subject to imprisonment of up to a year and/or a fine not exceeding €30,000. Section 11 of Law 55(I)2006 stipulates that the normal working hours of shop employees must not exceed 38 hours weekly, whereas section 10 of Law 55(I)/06 provides that the normal daily working hours should not exceed 8 hours; an employee may, with his consent, be employed as overtime for 2 additional hours daily and up to a total of 8 hours per week.

203. The daily working schedule of each employee is continuous (section 14 of Law 55(I)/06), with only one break which must last between 15 minutes and 1 hour (section 13 of Law 55(I)/06); if, however, the shop decides to apply the afternoon recess between 2.00 p.m. and 5.00 p.m. during the period 15 June to 31 August, the break may be extended during such afternoon recess (section 24 of Law 55(I)/06). Each shop employee is entitled to a minimum daily period of rest of 11 continuous hours and to a minimum weekly rest of at least 24 continuous hours per week, i.e. Sunday off (section 12(1) of Law 55(I)/06). In addition, employees of a shop that does not open on Sundays, but opens six days a week, have the right to receive either three mornings or afternoons off per week, or an additional 24-hour rest together with a morning or afternoon off per week, pursuant to section 15 of Law 55(I)/06; an afternoon off is obligatorily given on one Saturday per fortnight. Employees of shops that open only five days a week are entitled to one morning or afternoon off. The duration of a morning off is until 2.00 p.m. on a specific day and

---

256. *Attorney-General* v. *Kongorozis* [2006] 1 CLR 457 (in Greek).

257. C-101/04, *Dellas and others* v. *Premier ministre and Ministre des Affaires sociales, du Travail et de la Solidarité* [2005] ECR I-253, Case C-437/05, *Vorel* v. *Nemocnice Cesky Krumlov* [2007] 1 ECR-331.

the employee must not take up work before this time, whereas an afternoon off must be taken after 2.00 p.m. and the employee must not take up work after this time during that day.

204. Law 70(I)/15 which amended Law 55(I)/06, introduced provisions for employees who work in general shops which remain open all days of the week, including Sunday; in the latter cases, the minimum weekly rest of the employee is 48 hours per week, which could be either continuous, or split into two separate 24-hour periods. Effectively, Law 70(I)/15 secures the right of shop employees to work for no more than five days a week, despite the fact that the shop might stay open seven days a week. If an employee of a general shop works on a Sunday, then the employee should take one Sunday off per fortnight; an employee of a special shop working on a Sunday, should take one Sunday afternoon off per fortnight. If due to special reasons, an employee had to irregularly work on a Sunday which was part of his weekly rest, he should receive overtime compensation. Employees are additionally entitled to a morning or afternoon off per week. Shop employees who were employed prior to 15 May 2015 when Law 70(I)/2015 came into force, can only work on a Sunday with their consent.

III. Hotel and Catering Employees

205. The Hotel Employees (Conditions of Service) Regulations 136/1972 were enacted in accordance with the Hotels and Tourist Establishments Law 40/1969 and provide for the working hours of employees in hotels, other than the hotel manager, but including employees of restaurants or kitchens situated in the hotel and mainly used for the service of customers of the hotel. The maximum daily hours of work for hotel employees are eight, whereas the maximum weekly hours of work are 48; however, the maximum weekly hours for employees at the accounting office of the hotel and for personal secretaries are 45. There can be no continuous employment for more than 14 hours per day, with no more than two breaks per day (three shifts). Overtime work may amount to up to nine hours per week. Every employee is further entitled to one day off a week with full pay; during the summer months, however, from 15 June to 15 September, the employee may work during two of the days off per month. Violation of the obligations of the employer amounts to a criminal offence punishable by imprisonment of up to a month and/or a fine of up to €3,400.

206. The Catering Employees (Conditions of Service) Regulations of 1968 are attached to the Catering Employees (Conditions of Service) Law 80/1968[258] and provide for the working hours of employees in restaurants, coffee shops, night clubs, taverns, music clubs, cabarets, confectioneries, places serving alcohol and any other place selling food or drinks. The maximum daily hours of work for employees are 8, whereas the maximum weekly hours of work are 48 including overtime work.

258. As amended by Laws 58/1978, 65(I)/2002, 73(I)/2002 and 131(I)/2009.

Overtime work may amount to up to eight hours per week; however, overtime work may increase to up to 10 hours per week in exceptional circumstances. The working week consists of six days per week and every employee is further entitled to one day off a week with full pay. There can be no more than one break per day (two shifts). Violation of the obligations of the employer amounts to a criminal offence punishable by imprisonment of up to a year and/or a fine of up to €3,400. There can be no continuous employment for more than 14 hours per day, with no more than two breaks per day (three shifts). The Republic of Cyprus has further ratified Convention No. 172 concerning Working Conditions in Hotels, Restaurants and Similar Establishments by Law 7(III)/1997, which applies to both hotel and catering employees.

IV. Office Employees and Workers in Quarries and Mines

207. The Working Hours Law Cap. 182, as amended by Law 15/1967 and Law 62(I)/2002, provides that subject to the provisions of Law 63(I)/02, the Council of Ministers may issue a decree setting the daily, weekly or monthly hours of persons employed in any professional activity; any person violating the terms of the decree commits a criminal offence punishable by imprisonment of up to six months and/or a fine of up to €765. The Minister of Labour, Welfare and Social Insurance may appoint inspectors to oversee the implementation of the Decree and if any person impedes the exercise of the inspector's duties he shall be subject to imprisonment of up to two months and/or a fine of up to €170.

208. The existing Working Hours of Employees Decree applies to all offices where any commercial or banking activity, or any liberal profession, takes place, but not to industrial enterprises, or places for the treatment and care of the poor, or to professions which are governed by specific legislation; and the Decree refers to the work of a clerk, secretary, or administrative or executive work, including the work of an usher. The Decree sets the working hours of employees to a maximum of 44 hours per week, or 8 hours per day, excluding meal breaks; exceptions refer to cases where there are special circumstances of unexpected pressure of work, or *force majeure*, or urgent need for work.

209. Another Decree issued by virtue of Cap. 182, refers to the working hours of mine and quarry workers; the Decree provides that no mine worker shall work underground for more than eight hours per day, or 40 hours per week, excluding meal breaks. Furthermore, no mine worker shall work over the earth's surface for more than 44 hours per week and 8 hours per day. The maximum number of daily working hours for a quarry worker are 8 per week, whereas the respective weekly maximum is 44 per week. Exceptions refer to urgent or unexpected work which cannot be postponed, or which cannot be performed during normal working hours. Any violation of the Decree by the employer amounts to a criminal offence punishable by imprisonment of up to six months and/or a fine not exceeding €765.

V. Seafarers, Flying Personnel and Mobile Workers

210. Seafarers are covered by the provisions of the Merchant Shipping (Organization of Working Time of Seafarers) Law 79(I)/2003, which incorporates Directive 1999/63/EC in the Cypriot public order.[259] The Directive implements the relevant ILO Conventions[260] and provides for minimum rules for the organization of work in the marine sector. Collective agreements may further provide for more favourable protection. Law 79(I)/2003 applies, in accordance with section 4, to the seafarers of any ship, whether publicly or privately owned, which is registered in Cyprus, which is ordinarily engaged in commercial maritime operations. The relevant provisions on working time further apply to the seafarers of seagoing ships and sea vessels which are ordinarily engaged in commercial maritime operations and carry the flag of another state, if they are calling at the ports of Cyprus.[261]

211. The average working hours of a seafarer should not exceed 8 hours per day, with one day off per week; seafarers should enjoy minimum hours of rest not less than 10 hours in any 24-hour period and 77 hours in any seven-day period (section 5(2) of Law 79(I)/03).[262] Hours of rest may be divided into no more than two periods per 24 hours, one of which shall be at least 6 hours in length and the interval between consecutive periods of rest shall not exceed 14 hours. When a seafarer is on call, he shall have an adequate compensatory rest period if the normal period of rest is disturbed by call-outs to work. Seafarers under 18 years of age should not work at night (section 6 of Law 79(I)/03).[263] Violation of any of the above provisions amounts to a criminal offence punishable by imprisonment of up to 12 months and/or a fine not exceeding €6,800 (section 34 of Law 79(I)/03). The IDT has jurisdiction for the settlement of industrial disputes of a civil nature by virtue of the provisions of Law 79(I)/03 (section 33 of Law 79(I)/03).

212. The master of a ship shall, however, have the right to require a seafarer to perform any hours of work necessary for the immediate safety of the ship, persons on board or cargo, or for the purpose of giving assistance to other ships or persons in distress at sea and may accordingly suspend the schedule of hours of work or

259. Council Directive 1999/63/EC of 21 June 1999 concerning the Agreement on the organization of working time of seafarers concluded by the European Community Shipowners' Association (ECSA) and the Federation of Transport Workers' Union of the European Union (FST). It also harmonizes Cypriot law with Directive 1999/95/EC of the European Parliament and of the Council of 13 December 1999 concerning the enforcement of provisions in respect of seafarers' hours of work on board ships calling at Community ports.
260. Convention 180/1996 on Seafarers' Hours of Work and the Manning of Ships and the Maritime Labour Convention of 2006; the Maritime Labour Convention has been ratified by the Republic of Cyprus with Law 6(III)/2012, whereas Convention 180 has not yet been ratified by the Republic of Cyprus.
261. In the event of doubt as to whether the ship is regarded as seagoing ship, or engaged in commercial maritime operations, the question shall be determined by the competent authority of the state whose flag the ship flies.
262. The protection is increased compared to Article 5 of Directive 1999/63/EC which refers to 72 hours of rest per seven-day period.
263. I.e. from midnight to 5.00 a.m. No person under 16 years of age may work as a seafarer.

hours of rest and require a seafarer to perform any hours of work necessary until the normal situation has been restored. As soon as practicable after the normal situation has been restored, any seafarer who has performed work in a scheduled rest period should be provided with an adequate period of rest (section 7 of Law 79(I)/03). Records of daily hours of work and rest should be properly maintained.

213. The Organization of Working Time of Flying Personnel of the Civil Aviation Law 12(I)/2004, as amended by Law 16(I)/2007, implements Directive 2000/79/EC in the Cypriot legal order.[264] The Directive implements the European Agreement on the organization of working time of mobile staff in civil aviation concluded on 22 March 2000 between the organizations representing management and labour in the civil aviation sector and provides that the maximum annual working time, including some elements of standby for duty assignment as determined by the applicable law, shall be 2000 hours in which the block flying time shall be limited to 900 hours (section 9(2) of Law 12(I)/04).

214. It is further provided that mobile staff in civil aviation shall be given days free of all duty and standby, which are notified in advance, as follows: (i) at least 7 local days in each calendar month, which may include any rest periods required by law; and (ii) at least 96 local days in each calendar year, which may include any rest periods required by law (section 10 of Law 12(I)/04). The IDT has jurisdiction for any civil dispute arising out of the application of Law 12(I)/04 (section 11), whereas any violation of the provisions of Law 12(I)/04 by the employer amounts to a criminal offence punishable by imprisonment of up to a year and/or a fine not exceeding €3,400 (section 12 of Law 12(I)/04). The Minister of Labour, Welfare and Social Insurance may appoint inspectors for monitoring the proper application of Law 12(I)/04 (section 13).

215. The Organization of the Working Time of Persons Performing Mobile Road Transport Activities Law 47(I)/2005, as amended by Law 21(I)/2009, implemented in the Cypriot legal order the provisions of Directive 2002/15/EC.[265] Law 47(I)/05 applies to any mobile workers employed by undertakings established in Cyprus and participating in road transport activities;[266] it applies subject to any provisions in collective agreements which are more favourable to the employees. The average weekly working time of a mobile worker (including apprentices and trainees in

264. Council Directive 2000/79/EC of 27 November 2000 concerning the European Agreement on the Organization of Working Time of Mobile Workers in Civil Aviation concluded by the Association of European Airlines (AEA), the European Transport Workers' Federation (ETF), the European Cockpit Association (ECA), the European Regions Airline Association (ERA) and the International Air Carrier Association (IACA).
265. Directive 2002/15/EC of the European Parliament and of the Council of 11 March 2002 on the organization of the working time of persons performing mobile road transport activities.
266. Covered by Regulation (EEC) 3280/85 of 20 December 1985 on the harmonization of certain social legislation relating to road transport, or failing that by the European agreement concerning the work of crews of vehicles engaged in international road transport (AETR).

accordance with section 7 of Law 47(I)/05) may not, as a principle, exceed 48 hours; it may, however be extended to 60 hours per week, if the average of 48 hours per week is not exceeded over a period of four months. Working time in cases of different employers is the sum of the working hours; accordingly, the employer should ask the mobile worker concerned in writing for an account of time worked for another employer and the mobile worker should also provide such information in writing (section 5 of Law 47(I)/05).

216. Mobile workers should under no circumstances work for more than six consecutive hours without a break; furthermore, working time shall be interrupted by a break of at least 30 minutes, if working hours total between six and nine hours, and by a break of at least 45 minutes, if working hours total more than nine hours. Breaks may be subdivided into periods of at least 15 minutes each (section 6 of Law 47(I)/05). Moreover, if night work is performed, the daily working time should not exceed 10 hours per 24-hour period (section 8 of Law 47(I)/05); compensation is given for night work in accordance with collective agreements, on the condition that such compensation is not likely to endanger road safety. Any employer failing to comply with the provisions of Law 47(I)/05 is guilty of a criminal offence which is punishable by imprisonment of up to six months and/or a fine not exceeding €3,400.

§2. Annual Leave and Holidays

I. General Legislation

217. The Law on Annual Leave with Pay (8/1967) provides for annual holidays with pay for all employees of the private and public sector, including trainees. The provisions of Law 8/67 in no case hinder more favourable provisions for annual leave with pay provided for by collective agreement or otherwise. By virtue of section 5 of Law 8/67, any employee who has worked for 48 weeks is entitled to annual holidays with pay for four working weeks; in other words, employees who have a 5-day working week are entitled to 20 days of annual holidays with pay, whereas those who have a 6-day working week are entitled to 24 days of annual holidays with pay. When an employee has worked for less than 48 weeks per year, the annual leave he is entitled to shall be calculated proportionally (section 5(3) of Law 8/67); if, however, the employee has worked for less than 13 weeks per year, then he is not entitled to annual leave. The payment of an allowance in lieu of the period of annual leave is prohibited.[267]

218. It should be noted that, temporary absence owing to sickness or accident, or while on maternity leave or family leave, are considered as period of employment for the purposes of Law 8/67 and are not calculated as part of the period of

267. See also Case C-194/12, *Concepcion Maestre Garcia* v. *Centros Comerciales Carrefour SA* EU, C-2013: 102.

annual leave.[268] The same is true with regard to public holidays, leave on grounds of *force majeure*, period during which employees were on strike, or the period of warning for termination of employment; these periods are also not considered to be part of the period of annual leave (section 6 of Law 8/67). It is further provided that leave should include at least a period of no less than nine continuous days and that the employer and employee may agree that the leave may be accumulated for a maximum of the annual leave that the employee is entitled to for two years (section 8 of Law 8/67); if there is no such agreement and the employment relationship does not provide for such accumulation, then the employee shall not be entitled to receive accumulated holiday leave.[269]

219. During the period of annual holidays, the employee must be paid by the Central Holiday Fund to which the employers are obliged to pay contributions, unless the employer has been exempted from the obligation to contribute to the Central Holiday Fund on the ground that he provides annual leave to his employees under more favourable terms than those provided by Law 8/67;[270] in the latter case the employer shall pay the employees the normal wage or salary for the period of leave. The employer's contribution to the Central Holiday Fund depends on the duration of leave the employee is entitled to; for the typical four-week annual leave, the contribution of the employer shall amount to 8 per cent of the total gross earnings of the employee and this is the amount payable to the employee by the Central Holiday Fund. The rate of contribution is adjusted in accordance with an increase or reduction in the days of annual leave to which an employee is entitled.[271] The Central Holiday Fund is established by the Council of Ministers and has its own legal personality.

220. The Minister of Labour, Welfare and Social Insurance may appoint inspectors to monitor the proper application of Law 8/67 (section 13). Any employer who fails to provide annual leave to his employee, or, without due cause, fails to pay the contributions to the Central Holiday Fund, is guilty of a criminal offence punishable by imprisonment of up to a year and/or a fine not exceeding €3,400.[272] If the employer intentionally or negligently makes a false statement under oath regarding the application of Law 8/67, he is subject to imprisonment not exceeding six months and/or a fine not exceeding €765. Any person who impedes the carrying out of the duties of an inspector, or neglects to provide information under the law, or unjustifiably refuses to answer any questions posed to him by the inspector, is subject to a fine not exceeding €1,275. The IDT has jurisdiction for any civil dispute arising from the application of Law 8/67.

268. This is consistent with Case C-282/10, *Dominguez* v. *Centre Informatique du Centre Quest Atlantique* EU, C-2012: 33.
269. *Kofterides* v. *Cyprus Airways Ltd* [2005] 1 CLR 443 (in Greek).
270. *Georgiou and others* v. *Pelagos Disalination Services Ltd* [2008] 1 CLR 732 (in Greek).
271. See also OEB, *Handbook of Officer of Labour Relations:Basic Industrial Legislation* (Nicosia, 2015, in Greek): 18–19.
272. *HjiMichael* v. *District Labour Office* [1973] 2 CLR 72.

II. Working Time Legislation

221. The Organization of Working Time Law 63(I)/2002 is consistent with the provisions of Law 8/67; it provides that every worker is entitled to paid annual leave of at least four weeks in accordance with the conditions provided under national legislation and practice and that the minimum period of paid annual leave may not be replaced by an allowance in lieu of payment, except where the employment relationship is terminated (section 8 of Law 63(I)/02).[273] The rule of *pro rata temporis* applies to the conditions of employment of part-time workers; the granting of annual leave for a period of part-time employment, by the reduction of annual leave in comparison with that granted for a period of full-time employment, is justified on objective grounds.[274]

222. It has been held that a worker who is on sick leave during a period of annual leave scheduled unilaterally by the employer, has the right, following the end of his sick leave, to take his annual leave at a time other than that originally scheduled.[275] The right to paid annual leave cannot be extinguished at the end of the year, when the worker has been on sick leave and where his incapacity to work has persisted until the end of the employment relationship, which was the reason why he could not exercise the right to paid annual leave.[276] In case of death of the employee, the entitlement to paid annual leave should confer an entitlement to an allowance in lieu of leave.[277]

223. During the annual leave, the employee is entitled, not only to the maintenance of his basic salary, but also, to all the components intrinsically linked to the performance of the tasks which he is required to carry out under his contract of employment and in respect to which a monetary amount, included in the calculation of his total remuneration, is provided and, second, to all the elements relating to his personal and professional status.[278] It has been held that a worker whose remuneration consists of a basic salary and commission, the amount of which is fixed by reference to the contracts entered into by the employer as a result of sales achieved by

273. Law 63(I)/02 further applies to public servants. See also Case C-337/10, *Neidel* v. *Stadt Frankfurt am Main* EU, C-2012: 263, Case C-519/09, *May* v. *AOK Rheinland/Hamburg-Die Gesundheitskasse* [2011] ECR I-2761.

274. Case C-486/08, *Zentralbetriebsrat der Landeskrankenhäuser Tirols* [2010] ECR I-3527 which references Directive 97/81/EC of the Council, of 15 December 1997, concerning the Framework Agreement on part-time work concluded by UNICE, CEEP and the ETUC. See also C-229/11 and C-230/11, *Heimann and Toltschin* v. *Kaiser GmbH* EU, C-2012: 693.

275. Case C-194/12, *Concepcion Maestre Garcia* v. *Centros Comerciales Carrefour SA* EU:C: 2013: 102, Case C-277/08, *Pereda* v. *Madrid Movilidad SA* [2009] ECR I-8405.

276. Case C-350/06, *Schultz–Hoff* v. *Deutsche Rentenversicherung Bund* [2009] ECR I-179.

277. Case C-118/13, *Bollacke* v. *K + K Klaas & Kock B.V. & Co. KG* EU, C-2014: 1755.

278. Case C-155/10, *Williams and others* v. *British Airways plc* [2011] ECR I-8409. The case concerning an airline pilot refers to both Article 7 of Directive 2003/88/EC and Clause 3 of the Agreement annexed to Council Directive 2000/79/EC.

that worker, is entitled, in respect of his paid annual leave, to a remuneration composed both of his basic salary and commission; the method of calculating the commission payable to the worker in respect of his annual leave should be determined on the basis of an average over a representative reference period.[279]

224. In the event of an increase in the number of hours of work performed by a worker, there is no obligation to retroactively recalculate the entitlement to paid annual leave already accrued, and possibly taken, according to that worker's new work pattern; however, a new calculation must be performed for the period during which working time increased. It is further noted that the calculation of the entitlement to paid annual leave is to be performed according to the same principles, whether what is being determined is the allowance in lieu of paid annual leave not taken where the employment relationship is terminated, or the outstanding annual leave entitlement where the employment relationship continues.[280]

III. Specific Legislation

225. The provisions of Law 8/67 generally apply to both hotel and catering employees by virtue of The Hotel Employees (Conditions of Service) Regulations 136/1972 and Catering Employees (Conditions of Service) Regulations of 1968 respectively; thus, hotel and catering employees are generally entitled to an annual leave of four weeks with full pay. The same rights are granted to mobile staff in civil aviation in accordance with section 4 of Law 12(I)/04. With respect to seafarers, section 13 of Law 79(I)/03 provides that every seafarer shall be entitled to paid annual leave of at least four weeks, or a proportion thereof for periods of employment of less than one year, in accordance with the conditions for entitlement to, and granting of, such leave provided by national legislation and collective agreements; the minimum period of paid annual leave may not be replaced by an allowance in lieu, except where the employment relationship is terminated.

IV. Holidays

226. Public holidays are normally governed by individual or collective agreements between employers and employees. However, a list of public holidays, can be found in specific legislation. Official public holidays for the public and semi-public sector, which are also observed regularly by private enterprises, are the following: 1 January, 6 January (Epiphany), the national holidays of 25 March (start of Greek independence war), 1 April (start of EOKA struggle) and 28 October (Greek rejection of Mussolini's demand to surrender), 1 May, 15 August (Dormition of Theotokos), 1 October (Independence Day), Christmas Eve, Christmas and Boxing Day (24, 25 and 26 December), as well as the movable holidays of Green Monday, Good Friday, Easter Monday, Monday of the Holy Spirit, a total of

279. *Z.J.R. Lock* v. *British Gas Trading Ltd* EU, C-2014: 351.
280. *Greenfield* v. *The Care Bureau Ltd* EU, C-2015: 745.

15 days, as well all Saturdays and Sundays for a total of 119 days. Bank holidays do not include Christmas Eve, but replace it with 2 January for the same total of public holidays.

227. The list of public holidays for catering employees, in accordance with the Catering Employees (Conditions of Service) Regulations of 1968 does not include 24 December (or 2 January). The list, however, still provides for 15 public holidays because Easter Sunday is included; Sundays and Saturdays are not normally considered as public holidays for catering employees, unless there are different provisions in the relevant individual or collective agreements in force. With regard to shop employees, section 16 of Law 155(I)/06 for the Regulation of the Operation of Shops and Conditions of Employment of Shop Employees does not include Good Friday, but includes 2 January and Easter Sunday for a total of 15 public holidays. Saturdays are not normally public holidays for shops, unless there are different provisions in the relevant individual or collective agreements.

228. It should be noted that the operation of shops on Sundays has sparked great controversy. The Minister of Labour, Welfare and Social Insurance issued several decrees allowing for shops all over Cyprus to remain open on Sundays for the entire period of 2 May 2013–31 December 2015; the Minister has consistently maintained and supported by statistical data, that the decrees have helped to reduce unemployment since a significant number of formerly unemployed persons were hired due to the increased sales and additional working hours of shops. The Ministry has further announced that it would intensify inspections for safeguarding compliance with the existing legislation regarding the rights of employees and during 2014 there were more than 2000 inspections and 210 criminal prosecutions regarding failure by employers to protect the rights of employees. The majority of the House of Representatives removed the power of the Minister to issue decrees by Laws 36(I)/15 and 55(I)/15 and enacted a new legislation which provided for shops, with the exception of some specific areas characterized as touristic, to be closed on Sundays; however, the legislation was unanimously held to be unconstitutional by the Full Bench of the Supreme Court as falling outside the competences of the House of Representatives and amounting to an interference with the powers of the executive.[281]

229. Despite the ruling of the Supreme Court, the House of Representatives has steadfastly refused to approve the Regulations submitted by the Minister for maintaining the shops open on Sundays and accordingly from 1 January 2016, Law 55(I)/06 provides that the shops should remain closed on Sundays. The Attorney-General once again applied to the Supreme Court, while the shop owners decided to keep their shops open on Sundays, since on the basis of the ruling of the Supreme Court, existing legislation preventing the shops to open on Sundays would most probably also be declared as unconstitutional. It should be noted, however, that whereas one

281. *President of the Republic* v. *House of Representatives*, reference 1/2015, ruling of 3 December 2015.

of the major arguments of the majority of the House of Representatives for opposing the operation of shops on Sundays is the protection of employees, it is sufficiently clear that Law 70(I)/15 fully safeguards the rights of the employees and provides increased protection for employees working on a Sunday; the only question is thus the extent of implementation of the legislative provision in actual practice, but this is only indirectly related to the opening of shops on Sundays.

Chapter 4. Remuneration and Benefits

§1. Protection of Wages

230. The Protection of Wages Law 35(I)/2007, as amended by Law 200(I)/2012, provides for the manner of payment of wages by the employer and effectively incorporates the provisions of the ILO Protection of Wages Convention 95/1949 in the Cypriot legal order. The IDT is the competent court for any civil dispute arising from the application of the Law (section 19 of Law 35(I)/07). Law 35(I)/07 provides that the employees' wages must be paid in cash in a legal tender; this includes currency notes and coins, payment through salaries accounts, bank cheques and postal drafts (section 3 of Law 35(I)/07). 'Wages' are defined in section 2 of Law 35(I)/07, as any remuneration in money as a result of the employee's employment and any gain from such employment capable of being attributed a monetary value; it includes the provident fund contribution, as well as the contribution payable to the Central Holiday Fund.

231. As far as payment of wages in kind is concerned, section 4 (2) of Law 35(I)/07 stipulates that, where this is customary in the industry or occupation concerned, payment of part of the wage may be made in kind provided that: (i) allowances in kind, considering their amount and quality, are appropriate for, and benefit, the employee and his family, (ii) the value attributed to them is fair and reasonable and (iii) the employee's consent has been obtained; in no case can payment of wages be made, either wholly or partly, in the form of alcoholic drinks or other dangerous substances (section 4(1) of Law 35(I)/07).

232. Wages must be paid directly to the employee, except in cases where the employee has agreed in writing to the contrary (section 5 of Law 35(I)/07). In cases where payment is in cash, it can only be made during working hours, at or near the workplace, unless it is otherwise provided by another law, regulation or collective agreement; payment of wages is prohibited in catering or similar establishments and, where necessary to prevent abuse, in shops for the retail sale of goods, except in the case of persons employed in such shops (section 8 of Law 35(I)/07). The employer has no right to limit in any manner, whether directly or indirectly, the employee's freedom to dispose of his wages, except where and to the extent permitted by the Law itself (section 6 of Law 35(I)/07). Furthermore, in cases where the employer operates stores for the sale of goods or services to the employees, the latter cannot be coerced into making use of these stores or services (section 7 of Law 35(I)/07).

233. The payment of wages must be made at least every week, except in the case of monthly paid employees, where wages must be paid at least once a month; it is, however, possible for collective agreements to provide for different frequencies of payment. In the case of employees whose wages are fixed on a piece-work basis or on a production basis, the maximum intervals of payment of wages must be, as far as possible, such as to allow payment at least twice per month; intervals between such payments should not exceed 16 days (section 9 of Law 35(I)/07). The assignment of wages is prohibited, except if otherwise provided by existing law or regulation; in any event, no assignment can be made to such an extent that the maintenance of the employee and his family might be hindered (section 11 of Law 35(I)/07).

234. It is further prohibited to make any deductions from wages, unless such deductions are provided for by existing legislation or regulation, or by order of the court, or are made in accordance with the rules of a pension fund, provident fund and medical fund, or they are for damages owing to a loss suffered by a business as a result of the intentional act or gross negligence of the employee; other deductions may be made subject to the employee's consent. Deductions should be in any case restricted to the extent that the employee shall be in a position to maintain himself and his family (section 10 of Law 35(I)/07). Before any deductions from wages for damages to the employer are made, consultations must take place with the employees' representatives, or, in the absence of a representative, with the employee himself; if these consultations fail to produce results, then the dispute is referred to the Minister of Labour, Welfare and Social Insurance for mediation and, if no agreement is reached at the mediation stage, the Ministry refers the dispute to the IDT.

235. The employer should keep proper records showing the gross and net wages of every employee and any deductions from their wages, as well as the reasons for such deductions (section 12 of Law 35(I)/07). The Minister of Labour, Welfare and Social Insurance may appoint inspectors for monitoring the implementation of Law 35(I)/07; those inspectors have the power to be provided with information and inspect books, records and other documents of the employer; they may also inspect, enter, examine, investigate any matter relevant to the application of Law 35(I)/07 (section 13-18 of Law 35(I)/07). Any employer who violates the provisions of Law 35(I)/07 is guilty of a criminal offence and is subject to imprisonment of up to six months and/or a fine not exceeding €15,000; the court may further order the employer to pay the sums owed to the employee. Furthermore, any employer who abuses the right of instituting insolvency proceedings, with a view to depriving the employee of his rights to wages, is subject to imprisonment of up to six months and/or a fine not exceeding €10,000; the same penalty is incurred by any person who obstructs inspectors in the exercise of their powers (section 20 of Law 35(I)/07). The IDT may further grant orders requiring the employer to pay the wages (section 19(2) of Law 35(I)/07).

§2. Minimum Wage

236. The minimum wage for a given profession may be fixed by a Decree of the Council of Ministers, issued in accordance to the provisions of section 3(1) of the Minimum Wage Law, Cap. 183; the Council of Ministers may also change or repeal the minimum wage. The purpose of setting a minimum wage is to protect employees in non-unionized occupations, where the conditions of employment are not sufficiently regulated by collective agreements, or where there is risk of exploitation of workers by the employers. The Decree in force, issued by the Council of Ministers in 2012 (180/2012), sets out minimum wages for seven categories of workers: (a) clerks, (b) sales-persons, (c) nursing aids, (d) school aids, child minders and nannies,[282] (e) care workers, (f) cleaners and (g) security guards. The spouse, child or parent of the employer, do not fall within the definition of a clerk, sales-person, nursing-aid, school-aid, child minder and nanny. There is no minimum wage for other categories of workers, where wages are regulated exclusively by individual and collective agreements. A minimum wage has, however, been set for non-Cypriot domestic workers at €460 from 1 July 2013 by a decision of the Civil Registry and Migration Department and the relevant Committee of Ministers.[283]

237. The minimum wage is set at €870 for a clerk, sales-person, nursing-aid, school-aid, child minder and nanny, or a clean worker, whereas the minimum hourly wage of a security guard is set at €4.90 and of a cleaner €4.55. On completion of continuous employment of six months at the same employer, the minimum wage of a clerk, sales-person, nursing-aid, school-aid, child minder and nanny, or clean worker increases to €924, whereas the minimum hourly wage for a security guard increases to €5.20 and of a cleaner to €4.84. Part-time clerks, sales-persons, nursing-aids, school-aids, child minders and nannies, or cleaning workers shall be paid proportionally. Any employer and/or representative of the employer, who pays less than the minimum wage to an employee belonging to any of the occupations covered, is guilty of a criminal offence punishable by a fine not exceeding €170 and to an additional fine not exceeding €42 for each day of contravention of the Decree following conviction (sections 5 and 7 of Cap. 183). The employer cannot pay less than the minimum wage even if the employee consents.

238. The employer may also be ordered, upon conviction, to pay any difference between the wages paid to the employee and the wages which ought to have been paid in accordance with the minimum wage in force during the past two years prior to the submission of the complaint by the employee (sections 5(2) and 6(1) of Cap. 183). In case the employee has neglected to apply before the court, or file a complaint in accordance with the provisions of Cap. 183 and if there are sums that should have been paid as wages for a period longer than two years, the Attorney-General may file a civil action in the name of the employee to claim such amount (section 6(2) of Cap. 183). It further amounts to a criminal offence for the employer to receive any payment by way of premium by an employee for whom the minimum wage applies, if the latter happens to be an apprentice or learner; the only exception is if such payment is made in accordance to an apprenticeship agreement executed not later than four weeks after the commencement of employment. In case of conviction, the employer shall be subject to a fine not exceeding €170 and the court may additionally order the employer to pay the employee the sum improperly received by way of premium (section 8 of Cap. 183).

---

282. Defined as any person who takes care of infants or children or assists in their care, in a kindergarten, child-care or day-care facility.

283. The setting of a minimum wage only for non-Cypriot domestic workers and at a level lower than the respective minimum wage for Cypriot workers raises issues of discrimination. See also Equality Authority of Cyprus, *Annual Report for 2005* (Nicosia, 2006, in Greek): 17.

239. For the purpose of calculating the amount of wages payable in the case of a worker employed in any work for which a minimum wage has been fixed, the worker will be deemed to have been employed there during all the time for which he was present on the premises of the employer, unless the employer proves that he was present without the employer's express or implied consent, or that he was present for a purpose unconnected with his work and other than that of waiting for work to be given to him to perform. Where an employee resides on the premises of the employer he will not be deemed to be employed during the time that he is present on the premises by reason only of the fact that he resides there; furthermore, an employee that is present during normal meal times in a room or place where no work is being conducted, will be deemed to be present for a purpose unconnected with his work (section 9 of Cap. 183).

240. It is further provided that remuneration received by any person in respect of work carried out for any shopkeeper, dealer or trader, after allowing for the necessary expenditure in connection with the work, will be deemed as wages and the person shall be considered as the employer for the purposes of Cap. 193 (section 10 of Cap. 193). In order to prevent abuse, section 11 of Cap. 193 provides that the employer has the burden, in any criminal prosecution, to prove that wages have been paid, at least, at the minimum wage; it is the duty of any employer to keep such records of wages as are necessary in order to show that the provisions for a minimum wage are being complied with and if the employer fails to do so then he is subject to a fine not exceeding €43 and to an additional fine of €43 for each day during which the offence continues after conviction (section 12 of Cap. 193). The Council of Ministers may appoint officers for the purpose of investigating any complaints and for the purpose of securing the proper observance of the provisions of Cap. 189 (section 13 of Cap. 189); if any person impedes the exercise of the powers of such officers, he shall be guilty of a criminal offence and subject to a fine not exceeding €43.

§3. Overtime

241. Overtime payment is not generally governed by statute, but by individual or collective agreements. However, there are certain exceptions. Law 155(I)/06 provides that overtime work of shop employees is compensated on an 1:2 ratio (overtime work equals two working hours per hour) for every employee who consents to work on a Sunday, or on a morning or afternoon off, or on a public holiday and on a 1: 1.5 ratio (overtime work equals one and a half working hours per hour) for other days (section 18 of Law 55(I)/06). Overtime work for hotel employees and catering employees is compensated at a ratio of 1:1.5 in accordance with Regulations 136/72 and 80/68 respectively. In *Kofterides* the employee, after resigning from his employment, claimed damages for holiday leave which had not been given to him and for overtime work he had performed during his employment. The Supreme Court held that there is no general rule in private law that overtime work should be payable;[284] the question should therefore be determined on the basis of the employment relationship and in the case at hand there was no such term in the employment relationship.[285]

§4. 13TH SALARY AND BONUSES

242. There is no legislation imposing a duty upon the employer to pay a 13th salary to an employee and, accordingly, this is regulated by individual or collective employment agreements, or the practice followed by the employer. However, if there is a practice in accordance to which a 13th salary is paid, this should in principle be given to all employees, unless there are differentiations due to the duties assigned, or the years of service. The Ministry of Labour, Welfare and Social Insurance considers that when the 13th (and/or 14th salary) is paid, even as a matter of practice, the employer is obliged to continue to pay the 13th salary, as this is included within the definition of 'wages' under section 2 of Law 35(I)/07.[286]

243. The definition of 'wages' in accordance with section 2 of Law 35(I)/07 does not, however, include occasional commissions, bonuses and ex gratia payments. An obligation of the employer to pay commission to the employee in accordance with the terms of the employment contract is a claim arising from the employment relationship and falls under the jurisdiction of the IDT. In *Global* the question referred to the interpretation of the term of the employment contract which stated that: 'the employee shall also receive 50 per cent of gross commission generated from clientele introduced by him directly to the employer at the end of each month'. The employer argued that the term 'generated' implied that the commission would be paid only once they collected the money from the clients that the employee had introduced; the Supreme Court disagreed and held that, in accordance with the terms of the contract, once the employee had introduced the client and a binding transaction had taken place between the client and the employer, the employee had a right to receive his commission.[287]

284. The Court distinguished *Papayiorgis* v. *Electricity Authority of Cyprus* [1996] 3 CLR 563 (in Greek) and *Electricity Authority of Cyprus* v. *Filiastides* [2003] 3 CLR 342 (in Greek), which refer to recognized legal rights in the public sector.

285. *Kofterides* v. *Cyprus Airways Ltd* [2005] 1 CLR 443 (in Greek).

286. See Minister of Labour: 'Criminal Offence not to Pay 13th Salary', *Phileleftheros* 2/12/2013 (in Greek).

287. *Global Capital Ltd* v. *Paraskeva* [2007] 1 CLR 986 (in Greek).

Chapter 5. Incapacity to Work

§1. Sick Leave

244. Sick leave is regulated by individual or collective agreements and not by statutory law, with the exception of hotel and catering employees; however, the termination of employment of an employee who is absent from work due to sickness, or other incapacity, is prohibited for a period of up to six months from the commencement of such incapacity (section 9(6) of Law 24/67). The Hotel Employees (Conditions of Service) Regulations 136/1972 and Catering Employees (Conditions of Service) Regulations of 1968 govern specifically the sick leave of hotel and catering employees. Hotel employees with service between six months and three years are entitled to 15 days of sick leave per year and those with more than three years of service are entitled to 24 days of sick leave per year. Catering employees with service between six months and three years are entitled to 10 days of sick leave per year and those with more than three years of service 18 days per year.

245. In *Keo* the employee, a member of the Medical Fund of the employer, had undergone an open heart surgery abroad; it was undisputed that if the surgery had taken place in Cyprus the employer would have to pay the costs. It was held that since the Medical Fund was not registered, the employee had essentially entered a contractual relation with the employer, with the charter constituting the terms of the contract; the proper interpretation of the charter showed that the employee had complied with all the requirements set out in the charter and had undertaken surgery abroad following the recommendation of a doctor chosen by the Fund. Furthermore, there was no provision expressly limiting the right of the employee to receive compensation when the medical operation was carried outside Cyprus. It was further held that the document signed by the employee when his employment was terminated on grounds of redundancy never provided that the employee would not claim compensation for medical treatment.[288]

246. Any employee on sick leave, who is not entitled to old-age pension, and who fulfils the legislative insurance criteria, is granted a sickness benefit from the Social Insurance Fund for a period not exceeding 156 days. Section 31(1) of the Social Insurance Law 59(I)/2010 provides that a sickness benefit is payable to any insured person for each day that he is incapable to work; nobody is entitled to a sickness benefit, however, during the first three days of sickness; it was considered that there was too much potential for abuse if sick leave was paid for sick leave of less than three days. Sick leave will be paid if the employee can prove that due to illness, or physical or mental incapacity, certified by a medical doctor, he is not capable of performing the work he normally performs and that during such illness his wages are not fully paid by his employer. Insured employees who receive part of their earnings from their employer for the period they are entitled to sickness

288. *Keo Ltd* v. *Mouzouri* [2008] 1 CLR 1195 (in Greek).

benefit, have the benefit reduced so that the total amount of the earnings plus the benefit does not exceed the insured person's full earnings.

247. The employer is not required to pay the wages of the employee for sick leave of less than three days for which he is not entitled to payment by the Social Insurance Services, unless the individual or collective employment agreements otherwise provide; however, some employers will, as a matter of practice, cover part of the sick leave of the employee in such cases. As a matter of good practice, employers might also compensate the employee for sick leave and then receive the amount paid by the Social Insurance Fund, so as to avoid any delay that employees may face receiving the sickness benefit from the Social Insurance Fund.[289] An employee who has completed 156 days of sick leave, reclaims the right to a sick leave following employment for 13 weeks and the payment of the necessary contributions to the Social Insurance Fund. A person who becomes permanently incapable for work may be entitled to invalidity pension in accordance with section 40 of Law 59(I)/2010.

§2. Accidents at Work

248. The period of notice for termination of employment is suspended in the case of an employee who becomes incapable to work as a result of an occupational accident occurring during the period of notice, by virtue of section 9(7) of Law 24/67. An employee who is unable to work due to an occupational accident is entitled to receive a benefit from the Social Insurance Fund.[290] An occupational accident is defined, by virtue of section 47(1) of the Social Insurance Law 59(I)/2010 as an accident caused during and because of the employee's occupation; the term even includes accidents which occurred while the employee was acting against the instructions of his employer, or which took place while the employee was on his way to work, or returning to work.[291]

249. An employee of any age who suffers injuries caused by an occupational accident is granted an employment injury benefit for a period of up to 12 months from the day that the accident occurred; the benefit is not payable, however, for the first three days of interruption of employment (section 48 of Law 59(I)/10). An employee is not entitled to employment injury benefit for any day during which he receives full salary from his employer. In case he received part of his salary, the employment injury benefit is reduced, so that the sum of the benefit and the salary does not exceed the amount of full salary of the employee. An employee who becomes disabled, may be entitled to a disablement benefit, either a grant or a disablement pension, depending on the degree of disablement (sections 49 and 50 of

289. See also OEB, *Handbook of Officer of Labour Relations: Industrial Policies and Good Practices* (Nicosia, 2015, in Greek): 26.
290. See also the ILO Employment Injury Benefits Convention 121/1964 ratified by Law 38/1966.
291. But not if the employee left from work during working hours for reasons unrelated to his work.

Law 59(I)/10). If the employee has died as a result of the accident, then a death benefit is payable to the surviving spouse, children or parents of the employee.[292]

§3. Leave for Grounds of *Force Majeure* and Without Pay

250. An employee is entitled to receive leave on grounds of *force majeure* in accordance with section 12 of the Parental Leave and Leave on Grounds of *Force Majeure* Law 47(I)/2012; such leave is due to urgent family reasons which refer to illness or accident of dependent members of the employee's family and which necessitate his immediate presence. The leave is granted to the employee, either once or in segments; in case of spouses who are entitled to leave on the same grounds, the leave is granted separately to each spouse. An employee intending to apply for leave on grounds of *force majeure*, should inform his employer as soon as possible (section 13 of Law 47(I)/12). An employer who violates the provisions of Law 47(I)/12 is guilty of a criminal offence punishable by a fine not exceeding €7,500. An employee may also request leave without pay in cases of serious medical grounds, education or other reasons; leave without pay is typically requested in cases where the annual leave does not suffice. The granting of an annual leave without pay shall be regulated by the individual or collective employment agreement, or the practice of the employer; annual leave without pay does not interrupt continuous employment.[293]

§4. Leave due to Military Obligations

251. With respect to military obligations, section 72 of the National Guard Law 19(I)/2011 stipulates that the employment of any person conscripted to the National Guard of the Republic for carrying out military service, is suspended for as long as he serves in the National Guard; this applies only for employees who had been employed in a permanent or temporary position for over six months. If the employee requests from the employer to continue his employment within one month from his release from military service, the employer is required to provide him with the same, or similar occupation as before and with no less favourable terms; if the employment prior to conscription was of indeterminate duration, the re-employment should last for at least six months. The same rules apply also in regard to reservists; additionally, the employer should consider that the time served by the reservist in the National Guard during working hours amounts to hours worked for the employer and he should accordingly pay such wages to the employee, plus three hours following the end of such service.

292. See also OEB, *Social Insurance* (Nicosia, 2015, in Greek): 36–41.
293. See also OEB, *Handbook of Officer of Labour Relations:Industrial Policies and Good Practices* (Nicosia, 2015, in Greek): 27 where it is suggested that as a matter of good practice, if the employee shall be on leave without pay for a lengthy period of time, the employer should notify the Social Insurance Services that the employee is on leave without pay, in order to safeguard the continuous nature of his employment.

Chapter 6. Job Security

§1. Seniority

252. Seniority is not governed by legislation, but rather by collective agreements, or the employer's practice. Seniority might, depending on the case, lead to assignment of work of increased responsibility, or setting working hours, or shift work at more convenient times. Seniority might also be important for redundancy purposes, since as a rule the employer should dismiss first the person who was hired last and should dismiss last the person who was hired first and who is an employee for the longest period of time. However, this rule may not apply in cases of modernization, or any other change in the method of production or organization, if the employees who have been working for the longest period of time do not have the necessary qualifications, or cannot adapt to the changes. Similarly, the aforementioned rule may not apply when there are other considerations which should be weighed, such as health problems, financial or family reasons and limited possibility for a more recently hired employee to be employed elsewhere.

§2. Lifetime Employment

253. As a matter of principle, a contract of employment is governed by its contractual terms; in this respect, the fact that the employer has set an age of retirement does not imply that the employer is bound to employ his staff until they reach that age.[294] Furthermore, it has been held that a provision for 'permanent employment' does not normally mean for life or until the normal age of retirement;[295] accordingly, unless there is a special provision in the contract, such employment may be terminated by reasonable notice or because of redundancy. The only permanent employees are those employed in the public sector as permanent public servant; the latter may not be declared as redundant by definition, since their service is safeguarded until their retirement in accordance with legislation.[296]

§3. Different Methods of Terminating the Employment Relationship

254. Termination of employment may occur by a dismissal (including on grounds of redundancy) or resignation of the employee.[297] In *Christodoulou* the trial court had interpreted the term 'termination of employment' of section 21 §2 of the

294. *Stylianides* v. *British American Insurance Co Ltd* [1990] 1 CLR 517 (in Greek).
295. *Pitsillides* v. *National Bank of Greece (Cyprus) Ltd*, Civ. Appeal 199/09, dated 3 July 2012 (in Greek), *Charalampous and others* v. *Attorney-General of England and Wales and another* [2004] 1 CLR 90, *Synergatikos Organismos Diatheseos Ampelourgikon Proionton Ltd* v. *Karellis* [1971] 1 CLR 248, *Savvides* v. *SEK and others* [2004] 1 CLR 57 (in Greek).
296. *Meliniotis* v. *Redundancy Fund* [2006] 1 CLR 144 (in Greek).
297. See in general the comprehensive M. Antoniou, *Termination of Employment Law in Cyprus* (Nicosia: OEB, 2000, in Greek), OEB, *Handbook of Officer of Labour Relations: Termination of Employment* (Nicosia, 2015, in Greek).

Provident Funds Law 44/81 as covering only the unilateral termination of employment by the employer. The Supreme Court reversed this decision and held that the term includes both dismissal of the employee by the employer and resignation of the employee.[298] Once the employment relationship has been terminated, it may not be revived unilaterally, but only following an agreement of the parties; it was accordingly held that the employee had no obligation to return to his employer as the latter had unilaterally revoked the termination of employment.[299] Irrespective of the grounds of termination of employment, the employee has a right to receive a certificate detailing the dates of employment and the work that he carried out; the certificate may not include anything negative for the employee (section 8 of Law 24/67).

§4. Terms of Notice in the Event of Termination or Dismissal

255. By virtue of the relevant principles of the English common law, a contract of employment of indefinite duration is subject to an implied term that the contract may be terminated following reasonable notice; what constitutes reasonable notice in each case shall depend on the nature of the employment, the market available for the service offered by the employee and the duration of his employment. The required notice, in cases where the District Court has jurisdiction, might range from one to 12 months, the latter being the case in exceptional circumstances for managerial positions only.[300]

256. Where the IDT has jurisdiction by virtue of Law 24/67, the notice period given by the employer to the employee in case of dismissal shall be calculated on the basis of the time of continuous employment of the employee. Notice should always be given in writing and cannot be waived by an agreement of the parties; it can, however, be extended by virtue of the terms of the individual or collective agreement. No notice need be given for employment on a trial basis, if at the end of the provisional employment the employer decides not to hire the employee; however, the trial period shall not exceed 26 weeks, unless there is a written agreement extending it to up to 104 weeks. The burden of proof is on the employer to prove that the employment was on a trial basis.

257. The notice period required in accordance with section 9 of Law 24/67 is the following: (i) one week for continuous employment between 26 and 51 weeks, (ii) two weeks for continuous employment between 52 and 103 weeks, (iii) four weeks for continuous employment between 104 and 155 weeks, (iv) five weeks for continuous employment between 156 and 207 weeks, (v) six weeks for continuous employment between 208 and 259 weeks, (vi) seven weeks for continuous

298. *Christodoulou* v. *Provident Fund of the Employees of the New Co-Operative Society of Kaimakli*, Civil App. 197/08, dated 17 March 2011 (in Greek).

299. *A. Iasonos Ltd* v. *Christou and others* [1994] 1 CLR 703 (in Greek).

300. *Stylianides* v. *British American Insurance Co Ltd* [1990] 1 CLR 517 (in Greek), citing with approval *Dobie* v. *Burns International* [1984] 3 All ER 333, *Savvides* v. *SEK and others* [2004] 1 CLR 57 (in Greek) where it was held that a 12-month notice ought to be given.

employment between 260 and 311 weeks, (vii) eight weeks for continuous employment over 312 weeks. The employee should also provide minimum notice in case of resignation, in accordance with section 10 of Law 24/67, as follows: (i) one week for continuous employment between 26 and 51 weeks, (ii) two weeks for continuous employment between 52 and 259 weeks, (iii) three weeks for continuous employment of more than 260 weeks.

258. The employer may opt to make payment to the employee in lieu of notice (section 11 of Law 24/67). Payment in such case is calculated in accordance with the Third Schedule of Law 24/67. In general the employee is entitled to receive the wages he would have received during the period of notice. If the employee is paid on an hourly base, the payment shall be determined on the basis of the average of the employee's weekly wages during the past 12 weeks of full employment.[301] If the employee has no determined wages or hourly fee, then he is entitled to receive for each week of notice, not less than the average of weekly wages during the past 12 weeks of full employment.

259. The legal provisions regarding notice or payment in lieu of notice, are obligatory for the employer and, accordingly, any agreement made which absolves the employer from such an obligation is void; in *Odessa Hotels* it was held that the arrangement to compensate the employees with one month salary was made in order for the employer to circumvent his legal obligations. It was accordingly held that the written agreement between the employer and the employee was illegal and void.[302] The employment relationship continues to be applicable until the notice period has expired, even if the employer has opted to make payment in lieu of notice; the employee shall continue to be considered as an employee of the employer until the expiry of the period of notice which he would have been given if he had not received payment in lieu of notice. It is noted that individual or collective agreements may provide for additional notice periods to the statutory minimum notice period.[303]

260. By virtue of section 11 § 2 of the Law, if the employee to whom notice has been given is offered new employment by a different employer, he may opt to quit his current employment before the expiry of the notice in order to begin his new employment; in such a case the employee shall abandon his right to be paid in lieu of the remaining notice period. Furthermore, during the notice period, the employee may leave from work during working hours, following an agreement with his employer, for up to 8 hours a week, in order to seek new employment, provided that the total hours of his absence during the entire notice period shall not exceed 40 hours (section 12 of Law 24/67).

261. An interesting case is *Ioannou.* The employer sent a written notice of termination of employment to the employee; however, before the notice had expired

---

301. A week of full employment is a week during which the employee has worked at least 18 hours.
302. *Odessa Hotels Ltd* v. *Pino* [2007] 1 CLR 1277 (in Greek). See also *Karmios and others* v. *Attorney-General of England and another* [2006] 1 CLR 768 (in Greek).
303. *Famalift Shipyard Ltd* v. *Pavlides and others* [1991] 1 CLR 161 (in Greek).

and while the employee was still employed at the employer, they offered him work in another one of their establishments. The employee rejected that offer as he would need to travel 16 km to go to work. The employer proved before the IDT that there had been substantial constriction of their volume of work, which justified the redundancy of the employee. It was further held that the alternative work offered to the employee was suitable and appropriate as the duties to be allocated to the employee were within his specialty and the distance of 16 km was not inappropriate under the circumstances; his rejection of the offer deprived him of the right to claim payment from the Redundancy Fund.

262. The employee argued that since the offer had been made during the notice period, it should not have been taken into account. The Supreme Court rejected this argument and held that the effective date of termination of employment, when the contract has been terminated by notice, is the expiry of the notice period; if the contract has been terminated without notice, then this is the date on which the termination takes effect. The period of notice falls for all purposes within the scope of the employment relationship, as the termination becomes applicable only at the expiry of the notice.[304]

§5. Wrongful Dismissal

I. Continuous Employment

263. If the employer dismisses, without just cause, an employee who has been continuously employed by him for not less than 26 weeks, the employee shall have, by virtue of section 3 of Law 24/67, a right to compensation calculated in accordance with the First Schedule of Law 24/67. However, the minimum period of continuous employment required may be extended from 26 weeks to a maximum of 104 weeks, by a written agreement made at the time the employee commences employment. The calculation of continuous employment is therefore of importance for determining whether an employee has a right to compensation; it further remains relevant in order to assess the amount of the compensation to be awarded. The principles for calculating continuous employment remain the same in cases of redundancy, where the employee has a right to compensation from the Redundancy Fund if he had been continuously employed for a period of at least 104 weeks. Accordingly, the principles analysed herewith apply both in cases of wrongful dismissal and redundancy.

264. Part II of the Second Schedule provides that the employment remains continuous irrespective of absences owing to: (i) obligatory military service, (ii) illness, disease, injury or pregnancy, (iii) paid or unpaid leave, (iv) parental leave or leave on grounds of *force majeure*, (v) temporary interruption of work, (vi) occupation abroad on an undertaking owned completely, or mainly, by the employer, (vii) *force majeure*, warfare, insurrection or act of God, (viii) industrial dispute,

304. *Ioannou* v. *Vesta Holidays Ltd and another* [2001] 1 CLR 909 (in Greek).

(ix) circumstances which in accordance with custom, arrangement or law, do not interrupt the continuous nature of the employment relationship, (x) transfer within the meaning of the proviso of section 3 of Part I of the Second Schedule of Law 24/67. The proviso of section 3 of Part I of the Second Schedule provides that when the enterprise, or part of the enterprise, of the employer, is transferred to another employer, or when the employee is transferred from one company to another, then all weeks of employment at the first employer shall be deemed as employment at the second employer in the calculation of the period of employment. This forms an exception to the rule that the employment should be continuous for the same employer.

265. For the calculation of the 'weeks' of continuous employment, only weeks during which the employee, has either: (a) worked for at least 18 hours, or (b) was absent from work due to illness, injury, pregnancy or disease, parental leave, temporary interruption of work, or in circumstances which in accordance with custom, arrangement or law, do not interrupt the continuous nature of the employment relationship, shall be taken into account (section 2 of Part I of the First Schedule). It is suggested that circumstances of leave on grounds of *force majeure*, obligatory military service, paid or unpaid leave, should properly be considered as circumstances during which the continuous nature of the employment relationship is not interrupted for the purposes of the calculation under section 2 of Part I of the First Schedule; however, section 3 of Part I of the First Schedule explicitly excludes weeks during which the employee was absent due to an industrial dispute. The 'continuous' character of employment is not affected by any change in the conditions or terms of employment.[305]

266. The requirement of 'continuous employment' was considered in *Egglezou.* The employees were employed in a hotel from April until October each year for four years, until their employment was eventually terminated on grounds of redundancy; from November until March they registered in the unemployment office and received unemployment benefits. The Supreme Court held that the employees had not been continuously employed by the same employer for 104 weeks, since their employment was being discontinued each year, and not simply suspended. Whereas it was true that many hotels suspend their operations during winter, the parties had not abided by the terms of the collective agreement between the trade unions and the employers; the collective agreement provided that the employers should have retained 25 per cent of the salary of the employees in October and return it to them in April and the employees should have stated this to the unemployment office in order to receive a reduced allowance during winter. Since the parties had not abided to such terms, it could not be considered that the employment had been a continuous one.

267. The determination of whether the employment was continuous has to be made on the basis of objective criteria; accordingly whether the employer and the

305. *Famalift Shipyard Ltd* v. *Pavlides and others* [1991] 1 CLR 161 (in Greek).

employee have characterized the absence as unpaid leave is not conclusive. Unpaid leave implies temporary absence from the service of the employer; the length of the leave, its circumstances, the grounds on which it was given and whether the employer had some direct or indirect interest or whether it merely served the interests of the employee, are all factors to be considered in order to conclude whether the employee was absent with unpaid leave. The tribunal has to be convinced that during the period of absence, the employment relationship continues, despite being temporarily suspended. In *Louca* the Supreme Court held that the six year absence of the employee from the service of the employer, in order to be employed abroad for a different employer without any relationship with his original employer, had interrupted the period of continuous employment of the employee, irrespective of whether the employee returned to the service of the employer six years later. Accordingly, the period during which the employee was absent abroad should not be calculated in order to compensate the employee from the Redundancy Fund.[306]

268. In *Onisiforou* the employee, initially employed by company A, was transferred for 11 months to company B, which had the same shareholders and directors as company A; following the 11-month period, she returned to company A. When her employment was terminated on grounds of redundancy, the question arose whether her employment in company A had been interrupted for those 11 months, in such a way that would not entitle her to receive compensation from the Redundancy Fund on the ground that she would not have completed 104 weeks of continuous employment relationship with the employer in accordance with section 16 §1 of the Law. The IDT found in favour of the employee; the Fund appealed before the Supreme Court.

269. The Supreme Court noted that company B was neither a holding company nor a subsidiary of company A, so as to justify the lifting of the corporate veil.[307] The two companies were separate entities, despite the fact that the shareholders and the directors were identical. Furthermore, the facts of the case did not constitute an arrangement, namely a case where the employee was loaned by his general employer to a temporary employer for a limited period of time, the understanding and intention being that she would later return into the employment of her general employer; the transfer of the employee to company B was for an indefinite period of time, irrespective of the fact that it eventually lasted 11 months. As a result, the employee had changed employer and was not to be awarded any payment from the Redundancy Fund.[308]

306. *Louca* v. *Redundancy Fund* [1995] 1 CLR 90 (in Greek).
307. For the lifting of the corporate veil in Cypriot law see generally K. Ioannides, 'Lifting the Corporate Veil in the Cypriot Courts' [2013] *Yearbook of Cyprus and European Law*: 217–224 (in Greek).
308. *Redundancy Fund* v. *Onisiforou* [1989] 1 CLR 504 (in Greek), citing with approval *Spanlite Structures Ltd.* v. *Jarrett* (1973) ITR 511, *Secretary of State for Employment* v. *Globe Elastic Ltd* (1979) IRLR 2.

II. Compensation

270. Paragraph 4 of the First Schedule of Law 24/67 provides that the IDT has a wide discretion in determining the compensation awarded; in exercising such discretion, the IDT should take into account the daily wages and other earnings of the employee, the period of employment, the employee's loss of career, the factual circumstances of the termination of employment and the employee's age. The discretion of the IDT to award compensation is wider than the dependence upon the general contractual principles for awarding compensation.[309] The calculation of the compensation that an employee is entitled to may include periods of service prior to the date on which Law 24/67 came into force, i.e. 1 February 1968.[310] The compensation shall be further calculated on the basis of the salary he received on the day when the employment was terminated.[311]

271. The minimum compensation to be awarded is the one that would be paid in case of redundancy, whereas the maximum compensation amounts to wages of up to two years.[312] The compensation to which the employee shall have a right, is payable by the employer to the extent that it does not exceed the wages of the employee for one year, and by the Fund to the extent that it exceeds the wages of the employee for one year. In *Cabras* the Supreme Court held that whereas the IDT had stated its findings in its judgment, its analysis was a cursory one; with respect to the determination of the calculation of the compensation of the employee, the IDT took into account only the period of employment and the salary of the employee and did not evaluate or assess the other grounds that should be taken into account by virtue of paragraph 4 of the First Schedule.[313]

272. If at the time when a case is adjudicated by the IDT, bankruptcy or liquidation procedures against the employer have commenced, the employee shall receive the totality of the sum adjudicated in his favour by the Redundancy Fund (section 31 §3 of Law 24/67); this sum refers to the amount payable due to the termination of employment and not to any other amounts which the employer owes to the employee by virtue of other laws, or with regard to accrued rights which arose during the employment relationship and not because of its termination.[314] All the rights of the employee against the employer are then transferred to the Redundancy Fund. In *Georgiou* the Redundancy Fund argued that it should not have the obligation to compensate the employee simply because an application for bankruptcy or liquidation has been filed, but that such obligation should apply only once the

309. *Louis Tourist Agency Ltd* v. *Elia* [1992] 1 CLR 98 (in Greek).
310. *Avgi Yerolakkos Buses Co Ltd* v. *Administrators of the Estate of Christou* [1971] 1 CLR 1.
311. *Famalift Shipyard Ltd* v. *Pavlides and others* [1991] 1 CLR 161 (in Greek).
312. See, however, *Papadopoulos* v. *N.I. Demetriou (Insurance) Ltd and another* [2001] 1 CLR 1994 (in Greek), where oddly compensation for unlawful termination of employment was calculated as amounting to five months' salary, whereas the minimum would be ten weeks' salary in accordance with section 1(a) of the First Schedule.
313. *JA Cabras & Bros Ltd* v. *Charalampous* [1992] 1 CLR 302 (in Greek), *Mouzouris* v. *KosmoPlast and Co and another* [2007] 1 CLR 896 (in Greek).
314. *Kyriakou and others* v. *Redundancy Fund* [1993] 1 CLR 1020 (in Greek).

bankruptcy or liquidation has been ordered by a court; otherwise, an employer might abuse the system through the filing of sham applications for bankruptcy or liquidation. The Supreme Court disagreed; it was held that the legislator clearly referred to the commencement of bankruptcy or liquidation procedures and not to an order having been granted.[315]

§6. Reinstatement

273. Unlike contracts of employment governed by public law, wrongful dismissal in the domain of private law causes the termination of the contract of employment; no question of reinstatement to their position arises.[316] In fact, no such jurisdiction vests in the IDT; its jurisdiction is confined to the award of damages for wrongful dismissal in accordance with the provisions of the law.[317] However, section 3 §1 of Law 24/67, as amended, now provides that the court may reinstate the employee if the termination of employment was either flagrantly unlawful, or unlawful and made in bad faith; the IDT should further consider whether reinstatement is required in view of the circumstances of the case. Reinstatement may be ordered if the employer employs more than 19 employees and the employee himself seeks to be reinstated.

274. In *Patsalides* it was held that the dismissal was neither flagrantly unlawful, nor made in bad faith; moreover, it was not required in view of the circumstances of the case, since the employee's conduct had been inappropriate and the termination of his employment had only been declared unlawful because of the delay of the employers to reach the decision to dismiss him.[318] Reinstatement shall also be ordered in case where the provisions of Law 205(I)/02 have been violated and the dismissal was because of gender discrimination (section 15(3) of Law 205(I)/02), if the employee has sought such remedy; the good, or bad faith of the employer is in such a case irrelevant.

§7. Termination for a Just Cause

275. A termination of employment shall not provide a right to compensation, if the employer dismissed the employee for just cause; as provided in section 5 of Law 24/67: (a) where the employee fails to carry out his work in an adequately satisfactory manner, (b) where the employee became redundant, (c) where the termination of employment is due to *force majeure*, warfare, insurrection, disaster or destruction of the facility due to fire unintentionally or negligently caused by the employer, (d) where the employment is terminated at the end of a fixed-term contract of

315. *Redundancy Fund* v. *Georgiou* [2006] 1 CLR 115 (in Greek).
316. *Pattikis and another* v. *The Municipal Committee of Nicosia* [1988] 1 CLR 103, *Talia* v. *SODAP* [2008] 1 CLR 560 (in Greek).
317. *Pattikis and another* v. *The Municipal Committee of Nicosia* [1988] 1 CLR 103.
318. *Patsalides* v. *Cyprus Airways*, Civ. Appeal 406/2008, dated 21/2/2012 (in Greek).

employment,[319] or when the employee completes the normal age of retirement on the basis of the law, custom, collective agreement, contract, employment regulations or otherwise, or (e) where the employee so conducts himself as to render himself liable to dismissal without notice. The grounds of termination of employment for redundancy and misconduct under (b) and (e) above shall be examined separately.

276. Termination of employment under section 5(a) of Law 24/67 where the employee fails to carry out his work in an adequately satisfactory manner, is subject to the proviso that temporary incapacity due to illness, injury, pregnancy or disease does not give rise to a just cause for dismissal. Thus, the justified absence of the employee from work in specific dates cannot give rise to a lawful dismissal.[320] However, in *Nicola* the Supreme Court held that the termination of employment of the employee was justified, since it was proven he had not performed his work in a reasonably satisfactory manner; the frequent and continuous absence of the employee from work on health grounds did not amount to temporary incapacity within the meaning of section 5 (a) of the Law and could thus be taken into account as indicating that the employee's work had not been satisfactorily performed.[321]

277. With regard to termination of employment on the grounds that the employee has reached the normal age of retirement by virtue of section 5(b) of Law 24/67, there are two interesting judgments of the Supreme Court. In *Charalampous* the employment relationship was terminated once the employee reached his 60th year of age. The employee argued that his contract of employment did not provide for mandatory retirement at 60 years, and that accordingly section 2 of the Social Insurance Law 41/80, which provided that the age of retirement is the 65th year of age, should be applicable. The Supreme Court held that whereas the contract of employment did not provide for the age of retirement, it was an established and known practice of the employer that all employees would retire once they reached their 60th year of age.[322]

278. In *Iracleous* the employment of the employees was terminated once they reached their 63rd year of age and they were given a bonus in accordance with the employer's regulations. The employees argued that they were entitled to work until the 65th year of age by virtue of section 2 of the Social Insurance Law 41/80,[323] whereas the employer claimed that at the material time a collective agreement between the employer and the employees' trade union was in force, in accordance with which the employees should have retired once they reached their 63rd year of age. The Supreme Court, reversing the judgment of the IDT, held that the said employees had objected and never consented with the terms of the collective agreement, as they considered it contrary to their interests. Accordingly, they were not

---

319. Unless by virtue of Law 98(I)/03 the contract should be considered as one of indefinite duration.
320. *Shoemex Ltd* v. *Georghiou* [1987] 1 CLR 509.
321. *Nicola* v. *Central Slaughterhouse of Kofinou* [2001] 1 CLR 810 (in Greek).
322. *Charalampous* v. *Michael Automotive Ltd* [2009] 1 CLR 102 (in Greek).
323. As it was in force at the time.

bound by the terms of the collective agreement; neither did the fact that they had received a bonus imply by itself that they could not file an application against their dismissal.[324]

279. The employer shall have, by virtue of section 6 of Law 24/67, the onus to prove before the IDT that the termination of employment was for a just cause and if he fails to do so, the termination of employment shall be unlawful.[325] The following shall never constitute a just cause for termination of employment: (i) membership in a trade union, or participation in trade union activities outside working hours or during working hours with the consent of the employer, or membership in a safety committee, (ii) representation of the workers or acts made by a representative of workers, (iii) submission of a complaint in good faith, or participation in procedures against the employer for alleged violation of civil or criminal responsibility, or recourse to a competent administrative authority, (iv) race, gender, national origin, religion, ethnicity, family status, religion, political views, or social origin, (v) pregnancy or motherhood,[326] (vi) parental leave or leave on grounds of *force majeure*.

§8. Misconduct

I. Nature and Degree of Conduct

280. Without prejudice to the generality of section 5(e) of Law 24/67, section 5(f) provides that the following may, *inter alia*, constitute grounds for dismissal without notice, all the circumstances of the case being taken into consideration: (i) any conduct on the part of the employee which makes it clear that the employer–employee relationship cannot reasonably be expected to continue, (ii) gross industrial misconduct, (iii) commission by the employee in the course of his duty of a criminal offence without the agreement, express or implied, of his employer, (iv) immoral behaviour by the employee in the course of his duties, (v) serious or rebated contravention or disregard of work or other rules in relation to the employment. It is further provided, under section 5(e) of Law 24/67, that where the employer does not exercise his right of dismissal within a reasonable period following the matter which gave rise to this right, he shall be deemed to have waived his right to dismiss the employee.

281. It has been held that paragraphs (e) and (f) of section 5 substantially reproduce the English common law regarding summary dismissal for misconduct;[327] subsection (f) merely sets out, in a rather arbitrary manner, certain common law

324. *Irakleous and another* v. *Municipality of Limassol* [2005] 1 CLR 479 (in Greek).
325. *Palinex Information Technology Ltd* v. *Nicolaides* [2003] 1 CLR 1868 (in Greek).
326. See also section 4 of Law 100(I)/97.
327. *KEM (Taxi) Ltd* v. *Anastassis Tryphonos* [1969] 1 CLR 52.

provisions, in order to provide guidance to the general public, rather than to the lawyer;[328] it is submitted, however, that such a continental law style sub-classification is helpful in clarifying the meaning of complex terms. Termination of employment under section 5(e) of Law 24/67 may occur even if the employee is temporarily absent from work due to illness, disease, or injury, contrary to what is the case under section 5(a) of Law 24/67 regarding failure of the employee to carry out his work in an adequately satisfactory manner. It was accordingly held that the behaviour of the employee, who had unjustifiably retained saws which were the property of the employer, was conduct which justified dismissal without notice even while he was sick.[329]

282. Dismissal without notice is considered as a drastic measure and should accordingly be used only in serious cases, where this is justified.[330] Conduct falling short of 'dishonesty' may nevertheless be of such a grave and weighty character so as to amount to a breach of the confidential relationship between employer and employee, such as would give the employer the right to immediately discharge the employee.[331] The burden of the employer is on the balance of probabilities to prove that his confidence and trust towards the employee have been irrevocably breached due to the conduct of the employee; the employer need not, however, prove that he has suffered damage as a result of the conduct of the employee.[332] The correct test is thus for the tribunal to consider whether it was correct for the employers to dismiss the employee.[333] The question of reasonableness should be considered objectively and not on the basis of what the tribunal would have done, if it was the employer; it is not for the tribunal to substitute itself as an employer, but to consider by the standards of a reasonable person whether reasonable grounds have been established for the belief that the employee should be dismissed.[334]

283. In *KEM* it was held that there is no fixed rule of law defining the degree of misconduct which could justify dismissal without notice; whereas misconduct inconsistent with the fulfilment of the express or implied conditions of service will justify dismissal, an isolated act of neglect or misconduct will not justify it unless attended by serious consequences. The tribunal must determine whether the misconduct of the employee was such as to interfere with and to prejudice the safe

328. JB Cronin, 'ILO Recommendation 119: Job Security in Cyprus' (1968) 17 *International and Comparative Law Quarterly Review*: 760, cited with approval in *Constantinidou* v. *FW Woolworth & Co Cyprus Ltd* [1980] 1 CLR 302.
329. *Demetriou* v. *Nikos E. Klappis & Sons Ltd* [2006] 1 CLR 1358 (in Greek).
330. *Patikkis* v. *Nicosia Municipal Committee* [1988] 1 CLR 103, *Kasapis* v. *Technoplastics Ltd* [1992] 1 CLR 919 (in Greek), *Kanika Developments Ltd* v. *Louca* [2004] 1 CLR 603 (in Greek), *Charalampous* v. *Republic* [2007] 1 CLR 752 (in Greek).
331. *Sinclair* v. *Neighbour* [1966] 3 All ER 988.
332. *Fotiades* v. *Alpha Bank Ltd*, Civ. Appeal 319/09, dated 26 September 2013 (in Greek).
333. *British Leyland (U.K.) Ltd* v. *Swift* [1981] 1 RLR 91, cited with approval in *Kakofeggitou* v. *Cyprus Airways Ltd* [2005] 1 CLR 1478 (in Greek), *Fotiades* v. *Alpha Bank Ltd*, Civ. Appeal 319/09, dated 26 September 2013 (in Greek).
334. *Galatariotis Telecommunications Ltd* v. *Vasiliou* [2003] 1 CLR 318 (in Greek).

and proper conduct of the employer's business and accordingly to justify immediate dismissal; the test to be applied may vary, depending on the nature of the business and the position held by the employee. A single act of disobedience or misconduct shall not justify dismissal, unless it is of such nature that it might in effect be considered that the employee is repudiating the employment contract or one of its essential conditions.[335] Refusal to obey instructions and continuous absence from work might, depending on the circumstances of the case, justify immediate dismissal.[336]

284. Wilful disobedience of a lawful and reasonable order of the employer shows a complete disregard of a condition essential to the contract of service, namely that the employee must obey the proper orders of his employer. Accordingly, the question of whether the conduct of the employee was such as to make it clear that the employment relationship cannot reasonably be expected to continue, must depend upon the facts and circumstances of the particular case; and the conditions prevailing at the time and place where the matter has occurred. The tribunal should thus take into account the local conditions in order to determine how a reasonable employer in Cyprus would be expected to react in similar circumstances, considering the position held by the employee and the nature of the business.[337]

II. Specific Cases

285. Bad language, insolence or insubordination in the course of employment may amount to misconduct, but this may also depend on the environment in which they were used; the moderation of language to be expected in a mine in the absence of customers is not the same as in a transport office in the presence of customers. In *KEM* it was held that on the basis of the facts of the case the language used by the employee in the presence of the employer's customers was terribly obscene and insolent and the employee's conduct was held to be insulting and insubordinate to such a degree so as to be incompatible with the continuation of the employment relationship. Whereas, it might have been an isolated act of misconduct, it was of such intensity so as to interfere with the proper conduct of the employer's business, as the employee had essentially undermined the quality of the vehicles of his employer's transport company in the presence of their customers; this amounted to such a deliberate disregard of the conditions of service as to justify summarily dismissal.[338]

286. Similarly, in *Constantinidou* it was held that the violation of regulations and instructions which set out a mode of security for the safety of the goods in a

335. *KEM (Taxi) Ltd* v. *Anastassis Tryphonos* [1969] 1 CLR 52.
336. *Makris* v. *Makrisbros Ltd* [1980] 1 CLR 238.
337. *KEM (Taxi) Ltd* v. *Anastassis Tryphonos* [1969] 1 CLR 52.
338. *KEM (Taxi) Ltd* v. *Anastassis Tryphonos* [1969] 1 CLR 52, referencing *Clouston & Co Ltd* v. *Corry* [1906] AC 122; *Jupiter General Insurance Co Ltd* v. *Shroff* [1937] 3 All ER 67; *Laws* v. *London Chronicle Ltd* [1959] 2 All ER 285.

supermarket amounted to sufficient grounds for justifying summary dismissal.[339] In *Lambrianou* the employee had attempted to cover his own unsatisfactory work performance by falsely accusing his supervisor for appropriation of money of the employer; the Supreme Court held that the conduct of the employee had made it impossible for the employee and his supervisor to continue working together and had breached the confidence of the employer towards the employee. Accordingly, the dismissal without notice was warranted.[340]

287. In *Demstar* the IDT held that the employers had unlawfully terminated the employment of their employee. The Supreme Court reversed the decision; it was held that the employee had shown improper behaviour towards the director of the employer, as he rudely declined to obey an order of the director to be accompanied by one of his colleagues during the installation of the telephone operation of an important client of the employer, so that if at any time the employee was absent from work, his colleague would be able to serve the needs of the client. [341] The Supreme Court noted that the employee had wilfully refused to obey a reasonable order from the director of the employer, in a way which amounted to disrespect and indifference for the manner in which the employer expected the work to be carried out and offended the dignity and prestige of the employer; the behaviour of the employee had reasonably caused the employer to lose confidence in the employee and breached the foundations of the employment relationship.

288. On the other hand, in *Dias* the employment relationship of the employee was terminated because he had a dispute with and used offensive language to another employee, which resulted in the latter hitting him in the mouth; the Supreme Court held that the offensive words used by the employee towards his colleague while they were alone in their office, could not be considered by themselves as conduct which justified dismissal without notice.[342] Similarly, in *Louca* the employee was dismissed without notice for having slapped another employee who deliberately refused to follow his instructions. It was held that the dismissal was not reasonable under the circumstances; the employee had been offering his services to the employers for 10 years without any problems and whereas his conduct was improper, it was an isolated incident and it should accordingly be viewed within the wider context of the employee's career and personal attributes.[343]

289. An employee may in general act as he wishes during his non-working hours, provided he does not hinder the interests of his employer and to the extent that the employer has not expressly and lawfully prohibited the employee from doing something. However, the provision of services by the employee to a competitor in a manner which runs contrary to the interests of his employers constitutes

339. *Constantinidou* v. *FW Woolworth & Co Cyprus Ltd* [1980] 1 CLR 302.
340. *Lambrianou* v. *Photos Photiades Distributors Ltd* [2011] 1 CLR 763 (in Greek).
341. *Demstar Information Group Ltd* v. *Anastasiades* [2008] 1 CLR 1146 (in Greek).
342. *Dias Publishing House Ltd* v. *Koyia* [2006] 1 CLR 1227 (in Greek).
343. *Kanika Developments Ltd* v. *Louca* [2004] 1 CLR 603 (in Greek).

lawful and justified grounds for termination of employment by the employer.[344] In *Crown Resorts* the employer terminated the employment of the employee because he had given 37 documents to the former manager of the hotel of the employer; the employer alleged that the documents contained confidential information and data. The IDT held that the termination of the employment was unlawful; it was found as a matter of fact that the employee had delivered the documents with the consent of the managing director of the employer and that the documents contained no confidential information; accordingly, no reasonable employer would have terminated the employment relationship.[345]

290. In *Papaphilippou* it was held that if the employee is in a position to be fully aware of the grounds on which he is dismissed without notice, there is no need to notify him. The employee, secretary in a law firm, had taken a folded paper from the office of her employer and photocopied it without his permission or knowledge; the IDT held that the employee's dismissal without notice was not justified, since that was an isolated incidence. The Supreme Court reversed the IDT's judgment and held that the employment relation has been irrevocably broken down, since there was no longer any confidence or trust between employer and employee; taking into account the obligations of a secretary in a law firm, which refer to the handling of confidential information of clients, the employee owed to the employer an increased duty of confidentiality and her behaviour constituted grounds for immediate dismissal.[346]

291. In *Christou* the employee was a maid in a hotel administered by the employer. She had found a golden watch that a client of the hotel had forgotten in his room and only delivered it to the employer after one week, when the client called the hotel mentioning that he had forgotten his watch. The employee alleged that she had put the watch in her trolley, but neglected to deliver it due to work pressure. The employer terminated her employment without notice for failing to deliver the watch immediately to the employers; it was held, however, that such an isolated incident in her seven years of service to the employers could not justify the drastic measure of dismissal without notice.[347]

292. If the employment has been terminated due to mere suspicion that the employee has behaved in a certain way, the termination is considered to be unlawful. In *Petrides* the Supreme Court held that the termination of employment of the employee on the basis of suspicion that he had leaked confidential information to third parties was, in the absence of proof of such conduct, unlawful. It was further held that the right of the employer to dismiss the employee without notice should be exercised within reasonable time; otherwise, the termination of employment shall be unlawful. In the circumstances of the case it was not reasonable for the employer

344. *Antenna Ltd* v. *Constantinou* [2010] 1 CLR 392 (in Greek).
345. *Crown Resorts Ltd* v. *Kallis* [2011] 1 CLR 1369 (in Greek).
346. *L. Papaphilippou & Co* v. *Louca*, Civ. Appeal 59/2010, judgment of 20 June 2014 (in Greek).
347. *Kynigos Hotels Ltd* v. *Christou* [2004] 1 CLR 665 (in Greek).

to dismiss the employee four months after their suspicions had been established.[348] Reasonable time is a matter of fact and is determined on the basis of the totality of the circumstances.[349]

293. In *Andreou* the employers, hotel owners, dismissed the employee on the grounds that he had an affair with the daughter of a client, who often stayed in the hotel where the employee was working; when the client and his daughter found out that the employee was married, they were distressed. The client sent a letter to the employers demanding that they dismiss the employee. The Supreme Court, affirming the IDT's judgment, noted that the employee had the affair at a time when he was single and got married at a later stage, when he was no longer having an affair with the daughter of the client. It was held that whereas the employee has obligations towards his employers, he is still an independent personality who has the right to a private and persona life; the fact that the meeting between the employee and the client's daughter took place in the hotel was irrelevant. The termination of employment was unlawful.[350]

III. Disciplinary Procedure: Right to be Heard

294. Whereas there is no obligation for the employer to adopt a detailed disciplinary code, if such code is adopted, then the employer shall be nevertheless expected to apply the procedure provided in the disciplinary code. It should be noted that Law 24/67 does not provide for the imposition of any other disciplinary sanctions other than termination of employment, when such might be imposed; accordingly, additional sanctions in appropriate cases might be adopted by virtue of collective agreements. Disciplinary codes are normally introduced following consultation with the employees or their representatives and any individual employee is expected to be properly informed on the application of the disciplinary code at the time of commencement of employment.[351]

295. Early case law suggested that there is no rule prescribing that an employee should always be given a fair hearing before dismissal.[352] However, subsequent case law concluded that there is a right to be heard prior to termination of employment by virtue of Article 7 of the Ratification Law of the Convention on the Termination of Employment 45/85.[353] Article 7 of Law 45/85 provides that the employment should not be terminated on grounds relevant to the conduct or work of the employee, before he has an opportunity to be heard and defend himself against the

348. *Kyprianou and Co* v. *Petrides* [2007] 1 CLR 607 (in Greek).
349. *Demetri and others* v. *Beven and others* [1999] 1 CLR 663 (in Greek), *CTC/ARI Airports Ltd* v. *Ioannidou*, Civ. Appeal 24/2011, judgment of 16 December 2015 (in Greek).
350. *Thanos Hotels Ltd* v. *Andreou* [2002] 1 CLR 1000 (in Greek).
351. See also OEB, *Handbook of Officer of Labour Relations: Industrial Policies and Good Practices* (Nicosia, 2015, in Greek): 15–21 for a sample disciplinary code.
352. *Constantinidou* v. *FW Woolworth & Co Cyprus Ltd* [1980] 1 CLR 302.
353. *Crown Resorts Ltd* v. *Kallis* [2011] 1 CLR 1369 (in Greek).

charges, unless it cannot reasonably be expected from the employer to give him that opportunity.[354]

296. It has been held that Article 7 of Law 45/85 does not imply that a disciplinary trial should be conducted similarly to what is the case in the public service, nor that some specific procedure should be followed; in private law the aim is not to prove that a disciplinary offence has taken place, but merely that a reasonable employer would dismiss the employee under the circumstances of the case. There is thus no obligation for the employer to hear the employee in the presence of his lawyer, or to provide the employee with the material under investigation in advance. What is important is whether the employee had been given the opportunity to present his views and whether, on the basis of the circumstances, it was reasonable for the employer to dismiss the employee.[355]

297. In *Pattikis* the Supreme Court held that the employer, by his representations and practice, created a legitimate expectation in the mind of the employees that they would not be dismissed for an alleged misdeed, unless prior opportunity was given to them to be heard in the matter of the complaint; they were even led to believe that a disciplinary procedure would be followed for the establishment of misconduct and the imposition of sanctions including termination of the contract of employment. In the circumstances, the right to be heard should be deemed to have been implicitly incorporated in their contract of employment.[356] In *Koilaras* the Supreme Court held that there was no violation of the right to be heard, since the employee had been informed of the charges against him and he had admitted them. It was further held that the employee had a second job without the knowledge of the employer, using the company's car for carrying this other work; his performance in his work had also been negatively affected.[357]

298. The question whether the employee has a right to silence was considered in *Galatariotis*. The employee was dismissed because his mother held shares in a competitive company, which was founded by a former employee of the employers; it was alleged by the employer that the overall conduct of the employee convinced them that the continuation of the employment relationship was not possible, as the employee could no longer be trusted in good faith. The IDT held that the termination of employment was unlawful. The employers appealed and argued that the silence of the employee, when requested by the employer, meant that the charges were true.

299. The Supreme Court noted that if charges are pronounced against a person outside the court, his affirmative reply might be used as admission of the charges; his silence might also be interpreted as admission of the charges, if the

354. *Andreas Prokopiou Ltd* v. *Toumazou* [2001] 1 CLR 1125 (in Greek).
355. *Kakofeggitou* v. *Cyprus Airways Ltd* [2005] 1 CLR 1478 (in Greek), *Sieli* v. *Bank of Cyprus Ltd*, Civ. Appeal 348/08, dated 8 March 2012 (in Greek), *Fotiades* v. *Alpha Bank Ltd*, Civ. Appeal 319/09, dated 26 September 2013 (in Greek).
356. *Pattikis and another* v. *The Municipal Committee of Nicosia* [1988] 1 CLR 103.
357. *Koilaras* v. *Pharmaceutical Organization of Cyprus Ltd* [2010] 1 CLR 869 (in Greek).

circumstances are such that some explanation or even denial would reasonably be expected. It was, however, held that the trial court was correct to consider that under the totality of the evidence and the circumstances, the silence of the employee could not be construed as admission of the charges. In this respect the Court noted that a critical factor in deciding whether silence amounts to acceptance of the charges is whether the parties were on equal terms, namely whether one is not in a position of authority over the other; conversely, in the context of an employment relationship the employer is in a position of authority over an employee.[358]

IV. Without Notice

300. Dismissal for conduct envisaged by section 5 of Law 24/67 may occur without notice. In *Agapiou* the IDT held that the employee was guilty of the conduct envisaged by section 5 of Law 24/67, but nevertheless held that the dismissal of the employee without notice was not lawful and accordingly awarded to the respondent four weeks wages in lieu of notice of dismissal. The Supreme Court reversed the IDT's judgment and held that termination of employment for any of the grounds set out in section 5 of Law 24/67 does not give rise to a right to compensation; since the IDT had held that the employee had repeatedly contravened her rules of employment and had failed to carry out her work in a reasonably efficient manner, she could not receive the benefits provided for in section 9 of Law 24/67.[359]

301. In *Kasapis* the employee was dismissed for not turning up to work for a week without reasonable justification. The IDT held that the termination of employment without notice was justified in accordance with section 5 of Law 24/67 and that the employee should not receive any compensation; it was held, however, that the employee should have been given notice in accordance with Article 11 of the Convention on Termination of Employment of 1982 which was ratified with Law 45/85. The Supreme Court affirmed that the dismissal of the employee had been justified under the circumstances. It was held, however, that, contrary to the IDT's perspective, Article 11 of the Convention did not introduce different criteria than section 5 of Law 24/67; if the conduct of the employee was of such nature as to justify immediate termination of employment without notice, he is not entitled to receive payment in lieu of notice as that would be contradictory.[360]

302. A similar conclusion was reached by the Supreme Court in *Kleovoulou*, where it was held that there are differences or conflict between Article 11 of the Convention and section 5 of Law 24/67; it was held that the act of the employee to carry out competing work for a client of the employer without the consent or knowledge of the employer and to use without authorization raw materials owned by the

358. *Galatariotis Telecommunications Ltd* v. *Vasiliou* [2003] 1 CLR 318 (in Greek).
359. *Pancypria Eteria Artopion Ltd* v. *Agapiou* [1985] 1 CLR 196.
360. *Kasapis* v. *Technoplastics Ltd* [1992] 1 CLR 919 (in Greek).

employee in order to carry out such work, justified immediate dismissal.[361] It should be noted that in *KEM* Josephides J. suggested that the law be amended so as to enable, in a proper case, the employee to lose only his right to payment in lieu of notice and not to lose his right to compensation, even if his employment has been deemed to be lawfully terminated by the employer without notice; it was suggested that the IDT should have discretion to decide whether on the basis of all circumstances, including length of service, it would be fair for the employee to be awarded compensation, in full or in part.[362] However, no amendment was introduced.

V. Constructive Dismissal

303. An employee may lawfully terminate his employment with an employer because of the conduct of the employer by virtue of section 7(1) of Law 24/67; in this latter case, the termination shall be deemed to be termination by the employer. Accordingly, if the employer's behaviour has become so intolerable that the employee has no option but to resign, then constructive dismissal shall have occurred and the employer shall be liable to compensate the employee. The onus is on the employee to prove that his resignation was due to improper conduct by the employer. Section 7 §1 of Law 24/67 refers to a conduct of the employer which objectively is of such a nature that it shakes the foundations of the employment relationship; this might be due to a breach of fundamental terms of the employment relationship, or because of a conduct which is inconsistent with the accepted framework that should govern the relationship between an employer and an employee.[363] The non-payment of salaries and contributions by the employer is a conduct that falls within the ambit of section 7 §1 of the Law.[364]

304. In *Alouet* the employer had unilaterally suspended the operation of the contract of employment of his employees without payment of their wages to them and without them having consented to such suspension. It was held that the employer's conduct amounted to a breach of fundamental terms of the contract of employment of his employees, which entitled them to terminate the employment under section 7 §1 of the Law and to pursue their right to compensation calculated in accordance with section 3 of the Law, in the same way in which they would have been entitled to do had their employment been unlawfully terminated by their employers themselves. Neither the fact that the applicants were making enquiries as to whether, or when, they would return to work, nor the meeting they had with their employers in an effort to reach an amicable settlement of their claims, nor the fact that they considered themselves as having been dismissed from their employment after the meeting in the manager's office, nor the fact that, prior to this meeting, the employee

361. *Kyros Manufacturing Ltd* v. *Kleovoulou* [1992] 1 CLR 936 (in Greek).
362. *KEM (Taxi) Ltd* v. *Anastassis Tryphonos* [1969] 1 CLR 52.
363. *Louis Tourist Agency Ltd* v. *Elia* [1992] 1 CLR 98 (in Greek).
364. *JA Cabras & Bros Ltd* v. *Charalampous* [1992] 1 CLR 302 (in Greek).

found temporary employment elsewhere, changed the situation or affected in any way their right to claim compensation.[365]

305. In *Dias* the Supreme Court held that the employment relationship had been lawfully terminated by the employee because of the conduct of the employer; it was found that the employer had gradually and consistently undermined the employee to such an extent that it had shaken the foundations of the employment relationship and the confidence between employer and employee. The Court noted that constructive dismissal does not depend upon the actual intention of the employer to force the employee to resign, but on whether the conduct of the employer is objectively of such a nature as to preclude the continuation of the employment relationship.[366] Similarly, in *Elia* it was held that the pressure exercised by the employer, who stated to the employee that they do not trust her anymore and that she had better resign in order to avoid negative consequences, amounted to constructive dismissal; the employee had lawfully terminated the employment relationship.[367]

306. However, in *Gregoriou* the employer sent a letter to the employee, who was their general manager, stating that they intend to follow his suggestions and terminate his employment on grounds of redundancy as soon as possible, in view of the employer's bad financial situation. The employee replied that he had never suggested such course of action. A meeting then took place between the parties and the employer clarified that they never intended for him to leave; however, the employee never returned to his employment despite the employer repeatedly suggesting to him to do so. The Supreme Court affirmed the IDT's decision that, in view of the circumstances, the employer had never terminated the employment of the employee and that the employee had voluntarily and without justification resigned.[368]

307. In *Salamis Tours*, following a lengthy leave of absence on medical grounds, the employee, a bus driver, delivered to his employer, a medical certificate in accordance to which he would be able to gradually begin to work again, albeit for limited hours per week. The employer noted that the medical certificate was vague and requested the employee to furnish them with a medical certificate confirming that it would be safe for him to return to work and specifying precisely how many hours a day he could work. The employee resigned due to the refusal of the employer to let him return to work. The IDT held that the employer had a duty to conduct a proper inquiry in order to determine the medical status of the employee, which they failed to discharge; accordingly, there was constructive resignation due to the conduct of the employer and their refusal to allow the employee to resume work.

308. The Supreme Court reversed the IDT's judgment; it was held that the clarifications requested by the employer were reasonable, whereas the insistence of the

365. *Alouet Clothing Manufacturers Ltd* v. *Athanasiou and another* [1988] 1 CLR 626.
366. *Dias Publishing House Ltd* v. *Papachristodoulou* [2006] 1 CLR 625 (in Greek).
367. *Louis Tourist Agency Ltd* v. *Elia* [1992] 1 CLR 98 (in Greek).
368. *Gregoriou* v. *Boyiadjis and Co Ltd* [2003] 1 CLR 1924 (in Greek).

employee not to furnish a less vague certificate was unreasonable. It was further held that the employee has the obligation to provide the employer with the relevant data. Moreover, it was held that the finding that the employer had an obligation to conduct an inquiry was thus arbitrary and might lead to complications; if the employers were to have the employee examined by their own doctor and there were conflicting medical opinions, the employer could not force the employee to resume work full-time, as potentially recommended by the employer's doctor, if the employee's doctor suggested that this might endanger the employee's health, and vice-versa. The employer was accordingly not liable to pay compensation.[369]

§9. Redundancy

I. Grounds

309. When the employment of an employee, who had been continuously employed for a period of at least 104 weeks by the same employer, has been terminated on grounds of redundancy, the employee shall be compensated by the Redundancy Fund (section 16 §1 of Law 24/67).[370] Accordingly, redundancy can only be justified if the employee has been continuously employed by the same employer for a continuous period of at least 104 weeks. Redundancy will only be declared if it is based upon at least one of the following grounds for dismissal: (a) the employer has ceased or intends to cease to operate the business, or the place (location) where the employee is employed, (b) modernization, mechanization, or any other change in the method of production or organization, (c) abolition of a specific department, or (d) reduction in the turnover of the business, or difficulties in placing products in the market, or credit difficulties, or lack of orders or lack of raw materials.

310. The above are the only grounds on the basis of which redundancy may be declared. Whereas there might be cases where the circumstances of the employer's business might fall in more than one of the grounds for redundancy, an employee cannot be redundant unless at least one of the grounds is fulfilled, when considered independently of any other ground.[371] The Supreme Court has noted that when deriving guidance from decisions in English cases on matters of redundancy, the courts should always bear in mind that the English law of redundancy differs substantially from the respective Cypriot law.[372] Events which followed the dismissal of the employee are irrelevant.[373]

311. Grounds for redundancy are further analysed below. An employer shall be considered to cease, or intend to cease, to operate the business where the employee

369. *Salamis Tours Ltd* v. *Polykarpou* [2010] 1 CLR 1091 (in Greek).
370. See in general A. Emilianides, 'Redundancy Law in Cyprus', in Van Kempen *et al.* (eds.), *Redundancy Law in Europe* (The Hague: Kluwer, 2009): 29–37.
371. *Hadjisavvas* v. *Redundancy Fund* [1989] 1 CLR 145.
372. *Hadjisavvas* v. *Redundancy Fund* [1989] 1 CLR 145.
373. *Hadjichristofi* v. *Georgiou and another* [2002] 1 CLR 873 (in Greek).

is employed, if he is subject to bankruptcy or similar proceedings and in addition the business should be part of the property which is subject to bankruptcy. It also applies to circumstances where the employer ceases to operate altogether the business, without transferring such business.[374] However, it does not apply in circumstances where the employer has ceased, or intends to cease, to operate the business where the employee is employed, due to transfer of, or part of, a business, because such a transfer is no longer a ground of dismissal on the basis of redundancy.

312. In *Papadopoulos* the IDT held that the employee had been dismissed on grounds of redundancy, because of the merger between his employer and another company. The Supreme Court reversed the judgment of the IDT and held that the merger between two companies or the fact that a company bought shares in the other company, are not grounds of redundancy by virtue of section 18 of the Law. Accordingly, the termination of employment was unlawful.[375] It should be noted, however, that by virtue of section 10 of Law 104(I)/00, in the circumstances where a transfer of an undertaking or business or part of an undertaking or business has taken place in accordance with the provisions of Law 104(I)/000, dismissals on grounds of economic, technical or organizational reasons entailing changes in the workforce under section 5 of Law 104(I)/00, shall be considered as grounds of redundancy.

313. If the employer has ceased, or intends to cease, to operate the business at the place (location) where the employee is employed, the IDT has judicial discretion to decide under what circumstances it is reasonable for the employee to continue to be employed, despite the change of the location of employment. The decision whether continuation of employment would be reasonable, should take into account the personal circumstances of the employee, the costs and risks involved and the degree of the change of location of employment. If the location of business changes substantially, the Court will normally accept that there is a justified ground for dismissal on the basis of redundancy.

314. Modernization, mechanization, or any other change in the method of production or organization, which necessitates a reduction in the number of employees, or a change in the products, the method of production, or the expertise required by the employees, constitutes a ground for redundancy. The employers have the discretion to choose the methods of production or organization, which would lead to a better overall efficiency of their business, so long as the change of method is substantive and has become necessary due to technological, market, or other similar developments. Such change of method constitutes a justified ground for dismissal on the basis of redundancy, so long as it relates to the proper functioning of the business and it also objectively necessitates a reduction in the number of employees.

315. The simple aim of the employer to hire new (younger or with lower pay) employees instead of the existing employees, does not amount to a change in the

---

374. *Savvides* v. *SSP Catering Cyprus Ltd and others*, Civ. Appeal 179/09, dated 20 September 2012 (in Greek).
375. *Papadopoulos* v. *N.I. Demetriou (Insurance) Ltd and another* [2001] 1 CLR 1994 (in Greek).

method of production or organization and does not justify dismissal on the basis of redundancy. Similarly, the dismissal of an employee in order to delegate to another existing employee with his/her duties, does not amount to a change of organization, nor to a justified ground of dismissal due to redundancy. In *Colocassides* the employers raised as ground of redundancy that the employment was terminated due to modernization, mechanization or any other change in the production or organization methods, which diminishes the number of required employees; it was held that the duties of the position of the dismissed employee had not been in reality abolished, but were rather carried out by another employee.[376]

316. In *Fotiades* it was held that the employment had been terminated two years prior to the mechanization of the employee's department; thus, it was not convincing to argue that the redundancy was due to such mechanization. Furthermore, until his employment was terminated, the employee worked overtime, a fact which showed that the volume of work of his department had not been reduced.[377] Similarly, in *Galatariotis* it was held that the evidence produced by the employer had not proven in a convincing manner that the volume of work of the employer had been diminished.[378]

317. Abolition of a specific department shall amount to a valid ground for redundancy, so long as such abolition does not arise from a transfer of such department to another legal entity, as a result of a merge, or a legal transfer. Abolition of a department which is the result of a change of organization or of the business changing the ambit of its activities, would be considered as a justified ground for dismissal due to redundancy. However, abolition of a specific position does not amount to grounds for redundancy.

318. Finally, reduction in the turnover of the business, or difficulties in placing products in the market, or credit difficulties, or lack of orders or lack of raw materials would also amount to grounds for redundancy. Credit difficulties should be interpreted as referring to the failure to find loans, since such failure affects directly the operation of the employer; on the contrary, failure to repay existing loans affects the operation of the employer only indirectly and as such does not amount to grounds for redundancy.[379] An employee shall not become redundant if there is a temporary reduction in the turnover of the business, but only so long as there is a permanent reduction and the reverse of such reduction cannot be foreseen soon.

319. Thus, a temporary reduction in the turnover, which is due to the fact that the nature of the business is seasonal, or a temporary recess of the activities of the business, are not justified grounds for dismissal due to redundancy; the volume of

---

376. *S & G Colocassides Ltd* v. *Lazarides and another* [1999] 1 CLR 2181 (in Greek), *Paphos Stone C Estates Ltd and another* v. *Christodoulides and another* [2000] 1 CLR 2110 (in Greek).
377. *Fotos Fotiades Breweries Ltd* v. *Antoniades and another* [2002] 1 CLR 1490 (in Greek).
378. *Galatariotis Bros Ltd* v. *Gregora and another* [2001] 1 CLR 1985 (in Greek).
379. *Skyrianides Hotels Ltd* v. *Polyviou and another* [2003] 1 CLR 820 (in Greek).

work should thus be evaluated compared with a fixed denominator which represents the volume of work within a normal cycle of business activity, such as an accounting year.[380] In *Hadjisavva* the employee alleged that he had been dismissed on grounds of redundancy due to the contraction of the volume of work or business of his employer; it was held that this was not substantiated as at the material time of the termination of employment there was an increase and not a reduction of the employer's business, which had led the employers to hire three additional employees in order to cope with the volume of work.[381]

320. The fact that losses incurred, or that the employer had set higher aims with respect to profits, or turnover, or that the employer aims to have more profit, or that the employee receives a high salary, do not prove reduction in the turnover and do not constitute justified grounds for dismissal on the basis of redundancy. Accounting loss might be attributed to a number of factors and is not the same as reduction in the volume of work of the employer for redundancy purposes; the most accurate indication of the volume of work for an employer is the value of the work carried out.[382] Reduction of the volume of work of the employee, but not of the business, does not in any event amount to a justified ground for dismissal due to redundancy; when the law provides for the reduction of volume of work, it refers to the contraction of work of the given employer and not the reduction of work of the specific employee; it is only the volume of work of the employer that is of interest for redundancy purposes.[383]

II. Offer of Position, Transfer or Renewal

321. The fact that the employer had hired new employees after effecting dismissals that were due to redundancy, does not prove by itself that the alleged legal grounds for dismissal due to redundancy had not existed. The employee shall not, however, be entitled to receive compensation from the Redundancy Fund if before the termination of the employment contract, the employer offers to the employee a new adequate position or location of employment and the employee unreasonably rejects such offer. The new position or location of employment should be adequate, in the sense that the terms of employment, the salary and other benefits should be similar to those of the previous employment contract. Similarly, the test of unreasonableness of rejection shall depend upon the particular personal circumstances of the employee concerned.

322. The employee shall not further be entitled to receive compensation from the Redundancy Fund, if the employment contract has been terminated due to a change of employer, despite the fact that the new employer renewed the existing

380. *A. Iasonos Ltd* v. *Christou and others* [1994] 1 CLR 703 (in Greek), *Hadjichristofi* v. *Georgiou and another* [2002] 1 CLR 873 (in Greek).
381. *Hadjisavvas* v. *Redundancy Fund* [1989] 1 CLR 145.
382. *Tryfonos* v. *Takis Vashiotis Ltd* [1999] 1 CLR 1953 (in Greek).
383. *Hadjichristofi* v. *Georgiou and another* [2002] 1 CLR 873 (in Greek).

employment contract.[384] The employee shall be entitled to receive compensation from the Redundancy Fund, only if he proves to the IDT that the reason for not accepting the offer of the new employer for renewal of the existing employment contract was based upon reasonable grounds. In *Kastrappis* the employment of the employees was terminated on grounds of redundancy, because of the merger of their employer with another company; it was offered to them that they continue their employment after the merger, so long as their workings hours were increased for one hour a week. The employees rejected the offer due to the increase of their working hours and applied before the IDT against the Redundancy Fund.

323. The IDT held that the refusal of the employees to work for the new employer was without good cause, as it considered that the one hour difference in the working hours was not that significant. The Supreme Court reversed. It was held that a renewal of a contract of employment within the notion of section 20(b) refers to a renewal or extension upon identical terms as the old contract; the only different element in the contract should be the identity of the employer. Furthermore, a mere request to stay on for a short while does not constitute a renewal. Since the new offer would amount to a change in the working hours of the employees, it could not constitute a renewal.[385]

324. Furthermore, the employee shall not be entitled to compensation if the employer is a company and transfers the employee to another affiliated company, which is either a parent company, or a subsidiary, or they both belong to the same group of companies; in the latter case all the weeks that the employee was employed under the first employer shall be calculated as employment in the second employer. Two companies shall be defined as affiliated, either if one is a subsidiary of the other, or if they are both subsidiary of a third company. A subsidiary is defined by section 148 of the Companies Law, Cap. 113, which provides that a company shall be deemed to be a subsidiary of another if: (a) either (i) the latter is a member of the former and controls the composition of its board of directors;[386] or (ii) more than half of the equity share capital[387] of the former is held by the latter; or (b) the first company is a subsidiary of any company which is a subsidiary of the latter. In *Toumazou* it was held that the employees had been employed continuously, as they had continued to work for a second employer who had undertaken the reputation,

384. *Kyriakides and another* v. *Redundancy Fund* [1990] 1 CLR 20 (in Greek).

385. *Kastrappis* v. *Apostolides and another* [2003] 1 CLR 509 (in Greek), *Proiki* v. *Michaelidou* [2002] 1 CLR 736 (in Greek).

386. The composition of a company's board of directors shall be deemed to be controlled by another company if that other company, without the consent or concurrence of any other person, can appoint or remove the holders of all or a majority of the directorships; that other company shall be deemed to have power to appoint to a directorship with respect to which any of the following conditions is satisfied: (a) that a person cannot be appointed thereto without the exercise in his favour by that other company of such a power as aforesaid, or (b) that a person's appointment thereto follows necessarily from his appointment as director of that other company, or (c) that the directorship is held by that other company itself or by a subsidiary of it.

387. Equity share capital means the company's issued share capital excluding any part thereof which, neither as respects dividends nor as respects capital carries any right to participate beyond a specified amount in a distribution.

clientele, turnover and equipment of the first employer; accordingly, they were not entitled to receive compensation from the Redundancy Fund.[388]

325. In *Demades* the IDT held that the first employers of the petitioner were affiliated to her second employers and that accordingly the petitioner's service in the first employers should be calculated towards the compensation of the employee; the IDT based that finding on the fact that the first employer was the founder and major shareholder of the second employer and controlled the function and accounts of the second employer. The Supreme Court reversed the IDT's judgment and noted that the trial court had not used the criteria set out in the legislation; it was further noted that the first employer held only 1/3 of the share capital of the second employer and not more than half as required by Cap. 113. Since the proviso in paragraph 3 applied only in case of affiliated companies, the IDT had erred in its findings.[389]

III. Procedural Requirements

326. The right to terminate employment on grounds of redundancy is grounded in the employment relationship itself; such termination of employment on grounds of redundancy is not therefore dependent upon the consent of the employees.[390] However, the employer has the obligation to provide information and to engage in consultations before redundancies take place. An employer who intends to dismiss employees on grounds of redundancy is required, in the first place, to notify the Minister of Labour, Welfare and Social Insurance of any proposed redundancies at least one month before such dismissals occur. The notification should include the number of employees affected, the specific departments of the business in which the affected employees work, the specialization and the names of the employees affected, as well as their family obligations, and the reasons for the redundancy.

327. Once the notification is sent, the Ministry may contact the employer to see if there is any alternative arrangement other than the dismissal. If no solution is found, the employer may proceed with the redundancies. The above provision applies to both individual and collective redundancies. The IRC further provides that the employer should notify the trade union at least two months before the date of redundancy; after notification, consultation should be carried out with the unions and the employees, as soon as possible. Whereas failure to abide by the provisions of the IRC, or the relevant legislation on the obligation to timely provide the relevant information to and to consult with the representatives of the employees, does not invalidate the termination of employment, the non-compliance may be taken into account in order to assess the overall conduct of the employer.

388. *Toumazou and others* v. *Redundancy Fund* [2003] 1 CLR 1078 (in Greek).

389. *Demades Auto Supplies Limassol Ltd* v. *Ioannidou* [1996] 1 CLR 228 (in Greek).

390. *Charalampous and others* v. *Attorney-General of England and Wales and another* [2004] 1 CLR 90.

328. In *Stavrou* the IDT held that the overall behaviour of the employer, including non-compliance with the IRC, showed that he did not want to negotiate; he effectively informed the trade unions only when he delivered the notices for dismissal. The abolition of sections of the hotels by the employers essentially amounted to deliberate action to reduce labour costs; it was thus held that the termination of employment was not on grounds of redundancy and that the employer was liable to pay for unfair dismissal. The Supreme Court affirmed the IDT's judgment and noted that the finding that an existing section of the business of the employer had been abolished could not be separated from the overall conduct of the employer; the test to be applied was an objective one on the basis of the actual requirements of the business and not the opinion of the employer.[391] Accordingly, the dismissals were unlawful.[392]

329. When an employee is dismissed due to redundancy, the employee must file an application with the Redundancy Fund for compensation. The Redundancy Fund is a public law legal entity, which is established by the Council of Ministers and which compensates employees who were dismissed on grounds of redundancy. Each employer is obliged to contribute to the Redundancy Fund. The form of application is completed by the employer and contains specifically the grounds leading to the termination of the employment contract on the basis of redundancy. If the Fund accepts the grounds stated by the employer and pays the employee, then the employee is redundant. If, however, the Fund rejects the application, the employee has to file an action to the IDT claiming compensation for redundancy against the Fund, or alternatively compensation for unfair dismissal against the employer. Thus, the action is normally filed against both the employer and the Redundancy Fund.

IV. Burden of Proof

330. In order to claim compensation from the Redundancy Fund, it has to be proved that the employer unilaterally terminated the employment relationship of his employee on grounds of redundancy; the employee carries the burden to prove that he was dismissed from his employment, whereas the employer has the burden to prove the grounds on which the employment was terminated. It is a cardinal rule, that the person alleging that the termination of employment was on grounds of redundancy should have the burden to prove such allegations on the balance of probabilities; this is consistent with section 6 §1 of Law 24/67 which establishes a presumption that the employment was not terminated on grounds of redundancy. Accordingly, if the employee is alleging that his employment was terminated on grounds of redundancy, the burden of proof lies with him and not with the Redundancy Fund.[393]

391. *Hindle* v. *Percival Boats Ltd* [1969] 1 All ER 836 was cited with approval.
392. *United Hotels Ltd* v. *Stavrou and others* [2003] 1 CLR 515 (in Greek).
393. *Hadjisavvas* v. *Redundancy Fund* [1989] 1 CLR 145.

331. The fact that the employee applied before the Redundancy Fund does not prove that the termination of employment was justified; any employee has a right to assert what he considers to be his rights, but the question whether the employment was terminated on grounds of redundancy will be considered on the merits.[394] If the employee does not claim that he was unjustifiably dismissed by the employer and claims relief only on grounds of redundancy, he might risk that the employer might not appear during the hearing, since he is no longer affected by the action; this might accordingly make it more difficult for the employee to prove his case, as the employer may not be called upon in order to provide the necessary evidence.[395] If the employer fails to prove one of the aforementioned grounds, or if the dismissal is based upon another ground, the dismissal of the employee shall be deemed unfair and the employer will be liable to compensate the employee by paying compensation.

332. In *Kyriakou* the employer terminated the employment of the employee on grounds of redundancy. The IDT held that there was no redundancy, but further held that the termination of the employment was lawful as the employee had refused to be transferred in another town. The Supreme Court reversed the first instance judgment and held that the finding of the IDT, that the termination of employment was lawful because of her conduct, was arbitrary and erroneous; it was noted that the employer himself had dismissed the employee on grounds of redundancy and not on account of her conduct. It was further held that the alleged constriction of the volume of work of the employer referred only to one of the offices of the employer and not to the business as a whole. Accordingly, the termination of employment was unlawful.[396]

333. Should the IDT reach the decision that the employer and the employee had jointly agreed to terminate the employment contract, falsely alleging that there existed grounds amounting to redundancy, the employee might not be entitled to any compensation by either the Redundancy Fund, or the employer. In *Aristeidou* the IDT rejected the claim of the employee to receive compensation from the Redundancy Fund. It was noted that the termination of employment was the result of an agreement between the employer and the employee and collusion between them in order to defraud the Redundancy Fund; the termination of the employment thus took place with the consent of the employee and furthermore no evidence was admitted proving the alleged reduced turnover of the employer. The Supreme Court affirmed the first instance judgment.[397]

334. However, in *Kakoyiannis* the Supreme Court reversed the findings of the IDT that the employer still needed the services of the employee and that the dismissal of the employee occurred in collusion so as to help the employee to be compensated by the Redundancy Fund. The Court held that it had not been disputed that

394. *Hadjichristofi* v. *Georgiou and another* [2002] 1 CLR 873 (in Greek).
395. *Chrysanthou and others* v. *Petros Pitsillis Glass Market Ltd and another* [2001] 1 CLR 383 (in Greek).
396. *Kyriakou* v. *AG Patsalides Ltd and another* [1995] 1 CLR 116 (in Greek).
397. *Aristidou* v. *RK Super Beton Ltd and another* [1999] 1 CLR 114 (in Greek).

the employee was the personal driver of the senior partner of the employer, whose age and health had caused him to restrict his travelling to the extent that a driver was no longer needed; accordingly the services of the employee were no longer needed and he had become redundant. It was further held that there was no evidence of collusion and that such an arbitrary finding could not be supported by the mere fact that both the employer and the employee agreed during the hearing that the dismissal was on grounds of redundancy. The Supreme Court held that the employment had been terminated on grounds of redundancy.[398]

335. Any kind of evidence might be admitted in order to determine whether the termination of employment was on grounds of redundancy; thus, not only accounting data and balance sheets, but also letters or oral testimony or other evidence might be presented and can be taken into account. In *Chrysanthou* the IDT had considered that the only relevant evidence would be the presentation of balance sheets in order to prove redundancy; this approach was not supported by the Supreme Court, which held that the IDT should have also taken into account the evidence that had been presented which proved that the employer had shut down his business.[399]

V. Selection Criteria

336. The employer is required to consider whether there are other solutions which shall result in a less drastic measure, before terminating the employment contract due to redundancy. When dismissal is unavoidable, the employer should, as already indicated, as a rule dismiss first the person who was hired last and should dismiss last the person who was hired first and who is an employee for the longest period of time. However, this rule may not apply in cases of modernization, or any other change in the method of production or organization, if the employees who have been working for the longest period of time do not have the necessary qualifications, or cannot adapt to the changes. Similarly, the aforementioned rule may not apply when there are other considerations which should be weighed, such as health problems, financial or family reasons and limited possibility of a more recently hired employee to be employed elsewhere. In case the employer wishes to hire new employees of the same specialization within a period of eight months after the dismissal, he must give priority to employees who were dismissed on grounds of redundancy (section 22 of Law 24/67).

VI. Notice and Compensation

337. Employers are required by section 9 of Law 24/67 to give a minimum notice period in cases of redundancy; the minimum notice period is calculated in accordance with the period during which the employee had been continuously

398. *Christodoulou* v. *P.L. Cacoyiannis and Co and another* [2001] 1 CLR 188 (in Greek).
399. *Chrysanthou and others* v. *Petros Pitsillis Glass Market Ltd and another* [2001] 1 CLR 383 (in Greek).

employed by the employer and is the same as the minimum notice period required in cases of dismissal. The notice must always be given in writing. If the employer does not give the minimum notice period, or part of it, the employee shall be entitled to be paid such notice period, or such part of the notice period. The employer may choose to pay the notice period, in which case the employee is required to accept payment in lieu of notice.

338. If the employer proves that the dismissal was based upon one of the specific legal grounds relating to redundancy, then the Redundancy Fund shall compensate the dismissed employee. Otherwise, the employer shall pay compensation for unfair dismissal. The amount of compensation awarded depends principally on the number of years that the employee had been employed. Therefore, the employee shall be entitled to two weeks salary for each year of the first four years of continuous employment, to two and a half weeks salary for each year between the 5th and the 10th year of continuous employment, to three weeks salary for each year between the 11th and the 15th year of continuous employment, to three and a half weeks salary for each year between the 16th and the 20th year of continuous employment and to four weeks salary for each year between the 21st and the 25th year of continuous employment. If any remaining period of continuous employment does not amount to 52 weeks, then a remaining period of 26 or more weeks, shall amount to one full year of continuous employment for the purposes of awarding compensation. Any agreement between an employer and an employee to the effect that the latter will not claim any redundancy payment in return for any benefit provided by the employer is void and will have no effect.

339. The employee shall not be compensated by both the Redundancy Fund and the employer; in cases where compensation is to be paid by both the employer and the Redundancy Fund, it would be proper for the trial court to allocate in the judgment the sum that each party is obliged to pay to the employee, so as to avoid any misunderstandings.[400] The double payment of employees is prohibited in accordance with section 17(b) of Law 24/67.[401] Therefore, an employee who has received benefits from the Redundancy Fund may not also be compensated by the employer, or any other source, unless the compensation which would be received by the employer would be in excess of what the employee has received from the Redundancy Fund; in such a case he may receive the surplus, and only the surplus, from the employer. If the compensation which would be received by the employer does not exceed the amount received by the Redundancy Fund, the employee may not also be compensated by the employer.[402]

340. In *Karmios* the termination of employment of the employees was terminated on grounds of redundancy. The employer provided to the employees all their benefits and in addition paid a lump sum amount; in consideration, the employees accepted that the lump sum discharged all financial obligations in respect of the

400. *Fotos Fotiades Breweries Ltd* v. *Antoniades and another* [2002] 1 CLR 1490 (in Greek).
401. *Mouzouris* v. *KosmoPlast and Co and another* [2007] 1 CLR 896 (in Greek).
402. *Koliou* v. *George Kounnas and Sons Ltd* [1996] 1 CLR 1117 (in Greek).

redundancy and undertook not to pursue any action for additional claims. Subsequently, the employees filed an action against the employers before the District Court, arguing that the termination of employment was unlawful. It was held that the employees were estopped from claiming additional compensation in view of the contract they had signed in consideration of the lump sum. It was further held, however, that the employees were entitled to a notice of an additional three months, since only three weeks of notice had been given, instead of six.[403]

341. When trade union officials have received authorization to negotiate a settlement or dispute on behalf of a few employees who are identified by name, it is legitimate to consider that the trade union acts as an agent of the employee; in *Lanitis* it was held that the employer had negotiated with the trade unions and mutually agreed the termination of employment of specific employees, in consideration of compensatory benefits to be enjoyed by the employees whose employment was terminated; accordingly, the employees were not entitled to any other benefits under Law 24/67 because of redundancy.[404]

§10. Collective Dismissals

342. Collective Dismissals Law 28(I)/01 transposed Directive 98/59/EC into the Cypriot legal order.[405] Collective redundancies are defined in section 2 of Law 28(I)/01 as dismissals effected by an employer for reasons not related to the individual workers concerned, where the number of redundancies amount to: (a) at least 10 employees in employers who employ more than 20, but less than 100 employees,[406] (b) at least 10 per cent of the number of employees in employers who employ more than 100, but less than 300 employees, or (c) at least 30 employees in employers, who employ more than 300 employees.[407] In the calculation of employees, a wide definition should be adopted, including also trainees and directors.[408] Unilateral changes to essential elements of the employment contract by the employer amount to redundancy for the purposes of Law 28(I)/01.[409]

343. Law 28(I)/01 does not apply to: (i) collective redundancies effected under contracts of employment concluded for limited periods of time or for specific tasks

403. *Karmios and others* v. *Attorney-General of England and another* [2006] 1 CLR 768 (in Greek). See also *Hatzistylli* v. *Cyprus Airways Ltd*, Civ. Appeal 38/09, dated 22 May 2012 (in Greek).
404. *Lanitis Bros Co Ltd* v. *Ioannides and others* [1979] 1 CLR 815.
405. Council Directive 98/59/EC of 20 July 1998 on the approximation of the laws of the Member States relating to collective redundancies.
406. Terminations of an employment contract for reasons not related to the individual workers shall be assimilated to redundancies, provided that there are at least five redundancies.
407. Cyprus thus implemented Article 1(1)(a) of Directive 98/59/EC by opting for the definition under (i). For the definition of employer under the Directive see Case C-270/05, *Athinaiki Chartopoiia AE* v. *L. Panagiotides and others* [2007] ECR I-499, Case C-44/08, *Akavan Erityisalojen Keskusliitto AEK ry and Others* v. *Fujitsu Siemens Computers Oy* [2009] ECR I-8163.
408. Case C-229/14, *Balkaya* v. *Abbruch* EU, C-2015: 455.
409. Case C-422/14, *Rivera* v. *Gestora Clubs Dir SL* EU, C-2015: 743.

except where such redundancies take place prior to the date of expiry or the completion of such contracts,[410] (ii) workers employed by public administrative bodies or by bodies governed by public law, or (iii) the crews of seagoing vessels. An employer who contemplates collective redundancies should begin consultations with the workers' representatives in good time with a view to reaching an agreement; the consultations should at least cover ways and means of avoiding collective redundancies or reducing the number of workers affected, and of mitigating the consequences by recourse to accompanying social measures aimed, *inter alia*, at the provision of aid for redeploying or retraining workers made redundant (section 4 of Law 28(I)/01).[411]

344. In order to enable workers' representatives to make constructive proposals, the employer should supply them with all relevant information and notify them in writing of the reasons for the redundancies, number and categories of workers normally employed and to be made redundant, the period over which the redundancies are to be effected, the criteria for the selection of workers and the method used for calculating redundancy payments (section 5 of Law 28(I)/01). All information is confidential (section 11 of Law 28(I)/01). The employer should further notify the Minister of Labour, Welfare and Social Insurance of any intention for collective dismissals and the information referred to above (section 6 of Law 28(I)/01).

345. No dismissals shall take effect prior to 30 days from the date on which the Ministry was notified; the Ministry shall utilize this period in order to attempt to reach solutions to the problems caused due to the collective dismissals (sections 8 and 9 of Law 28(I)/01); however, no waiting period is needed if the dismissals are due to the termination of the activities of the undertaking in accordance with a court's decision (section 10 of Law 28(I)/01).[412] It should be noted that the obligations of the employer, by virtue of Law 28(I)/01, apply irrespective of whether the decision regarding collective redundancies is taken by the employer, or by an undertaking controlling the employer (section 7(1) of Law 28(I)/01).

346. Following the completion of the consultation procedure and the notification period, the employer may carry out the collective redundancies.[413] An employer who violates the provisions of his obligations to inform and consult the representatives of the employees, or the Minister, shall be guilty of an offence punishable by a fine not exceeding €1,000, whereas if the employer violates the provisions relevant to the 30-day waiting period, he is subject to a fine not exceeding €2,000 (section 13 of Law 28(I)/01). It is no defence on the part of the employer that the necessary information had not been provided to him by the undertaking which made the decision leading to the collective redundancies (section 7(2) of Law 28(I)/01).

410. Case C-392/12, *Canas* v. *Nexea Gestion Documental SA* EU, C-2015: 318.
411. Case C-12/08, *Mono Car Styling SA* v. *Dervis Odemis and Others*[2009] 1 ECR-6653.
412. Cases C-235 and 239/10, *Claes and others* v. *Landsbanki Luxembourg SA* [2011] ECR I-1113.
413. Case C-188/03, *Junk* v. *Kühnel* [2005] ECR I-885.

§11. Special Protection for Employees' Representatives

347. As already noted, membership in a trade union, or participation in trade union activities outside working hours or during working hours with the consent of the employer, or membership in a safety committee, or seeking to represent the workers, or acts made by a representative of workers, can never constitute lawful grounds for termination of employment. Trade union representatives, or representatives of employees, also enjoy similar protection on the basis of Article 21 of the Constitution and the provisions of various ILO Conventions ratified by the Republic of Cyprus. Furthermore, an employer may not terminate the employment because the employees exercise their constitutional right to strike, in accordance with Article 27 of the Constitution. In line with the relevant constitutional provisions, section 50 of the Trade Union Law (71/65) provides that it is illegal to discriminate against employees for their participation in the activities of a trade union. Similar protection is afforded to works councils members and, under Law 106(I)/11, to other employees' representatives.

348. It should be noted, however, that this should not imply that special protection is afforded to employees' representatives; employees' representatives and trade unionists could be dismissed similarly to any other employee, so long as the grounds for their dismissal is not their status as employee representatives. An interesting case discussing the limits of this approach is *Mikrou*, which refers more generally to activities of workers in the exercise of their collective rights. The IDT held that the employers had lawfully terminated the employment of the employees without notice, because they had participated in a general assembly which approved to send a letter to the Minister of Labour, Welfare and Social Insurance was containing unproven allegations which defamed and undermined the employer; the letter was leaked and was disseminated widely, so as to cause damage to the employer. The employees appealed and argued that the IDT does not have jurisdiction to consider whether an act is defamatory and that the termination of their employment was unlawful.

349. The Supreme Court affirmed the IDT's judgment and held that there is no restriction to the legal issues that may be adjudicated by the IDT; accordingly, the IDT may determine incidentally whether there is defamation, if this is relevant to its judgment. The Court further held that section 41 of the Trade Unions Law 71/65 did not apply; section 41 provides that an act performed by a person in contemplation or furtherance of a trade dispute shall not be actionable on the ground only that it induces some other person to break a contract of employment, or that it is an interference with the trade, business or employment of some other person, or with the right of some other person to dispose of his capital or his labour as he wishes. The Court held that section 41 of Law 71/65 applied only when the act of interference amounted to a tort solely because of that interference; it did not, however, protect acts where the interference was brought about by unlawful intimidation or other illegal means.[414] Since the interference was the result of the tort of defamation, section 41 was inapplicable.[415]

350. The dissenting judgment in *Mikrou* held that the IDT has no jurisdiction to determine whether a publication is defamatory or not, since it is the District Court that enjoys such jurisdiction. It was considered that the approach of the IDT reversed the burden of proof as it assumed that the employees had to prove the truth of their allegations. It was further held that if the employees had defamed the employer, they should apply before the District Court for defamation. The dissenting judgment further noted that it would not be proper to consider that the expression of unproven allegations by the employees or the employers, through their trade unions, during an employment dispute, amounted to grounds for termination of employment. It is submitted that the reasoning of the dissenting judgment seems more convincing than the opinion of the majority of the Supreme Court. The issue to be examined by the IDT was not whether there existed defamation, which is a question to be determined by the District Court, but whether the conduct of the employees justified their immediate dismissal.

351. In this respect it is pointed out that if a publication has been made in good faith and the relation between the parties by and to whom the publication is made is such that the person publishing the matter is under a legal, moral or social duty to publish it to the person to whom the publication is made and who has a corresponding interest in receiving it, then the publication enjoys qualified privilege from defamation. This aspect was not examined by the IDT, despite the fact that the trade unions clearly had a duty to send a letter to the Ministry of Labour, Welfare and Social Insurance stating their concerns. In agreement with the dissenting judgment, it is submitted that if the expression of unproven statements by the trade unions against the employer, which are stated not to the public, but to the Ministry of Labour, Welfare and Social Insurance, which is the competent person to solve labour disputes, could amount to grounds for immediate dismissal, this would unreasonably restrict the freedom of trade unions and employees to express their views and demands against the employer, potentially in violation of the rights safeguarded by Article 21 of the Constitution.

414. *Rookes* v. *Barnard and others* [1964] AC 1129 (HL).
415. *Mikrou and others* v. *Meridian Hotels Ltd* [2003] 1 CLR 1320 (in Greek).

Chapter 7. Protection of Certain Categories of Worker: Protection against Discrimination in Employment

§1. PROTECTION OF CERTAIN CATEGORIES OF WORKER

I. Young Workers

352. The working time of minors is governed by the Protection of Young People at Work Law 48(I)/2001 which transposed Directive 94/33/EC.[416] In some cases the limits specified in Law 48(I)/01 are more protective when compared to the limits set out in Directive 94/33/EC. Cyprus has also ratified the ILO Minimum Age Convention 138/1973 by Law 17(III)/1997 and the ILO Convention concerning the prohibition and immediate action for the elimination of the worst forms of child labour 182/1999 by Law 31(III)/2000.

353. Children below 15 years of age, who are employed in cultural, artistic, sport or advertising activities in accordance with section 7 of Law 48(I)/01 cannot be occupied for more than: (a) two hours a day for children no more than six years old, (b) three hours a day for children between 7 and 12 years of age, (c) four hours a day for children between 13 and 15 years of age; those hours cannot coincide with teaching time during school term (section 7(4) of Law 48(I)/01). No child should participate in those activities during night time.[417] Children are entitled to a minimum rest of 14 continuous hours for every 24-hour period (section 9 of Law 48(I)/01) and to a weekly minimum rest of at least 48 continuous hours, including on a Sunday, unless organizational or technical grounds necessitate the occupation of the child to take place on a Sunday (section 10 of Law 48(I)/01). The maximum daily occupation of a child is 7 hours and 15 minutes, whereas the maximum weekly occupation is 36 hours (section 8(1) of Law 48(I)/01).

354. The daily working time of teenagers between 15 and 16 years of age should not exceed 7 hours and 15 minutes daily and their weekly working time should not exceed 36 hours; teenagers between 16 and 18 years of age may be employed for 7 hours and 45 minutes daily and up to 38 hours per week; if the teenager is employed by more than one employer, the time worked is accumulated. Overtime employment of teenagers is prohibited (section 15 of Law 48(I)/01). If the daily time of employment exceeds 4.5 hours, the teenagers should have a break of at least 30 minutes. Teenagers are entitled to a minimum rest of 12 continuous hours for every 24-hour period and to a minimum weekly rest of at least 48 continuous hours, including on a Sunday, unless organizational or technical grounds necessitate the occupation of the child to take place on a Sunday; the minimum weekly rest may be limited to 36 continuous hours if this is necessitated on organizational or technical grounds (section 18 of Law 48(I)/01). The daily employment of teenagers should

416. Council Directive 94/33/EC of 22 June 1994 on the protection of young people at work.

417. From 19.00 p.m. (or 20.00 p.m. between June-September) until 7.00 a.m. If the child attends educational courses at night, no occupation can take place after 16.00 on those days (section 6, 8(2) and 11 of Law 48(I)/01).

take place at least two hours prior to, or after commencement of school classes (section 15(5) of Law 48(I)/01). Teenagers shall not be employed at night (section 14 of Law 48(I)/01).[418]

355. Any person employing any minor in violation of the provisions of Law 48(I)/01 shall be guilty of a criminal offence, punishable by imprisonment of up to two years and/or a fine not exceeding €17,000 (section 30 of Law 48(I)/01); the minor's parents are also liable to a criminal offence punishable by imprisonment not exceeding six months and/or fine of up to €5,100, unless the court considers that the offence occurred without the consent, cooperation or wilful omission of the parent (section 31 of Law 48(I)/01). Furthermore, the owner, possessor or licensee of a public place where a child engages in itinerant trade shall also be liable to up to six month imprisonment and/or a fine not exceeding €5,100, unless he was unaware of the fact (section 32 of Law 48(I)/01). If a minor is found at any time on the premises of an undertaking, the employer shall have the burden of proving that the minor is not employed there (section 22 of Law 48(I)/01).

356. The Minister of Labour, Welfare and Social Insurance may appoint inspectors for monitoring the proper application of Law 48(I)/01; the inspectors have the power to enter any premises and proceed to any inspections, inquests, examinations or controls they consider necessary and request any person to provide information and facilitate them at the exercise of their duties. Any act which impedes the exercise of the functions of the inspectors amounts to a criminal offence punishable by imprisonment of up to a year and/or fine not exceeding €8,500 (section 33 of Law 48(I)/01). A Consultative Committee on Children Occupation consults the Minister on issues relevant to the application of Law 48(I)/01; the Committee is composed of five members appointed for a three-year term (section 31B of Law 48(I)/01).

II. Maternity

A. Maternity Leave

357. Maternity rights are safeguarded by the Protection of Maternity Law 100(I)/1997[419] which implemented Directive 92/85/EEC.[420] The rights under Law 100(I)/97 are safeguarded only for mothers and not for fathers.[421] In case of conviction for violation of any of the provisions of Law 100(I)/97, the employer is subject to a fine not exceeding €6,834. The IDT is the competent court for adjudicating disputes of a civil nature, whereas the Minister of Labour, Welfare and Social Insurance may appoint inspectors for monitoring the application of Law 100(I)/97.

418. From 23.00 p.m. until 7.00 a.m. (or 00.00–04.00)
419. Amended by Laws 45(I)/2000, 64(I)/2002, 109(I)/2007, 8(I)/2008, 43(I)/2008, 70(I)/2011 and 175(I)/2015.
420. Council Directive 92/85/EEC of 19 October 1992 on the introduction of measures to encourage improvements in the safety and health at work of pregnant workers and workers who have recently given birth or are breastfeeding.
421. See, however, Case C-5/12, *Montull* v. *Instituto Nacional de la Seguridad Social* EU, C-2013: 571.

358. A female employee who presents a certificate of a registered medical practitioner stating the expected week of birth is entitled to maternity leave in accordance with section 3(1) of Law 100(I)/97. Law 100(I)/97 safeguards minimum periods for maternity leave; this does not affect more favourable rights granted by individual or collective employment agreements. Maternity leave is provided for 18 weeks, 11 of which must compulsorily be taken at the beginning of the second week before the expected date of birth.

359. If the birth occurs after the expected week, the period of leave before the week of confinement is extended to include the period between the week of the expected confinement date and the week during which birth actually occurs; this does not affect the total duration of eight weeks which are compulsorily taken after confinement. If the confinement occurs earlier than the expected week of confinement, then the remaining maternity leave is taken after confinement, so that the total period of 18-week maternity leave is secured.[422]

360. If, immediately after confinement, the infant is hospitalized in an incubator as a result of premature childbirth, or as a result of any other health problem, the maternity leave period is extended by one week for every 21 days of required hospitalization for the infant. For this purpose, a certificate from a registered doctor of relevant specialization, as well as a certificate from the hospital where the infant was admitted, must be submitted. If the duration of the hospitalisation period after the first 21 days, lasts for a period less than 21 days then, an additional week of maternity leave is given whenever the days of hospitalization exceed 50 per cent of 21 days. This extension period of the maternity leave must be consecutive with the 18-week period, and cannot exceed six weeks.

361. As far as adoptive mothers are concerned, an employed woman who takes into her care a child less than 12 years of age for the purpose of adoption, is allowed to maternity leave of 16 consecutive weeks, provided that she has informed the Social Welfare Services of her intention and that she has informed her employer in writing of her intention to adopt a child, at least six weeks in advance; if this is not practically possible, then the employee informs her employer as soon as possible and provides a relevant confirmation from the Social Welfare Services that such information could not have been provided beforehand. It should be noted that the Application of Medically Assisted Reproduction Law 69(I)/2015 provides for a new framework for surrogate motherhood in Cyprus; however, it does not provide whether both the surrogate mother and the birth mother are entitled to maternity leave.[423]

422. See also Case C-116/06, *Kiiski* v. *Tampereen kaupunki* [2007] ECR I-7643, Cases C-512-513/11, *Terveys and another* v. *Teknologiateollisuus ry and Nokia Siemens Networks Oy* EU, C-2014: 73.

423. The right of the commissioning mother to maternity leave does not arise directly from Directive 92/85/EEC and accordingly it should be enacted by domestic legislation. See Case C-167/12, *CD* v. *ST* EU, C-2014: 169.

362. With respect to pay during the maternity leave period,[424] the insured woman is entitled to maternity allowance payable out of the Social Insurance Fund, subject to certain contribution and other conditions in accordance with the Social Insurance Law 59(I)/2010. Maternity allowance is payable for a period of 18 consecutive weeks, which may begin any week from the ninth to the second week, preceding the expected week of confinement (section 29(4)(a) of Law 59(I)/2010). Moreover, in accordance with section 28 of the Social Insurance Law, a woman who has given birth is also entitled to maternity grant in the form of a lump sum, provided that either she or her husband satisfies the relevant contribution conditions; a separate claim must be made not later than 12 months after the date of birth.

363. Maternity leave cannot prejudice the seniority of the employed woman, or her right to promotion, or her right to the work which she performed before the commencement of the maternity leave, and is without prejudice to the salary and benefits she received before her maternity leave, with the exception of any commissions received based entirely on the quantity and value of the work performed (section 7 of Law 100(I)/97). Furthermore, the period of absence on parental leave is deemed to be a period of employment in calculating the employee's annual leave with pay and for the purposes of Law 24/67. In addition to the maintenance of her basic salary, such a worker is entitled to pay components or supplementary allowances relating to her professional status, such as allowances relating to her seniority, her length of service and her professional qualifications.[425]

364. An employer is precluded from taking into account the period during which the mother was legislatively prohibited from working, so as to reduce a Christmas bonus pro rata.[426] It has further been held by the CJEU that it would be contrary to Directive 92/85/EEC to provide that an employer may send home a woman who is pregnant, although not unfit for work, without paying her salary in full, when he considers that he cannot provide work for her.[427] It is also noted that a worker should be able to take her annual leave during a period other than the period of her maternity leave, including where the period of maternity leave coincides with the general period of annual leave.[428] Moreover, it has been held that a clause in an employment contract which prohibits a woman from taking sick leave during the minimum period of maternity leave, unless she elects to return to work and thus terminate her maternity leave, is not compatible with Directive 92/85/EEC.[429]

424. See also Case C-194/08, *Gassmayr* v. *Bundesminister für Wissenschaft und Forschung* [2010] ECR I-6281.
425. Case C-471/08, *Parviainen* v. *Oyj* [2010] ECR I-6533.
426. Case C-333/97, *Lewen* v. *Denda* [1999] ECR I-7243.
427. Case C-66/96, *Handels- og Kontorfunktionærernes Forbund i Danmarkv.Dansk Handel & Service* [1998] ECR I-7327.
428. Case C-342/01, *Merino Gomez* v. *Continental Industrias del Caucho SA* [2004] ECR I-2605.
429. Case C-411/96, *Boyle and others* v. *Equal Opportunities Commission* [1998] ECR I-6401.

B. Termination of Employment

365. An employer is prohibited from terminating the employment of a woman, from the time she has notified him of the fact that she is pregnant, by producing to him the relevant medical certificate (section 4 of Law 100(I)/97). The prohibition lasts for a period of three months following the expiration of maternity leave. During this period an employer may not give notice of dismissal, dismiss, or take action, including preparatory steps,[430] aimed at the employee's permanent replacement; furthermore, a dismissal, or notice of dismissal must be retracted, regardless of whether the employer knew that the employee was pregnant or not, if the employed woman notifies her employer by producing to him the relevant medical certificate within five days from the day that she is informed about the dismissal or the intention to dismiss her.

366. Adoptive mothers are also protected against dismissal, by virtue of s. 4A of Law 100(I)/97, from the time that the employed woman notifies her employer of her intention to adopt by producing a relevant certificate from the Social Welfare Services; this prohibition also lasts for a period of three months after the expiration of the period of maternity leave. The CJEU has further held that the prohibition extends to preclude the dismissal of a female worker who, in circumstances such as those in the main proceedings, is at an advanced stage of *in vitro* fertilization treatment, if it is established that the dismissal is essentially based on the fact that the woman has undergone such treatment.[431]

367. The prohibition found in section 4 and 4A of Law 100(I)/97 complements the prohibition of section 6(e) of Law 24/67. However, the prohibition does not apply if: (i) the employee is guilty of serious misconduct, or (ii) the business has ceased functioning, or (iii) the duration of the employment contract has expired, except in cases where the non-renewal of the employment is due to the pregnancy, birth or maternity leave of the employee.[432] In any event, if the pregnant employee is unlawfully dismissed, the Redundancy Fund shall compensate the employee. In case of dismissal of the employed woman during the aforementioned period, the employer has to justify the dismissal in writing.

368. The CJEU has held that Directive 92/85/EEC precludes a worker from being dismissed on grounds of pregnancy where the worker was recruited for a fixed period; the dismissal was held to be precluded despite the fact that she failed to inform her employer that she was pregnant even though she was aware of this when the contract of employment was concluded, and that, owing to her pregnancy, she was unable to work during a substantial part of the term of that contract. The fact that the worker had been recruited by a very large undertaking which employs temporary workers frequently was held to be of no relevance to the issue.[433] It has

430. Case C-460/06, *Paquay* v. *Société d'architectes Hoet* [2007] ECR I-8511.
431. Case C-506/06, *Mayr* v. *Bäckerei und Konditorei Gerhard Flöckner OHG* [2008] ECR I-1017.
432. Case C-438/99, *Melgar* v. *Ayuntamiento de Los Barrios* [2001] ECR I-6915.
433. Case C-109/00, *Tele Denmark A/S* v. *Handels* [2001] ECR I-6993.

further been held that an employee has no obligation to inform her employer that she is pregnant, prior to returning to work from her parental leave, even if this would essentially mean that she shall be unable to carry out all of her duties.[434]

369. The extent of the prohibition was discussed in *Foka*, where the employee had been dismissed during the trial period of 26 months. The Supreme Court held that it was not necessary to decide whether section 4 of Law 100(I)/97 applies also to cases where the employee has not yet completed the twenty-six weeks of employment, since in that particular case the employee had not furnished in time a written notification of the pregnancy and accordingly the provisions of Law 100(I)/97 had not been activated.[435] The decision seems rather formalistic and it is notable that it did not discuss any of the CJEU case law. As to the substance of the dispute, it should be noted, that the wording of section 4 of Law 100(I)/97 does not introduce the criterion that an employee may not apply before the IDT for termination of employment prior to a period of continuous employment of 26 months. On the contrary, section 9A of Law 100(I)/97[436] expressly provides that for the purposes of Law 100(I)/97, neither a minimum period of employment, or work hours requirements, nor a maximum limit to compensation apply; any agreement between the employer and the employee providing otherwise, is void.

C. Other Provisions

370. In order to protect the safety and health at work of pregnant women and women who have recently given birth and are breastfeeding, employers are obliged to assess any risks at work and take protective measures (section 6 of Law 100(I)/97 in conjunction with the Maternity Protection (Safety and Health at Work) Regulations 255/2002) If the nature of the work involves any unavoidable risks, the employed woman must be transferred to another job. Where no alternative job is available, the employed woman is entitled to be absent from work as long as necessary, without prejudice to her remuneration. These obligations of the employer apply also in the case of night work, subject to the submission of a relevant medical certificate. No employer may force a pregnant or breastfeeding employed woman to perform any duties for which the risk assessment has revealed the involvement of a detriment to the safety and health exposure to specific agents and conditions, such as work involving exposure of the employed woman to lead, mercury, pesticides and other chemical substances, work in pressurized chambers, or work involving ionizing radiation.

371. For the purposes of breastfeeding and the increased needs of the child, an employed woman has the right to be absent from work for one hour daily, for a period of 9 months after the date of confinement, or the date of commencement of

434. Case C-320/01, *Busch* v. *Klinikum Neustadt GmbH & Co* [2003] ECR I-2041.
435. *Foka* v. *M.I. Motokinissi Ltd* [2004] 1 CLR 789 (in Greek). See, however, Case C-63/08, *Pontin* v. *T. Comalux SA* [2009] ECR I-10467.
436. Which, however, was added with Law 109(I)/2007.

the maternity leave in the case of adoption. This hour may be taken any time during the working day, or the employed woman may arrive at work an hour late, or leave an hour early; this hour is treated and remunerated as a working hour (section 5 of Law 100(I)/97). An employed woman is also entitled to be absent from work for pre-natal examinations, without prejudice to her salary, provided that such examinations need to be carried out during working hours; for this purpose the employed woman should give timely notice to her employer and further produce a relevant medical certificate (section 5A of Law 100(I)/97).

III. Parental Leave

372. In addition to the period of maternity leave, the Parental Leave and Leave on Grounds of Force Majeure Law 47(I)/2012 has harmonized Cypriot law with Directive 2010/18/EU.[437] Law 47(I)/12 gives the right to parental leave to all employees, men and women,[438] who have completed at least six months of continuous employment with the same employer, irrespective of whether the contract of employment is of an indefinite or definite duration (section 3 of Law 47(I)/12). More specifically, by virtue of section 4(1) of Law 47(I)/12, every eligible employee is allowed to take unpaid parental leave for a period not exceeding 18 weeks for each child; the parental leave is granted because of the birth, or adoption, of a child in order to raise and care for the child. If the parent is a widower, parental leave may last for up to 23 weeks.

373. The right is individual and non-transferable; however, where one parent has taken parental leave for at least two weeks, he/she may transfer to the other parent two weeks from the remaining of the total duration of his/her leave. In case of the birth of more than one child, there is a separate right to parental leave in respect of each child, i.e. 18 weeks for each child. In case both parents are employed by the same employer, they may decide, on every occasion, which of the two will take leave in turn and for how long; however, with the consent of the employer, they can both make concurrent use of the right to parental leave (section 4 of Law 47(I)/12).

374. The period when the parental leave is taken is as follows: (a) in the case of natural mothers, parental leave is taken after the end of the maternity leave and before the eighth birthday of the child, (b) in the case of natural fathers, parental leave is taken any time between the birth of the child and the child's eighth birthday, (c) in the case of adoption, parental leave by the adoptive mother is taken after the end of the maternity leave and within eight years from the date of adoption of the child, provided that the child has not attained the age of 12 years, whereas for adoptive fathers parental leave is taken immediately after adoption, (d) in cases where the child has a disability, parental leave may be taken until the child's 18th

437. Council Directive 2010/18/EU of 8 March 2010 implementing the revised Framework Agreement on parental leave.

438. See also Case C-222/14, *Maistrellis* v. *Ypourgos Dikaiosinis, Diafaneias kai Anthropinon Dikaiomaton* EU, C-2015: 473.

birthday. An employee may take parental leave for a minimum period of one week per calendar year; the maximum period for an employee who has one or two children is five weeks per calendar year, whereas for an employee with three or more children is seven weeks per calendar year (section 5 of Law 47(I)/12).

375. An employee who aims to exercise the right to parental leave is obliged to notify his employer in writing of the commencement and termination dates of the parental leave, at least three weeks before the commencement of the leave; in the event of serious illness/condition of the child, as specified in the Annex of Law 47(I)/12, the period of notification is reduced to one week (section 6 of Law 47(I)/12). The employer has the right to refuse in writing to grant parental leave, if he has reasonable cause to believe that the employee is not entitled to such leave; before refusing, however, the employer must inform the employee in writing of his intention and the employee may present his views within seven days. The employer has to take into account the employee's views and specify the reasons for his refusal (section 7 of Law 47(I)/12).

376. Following consultation with the employee, the employer may postpone the granting of parental leave for reasons related to the operation of the business, such as where the business is of a seasonal nature, where it is not possible to find a replacement for the period stated in the notice period, where a significant proportion of the workforce applies for parental leave at the same time, or where the specific duties of the employee are of strategic importance to the business. The employer must, within two weeks of the submission of the employee's application for parental leave, inform the employee in writing, of the reasons for postponing the leave; the period of postponement should not exceed a period of six months from the date that the employee is notified of the postponement (section 8 of Law 47(I)/12).

377. The employee may only use the parental leave for the purpose of caring for and raising the child for which the leave has been taken. Accordingly, the employer may terminate in writing the parental leave if he has reasonable grounds to believe that it is being used for a purpose other than that of caring for and raising the child. Prior to terminating the parental leave, the employer is obliged to inform in writing the employee concerned, of his intention to do so, and request that the employee presents his views within seven days. The employer must take into consideration the arguments of the employee before deciding whether or not to terminate the parental leave. The termination date of the parental leave should be at least seven days following the date of notification. In case of termination of the parental leave, the employee is obliged to return to work (section 9 of Law 47(I)/12).

378. After the end of the parental leave, the employee is entitled to return to work in the same or similar position, which in no case can be inferior to his position prior to the beginning of the parental leave. Rights acquired, or in the process of being acquired, by the employee on the date on which parental leave starts, will be maintained as they stand until the end of parental leave; at the end of parental leave, these rights, including any changes arising from national law, collective agreements or practice, will apply. It is further provided that upon his return, the employee may request changes to his time schedule, or the organization of his work for a specified time period; the employer responds to such requests taking into account the needs of both himself and the employee.

379. During the period of parental leave, the employer and the employee may keep in touch and make arrangements regarding specified measures to enable the employee's reintegration. The period of absence on parental leave, is recognised and credited as insurance period under the Social Insurance Laws. Furthermore, the period of absence on parental leave is deemed to be a period of employment in calculating the employee's annual leave with pay and for the purposes of Law 24/67 (section 10 of Law 47(I)/12). An employee who has taken any period of parental leave should, within three months of the expiration of such period, notify the Director of Social Insurance Department. The Minister of Labour, Welfare and Social Insurance may appoint inspectors for the proper application of Law 47(I)/12. Disputes of a civil nature are adjudicated by the IDT. An employer who violates the provisions of Law 47(I)/12 is guilty of a criminal offence punishable by a fine not exceeding €7,500.

IV. Disabled Workers

380. The rights of disabled workers are safeguarded by the Persons with Disabilities Law 127(I)2000,[439] which partly implements Directive 2000/78/EC.[440] The aim of Law 127(I)/00 is to take appropriate measures in order to eliminate disadvantages to persons with disabilities and for a person with a disability to have access to, participate in, or advance in employment, or to undergo training, unless such measures would impose a disproportionate burden on the employer. It is thus safeguarded by virtue of section 3 of Law 127(I)/00, that the principle of equal treatment of disabled persons shall apply; thus, there should be no discrimination whatsoever against any person on grounds of disability.

381. It is further provided that a person discriminates against another person if he treats such person: (a) less favourably than he treats or would have treated a person without a disability, in the same or in a similar situation, (b) on the basis of characteristics which generally belong to persons with such disability, or on the basis of an alleged characteristic which generally belongs to persons with such disability, or on the basis of an alleged characteristic generally attributed to persons with such

439. As amended by Laws 57(I)/2004, 72(I)/2007, 102(I)/2007, 63(I)/2014 and 22(I)/2015. See in general M. Florentzos, *The Legal and Social Position of Persons with Disability in the New Legal Order of the Republic of Cyprus as a Member State of the European Union* (Nicosia, 2005).

440. Council Directive 2000/78/EC of 27 November 2000 establishing a general framework for equal treatment in employment and occupation, especially Article 5. The Cypriot Law also takes into account the Standard Rules on the Equalization of Opportunities for Persons with Disabilities adopted by the 85th plenary meeting of the General Assembly of the UN on 20 December 1993 (48/96).

disability, or (c) based on the fact that this person does not satisfy, or is not in a position to satisfy a condition, the nature of which is such that a high percentage of persons who do not have such disability satisfy, or are in a position to satisfy, as opposed to persons who do have such disability and the existence of such condition is not justified by the circumstances of the case, or (d) contrary to any provision contained in a code of practice issued under Law 127(I)/00, or (e) in such a way that constitutes harassment.

382. In relation to employment, Law 127(I)/00 does not apply to the armed forces, to the extent that the nature of the work requires special abilities and it is not possible to be performed by persons with disabilities; furthermore, it does not apply to professional activities that, by reason of the nature or of the context in which they are carried out, a characteristic or an ability not possessed by a person with disability, constitutes a substantial and determining occupational requirement, provided that the aim is legitimate and the requirement is proportionate to that aim, taking also into consideration the possibility to adopt reasonable measures (section 3A of Law 127(I)/00).

383. Article 3B contains provisions for positive action. In order to ensure full equality in practice, positive measures may be taken under section 3B of Law 127(I)/00, to provide favourable treatment in employment; such measures, albeit seemingly indirectly discriminatory, are aimed at the prevention or compensation of disadvantages on grounds of disability and are accordingly consistent with the principle of equal treatment. In particular, the principle of equal treatment does not affect the maintenance or introduction of provisions on safeguarding health and safety in the workplace, or other measures that aim at the creation or maintenance of any conditions or facilities that have the purpose of safeguarding or encouraging the integration of persons with disabilities in the labour market.

384. Whereas section 4 of Law 127(I)/00 outlines the basic rights of persons with disabilities, section 5 concerns equal treatment and prohibition of discrimination in employment. It is provided that the principle of equal treatment applies to employment[441] and therefore any kind of discrimination against a person with disabilities is prohibited in relation to: (i) the conditions for access to employment, self-employment and occupation, including selection criteria and recruitment conditions, regardless of the sector or branch of activity and at all levels of the professional hierarchy, including promotion, (ii) access to all types and to all levels of vocational guidance, vocational training, advanced vocational training and retraining, including practical work experience, (iii) employment and working conditions, including dismissals and pay, (iv) membership of and involvement in an organization of workers or employers, or any other organization whose members practice a particular profession, including the benefits provided by such organizations.

441. The provisions of 5(1) do not apply to any kind of provisions made by state schemes or similar, including state social security or social protection schemes, except the professional schemes of social insurance.

385. In order to guarantee compliance with the principle of equal treatment for persons with disabilities, reasonable adjustments must be made. This means that the employer must take the appropriate measures according to the needs of a given situation in order to enable the persons with disability to have access to, participate in, or advance in employment, or to have access to training, unless this requirement creates a disproportionate burden on the employer. The burden may not be disproportionate when it is sufficiently remedied by measures existing within the framework of the state's disability policy.

386. The principle of equal treatment does not, among others, preclude: (a) the creation of employment opportunities with the introduction of employment schemes for persons with disability by providing incentives for the employers, or the creation of jobs in the governmental, semi-governmental and wider public sector to be filled exclusively by persons with disabilities, (b) the job reinstatement, where possible, of persons with disability in the same enterprises where the disability occurred during their employment, (c) special protection against dismissals, (d) the obligation to provide reasonable access and facilities in the workplace, including the necessary modifications or adjustments of accessibility to existing facilities, so as to make them accessible to persons with disabilities, the adjustment of work by creating working schedules of part-time occupation or modified working hours, with the acquisition of new, or the modification of existing, equipment, machinery, tools, means and any facilities or services, or the operation of special schemes of employment in the public and private sector, by providing economic incentives.

387. Anyone who commits any act, action or omission which constitutes direct or indirect discrimination against a person with disability in the field of employment, is guilty of an offence punishable with imprisonment of up to six months and/or with a fine not exceeding €6,800; however, where the offence is committed due to negligence, a fine not exceeding €3,400 shall be imposed. Clauses in individual, or collective agreements which are contrary to the provisions of Law 127(I)/00 must be abolished. The Minister of Labour, Welfare and Social Insurance may appoint inspectors for the monitoring of the application of Law 127(I)/00.

388. The IDT is competent for adjudicating any disputes of a civil nature; as far as burden of proof is concerned, section 9A specifically provides that, if the claimant establishes facts from which it may be presumed that there has been a breach, it shall be for the respondent to prove that there has been no breach of Law 127(I)/00. The IDT shall grant just and equitable damages which shall cover at least the whole material damage plus interest thereon as of the date of violation until full payment of damages. As far as extra-judicial protection is concerned, according to Article 9C, any person may submit a complaint to the Ombudsman acting as the Equality Authority. Any unfavourable treatment or impact against a complainant or a person involved in proceedings regarding the principle of equal treatment should be prohibited (Article 9E).

389. It should be noted that, pursuant to Law 127(I)/00, subsequent legislation has provided for specific protection of persons with disabilities, by providing for affirmative action with regard to the appointment of disabled persons in the wider public sector. The Appointment of Persons with Disabilities in the Wider Public Sector Law 146(I)/2009 has thereby provided for the creation of a separate list of candidates with disability, and stipulating that persons with disability shall be appointed in a ratio of 10 per cent of all available new positions in the wider public sector, a term which includes both public service and legal persons of public law; this shall not apply if the disabled persons have reached 7 per cent of all personnel in the sector concerned. The Supreme Court held that the differentiation provided in Law 146(I)/09 is reasonable and proportional and is therefore not inconsistent with Article 28 of the Constitution.[442]

V. Female Workers: Gender Discrimination

A. Equal Treatment

390. The Equal Treatment of Men and Women in Employment and Vocational Training Law 205(I)/2002[443] partly harmonizes Cypriot law with Directive 2006/54/EC.[444] Law 205(I)/02 provides for the application of the principle of equal treatment of men and women in the field of employment and, in particular, regarding access to vocational guidance, vocational education and training, as well as the terms and conditions in which they are carried out, access to employment, the terms and conditions of employment, including career development and the terms and conditions of dismissal (section 3 of Law 205(I)/02).[445] Law 205(I)/02 applies in principle to all employers and with regard to all activities related to employment; there are, however, certain exceptions in occupational activities where, by reason of the context in which they are carried out, gender constitutes a determining factor (section 4 of Law 205(I)/02).

391. Exempted occupational activities are listed in the Schedule of Law 205(I)/02 and refer to: (i) artistic activities where the filling of a post with a person of the other sex would cause a significant difference in the nature of the post, (ii) employment in a particular post when the duties of the post include the provisions of services outside Cyprus, in a state where legislation and culture are such that the particular services may not be logically rendered by a person of the other sex, (iii) personal services when it is imperative that these services employ persons of

442. *Tsikkas* v. *Republic*, Cases 1519-1520/2010, judgment of 3 September 2015 (in Greek).
443. As amended by Laws 191(I)/2004, 40(I)/2006, 176(I)/2007, 39(I)/2009 and 150(I)/2014.
444. Directive 2006/54/EC of the European Parliament and of the Council of 5 July 2006 on the implementation of the principle of equal opportunities and equal treatment of men and women in matters of employment and occupation (recast).
445. For the status of Cypriot law prior to harmonization see C. Tornaritis, *Gender Equality under the Law* (Nicosia, 1980, in Greek), *idem*, 'Women and Law, especially in the Republic of Cyprus' [1973] *Cyprus Law Tribune*: 3–8 (in Greek), P. Clerides, 'Comparative Study on Gender Equality amongst the Members of the Council of Europe' (1984) *Cyprus Law Review*: 977–1011 (in Greek), A. Loizou, 'The Working Woman, her Rights to Equality and the Protection of Maternity' (1983) 4 *Cyprus Law Review*: 697–707 (in Greek).

both sexes, or referring to the domestic care of elders, or persons with disability, (iv) employment in the post of warden in women's or men's prisons, (v) employment in the Security Forces or private security bodies when the employment of either sex is necessary to respect the dignity of a person, or in special forces[446] and (vi) employment of women in underground mining works.[447]

392. Men and women must enjoy equal treatment in the fields of employment, by virtue of section 5 of Law 205(I)/02. Lack of intention on the part of the employer does not preclude the illegal character of the discriminatory act. Contrary to indirect discrimination, direct discrimination is not subject to justification. Positive actions are lawful and encouraged; they may constitute the subject of collective agreements, or any other employer–employee agreements, or the subject of an equal opportunities and treatment programme that has been agreed upon between the employer and the employers' representatives at an enterprise or service, whether public or private (section 6 of Law 205(I)/02).

393. Any action amounting to direct, or indirect discrimination on the grounds of sex shall be prohibited, *inter alia*, in the following fields: (i) access to employment or work position, temporary, full-time or part-time employment and at all levels of an occupational hierarchy, (ii) the terms and conditions of employment, including qualifications and other terms, conditions and placement, permanency, accession, transfer, removal, detachment or promotion criteria, (iii) the terms and conditions of dismissal from any job or post, (iv) membership and participation in employees' or employers' representative organizations, or any organization whose members practise a specific profession, including any benefits granted by such organizations (sections 8, 9 and 9A of Law 205(I)/02).[448]

394. The Minister of Labour, Welfare and Social Insurance has a duty to inform workers, employers, as well as their organizations, through printed materials and other appropriate means, of the provisions of Law 205(I)/02. Trade unions have a similar obligation to inform the workers of the content of the law, whereas employers have a duty to facilitate the workers' organizations in order to provide workers with the information required (section 13 of Law 205(I)/02). The Minister further appoints inspectors who monitor the application of Law 205(I)/02 and safeguard the protection of workers by investigating relevant complaints and taking appropriate action.[449] An employer who violates any provision of Law 205(I)/02 is guilty of an offence punishable to imprisonment of up to six months and/or a fine not exceeding €6,834. Acts of retaliation by the employer against the employee are strictly prohibited (section 17 of Law 205(I)/02).

446. See E. Nicolaou, 'Appointment of Women in the Police Force and the Principle of Equality' (2007) 3 *Cyprus and European Law Review*: 534–553 (in Greek).

447. A general prohibition of the recruitment of women to specific posts in the mining industry and to posts involving work in a high-pressure atmosphere and as divers is precluded by the Directive; see Case C-203/03, *Commission* v. *Austria* [2005] ECR I-035.

448. See also Case C-595/12, *Napoli* v. *Ministero della Guistizia* EU, C-2014: 128.

449. See also *Alkiviadou* v. *Attorney-General* [2011] 1 CLR 2350 (in Greek).

395. The IDT is the competent court for disputes of civil nature, except with regard to administrative law disputes, and may award just and equitable compensation which covers at least the whole of the real damage, plus legal interest.[450] In case of a dismissal, the IDT may, apart from the award of compensation, order the re-employment of the worker and may compel the employer to accept his services, if the employee so wishes; if it is deemed necessary, the Court may also issue an order of recognition of the applicant's rights in relation to the reported violation (section 15 of Law 205(I)/02). For the purposes of Law 205(I)/02, no minimum period of employment, or work hours requirements, nor a maximum limit to compensation apply; any agreement between the employer and the employee providing otherwise, is void (section 16 of Law 205(I)/02).

B. Harassment

396. Any act, whether isolated or repeated, that constitutes harassment or sexual harassment, or causes direct or indirect discriminatory treatment owing to repulsion of an act of harassment or sexual harassment, or complaint against such an act, in relation, *inter alia*, to the field of employment, is prohibited by virtue of section 12 of Law 205(I)/02. 'Harassment' is defined, in section 2 of Law 205(I)/02, as any unwanted contact on the part of the person concerned, related to sex, with the purpose or effect of violating that person's dignity in employment. The fact that an individual repulses such an act may not be used as a basis for any decision that offends that individual.

397. Employers and representatives of trade unions and employers' associations must protect their employees, trainees, or apprentices, from any act of harassment caused by a supervisor, or by any other employee, trainee or apprentice, as well as against any act that causes discriminatory treatment owing to the repulsion of an act of harassment, or complaint against such an act. Moreover, employers and representatives of legal entities or organizations have an obligation to take every appropriate measure in order to ensure that such an act will not be repeated to remove its consequences and to take any timely measure possible in order to avert such actions. This can be achieved by a code of conduct concerning the avoidance of such actions, as well as practical measures for ensuring that the code can be put into effect (section 12 of Law 205(I)/02).[451]

398. The dismissal or any detrimental change to the conditions of employment of an individual, in case of a complaint concerning unequal treatment, including complains of violation of the law, or harassment or sexual harassment, is null and void, unless the employer proves that the dismissal or detrimental change has been

450. See also Case C-407/14, *Camacho* v. *Securitas Seguridad Espana SA* EU, C-2015: 831.

451. See also OEB, *Handbook of Officer of Labour Relations: Equality in Occupation and Combating Sexual Harassment in the Workplace* (Nicosia, 2015, in Greek): 66–86, E. Nicolaou, 'Sexual Harassment in the Workplace', in G. Serghides (ed.), *Property Relations between Spouses and Various Legal Issues* (Nicosia, 2010): 646–655 (in Greek).

made for reasons unrelated to the complaint or the repulsion of act of sexual harassment (section 17 of Law 205(I)/02).[452]

C. Equal Pay

399. The Equal Pay between Men and Women for the Same Work or for Work to which Equal Value is Attributed Law 177(I)/2002[453] partly harmonizes Cypriot law with Directive 2006/54/EC. The purpose of Law 177(I)/02 is to ensure the application of the principle of equal pay between men and women for equal work or equal value work (section 3 of Law 177(I)/02). It applies to all employees, for all activities related to employment (section 4 of Law 177(I)/02). Every employer must provide equal pay to men and women by virtue of section 5 of Law 177(I)/02, for the same work or for work to which equal value is attributed, irrespective of the sex of the employee; where a system of professional classification is used for the determination of pay, such a system must be based on common criteria for male and female employees and must be designed in such a manner that discrimination based on sex is excluded (section 5 of Law 177(I)/02).[454]

400. The comparator for the purposes of comparison between employees is an employee who is, or was, employed by the same employer, or in a business controlling the employer, during the two previous or subsequent years (section 5(3) of Law 177(I)/02). The introduction of the comparator described above clarifies that, the fact of whether there is equality in pay has to be determined by reference to a single employer, who is the point of reference and who employs the aggrieved person, and not in comparison with other employers. The Minister of Labour, Welfare and Social Insurance has a duty to inform workers, employers, as well as their organizations, through printed materials and other appropriate means, of the provisions of Law 205(I)/02. Trade unions have a similar obligation for informing the workers of the content of the law, whereas employers have a duty to facilitate the workers' organizations in order to provide workers with the information required (section 6 of Law 177(I)/02).

401. The Minister further appoints inspectors who monitor the application of Law 177(I)/02 and safeguard the protection of workers by investigating relevant complaints and taking appropriate action (section 10 of Law 177(I)/02). An employer who violates any provision of Law 205(I)/02 is guilty of an offence punishable with imprisonment of up to six months and/or a fine not exceeding €6,834 (section 24 of Law 177(I)/02); no employee should be dismissed, or discriminated against, for submitting a complaint, or contributing towards the prosecution of an employer who violates the provisions of Law 177(I)/02 (section 9 of Law 177(I)/02). The IDT is the competent court for disputes of civil nature, except with regard

452. The provisions of paras. 394–395 above also apply in the case of harassment.
453. As amended by Laws 193(I)/2004, 38(I)/2009 and 151(I)/2014.
454. The principle of equal pay between men and women is also found in Article 28 of the Constitution. See *Gregoriou* v. *Municipality of Nicosia* [1991] 4 CLR 3005 (in Greek).

to administrative law disputes, and may award just and equitable compensation which covers at least the whole of the real damage, plus legal interest; if it is deemed necessary, the Court may also issue an order of recognition of the applicant's rights in relation to the reported violation (section 22 of Law 177(I)/02). For the purposes of Law 205(I)/02, no minimum period of employment, or work hours requirements, nor a maximum limit to compensation apply; any agreement between the employer and the employee providing otherwise, is void (section 23 of Law 177(I)/02).

VI. Elderly Workers: Age Discrimination

402. The rights of elderly workers to non-discrimination are safeguarded through the framework of the Equal Treatment in Employment and Occupation Law 58(I)/2004, which transposes Directive 2000/78/EC.[455] Whereas the general provisions of Law 58(I)/04 also apply to age discrimination, there are also references specific to age discrimination.[456] Discrimination on grounds of age is unlawful with respect to employment by virtue of section 6 of Law 58(I)/04; this covers direct and indirect discrimination, harassment and victimization. Discrimination on grounds of age includes employees of whatever age; the prohibition of discrimination on grounds of age is not limited to a particularly old or young age, nor to an age after a certain threshold is exceeded.[457] However, section 8 of Law 58(I)/2004 introduces specific exceptions with respect to a difference of treatment on grounds of age; it is therefore provided that difference of treatment on grounds of age does not constitute discrimination if such difference is objectively justified by a legitimate aim, such as legitimate employment policy, labour market and vocational training objectives, and so long as the means of achieving that aim are appropriate and necessary.[458] Termination of employment contracts due to mandatory retirement of the employee do not amount to age discrimination.[459]

403. Such differences in treatment may include, among others: (a) the setting of special conditions on access to employment and vocational training, employment and occupation, including dismissal and remuneration conditions, for young people, older workers and persons with caring responsibilities, in order to promote their

455. Council Directive 2000/78/EC of 27 November 2000 establishing a general framework for equal treatment in employment and occupation.
456. See A. Emilianides, 'Age Discrimination Law in Cyprus', in Bokum *et al.* (eds.), *Age Discrimination Law in Europe* (The Hague: Kluwer Law International, 2009): 55–65.
457. See also Case C-229/08, *Wolf* v. *Stadt Frankfurt am Main* EU:C:2010:3, Case C-341/08, *Petersen* v. *Berufungsausschuss für Zahnärzte für den Bezirk Westfalen-Lippe* [2010] ECR I-47, Case C-388/07, *The Queen* v. *Secretary of State for Business* [2009] ECR I-1569, Case C-499/08, *Ingeniørforeningen i Danmark* v *Region Syddanmark* [2010] ECR I-9343.
458. See Case C-411/05, *Palacios de la Villa* v. *Cortefiel Servicios SA* [2007] ECR I-8531, Cases 250 and 268/09, *Georgiev* v. *Tehnicheski universitet* [2010] ECR I-11869. See, however, Case C-447/09, *Prigge and others* v. *Deutsche Lufthansa AG* [2011] ECR I-8003.
459. Case C-45/09, *Rosenbladt* v *Oellerking Gebäudereinigungsges.mbH* [2010] ECR I-9391.

vocational integration or ensure their protection, (b) the fixing of minimum conditions of age, professional experience or seniority in service for access to employment or to certain advantages linked to employment, (c) the fixing of a maximum age for recruitment which is based on the training requirements of the post in question or the need for a reasonable period of employment before retirement. The fixing for occupational social security schemes of ages for admission or entitlement to retirement or invalidity benefits, including the fixing under those schemes of different ages for employees or groups or categories of employees, and the use, in the context of such schemes, of age criteria in actuarial calculations, do not constitute discrimination on the grounds of age, provided these do not also result in discrimination on grounds of sex.

404. Age discrimination was considered in *Hadjiavraam*. The respondents had published an advertisement in the daily press in accordance with which they requested secretaries not older than 26 years of age; the claimant, who was 35 years old, alleged that she had suffered age discrimination. The IDT held that it had no jurisdiction to adjudicate the case, since an employment relationship had never been formed between the parties. The Supreme Court reversed the trial court's judgment and held that the IDT had exclusive jurisdiction by virtue of section 12 §1 of Law 58(I)/2004 and that accordingly it was irrelevant whether an employment relationship had been formed.[460] As far as compensation is concerned section 12 §3 of Law 58(1)/2004 provides that the IDT should award fair and just compensation, which shall cover at least all the positive damage caused by the discrimination.

405. The Supreme Court held that compensation should provide effective judicial protection which shall be analogous to the damage caused and which shall have deterrent effect.[461] In cases where the person who has actually been appointed had superior qualifications to the person discriminated against, the measure of compensation is not the same as in cases where the person discriminated against had superior qualifications than other candidates; in such cases the discrimination actually deprived the candidate of the opportunity to be appointed, whereas in the former the only damage was that his candidacy had not been duly considered.[462] A maximum compensation of three monthly salaries in cases where the employer proves that the person discriminated against would not have been appointed anyway due to the superior qualifications of the person who was actually appointed, has been considered as reasonable by the CJEU. On the facts of the case the appointed person had superior qualifications to the person discriminated against and it was thus held that the only damage to the applicant was that her candidacy had not been seriously evaluated.[463]

460. *Hadjiavraam* v. *Co-Operative Credit Company of Morphou* [2011] 1 CLR 1222 (in Greek).
461. Case-14/83 *Sabine von Colson and Elisabeth Kamann* v. *Land Nordrhein-Westfalen* [1984] ECR 1891.
462. Case C-180/95, *Draehmpaehl* [1997] ECR 1-2195.
463. *Hadjiavraam* v. *Co-Operative Credit Company of Morphou* [2011] 1 CLR 1222 (in Greek).

VII. Religious Ministers

406. Religious ministers primarily perform a spiritual function.[464] The status of a religious minister was considered by the Supreme Court in *Sideras*, which concerned a member of the clergy of the Greek Orthodox Church. In the aforementioned case it was held that the relationship between the religious minister and the church is one of employee and employer, irrespective of the fact that the main purpose of the working relationship is a spiritual one.[465] It was accordingly held that the purpose of the function carried out by a religious minister was not profit-making and accordingly a religious minister could not be considered as a self-employed person. In accordance with the decision, religious ministers are properly considered as employees, and thus, the general provisions of employment law are applicable with respect to their status as employees. This applies to ministers of all denominations and accordingly the status of religious ministers when working for their respective denominations will be the normal legal status of any other private law employee.

407. However, in view of the peculiar and unique characteristics that the status of a religious minister entails, certain exceptions from the general provisions of employment law might be recognized in the appropriate cases in order to apply the principles of collective and organizational religious freedom under Article 18 of the Constitution and Article 9 of the ECHR; the extent to which the principle of organizational religious freedom may circumvent the application of the general provisions of employment law has not yet been settled, and has to be examined on a case by case basis and in the light of all relevant considerations. This has been recognized also by Law 58(I)/04, harmonizing Directive 2000/78/EC, which applies to churches and other religious organizations as 'employers' and to religious ministers as 'employees'. Certain specific provisions have, however, been introduced with respect to religious organizations.

408. It is therefore provided under section 7 of Law 58(I)/2004 that in the case of occupational activities within churches and other public or private organizations whose ethos is based on religion or belief, a difference of treatment rooted in a person's religion or belief shall not constitute discrimination, provided that the nature of such an activity or treatment constitutes a genuine, legitimate and justified occupational requirement, with regard to the ethos of the organization. Hence section 7 of the Law allows for a requirement that a person should be of a particular religion or belief in order to be employed in a church or any other religious organization; the application of the principle of non-discrimination with respect to employment

464. In general see A. Emilianides, *Law and Religion in Cyprus* (2nd edn, The Hague: Kluwer, 2014), A. Emilianides and C. Ioannou, 'Law and Religion at the Workplace in Cyprus' in M. Rodriguez Blanco, *Law and Religion at the Workplace in the EU* (forthcoming).

465. *Sideras v. The Minister of Labour and Social Securities* [1989] 3 CLR (in Greek).

is relaxed in favour of the application of the principle of organizational religious freedom.[466]

409. Moreover, section 5 of Law 58(I)/2004, which corresponds to Article 4 of Council Directive 2000/78/EC, clarifies that a difference in treatment on any ground shall not constitute discrimination where, by reason of the nature of the particular occupational activities concerned or of the context in which they are carried out, such a characteristic constitutes a genuine and determining occupational requirement, provided that the objective is legitimate and the requirement is proportionate. It could be argued that section 5 of Law 58(I)/04 covers the case where a church refuses to employ women as members of the clergy; in this case it is indisputable that difference in treatment on grounds of sex is strictly related to the nature of the particular activities concerned and the context in which they are carried out, in view also of the principle of organizational religious freedom. However, whether the exemption could also apply with respect to other employees of the religious organization besides religious ministers is debatable; the church or the religious organization in question would have to prove that hiring a female layperson in order to perform certain duties might be problematic, for instance, due to the fact that this might be scandalizing for the male religious ministers who would have to work with the female employee. Whether in such a case, the criteria of the existence of a genuine and legitimate occupational requirement or the principle of proportionality are fulfilled, is quite doubtful.

410. It is further considered that, should section 5 be considered as a sufficient basis to justify differentiation of treatment on the grounds of sex, it could also justify differentiation on the grounds of sexual orientation, as long as such differentiation was explicitly based upon Canon Law provisions and was related to the principle of organizational religious freedom. Again, it is doubtful whether such differentiation in treatment might equally apply with respect to laypersons who are employed by the church or the religious organization without performing religious duties, such as accountants, secretaries, or legal counsels. Therefore, while section 7 of Law 58(I)/04 explicitly exempts cases where religious organizations differentiate between their employees, or refuse to hire employees on grounds of religion or belief, section 5 also provides an exemption, in the proper cases, with respect to difference in treatment on grounds of sex or sexual orientation.[467]

§2. Measures to Promote Equal Treatment: Non-discrimination

I. Article 28 of the Constitution

411. Article 28 § 2 of the Constitution ordains that every person shall enjoy all the rights and liberties provided for in this Constitution without any direct or

466. See in general R. Ahdar and I. Leigh, *Religious Freedom in the Liberal State* (Oxford: Oxford University Press, 2005): 305 ff.
467. A. Emilianides, 'Discrimination Law in Cyprus', in M. Hill, *Religion and Discrimination Law in the European Union* (Trier: European Consortium for State and Church Research, 2012): 79–85.

indirect discrimination against any person on the grounds of his/her community, race, religion, language, sex, political or other convictions, national or social descent, birth, colour, wealth, social class, or on any ground whatsoever, unless there is express provision to the contrary in this Constitution. Article 28 is similar to Article 14 of the ECHR; however, Article 28 is autonomous and its application is not dependent upon a finding of violation of another article of the Constitution, as is the case with Article 14 of the ECHR.[468] Article 1 of Protocol 12 of the ECHR, which has been ratified by the Republic of Cyprus, introduces a general and autonomous prohibition of discrimination, similarly to Article 28 of the Constitution.

412. In addition to the principle of non-discrimination, Article 28 §1 of the Constitution safeguards the complementing principle of equality, stating that all persons are equal before the law, the administration and justice and are entitled to equal protection thereof and treatment thereby. A violation of fundamental rights is actionable and thus, an aggrieved person may file an action in civil courts against those perpetrating the violation, with the aim to recover just and reasonable compensation for any pecuniary, or non-pecuniary damage that such person has suffered because of the discrimination; such discrimination may be either direct, or indirect. The person may further demand that the Court holds that any discrimination inflicted upon him, on the basis of a law, or an administrative act, is illegal and should thus be declared invalid and with no effect.

413. A difference in treatment is considered to be discriminatory, if it has no objective and reasonable justification; thus, the courts will conclude that a law, or an act, is discriminatory, if a difference in treatment does not pursue a legitimate aim, or if there is no reasonable relationship of proportionality between the means employed and the aim sought to be realised. The prohibition of discrimination refers to both direct and indirect discrimination. Indirect discrimination shall be taken to occur where an apparently neutral provision, criterion, or practice would put persons, at a particular disadvantage compared with other persons unless that provision, criterion, or practice, is objectively justified by a legitimate aim and the means of achieving that aim are appropriate and necessary. Indirect discrimination may occur where there is failure to treat different individuals or groups differently, without any objective justification, in such a manner that an apparently neutral provision which theoretically applies to everybody, in essence constitutes a disguised discriminatory provision which discriminates between the claimant and other persons.

414. For an assessment of whether indirect adverse treatment exists, it is accordingly necessary to compare with a group of comparators, and examine the hypothetically neutral provisions within the framework of the overall assessment of the

468. C. Tornaritis, 'The Right of Equality of Treatment and Absence of Discrimination', *Cyprus Law Tribune* 3–4 [1973]: 5–6, G. Pikis, 'Equality of Citizens before the Law as a Requirement of Safeguarding Rule of Law', in *Aspects of Cypriot Law*, v. II (Nicosia: Asselia, 1982, in Greek): 217–239, L. Loucaides, 'Guarantees against Racial Discrimination under the Legal System of Cyprus' *Cyprus Law Review* 17 (1987): 2659–2668.

particular age groups. Such difference in treatment will only constitute discrimination, however, so long as there is absence of justification, or lack of proportionality. In practice the requirements to be met for both direct and indirect discrimination on grounds of age may well coincide, so that in many cases it might be of theoretical value only to distinguish between the two forms of discrimination; indeed the ECHR does not use the terms direct, or indirect discrimination, but focuses on whether the differential treatment alleged has no objective and reasonable justification.[469]

415. The assessment as to whether a less favourable treatment exists must be based on a comparator and thus the notion of a 'comparable situation' is quite important; it should be proven that the claimant is treated less favourably than another person being in the same or essentially similar or comparable position as the claimant. The Supreme Court has repeatedly held that only persons in similar situations are entitled to equal treatment.[470] The principle of non-discrimination safeguards persons only when they are placed in an analogous situation and accordingly determined whether there has been discriminatory difference in treatment shall necessarily involve considerations of whether the groups of persons compared are indeed comparable.

416. It has repeatedly been held that the principle of equality safeguarded by Article 28 of the Constitution does not convey the notion of exact arithmetical equality, but it safeguards only against arbitrary differentiations and does not exclude reasonable distinctions which have to be made in view of the intrinsic nature of things.[471] The Court has to assess the material facts and particular circumstances of each case in order to conclude whether there has been unequal treatment and, bearing in mind if it was reasonably open to the Administration to treat the cases differently, the Court should not interfere by substituting its own views.[472].

417. However, Article 28 is violated only when the differentiation is not based on an objective and reasonable justification.[473] The existence of such justification must be assessed in relation to the aim and effects of the measure under consideration, regard being had to the principles which normally prevail in democratic societies. Article 28 is likewise violated when it is clearly established that there is no reasonable relationship of proportionality between the means employed and the aim sought to be realized. Bare equality of treatment regardless of the inequality of realities is neither justice nor homage to the constitutional principle. Where objects, persons or transactions essentially dissimilar are treated uniformly, discrimination may

469. *Abdulaziz, Cabales and Balkandali* v. *United Kingdom*, Judgment of 28 May 1985; (1985) 7 EHRR 471.
470. *Serghides* v. *Republic* [1991] 1 CLR 119 (in Greek), *Yiasemidou* v. *Municipal Board* [1996] 3 CLR 491 (in Greek),
471. *Kantara Shipping Ltd* v. *The Republic* [1969] 3 CLR 95, *Georghiades* v. *The Republic* [1979] 3 CLR 146.
472. *Kyriacou* v. *The Greek Communal Chamber* [1968] 3 CLR 280.
473. *Tsinontas* v. *Cyprus Land Development Corporation*[1987] 3 CLR 1766.

result.[474] The need for justification in cases of unequal treatment is thus considered to be of particular importance, in order to conclude whether the claimant is indeed treated less favourably.

418. The constitutional prohibition of discrimination extends also to the action of the administration. Article 28 of the Constitution and section 38 of the General Principles of Administrative Law, Law 158(I)/99, which safeguard the principle of equality of citizens entail that the administration must treat in an equal and uniform manner all citizens who are under the same or similar circumstances.[475] However, starting with *Dias*[476] the Supreme Court has repeatedly adhered to a rather limited approach on its jurisdiction to examine the constitutionality of laws allegedly violating the right to equality, which seriously undermines the constitutional guarantees against discrimination. It has been held that the Supreme Court has no jurisdiction to declare a provision as unconstitutional in administrative law recourse, if such a declaration would not automatically lead to the satisfaction of the petition, but that the House of Representatives would necessarily have to enact new legislation extending such right to persons in the case of the applicant.[477] The ECHR recently held that this approach amounted to a violation of the right to an effective remedy under Article 13 of the ECHR.[478]

419. In addition to the right to have access to courts, the Combating of Racism and other Discrimination (Commissioner) Law 42(I)/2004 vests the Ombudsman, who is an independent officer of the Republic with special competences, duties and powers for combating and eliminating discrimination in both public and private sectors. The powers of the Ombudsman have been extended to the entire range of non-discrimination legislation, such as 58(I)/04, 205(I)/02 and 177(I)/02. Any person or group of persons may lodge a complaint to the Equality Authority of the Ombudsman's Office for having been subjected to discrimination prohibited by any law of the Republic. The Ombudsman is therefore authorized with the supervision of the implementation of the human rights instruments which the Republic has ratified. The Ombudsman may also carry out investigations *ex proprio motu*, into incidents of discrimination, prepare codes of practice concerning specific public authorities or persons in the private sector, obliging them to follow practical measures aimed at promoting non-discrimination and equality of treatment.[479]

II. Equal Treatment in Employment and Work

420. The Republic of Cyprus has further enacted non-discrimination legislation in harmonization with EU law which prohibits discrimination, such as the Equal Treatment (Racial or Ethnic Origin) Law 59(I)/2004, which transposed Directive

474. *The Republic* v. *Maria Christoudia* [1988] 3 CLR 2622 (Ολ.).
475. *Jacovides* v. *The Republic* [1966] 3 CLR 212.
476. *Dias United Publishing Co Ltd* v. *Republic* [1996] 3 CLR 550 (in Greek).
477. *Tsiakka* v. *Republic* [2010] 3 CLR 510 (in Greek).
478. Vrountou v. Cyprus, App. 33631/06, Judgment of 13 October 2015.
479. E. Nicolaou, 'Ombudsman: The First Decade', *Cyprus Law Tribune* 2 [2001]: 29–33 (in Greek).

2000/43/EC,[480] and Law 58(I)/04 which transposed Directive 2000/78/EC. Law 58(I)/04 prohibits discrimination, specifically in the spheres of employment and occupation. The purpose of Law 58(I)/04 is, according to section 3 of the Law, to set out a framework in order to prevent discrimination on grounds of race or ethnic origin, religion or belief, disability,[481] age,[482] or sexual identity,[483] in the area of employment and occupation, so that the principle of equal treatment might be effected. However, different treatment on grounds of nationality is not in principle prohibited (section 5(1) of Law 58(I)/04).

421. Law 58(I)/04 extends to all public and private sector bodies and organizations; the notion of employee includes employees of whatever type, of definite duration, fixed-term, part-time, or on probationary period. Discrimination on any of the prohibited discriminatory grounds is unlawful with respect to access to employment, or occupation, including selection criteria and recruitment conditions, whatever the branch of activity and at all levels of the professional hierarchy, including promotion. Discrimination is further prohibited with regard to access to all types and to all levels of vocational guidance,vocational training, advanced vocational training and retraining, including practical work experience, employment and working conditions, including dismissals and pay, membership of, and involvement in, an organization of workers or employers, or any organization whose members carry on a particular profession, including the benefits provided for by such organizations (section 4 of Law 58(I)/04).

422. Direct discrimination on any of the discriminatory grounds is prohibited by virtue of section 6 of Law 58(I)/2004. Discrimination exists if a person is treated less favourably on one of the discriminatory grounds than another person is, has been or would be treated in a comparable situation. The assessment as to whether less favourable treatment exists must be based on a comparator and thus, the notion of a 'comparable situation' is important; it should be proven that the claimant is treated less favourably than another person performing the same or essentially similar or comparable work as the claimant. In order to conclude whether the claimant is treated less favourably, an overall comparison of all types of work to be performed under the contract should be undertaken. The mere fact that the claimant is

480. Council Directive 2000/43/EC of 29 June 2000 implementing the principle of equal treatment between persons irrespective of racial or ethnic origin.

481. See Case C-335 and 337/11, *HK Danmark* v. *Dansk almennyttigt Boligselskab* EU, C-2013: 222. It should be noted that sickness is not regarded as disability and accordingly dismissal on grounds of sickness is not prohibited by Law 58(I)/04. Case C-13/05, *Navas* v. *Eurest Collectividades SA* [2006] ECR I-6467. However, obesity might in some circumstances be considered as a disability. Case C-354/13, *Fag og Arbejde* v. *Kommunernes Landforening* EU, C-2014: 2463.

482. Age discrimination may also apply to younger and not only to elderly workers; in Case C-555/07, *Kücükdeveci* v. *Swedex GmbH & Co. KG* [2010] ECR I-365 it was held that domestic legislation, providing that periods of employment completed by an employee before reaching the age are not taken into account in the calculation of the notice period for dismissal, was discriminatory. See also Case C-417/13, *ÖBB Personenverkehr AG* v. *Gotthard Starjakob* EU, C-2015: 38.

483. See Case C-81/12, *Asociaţia ACCEPT* v. *Consiliul Naţional pentru Combaterea Discriminării* EU, C-2013: 275, Case C-267/12, *Hay* v. *Credit agricole mutuel de Charente* EU, C-2013: 823.

treated less favourably with respect to one aspect of the contract will thus not suffice if the claimant is treated more favourably with respect to other aspects; it is the overall assessment and comparison of the contract which is important. In the absence of a current comparator, comparators formerly employed have to be used for the comparison, before an assessment can be made.

423. A difference in treatment on one of the prohibited grounds shall not, however, constitute discrimination, where by reason of the nature of the particular occupational activities concerned or of the context in which they are carried out, such a characteristic constitutes a genuine and important occupational requirement, provided that the objective is legitimate and the requirement is proportionate. It is further provided that the provisions of Law 58(I)/2004 shall be without prejudice to measures laid down by national law which, in a democratic society, are necessary for public security, for the maintenance of public order and the prevention of criminal offences, for the protection of health and for the protection of the rights and freedoms of others. In addition Law 58(I)/2004 does not apply to payments of any kind made by state schemes or similar, including state social security or social protection schemes (section 5(2) and (3) of Law 58(I)/04).

424. Indirect discrimination is also prohibited; this would occur whenever an apparently neutral provision, criterion or practice would put persons of a particular group, at a particular disadvantage compared with other persons unless that provision, criterion or practice is objectively justified by a legitimate aim and the means of achieving that aim are appropriate and necessary. Indirect discrimination may occur where there is failure to treat different individuals or groups differently, without any objective justification, in such a manner that an apparently neutral provision which theoretically applies to everybody in essence constitutes a disguised discriminatory provision which discriminates between the claimant and other persons.

425. This would happen if the differentiation criterion has certain characteristics which are found much more frequently among members of one group, so that a significant number of such group, or even the whole group, is unable to comply with the requirement. In such a case it is presumed that membership of a particular group has been the decisive cause for the discrimination. Thus, for an assessment of whether indirect adverse treatment exists, it is necessary to compare with a group of comparators, and examine the hypothetically neutral provisions within the framework of the overall assessment of the particular age groups. Such difference in treatment will only constitute discrimination, however, so long as there is absence of justification, or lack of proportionality.

426. Any provisions in collective agreements or individual contracts of employment which violate the prohibition of discrimination are in principle void, pursuant to section 16, paragraph 5 of Law 58(I)/2004. Furthermore, by virtue of section 10 of Law 58(I)/2004, the employer may not subject the employees to discrimination or other adverse treatment on the ground that they have exercised their rights under the Law, such as complaining to the relevant authorities or being involved in any legal proceedings aimed at enforcing compliance with the principle of equal treatment. Consequently, victimisation of the employees by the employer is strictly prohibited. An instruction by the employer to apply discriminatory treatment on grounds of age is also prohibited, so that an employee may lawfully refuse to apply such a discriminatory instruction. Harassment based on one of the prohibited grounds is also expressly prohibited (section 6 of Law 58(I)/04).[484]

427. Positive action, with a view to ensure full equality in practice, does not constitute discrimination. Both measures to remedy existing disadvantages and preventive measures to prevent future disadvantages are in principle permitted, though the justification of preventive measures might, in most cases, prove to be difficult (section 9 of Law 58(I)/04). The competent court for any action by an employee subjected to discrimination on one of the prohibited grounds is the IDT, subject to the jurisdiction of the Administrative Courts on administrative law issues (section 12 of Law 58(I)/04). If the employee proves the existence of indications of discrimination on one of the prohibited grounds, the onus is on the employer to prove that there has been no discrimination (section 11 of Law 58(I)/04). Trade unions may exercise the judicial rights of the claimant with the latter's approval. An employer violating the provisions of Law 58(I)/04 is guilty of an offence punishable with imprisonment of up to six months and/or a fine not exceeding €6,834 (section 15 of Law 58(I)/04).

484. Case C-303/06, *Coleman* v. *Attridge Law* [2008] ECR I-5603.

Chapter 8. Covenants of Non-competition

428. Covenants of non-competition for the duration of an employment agreement will be considered as valid, and even, in some cases, be implied by the obligation of the employee to show fidelity towards the employee. However, the mere fact that an employee is seeking employment with a competitor would not amount to a breach of his duty to fidelity; such breach will occur if the employee discloses confidential information or trade secrets.[485] Similarly the employee will not be considered to breach his duty of fidelity if he has engaged in mere preparatory activities for future employment, or even competition against his former employer, if such acts are performed in the employee's own time, premises and equipment.[486] The employee, however, may not use the employer's premises or equipment, or engage in such activities during working hours. In all cases the position of the employee in the former employer's structure is relevant in determining the extent of his duty to fidelity; the acts of senior employees are accordingly much more likely to amount to a breach of a duty of fidelity on behalf of the employee.[487]

429. An employer cannot prevent an ex-employee from competing with him, nor from using the knowledge skill and experience gained during employment; thus technical skill, acquired by the employee's own observations and intelligence could not be the object of a covenant to not compete.[488] Post-employment covenants of non-competition would therefore normally be considered to constitute restraint of trade. However, a covenant would be considered as valid, if it is agreed prior to the end of the employment and if it contains reasonable restraints which are absolutely necessary in order to protect the legitimate interests of the employer.[489] In assessing the reasonableness of a covenant and accordingly whether it is enforceable, courts will consider the subject matter of the restraint, the length of time, the geographical area within which it will operate and whether it is narrowly worded, so as to safeguard only the reasonable concerns of the employer and not to impose an undue burden on the employee.[490]

430. The employer should therefore identify a potential or actual harm justifying the restraint, especially as any restraint of trade amounts to a restriction of the right to work as safeguarded under Article 25 of the Constitution of Cyprus. There are four legitimate interests in respect of which the employer is entitled to a form of narrow protection of this kind. These are: (a) non-disclosure of confidential

---

485. *Harris & Russell Ltd* v. *Slingby* [1973] 3 All ER 31.
486. *Balston Ltd* v. *Headline Filters Ltd* [1987] FSR 330, *Helmet Integrated Systems Ltd* v. *Tunnard* [2006] FSR 41.
487. *Nottingham University* v. *Fishel* [2000] All ER 269.
488. *Herbert Morris Ltd* v. *Saxelby* [1915] 2 Ch 57, *United Sterling Corp.* v. Felton [1973] FSR 409, *Wallace Bogan & Co* v. *Cove* [1997] IRLR 453.
489. See A. Emir, *Selwyn's Law of Employment* (17th edn, Oxford: OUP, 2012): 540ff.
490. *Fellowes & Son* v. *Fisher* [1976] QB 122, *Greer* v. *Sketchley Ltd* [1979] FSR 197, *Jack Allen (Sales and Service) Ltd* v. *Smith* [1999] IRLR 19.

information and trade secrets,[491] (b) non-solicitation, or enticing of clients of the employer;[492] the covenant will be unenforceable if it extends to clients with whom the employee did not have personal interaction during his employment, or to persons who were not clients of the former employer, (c) not working for direct competitors, so far as the covenant is narrowly worded and construed and does not extend beyond what is absolutely necessary to protect the employer,[493] and (d) not enticing existing employees of the employer, to the extent that the covenant refers to restraint on the enticement of specific employees within the limits of reason.[494]

491. *Forster & Sons Ltd* v. *Suggett* [1918] 35 TLR 87, *SBJ Stephenson Ltd* v. *Mandy* [2000] IRLR 233, *Thomas Marshall (Exports) Ltd* v. *Guinle* [1979] Ch 227.

492. *International Consulting Services (UK) Ltd* v. *Hart* [2000] IRLR 227, *GW Plowman & Sons Ltd* v. *Ash* [1964] 2 All ER 10, *WRN Ltd* v. *Ayris* [2008] EWHC 1080, *Marley Tile Co Ltd* v. *Johnson* [1982] IRLR 75,*Gledhow Autoparts* v. *Delaney* [1965] 3 All ER 288, *Scully UK Ltd* v. *Lee* [1998] IRLR 259.

493. *Littlewoods Organization Ltd* v. *Harris* [1978] 1 All ER 1026, *Associated Foreign Exchange Ltd* v. *International Foreign Exchange (UK) Ltd* [2010] IRLR 964, *Commercial Plastics Ltd* v. *Vincent* [1965] 1 QB 623.

494. *Hanover Insurance Brokers Ltd* v. *Schapiro* [1994] IRLR 82, *Alliance Paper Group plc* v. *Prestwich* [1996] IRLR 25.

Chapter 9. Inventions by Employees

431. With regard to creation of inventions under status of employment, section 11 of the Patents Law 16(I)/1998 provides that the patent right for any inventions invented during the execution of an employment contract belongs to the employer, unless there are different contractual provisions between the parties. The employee has a right to fair remuneration, taking into account his wages, the economic value of the invention and the profit made by the employer; if the parties disagree with respect to the amount of fair remuneration, this shall be determined by the Supreme Court.

432. More generally, for intellectual property works created in the course of employment, it is essential to consider whether the creation of the work during employment is a requirement of the employment contract, in which case the property rights are automatically transferred to the employer. It is essential to consider whether the work is carried out as a dependent creation *in order to* execute the employment contract and not incidentally because of the existence of the employment contract; the criterion is not when or where the work is created, but rather whether it is required in order to execute the employment contract.[495]

495. T.E. Synodinou and P. Jougleux, *Intellectual Property Rights in an Academic Environment: Comparative Approach of the French and Cypriot Legal Systems* (Nicosia: University of Cyprus, 2010, in French and Greek).

Chapter 10. Settlement of Disputes

§1. Grievance Procedures

433. The IRC provides that personal complaints, including complaints over dismissals, should be presented in the first instance by the employee to his immediate supervisor and if the complaint is not settled, or if it is of such nature that direct discussion between the employee concerned and his immediate supervisor is not considered appropriate, the employee has the right to demand that his complaint may be examined at one or multiple higher levels, depending on the nature of the complaint and the structure and size of the undertaking, provided that there is a real possibility of settling it. At all stages of the examination process of a complaint, the employee concerned is entitled to be accompanied, if he so wishes, by a local trade union representative or a trade union official. Similarly, the employer is entitled to be assisted, or represented, by an official of the relevant employer's association and/ or of the Cyprus Employers and Industrialists Federation (OEB). A settlement of a personal complaint may be challenged by the employers' or workers' organizations, which are signatories to the relevant collective agreement, as being contrary to the provisions of the said agreement, in which case the procedure specified in the IRC is followed.

434. A grievance not settled at the stage of direct negotiations may be submitted for mediation to the Ministry of Labour, Welfare and Social Insurance, in which case the Ministry undertakes to deal with it within a reasonable time and in any case not later than 15 days from the date of submission. If no settlement of the dispute is achieved by the Ministry within 15 days of the date it began dealing with it, the dispute should be submitted to binding arbitration. Grievances over dismissals should be dealt with as expeditiously as possible and the time limits should be halved.

435. It should be noted that with respect to disputes between employers and migrant workers, the mechanism of the Ministry of Labour, Welfare and Social Insurance provides for a compulsory system of quasi-mediation, in which third country nationals individually file a complaint to the competent authorities, and the mediator essentially files a report to the immigration authorities in order to determine the visa status of the migrant worker. Such a system fundamentally differs from the process of mediation in industrial disputes described above and cannot properly be considered as mediation.[496]

496. http://www.labourlawnetwork.eu/national_labour_law/court_decisions/court_decisions/prm/64/
v__
detail/id__1361/category__7/size__1/index.html, last accessed 10 December 2012.

§2. Role of the Courts

I. Courts of General Jurisdiction

A. District Courts

436. Whereas the District Courts, which are the general jurisdiction courts of the Republic of Cyprus, do not have jurisdiction to adjudicate disputes by virtue of specialized labour law legislation, they retain their general jurisdiction to adjudicate private law disputes arising out of contracts of employment on the basis of general legislation, such as the Contract Law, Cap. 149, or even the principles of common law. In *Stylianides* it was held that the aim of the Termination of Employment Law is to protect the employee from the unilateral termination of his employment; it was not the objective of Law 24/67 to abolish or restrict the application of other legislation which regulate the contracts of employment or their termination, in those cases where the District Courts have jurisdiction.[497]

437. In *Tony & Guy* the employers, who were hairdressers, filed a suit against the employee, who was a pupil hairdresser, before the District Court. They claimed that they had accepted the employee as a pupil hairdresser in their service for a period of a year in consideration of the employee paying them a specific sum of money; however, the employee had resigned before the end of the year and had failed to abide by the terms of the contract and pay the consideration. The District Court held that it had no jurisdiction as the matter fell under the exclusive jurisdiction of the IDT. The Supreme Court reversed the first instance judgment and held that for an independent claim to fall under the exclusive jurisdiction of the IDT, this should arise from the employment contract, or the employment relationship. However, the claim of the employer did not arise from the employment relationship and did not refer to the employment relationship of the parties; rather, the question was whether a contract had been breached and this fell under the jurisdiction of the District Court.[498]

438. Section 30(2) of Law 24/67 provides that an employee has the right to apply before the District Court of the district where he was employed when the dispute arose, if his claim is for compensation exceeding the employee's emoluments that the IDT has power to award by virtue of Law 24/67.[499] Thus, the District Court has jurisdiction for claimed damages in excess of the employee's emoluments for two years which the IDT is empowered to award. In addition, the District Courts have jurisdiction over all criminal prosecutions for violations of labour law legislation; the IDT does not exercise criminal jurisdiction.

439. In *Kapsou* the employee had been employed for less than 26 weeks; she filed an action before the District Court for wrongful dismissal. Under section 3 of

497. *Stylianides* v. *British American Insurance Co Ltd* [1990] 1 CLR 517 (in Greek).
498. *Tony & Guy Limassol Ltd and another* v. *Theodorou* [2008] 1 CLR 496 (in Greek).
499. *Belcy Company Ltd* v. *Louca* [2003] 1 CLR 871 (in Greek).

Law 24/67 an employee whose services are terminated after an employment of less than 26 weeks has no right to claim compensation under the provisions of Law 24/67. The Supreme Court held that section 3 had created a new statutory right regarding compensation for wrongful dismissal in substitution of the common law rights and consequently the jurisdiction of the IDT cannot be circumvented by an action before a District Court; the District Court accordingly lacked jurisdiction on the matter.[500]

440. In the subsequent *Elbee* case the employee, who had been employed for less than 26 weeks, filed an action before the District Court claiming accrued salaries. The Supreme Court held that the true meaning of *Kapsou* was not that no Court in the Republic would have jurisdiction in all cases that an employee had been employed for less than 26 weeks; otherwise, this would violate Article 30 of the Constitution providing for access to courts and would be contrary to the fundamental principle *ubi jus ubi remedium*. The *dictum* of *Kapsou* related only to the fact that there is no legal right for compensation for wrongful dismissal if an employee has been employed for less than 26 weeks; however, there was jurisdiction of the District Court to award accrued salaries to an employee.[501]

441. Accrued salaries or other benefits which have been created during the employment relationship, should accordingly be differentiated from the termination of employment which is governed by Law 24/67; accrued salaries are owed because of the employment relationship and not due to its termination.[502] In *Zavrou* it was held that the claim for accrued salaries is not an industrial dispute and since the IDT does not have jurisdiction for accrued salaries, the District Court has jurisdiction.[503] Following the *Zavrou* judgment, Law 8/67 was substituted by Law 79(I)/1996 which provides in section 12(e) that independent claims which arise from the employment contract and which include claims for annual leave, accrued salaries, ex gratia payment, 13th salary, or any other right accruing from law, regulation, custom, individual or collective employment relationship, is subject to the jurisdiction of the IDT. Accordingly, since 1996 it is the IDT, and not the District Court, which has exclusive jurisdiction for accrued salaries.[504]

442. In *Antoniou* the appellant filed an action before the District Court claiming to receive a specified sum on the basis of an agreement he had signed with his employer for the payment of overtime employment. The trial court held that the IDT had exclusive jurisdiction to try the dispute, as it related to accrued salaries of the employee. The Supreme Court reversed the first instance judgment; it was held that

500. *Kapsou* v. *Middle East Airlines Airliban* [1988] 1 CLR 152.

501. *Elbee Ltd* [1999] 1 CLR 149.

502. *Kyriakou* v. *Redundancy Fund* [1993] 1 CLR 1020 (in Greek).

503. *Zavrou* v. *Charalampous* [1996] 1 CLR 447 (in Greek), *Panayiotou* v. *DS Artokoulouropoieion Ltd* [2002] 1 CLR 1381 (in Greek).

504. *Elbee Ltd* [1999] 1 CLR 149. See also *Panayiotis Kountourides Ltd* v. *Awadalla and others* [2008] 1 CLR 852 (in Greek), whose reasoning is, however, unsatisfactory.

since the employment relations dispute was transformed to a contract for payment of a specified sum, it was the District Court that had jurisdiction and not the IDT.[505]

443. In the *Interamerican* case the employee, who had been employed for less than 26 weeks, filed an action before the District Court claiming damages in excess of her emoluments for two years; the District Court granted her three month compensation. The employer appealed and argued that the District Court had no jurisdiction. The Supreme Court held that the only requirement for the District Court to have jurisdiction is for the employee to claim more than what the IDT has jurisdiction to award, namely damages in excess of his emoluments for two years; the fact that the judgment given was for a lesser amount does not imply that the District Court shall be deprived of its jurisdiction *ex post facto*. It was further held that the *Kapsou* judgment should be distinguished, as the employee in that case had not filed a claim exceeding his emoluments for two years; the fact that the employee had been employed for less than 26 weeks did not deprive the District Court from jurisdiction. The *Interamerican* case has thus confirmed that a person who has been employed for less than 26 weeks may apply before the District Court for unlawful termination of employment, but only insofar as his claim exceeds his emoluments for two years.[506]

444. In *Vrahimis* the employee filed an action before the District Court claiming damages for breach of contract of employment. The initial claim was for salaries of less than two years, which would have granted exclusive jurisdiction to the IDT. The employee, however, requested that his statement of claim be amended, so as to increase the amount claimed to more than two years' worth of salaries, so that the District Court would enjoy jurisdiction. The employer sought leave for certiorari, claiming that the District Court did not have jurisdiction when the action was filed; accordingly the District Court did not have jurisdiction to entertain an application for amendment of pleadings in such a way as to subsequently acquire jurisdiction which it did not originally have. The Supreme Court rejected the application for certiorari and held that a defendant cannot be the judge of the amount claimed by the claimant; the District Court had not overstepped its authority by approving the application for amendment of the statement of claim.[507] In order to determine the amount claimed, the court should refer to the pleadings and submissions of the employee.[508]

445. An employee is deprived of the right to file an action to the District Court if he has filed an application before the IDT and vice versa. It used to be the case

505. *Antoniou* v. *ERE Electrical & Refrigeration Engineering Co Ltd* [2007] 1 CLR 1391 (in Greek), *Kozaki* v. *Kozaki* [2003] 1 CLR 1047 (in Greek).

506. *Interamerican Insurance Co Ltd* v. *Makridou* [2000] 1 CLR 1529 (in Greek).

507. *Apean of St Napa* [1991] 1 CLR 1100 (in Greek). With respect to the principles governing amendment of pleadings see *Iosifides* v. *Bernhard Schulte Shipmanagement Cyprus Ltd*, Civ. Appeal 239/11, dated 23 October 2013 (in Greek).

508. *Panayiotou* v. *DS Artokoulouropoieion Ltd* [2002] 1 CLR 1381 (in Greek), citing with approval *Sevegep Ltd* v. *United Sea Transport Ltd and another* [1989] 1 CLR 729, *Vounou* v. *Vounou* [1995] 1 CLR 168 (in Greek).

that the mere filing of an application before the IDT would bar any proceedings before the District Court by virtue of the proviso of section 30 of Law 24/67. In *Phassouri* it was held that since the employee had filed recourse before the IDT, he could not claim damages by filing an action before the District Court; the fact that he had withdrawn the recourse before the IDT was irrelevant.[509] In *Aspromallis* the employee had filed an action before the District Court which he later discontinued, reserving his rights to file new legal procedures. It was held that the subsequent recourse before the IDT was barred by the mere filing of the initial action before the District Court and should accordingly be dismissed.[510] Law 110(I)/2003 has abolished the proviso of section 30; accordingly an employee has the right, once he has discontinued or withdrawn an action before the District Court, to subsequently file an action before the IDT.[511]

446. The District Court has no jurisdiction to interfere with the execution of judgments of the IDT. In *Michaelides* the IDT had adjudicated compensation in favour of the employee, which was affirmed on appeal. When the employee proceeded to issue a writ of execution of the judgment, the employer applied *ex parte* before the District Court; the latter granted him an order which suspended the application of the writ of execution. It was held that the District Court has no jurisdiction to suspend the application of a writ of execution which was issued pursuant to a judgment of the IDT.[512]

B. Administrative Court

447. Prior to 1 January 2016 the Supreme Court exercised exclusive jurisdiction over administrative law recourses by virtue of Article 146 of the Constitution. Pursuant to the amendment of Article 146 of the Constitution by the Eighth Amendment of the Constitution Law (130(I)/2015) and by virtue of the Establishment and Function of the Administrative Court Law (131(I)/2015), the newly established Administrative Court exercises exclusive first-instance jurisdiction over all administrative law recourses. The employment relationships of permanent public servants are governed by public law and are not considered as part of labour law, but as part of administrative law. Accordingly, if the employee is employed under public law, then the IDT has no jurisdiction to adjudicate its termination of employment, as the act of termination will be one of administrative law which may be reviewed only by the Administrative Court.

448. An interesting question arose in *Meliniotis* concerning the jurisdiction of the IDT to adjudicate an application of the public law employee against the Redundancy Fund alleging that his dismissal was made on grounds of redundancy.[513] The

509. *Cyprus Phassouri Plantations Co Ltd* v. *Georgiou* [1982] 1 CLR 766.
510. *Aspromallis* v. *Freetown Hotels Ltd* [2003] 1 CLR 969 (in Greek).
511. *Argus Stockbrokers Ltd* v. *Hatzitheodosiou* [2009] 1 CLR 1514 (in Greek).
512. *Michaelides* [1997] 1 CLR 14 (in Greek).
513. *Meliniotis* v. *Municipality of Nicosia and another* [2003] 1 CLR 1067 (in Greek).

Supreme Court held, however, that whereas the IDT might enjoy jurisdiction, employees in the public sector may not be declared as redundant by definition, since their service is safeguarded until they retire in accordance with legislation. The employee in *Melioniotis* had consented to his early retirement in order to receive benefits and was not to be compensated by the Redundancy Fund.[514]

449. Not all persons employed by the government, municipalities or legal persons of public law are public servants or employees of such a public status; the state and legal persons of public law may employ, in addition to their permanent employees whose employment relationship is governed by public law, workers whose status is governed by contractual relationships of private law. The termination of employment of employees of the state, or of legal persons of public law, whose employment relationship is governed by private law, does not fall within the revisionary jurisdiction of the Supreme Court under Article 146 of the Constitution,[515] but under the jurisdiction of the IDT.[516] However, recourses challenging the appointment of persons to these positions would, in our view, properly fall under the jurisdiction of the Administrative Court, since a contractual relation has not yet been established in these cases at the stage of appointment and the issue is one of public law.

450. The period of service, the security of tenure, the nature of the duties and the view taken of the status of the employee by the employing authority, are all relevant factors to be weighed in order to reach a proper conclusion as to the legal status of the employee.[517] The fact that an appointment is made by contract does not necessarily alter the status of a public law employee.[518] In *Lemoniatis* it was further held that whether an employment relationship is governed by private law is a matter to be governed by the legislative provisions on the basis of which the employee was hired and not solely by the manner in which the parties themselves (i.e. the legal person of public law or the State on the one hand and the employee on the other hand) described or understood their employment relationship.[519]

451. *Apostolides* concerned the Termination of Employment (Temporary Restrictive Provisions) Law 50/74 and the Termination of Employment Law, 1/75

514. *Meliniotis* v. *Redundancy Fund* [2006] 1 CLR 144 (in Greek).
515. *Constantinou and another* v. *Republic* [2004] 3 CLR 577 (in Greek), *Loizou & Another* v. *CYTA*, 4 RSCC 48, *Chrysostomou and another* v. *Municipality of Limassol* [2005] 4 CLR 618 (in Greek), *Demetriou and another* v. *Eforia Ellinikon Ekpaideftirion Lemesou*, Case 4/11, dated 10 November 2011.
516. *Avraam* v. *Republic* [2008] 3 CLR 49 (in Greek), *Theatrical Organization of Cyprus* v. *Sofocleous*, Civ. Appeal 513/2012, dated 18 January 2016 (in Greek).
517. *Constantinou and another* v. *Republic* [2004] 3 CLR 577 (in Greek), *Loizou & Another* v. *CYTA*, 4 RSCC 48.
518. *Paschalidou* v. *Republic* [1969] 3 CLR 297, *Vassiliou & Others* v. *Republic* [1969] 3 CLR 417, *Papakyriakou* v. *The Health Services of Cyprus* [1970] 3 CLR 351, *Efstathiou* [1991] 4 CLR 3619.
519. *Lemoniatis and others* v. *Municipality of Limassol* [2005] 4 CLR 869 (in Greek), *Christofi and others* v. *Central Slaughterhouse of Kofinou*, Apps 643-645/96, dated 31 July 1997 (in Greek), *Araouzou* v. *Municipality of Kato Polemidia*, Apps 812-813/04, dated 22 December 2005 (in Greek), *Pattikis and another* v. *The Municipal Committee of Nicosia* [1988] 1 CLR 103.

which were enacted because of the Turkish invasion of 1974. Several companies were declared as stricken companies on the basis of Law 50/74, because their business was in the occupied areas and as a result their operations were suspended; this status gave them the right to dismiss their employees. Law 1/75 further provided for the suspension of redundancy payment to the workers dismissed. The Appellants in *Apostolides* had applied for a review of their case to the Director-General of the Ministry of Labour and Social Insurance, who, however, informed them that Law 1/75 conferred no discretion to anyone to allow redundancy payment to a worker dismissed immediately after and because of the Turkish invasion of 1974.

452. The Supreme Court held that the reply of the Director-General of the Ministry of Labour and Social Insurance was not an administrative act, since the Redundancy Fund has its own legal personality and is capable of suing and being sued in its own name; accordingly, no person may take a decision in its stead. It was further held that the temporary suspension of redundancy payments was a measure designed to protect the institution of redundancy payments for the sake of the longer-term interests of workers and was not contrary to Article 9 of the Constitution dictating to provide for workers and the poor a social security compatible with the means of the state. The grave emergency created by the Turkish invasion justified the suspension.[520]

C. Supreme Court

453. The Supreme Court is the highest court of the Republic and functions, since the constitutional crisis of 1963, both as the Supreme Constitutional Court and supreme appellate court of the Republic. The Supreme Court is composed of 13 judges, one of whom acts as the President and has jurisdiction to hear and determine all appeals from lower courts in civil and criminal matters. Appeals are heard by a panel of three judges. The hearing of the appeal is based on the record of the proceedings kept in the lower court; the Supreme Court only hears oral evidence in exceptional and very rare circumstances. In the exercise of its appellate jurisdiction, the Supreme Court may uphold, vary or set aside the decision appealed or it may order a retrial.

454. It has been held that the provisions of Law 24/67 should be read in conjunction with the Courts of Justice Law 14/60, which is the basic law providing for the vesting of original jurisdiction in the various courts of the Republic; section 19 of Law 14/60 provides that the Supreme Court shall have exclusive jurisdiction to try admiralty actions and, as a result the provisions of section 30 of Law 24/67, should be read as excluding from their scope admiralty actions. This construction is consistent with the principle *generalia specialibus non derogant*, since a specific legislative provision granting the Supreme Court jurisdiction over admiralty actions cannot be impliedly derogated by a general piece of legislation, such as Law 24/67. Accordingly, the Supreme Court shall have exclusive jurisdiction with respect to

520. *Apostolides and others* v. *Republic* [1982] 3 CLR 928.

actions for the recovery of wages and benefits of seamen from their employers or for the termination of employment of seamen.[521]

455. Any judgment of the IDT is subject to appeal before the Supreme Court within 42 days from the date that the judgment was issued; not only final judgments of the IDT, but also any interim judgments and decisions, may be appealed before the Supreme Court.[522] Rule 17 of the Rules of Procedure set out in the Arbitration Tribunal Regulations of 1968 used to provide for an appeal on a point of law by way of case stated. An appeal by way of case stated does not function in the same way as an ordinary appeal, where the Supreme Court, sitting as an appellate court, is not bound by any findings of fact made by the trial court and which, therefore, may be challenged before it by the appellant. In an appeal by way of case stated, findings of fact are not subject to review by the Supreme Court. The Supreme Court is conferred with power only to decide the legal point raised in the case stated and return the case to the President of the IDT together with its opinion thereon.

456. Law 110(I)/99 amended section 12 (11A) of Law 8/67 so that an appeal may be directly filed before the Supreme Court and not by way of case stated; however, the appeal may still be filed only on points of law;[523] the amendment to the Law followed repeated comments by the Supreme Court that the mechanism of an appeal by way of case stated should be considered as a failure, since it unreasonably delayed the appeals, put additional burdens on the IDT and caused it to justify its judgment through the case stated, thus leading to additional and unnecessary litigation against the decision of the IDT not to submit a case stated, or phrase a case stated in given manner.[524] The Supreme Court is thus not vested with jurisdiction to make its own findings of fact, either contrary or supplementary to those made by the Tribunal.[525]

457. In *HjiCostas* it was held that whenever an issue refers to the application of the law to given facts, it raises a pure question of law; thus, so long as the facts to which the court is required to apply the law are not disputed by the appellant, the point is a legal one, raising questions on the construction and scope of the law. It was thus held that the exploration of the ambit of the law is always considered as

521. *Ship Panayia Myrtidiotissa* v. *Sidiropoulou and another* [1993] 1 CLR 991 (in Greek), *Finiotis* v. *Greenmar Navigation Ltd and another* [1988] 1 CLR 114.

522. *Kosmos Press Ltd* [1993] 1 CLR 925 (in Greek), *PEO Federation* [1991] 1 CLR 1008 (in Greek).

523. *Christou* v. *Fairways Larnaca Ltd* [2005] 1 CLR 300 (in Greek), *Crown Resorts Ltd* v. *Kallis* [2011] 1 CLR 1369 (in Greek), *Economou Architects and Mechanics and others* v. *Demetriou* [2000] 1 CLR 853 (in Greek), *Zertali* v. *Redundancy Fund* [2003] 1 CLR 178 (in Greek), *Savvides* v. *SSP Catering Cyprus Ltd and others*, Civ. Appeal 179/09, dated 20 September 2012 (in Greek), *Faber Hoist Chemicals Ltd* v. *Kalimera*, Civil Appeal 190/2010, dated 24 February 2015 (in Greek).

524. *PEO Federation* [1991] 1 CLR 1008 (in Greek), *Kyriakides* [1992] 1 CLR 26 (in Greek), *Cyprus Workers' Confederation*[1996] 1 CLR 1030 (in Greek), *Takis Vashiotis Ltd* [1999] 1 CLR 5 (in Greek). See also *Economou Architects and Mechanics and others* [1999] 1 CLR 216 (in Greek), *Redundancy Fund* [1996] 1 CLR 899 (in Greek), *Redundancy Fund* [1990] 1 CLR 10 (in Greek).

525. *Alouet Clothing Manufacturers Ltd* v. *Athanasiou and another* [1988] 1 CLR 626, *Tryfonos* v. *Takis Vashiotis Ltd* [1999] 1 CLR 1953 (in Greek).

a question of law and not as a question of fact.[526] Acting on no evidence, or acting on evidence which ought to have been rejected, or failing to take into consideration evidence which ought to have been considered, or proceeding to findings which are clearly inconsistent with, or not supported by, the evidence presented,[527] are considered as matters of law and not of fact.[528]

458. A distinction should be made between primary facts and the conclusions arising from such facts. Primary facts are those which are observed by witnesses and proved by oral testimony, or facts proved by the production of a thing itself, such as a document. Their determination is essentially a question of fact and the only question of law that can arise on them is whether there was any evidence to support the finding. The conclusions from primary facts are, however, inferences deduced by a process of reasoning from them. Insofar as the correct conclusion to be drawn from primary facts requires, for its correctness, determination by a lawyer and not a layman, because, for instance, it involves the interpretation of documents, or because the law and facts cannot be separated, the conclusion is one of law on which the appellate court is competent to form an opinion in the same way as the first instance tribunal.[529]

459. It is therefore permissible to challenge the trial court's evaluation of the evidence before it, insofar as this relates to the construction of the legal principles. On the other hand, grounds of appeal which seek to challenge the findings of fact as such, which were made by the trial court, shall be rejected.[530] If the findings of the IDT are not arbitrary or inconsistent with the evidence presented, the Supreme Court may not interfere.[531] It has been held that the question whether the composition of the IDT was a proper one is a point of law.[532] Similarly, the question

526. *HjiCostas* [1984] 1 CLR 513, *Stylianides* v. *Paschalidou* [1985] 1 CLR 49. The above cases concerned cases stated under the Rent Control Tribunal, but were referred to with approval also with respect to the IDT. See e.g. *Alouet Clothing Manufacturers Ltd* v. *Athanasiou and another* [1988] 1 CLR 626.

527. *Christodoulou* v. *P.L. Cacoyiannis and Co and another* [2001] 1 CLR 188 (in Greek).

528. *Louis Tourist Agency Ltd* [1988] 1 CLR 454, *A.C.T. Textiles Ltd* v. *Zodhiatis* [1986] 1 CLR 89, *Kyriakides* [1992] 1 CLR 26 (in Greek), *Charalampous* [1998] 1 CLR 2290 (in Greek), *Loizou* v. *Stylson Engineering Co Ltd* [1998] 1 CLR 2077 (in Greek), *Stylson Engineering Co Ltd* [1997] 1 CLR 705 (in Greek).

529. *Aristeidou* [1997] 1 CLR 1264 (in Greek), *Kyros Manufacturing Ltd* v. *Kleovoulou* [1992] 1 CLR 936 (in Greek), *Louca* [1993] 1 CLR 216 (in Greek), *Alithia Ltd* [1992] 1 CLR 492 (in Greek), *British Launderer's Research Association* v. *Central Middlesex Assessment Committee* [1949] 1 All ER 21, *Argus Stockbrokers Ltd* v. *Hatzitheodosiou* [2009] 1 CLR 1514 (in Greek).

530. *Antenna Ltd* v. *Constantinou* [2010] 1 CLR 392 (in Greek), *Galatariotis Telecommunications Ltd* v. *Vasiliou* [2003] 1 CLR 318 (in Greek), *Panayiotis Kountourides Ltd* v. *Georgiou* [2003] 1 CLR 980 (in Greek), *Spinneys Cyprus Ltd* v. *Christou* [2004] 1 CLR 1833 (in Greek), *Eleftheriou* [1996] 1 CLR 490 (in Greek), *Famalift Shipyard Ltd* v. *Pavlides and others* [1991] 1 CLR 161 (in Greek), *Andreas Prokopiou Ltd* v. *Toumazou* [2001] 1 CLR 1125 (in Greek), *Michaelides* v. *Telegraphos Publishing Company Ltd* [1996] 1 CLR 1024 (in Greek), *CTC/ARI Airports Ltd* v. *Ioannidou*, Civ. Appeal 24/2011, judgment of 16 December 2015 (in Greek).

531. *Koilaras* v. *Pharmaceutical Organization of Cyprus Ltd* [2010] 1 CLR 869 (in Greek).

532. *Demades Auto Supplies Limassol Ltd* [1996] 1 CLR 1139 (in Greek), *Cyprus Workers' Confederation* [1996] 1 CLR 1030 (in Greek). In *Iracleous* it was held, erroneously in our view, that since there was conflicting evidence with regards to whether the President of the IDT had convened with

whether the trial court has properly accepted or rejected the admission of evidence,[533] or whether the trial court's judgment is sufficiently reasoned,[534] are points of law.

460. The question of whether the constitutional right of a party to have a fair trial, including the right to be heard, has been safeguarded, is a pure question of law, as it revolves round the application of the law to given facts.[535] However, if the question refers to whether the IDT has correctly exercised its discretion, the point is not a legal one, unless the allegation is that the IDT exceeded the limits of its discretion.[536] In *Kemal* the IDT held that the employment of the employee was not interrupted due to *force majeure*, but because of a decision of his employers which was unrelated to the *force majeure*. The Supreme Court held that the question concerned a matter of fact and could accordingly not be appealed.[537]

461. In *Agathocleous* the IDT held that the delay of the employer to exercise his right to dismiss the employee for one month from the date when his unjustified conduct took place was not reasonable under the circumstances and accordingly it was held that the employer waived his right to dismiss the employee without notice in accordance with section 5 of the Law; the employer appealed. The Supreme Court held that the ground of appeal did not concern a point of law, but rather a point of fact and dismissed the appeal.[538] It is submitted that the finding of the Supreme Court is not convincing; the finding of fact that the employer had not exercised his right to dismiss the employee for one month was undisputed; the question whether the delay was unreasonable concerned an interpretation of section 5 of the Law and whether the inferences and conclusions drawn by the trial court on the basis of the facts were proper, was clearly, in our view, a legal one.

462. As a general rule the discretion of the trial court to determine the amount of compensation to the employee is absolute and accordingly it is not subject to appeal,[539] unless the trial court erred in the principles and considerations which should have been taken into account when awarding compensation.[540] In *Theodorides* the Redundancy Fund intended to appeal against the finding of the IDT that the termination of employment of the employee was unlawful; the Supreme Court held that the appeal raised no legal point, as the employer had accepted before the court

---

the two lay members of the court (one member stated that he had, whereas the other stated that he had not), the question was not a pure point of law.

533. *Eliades* [1994] 1 CLR 184.
534. *Metaxa* [1997] 1 CLR 257 (in Greek).
535. *Kosmos Press Ltd* [1993] 1 CLR 925 (in Greek).
536. *Mintchev* v. *Georgiou* [2000] 1 CLR 469 (in Greek), *Bank of Cyprus* [1999] 1 CLR 1010 (in Greek).
537. *Kemal* v. *Redundancy Fund* [2004] 1 CLR 237 (in Greek).
538. *L' Union Nationale (Tourism and Sea Resorts) Ltd* v. *Agathocleous*, citing with approval *Edwards (Inspection of Taxes)* v. *Bairstow and another* [1955] All ER 48 (HL).
539. *Dias Publishing House Ltd* v. *Papachristodoulou* [2006] 1 CLR 625 (in Greek), *Demades Auto Supplies Limassol Ltd* v. *Ioannidou* [1996] 1 CLR 228 (in Greek).
540. *JA Cabras & Bros Ltd* v. *Charalampous* [1992] 1 CLR 302 (in Greek).

that the termination was unlawful and accordingly there was no legal provision to be further interpreted by the trial court.[541]

463. The fact that a party may not challenge the findings of fact of the trial court with an appeal does not imply that a person may challenge such findings before the Supreme Court with the prerogative order of *certiorari.*[542] A *certiorari* is an order by the Supreme Court which may review a judgment, order or decision of a lower court in cases where there is manifest illegality, or mistaken application of the Constitution or of a Law, or excess of jurisdiction, or where the impugned order was issued due to collusion between the parties or misleading the Court; unless such manifest illegality or excess of jurisdiction is proven, leave for *certiorari* shall not be granted.[543]

464. The grounds of appeal should be phrased in such a manner so as to show that they refer to a pure matter of law and not to a matter of fact; overtly generalized or vague grounds may be rejected, if it is impossible for the Court to determine their true nature and aims.[544] In any event, however, the consideration by the Supreme Court of the logical implications of a point of law is always possible, if it is considered as essential to resolve the dispute at hand.[545] In *Pattikis* the Supreme Court held that not only were the questions of law not clearly formulated, but the IDT had not established any facts, but rather restricted itself to a narration of the evidence. The Supreme Court, however, may not adjudicate on a question of law, unless all the factual circumstances have been resolved by the trial court; otherwise, it would be usurping the functions of the trial court. It was therefore essential for the trial court to resolve the factual questions for the legal questions to be decided on appeal.[546]

465. In *Colocassides* the applicants sought to be declared as a stricken business in the sense of the Termination of Employment (Temporary Restrictive Provisions) Law (50/74), but their application was rejected by the Minister of Labour and Social Insurance; the IDT upheld the decision of the Minister. When the applicants sought to appeal by way of case stated, the President of the IDT refused to state a case on appeal because section 4(a) of Law 50/74 provided that the decision of the Industrial Disputes Court shall be final, a provision which, according to him, excluded the right to an appeal before the Supreme Court. The Supreme Court issued the prerogative order of mandamus ordering the President of the IDT to state a case; it was

541. *Redundancy Fund* v. *Theodorides and another* [1997] 1 CLR 1005 (in Greek).
542. For prerogative orders see P. Artemis, *Prerogative Orders* (Larnaca, 2004, in Greek), C. Clerides, 'Prerogative Orders' *Cyprus Law Tribune* 3 [1994]: 297–312 (in Greek), L. Clerides, 'Prerogative Writs' *Cyprus Law Review* 14 (1986): 2195–2208 (in Greek), C. Tornaritis, 'The Prerogative Orders under the Constitution and the Law of the Republic of Cyprus' in T. Papadopoulos and G. Ioannides, *Proceedings of the Second International Cyprological Conference* (Nicosia: Society for Cypriot Studies, 1987): 641–650.
543. *Hadjiantoni* [1992] 1 CLR 484 (in Greek).
544. *Eleftheriou* [1996] 1 CLR 490 (in Greek).
545. *Kyriakou and others* v. *Redundancy Fund* [1991] 1 CLR 320 (in Greek).
546. *Pattikis* v. *The Municipal Committee of Nicosia* [1984] 1 CLR 802.

held that when a statute states that a decision of an inferior tribunal shall be final, this is on the assumption that the tribunal has observed the law and accordingly if the tribunal has erred in law, the Supreme Court will interfere. Thus, the finality clause did not preclude an appeal before the Supreme Court.[547]

II. Courts with Special Jurisdiction over Labour Matters: The IDT

A. *Jurisdiction*

466. The IDT was initially referred to as 'Arbitration Tribunal' under section 12 of the Annual Leave with Pay Law (8/1967). However, in *Keramourgia Aias* the Supreme Court held that the involvement of the executive in the appointment and specification of the terms of service of the Chairman of the Arbitration Tribunal, which is a judicial organ, offended against the principle of the separation of powers between the executive and the judiciary; as a result, it was held that the Arbitration Tribunal was set up in an unconstitutional manner and could not validly exercise any jurisdiction vested by virtue of section 30 of Law 25/67.[548] Section 2 of Law 5/1973 abolished the term 'Arbitration Tribunal' and introduced the IDT.

467. The IDT has exclusive jurisdiction to adjudicate on private industrial disputes arising by virtue of labour law legislation, such as Law 8/67 on annual leave, (24/67) on termination of employment, Law 63(I)/02 on organization of working time, Law 100(I)/97 on protection of maternity, Law 47(I)/12 on parental leave, Law 76(I)/02 on part-time employment, Law 98(I)/03 on fixed-term employees, Law 35(I)/07 on protection of wages, Law 177(I)/02 on equal pay between men and women, Law 205(I)/02 on equal treatment of men and women, Law 55(I)/12 on the recognition of trade unions, Law 104(I)/00 on transfer of enterprises, Law 100(I)/00 on written information on the terms of employment, Law 78(I)/05 on information and consultation of employees, Law 137(I)/02 on posting of workers, Law 208(I)/12 on professional pension funds,[549] Law 155(I)/06 concerning terms of employment of shop employees.

468. Except in cases of claims for damages for wrongful dismissal exceeding two years emoluments (for which the District Court has jurisdiction), the IDT has, by virtue of section 30 of Law 24/67, exclusive jurisdiction to decide on all industrial disputes arising out of the operation of Law 24/67, including any incidental or ancillary to such dispute matter, such as a dispute over the calculation of the sum to be paid to the employee under a collective agreement.[550] The IDT therefore has

547. *S & G Colocassides Co Ltd* v. *President of the Industrial Disputes Court* [1977] 1 CLR 59.
548. *Keramourgia Aias Ltd* v. *Christoforou* [1975] 1 CLR 38.
549. Law 208(I)/2012 on the Establishment, Register, Operation and Supervision of Funds for Occupational Retirement Provision and other provisions, implementing Directive 2003/41/EC of the European Parliament and of the Council of 3 June 2003 on the activities and supervision of institutions for occupational retirement provision.
550. *Stavrou* v. *Mobil LP Gas Cyprus Ltd* [1977] 1 CLR 120.

jurisdiction with regard to contracts of employment of both definite and indefinite duration,[551] as well as part-time work contracts.

469. By virtue of section 12 §1(c) of Law 8/67, the IDT shall have jurisdiction to adjudicate any labour dispute which is referred to it by the Minister of Labour, Welfare and Social Insurance an either on the consent of the parties, or in accordance with the terms of an existing collective agreement or of an arrangement which provides for the settlement of labour disputes through arbitration. It has been held that the IDT shall not have jurisdiction to adjudicate a dispute if this has been referred by one of the public servants of the Ministry of Labour, Welfare and Social Insurance and not by the Minister himself;[552] it is noted, however, that in the above case there was no evidence that the Minister had authorized the said employee to refer the dispute on his behalf, so it is not clear whether the same outcome would have been reached if there was evidence of such authorization.

B. Composition

470. The composition of the IDT is provided for in section 12 of Law 8/67. The IDT is presided over by a professional judge who is either a President, or a judge, and is a permanent member of the judicial service of the Republic, albeit not interchangeable with district court judges; they are specialized judges who serve only on the IDT. Both a President and a judge should be advocates of a high moral and professional character and are appointed by the Supreme Court; a President must have exercised advocacy for at least five years prior to appointment, whereas a judge should have exercised advocacy for at least three years. The remaining two members represent the employers and employees respectively and act as associated judges; these two members are appointed by the Supreme Court for a term of two years from a list submitted by the Minister of Justice. During their term, the associate judges are subject to the disciplinary control of the Supreme Court, similarly to permanent judges and may not appear as advocates in other cases pending before the IDT during their term.

471. In *Aspromalli* one of the associate judges of the IDT had been appointed for a period of two years; whereas the case at issue was not concluded within the two year term, he remained on the IDT until a judgment was issued. The Supreme Court noted that the fact that a member of the tribunal may not participate until the conclusion of a case, is problematic for the smooth administration of justice; however, section 12 §8 of the Law clearly specifies that the term of a member is for two years, unless the member is re-appointed prior to the end of his term. Since the term of the specific member had expired, he was no longer an associate judge and accordingly his participation in the composition of the IDT invalidated the first instance judgment. The Supreme Court suggested to the legislator that the law should be amended so as to enable a member to remain associate judge until the conclusion of

551. *Panayiotou* v. *DS Artokoulouropoieion Ltd* [2002] 1 CLR 1381 (in Greek).
552. *Louis Hotels Ltd* v. *Oyxev-Sek and Syxka-Peo* [2003] 1 CLR 1862 (in Greek).

a trial, irrespective of whether his term has expired.[553] Law 26(I)/97 amended section 12(8)(a) accordingly by adding a proviso to the effect that a member whose term has ended may lawfully continue to participate in the composition of the IDT for the adjudication of a pending dispute.

472. Rule 10 §1 of the Industrial Disputes Tribunal Procedural Rules of 1999 provides that in case of disagreement, the judgment of the IDT shall be taken by majority and shall be publicly pronounced by the judge who chaired the section of the IDT which adjudicated the dispute; any dissenting judgment should also be publicly pronounced. There is no requirement for the lay members of the IDT to sign the judgment; it is signed by the professional judge only;[554] what is important is that there is confirmation in the body of the judgment, either directly or indirectly, that the judgment also expresses the opinion of the lay judges.[555] With respect, however, to any points of law, the judgment of the professional judge who chairs the IDT is binding for the lay members of the IDT (section 12(2)(c) of Law 8/67). Grammatical or other inadvertent errors in judgments of orders may be corrected at any time by the court following an application by the interested party.

473. In *Aristeidou* the Appellant brought forward as evidence a written statement prepared by one of the laymen who acted as an associate judge of the IDT; the said associate judge claimed that he disagreed with the opinion, which was signed by the President of the IDT, as his understanding was that, since redundancy had not been proved, the termination of employment was unlawful. The first instance judgment rejected both the claim for redundancy and the claim for termination of employment. The Supreme Court considered that the laymen who act as associate judges have the right and duty to express their opinion, or disagreement, during deliberations with the President prior to the issue of a judgment; if they insist on such disagreement, this must be specified in the judgment. However, any disagreement which is expressed *a posteriori* is impermissible and shall not be taken into account.[556]

474. Rule 8 of the 1999 Rules provides that the President of the IDT may issue general directions to provide for the allocation of the cases to sections of the IDT and for the appointment of the members of each section, in a manner that safeguards impartiality. In *Cyprus Airways* the Supreme Court noted that prima facie the power of the President to appoint the members of the section by general directions was inconsistent with section 12 §2(b) which provides that the President should appoint the members for each case; it was thus arguable that the Regulation was *ultra vires* to section 12 §2(b). However, it was held that there was no need to reach a final decision on the issue, since in any event there was no proof that the President had appointed the members of the section of the IDT; accordingly, the Supreme

553. *Aspromalli* v. *Cyprus Workers Confederation* [1996] 1 CLR 1392 (in Greek).
554. *King's Head Development Co Ltd* v. *Christodoulou and another* [2001] 1 CLR 533 (in Greek).
555. *Salamis Tours Ltd* v. *Polykarpou* [2010] 1 CLR 1091 (in Greek).
556. *Aristidou* v. *RK Super Beton Ltd and another* [1999] 1 CLR 114 (in Greek).

Court granted *certiorari* which set aside the judgment of the IDT on the grounds that the composition of the IDT was defective.[557]

475. The case was remitted to another section of the IDT. During the hearing, the President of the IDT expressed her sorrow for the grounds upon which the *certiorari* was issued; the advocate for the employer, who had applied for the *certiorari*, requested her exemption from the trial. The President of the IDT held that since she was not the judge whose judgment was set aside by the *certiorari*, there was no grounds for her exemption from the case; her comment that she felt sorrow did not imply that she could not hear the case impartially. It was further commented that there were no other judges left to try the case. The employer applied once again for *certiorari*.

476. The Supreme Court noted that the criterion for exemption of a judge from a case is whether a well-informed and fair observer might consider that the judge might be biased; suspicions or assumptions are not sufficient.[558] In the circumstances, it was held that an objective observer might consider that there was a possibility of bias and ordered for the President of the IDT to be exempted from the case.[559] In the case of the *Cyprus Oil Distillery* the employer applied for *certiorari* alleging that the President of the IDT should be exempted from the case, because the employee had served as a lay member of the IDT in four cases which the same President chaired. The Supreme Court held that the participation of the President of the IDT in the adjudication of the case would lead an objective observer to conclude that there was a possibility of bias; it was ordered that the President of the IDT should be exempted from the case.[560]

C. Procedure

477. By virtue of Rule 3 of the Industrial Dispute Tribunal Procedural Rules 1/1999, the procedure commences by the filing of an application by the applicant-employee with the Registrar; the application should be in accordance with Form I and set out the grounds on which the application is based. It has been held that it is proper for the application to be signed by the advocate of the employee and there is no need for it to be signed by the employee himself;[561] the application must be accompanied by a retainer appointing the advocate. It has been held that the Legal Aid Law (165(I)/2002) does not include in its scope appeals against judgments of the IDT.[562] Rule 5 of the 1999 Rules provides that, if the respondent wishes to object to the claim or to part of the claim, he should submit an appearance before

557. *Cyprus Airways Public Company Ltd* [2010] 1 CLR 609 (in Greek).
558. *Cyprus Oil Distillery* [2004] 1 CLR 1676 (in Greek), *Typye* v. *Police* [2008] 2 CLR 279 (in Greek), *Pal* v. *Republic* [2010] 2 CLR 551 (in Greek) citing with approval *Hellow* v. *Secretary of State and another* [2008] UKHL 62.
559. *Cyprus Airways Public Company Ltd* [2010] 1 CLR 2025 (in Greek).
560. *Cyprus Oil Distillery* [2004] 1 CLR 1676 (in Greek).
561. *Fotos Fotiades Breweries Ltd* v. *Antoniades and another* [2002] 1 CLR 1490 (in Greek).
562. *Constantinou* v. *Republic* [2006] 1 CLR 927 (in Greek).

the Registrar in accordance with Form 3; the appearance should provide in detail the grounds on which the claim is disputed.[563]

478. Rule 6 of the 1999 Regulations provides that the IDT may, following an application by any of the parties or on its own accord, instruct any person (including any of the parties) to appear as a witness, or to demand the admission of any document related to the issue at hand, or to appoint an expert witness and instruct him to carry out all relevant action in order to provide an expert opinion, or issue any other directions it deems necessary. A witness not appearing before the IDT is subject to arrest. In *Agathocleous* the IDT called *ex proprio motu* a witness to give testimony. The Appellant argued that the court should not have called the witness at a stage when the parties had submitted all their evidence and called all their witnesses and were about to proceed to oral arguments. The Supreme Court disagreed. It was held that there was nothing arbitrary about the decision of the first instance court; it would rather have been paradoxical if the IDT had exercised its discretion to call a witness on its own accord before having the opportunity to hear the totality of the evidence and ascertaining whether this person would have been called by the parties themselves as a witness.

479. It was accordingly held that, contrary to other civil proceedings, the IDT has the discretion to instruct *ex proprio motu* any person to attend as a witness, without the consent of the parties and even if the parties expressly disagree. It was held, however, that once the IDT calls a witness, it has to allow the parties to cross-examine such witness; the only case when the court might not allow the parties to cross-examine would be if, despite the expectations of the court, the witness did not testify anything which is relevant to the issues at hand, in which case the court will treat the witness as if he had never been called. In all other cases, the parties should have a right to cross-examine; a different approach would violate the rights of the parties to examine and cross-examine witnesses, as safeguarded by Article 30 §3 of the Constitution. The refusal of the trial court to allow the cross-examination of the witness it had called on its own motion amounted to a material breach of procedural rules and led to a mistrial; the first instance judgment was annulled and it was ordered that the case should be re-tried by a different judge of the IDT.[564]

480. Rule 9 §4 of the Procedure Regulation of 1999 provides that, if the applicant fails to appear on the date of the hearing, the IDT may dismiss the case, and if the respondent fails to appear, the IDT may hear the case in his absence; in both cases, the IDT may postpone it to a future date if it considers that this would be in the interest of justice. In *Mitschev* the advocate for the employee requested a postponement of the hearing, because the employee was no longer residing in Cyprus and time was needed in order to arrange for him to travel to Cyprus in order to testify; the IDT dismissed the application for want of prosecution. The Supreme Court held that Rule 9 §4 was inapplicable, since the employee was present through his

563. *Menelaou* v. *Askanis Ltd* [2011] 1 CLR 312 (in Greek).
564. *Agathocleous* v. *Christodoulou* [1992] 1 CLR 176 (in Greek).

advocate and had requested for a postponement; the IDT had to consider the request for postponement and, if this was rejected, the advocate of the employee should have been given an opportunity to be heard before further decisions were taken.[565]

481. A trial before the IDT is governed by the inquisitorial and not the adversarial system as is the case with other civil disputes; thus, the IDT has wider powers to investigate the facts of the dispute. However, this does not change the rule that the issues under examination and the parameters of the trial are set out in the pleadings of the parties;[566] the IDT should always restrict itself to the disputes issued as these arise from the pleadings and not extend to other issues, or take decisions contrary to the admissions of the parties. If the IDT violates the above rule, its judgment may be reversed on appeal.[567] It has further been held that, although a judge may intervene in order to ensure that the proceedings follow the course ordained by the rules of evidence and procedure, he must avoid interfering beyond those limits and refrain from expressing unnecessary comments that might create the impression of bias and question his impartiality; a judge should accordingly maintain strictly his arbitral position and distance himself from the dispute.[568]

482. Whereas the powers of the judge in an inquisitorial system are wider, this does not imply that they are unlimited, or that they might include pressing examination and cross-examination and especially on issues which are not disputed. In *Athanasiou* it was held that the judge, having asked 156 questions to the Appellant in the form of cross-examination and many of them on issues which were not at stake, had abused his role.[569] Similarly, in *Epifaniou*[570] and *Gooda*[571] it was held that the President of the IDT had interfered with the examination and cross-examination of witnesses to such an extent and he had asked so many questions, that the principles of fair trial had been violated; in *Epifaniou* the President of the IDT had asked 355 questions, whereas in *Gooda* over 250 questions, many times aggressively.

483. In any procedure before the IDT it is presumed that the termination of employment was unlawful, until the opposite is proven (section 6 §1 of Law 24/67). Accordingly, the employee has the burden to prove that his employment has been

565. *Mintchev* v. *Georgiou* [2001] 1 CLR 361 (in Greek). For the principles governing postponement of the hearing see *DEOK* v. *Soteriades* [2001] 1 CLR 1829 (in Greek), *Hatziantoni* [1992] 1 CLR 484 (in Greek), *King's Head Development Co Ltd* v. *Christodoulouand another* [2001] 1 CLR 533 (in Greek). *Antoniou and others* v. *Rosabella Fashion Ltd* [2000] 1 CLR 150 (in Greek).

566. *Kouloumpri* [1992] 1 CLR 836 (in Greek), *Papageorgiou* v. *Loui Clappa Investment Services Ltd* [1991] 1 CLR 24 (in Greek), *Courtis and others* v. *Iasonides* [1970] 1 CLR 180, *Loucaides* v. *CD Hay and Sons Ltd* [1971] 1 CLR 134, *Republic* v. *Koukouri and others* [1993] 1 CLR 598 (in Greek).

567. *Athanasiou* v. *Reana Manufacturing & Trading Co Ltd and another* [2001] 1 CLR 1635 (in Greek).

568. *Evangelou and another* v. *Ambizas and another* [1982] 1 CLR 41.

569. *Athanasiou* v. *Reana Manufacturing & Trading Co Ltd and another* [2001] 1 CLR 1635 (in Greek).

570. *Fanos Epifaniou Ltd* v. *Melarta and others* [2002] 1 CLR 654 (in Greek).

571. *Panayiotis Kountourides Ltd* v. *Gooda* [2006] 1 CLR 1251 (in Greek).

terminated, whereas the employer has the burden to prove that the termination of employment was lawful.[572] The party who bears the burden of proof begins his case first. Therefore, the employee should be the first to present evidence, since he has to prove that his employment was terminated; however, if the employer has admitted that the employment was terminated, he shall present evidence first, as he shall have the burden of proof.[573] If the IDT has failed to properly identify the party who bears the burden of proof, its decision might be set aside on appeal.[574]

484. The IDT proceeds to the determination of a case in all reasonable speed, without being bound by any evidence rules[575] and to issue a reasoned opinion (section 12 §11 of Law 8/1967); the hearing takes place in a public trial. Rule 3(a) of the Procedural Rules for the Timely Issue of Judgments of 1986, as amended, provides that any judgment should be issued as soon as possible following the end of the procedure and should not be reserved for more than six months;[576] whether a judgment issued more than six months after it was reserved should be set aside on appeal, shall be determined on the basis of all the circumstances of the case, its character and complexity, as well as the conduct of the parties.[577] In *Kountourides* the judgment had been issued 15 months after it had originally been reserved; the Supreme Court held, after considering all the circumstances of the case, that the delay had not affected the final verdict of the court.[578]

485. By virtue of Rule 11 of the 1999 Rules, the IDT may, by exercising its discretion, issue any order which is necessary for the purposes of the case at hand. Furthermore, the IDT may, subject to the remaining provisions of the rules, determine its own procedure. Any interim petitions shall be served to the other party, unless there are exceptional circumstances which justify that they be dealt with ex parte; in such a case, the interim order shall be served to the other party who may appear before the IDT within seven days in order to request that the interim order be set aside. Any interim petition should be written in accordance with Form VI; however, it may also be oral if the IDT exceptionally considers that this is justified due to the circumstances (Rule 12 of the 1999 Rules). In *Eurofresh* the Supreme Court held that any interim petitions should be considered by the full IDT and not simply by the President of the IDT; accordingly, the President of the IDT does not have the jurisdiction to decide in the absence of the two lay members of the IDT.[579]

486. Regulation 14 of the Procedural Regulation provides that any notification or communication by the IDT should be in writing and should be either served or

572. *Louis Tourist Agency Ltd* [1990] 1 CLR 315 (in Greek), *Pitsillides* v. *National Bank of Greece (Cyprus) Ltd*, Civ. Appeal 199/09, dated 3 July 2012 (in Greek), *Skyrianides Hotels Ltd* v. *Polyviou and another* [2003] 1 CLR 820 (in Greek).
573. *Louis Tourist Agency Ltd* [1990] 1 CLR 315 (in Greek).
574. *Pavlou* v. *Josant Enterprises Hotel Ltd* [2006] 1 CLR 161 (in Greek).
575. *Panayiotis Kountourides Ltd* v. *Awadalla and others* [2008] 1 CLR 852 (in Greek).
576. *Victoros* v. *Christodoulou* [1992] 1 CLR 512 (in Greek).
577. *Pouyiouka and others* v. *Thrasyvoulou* [1998] 1 CLR 2014 (in Greek).
578. *Panayiotis Kountourides Ltd* v. *Awadalla and others* [2008] 1 CLR 852 (in Greek).
579. *Eurofresh Fruit & Vegetables Ltd* [2002] 1 CLR 682 (in Greek).

sent by double registered mail or delivered to the parties or their advocates. In *G&K Exclusive Fashions* it was held that the advocate of the employee had not been properly notified for the subsequent date of the hearing and thus the rights of the applicant, as safeguarded by Article 30 of the Constitution and the rules of natural justice, has been violated; there is an obligation to notify the parties not only of the first, but of every subsequent hearing date.[580]

487. The IDT has to keep detailed and accurate minutes of the procedure, which might enable the Supreme Court to exercise its powers of judicial review;[581] in this respect the IDT has to clearly record its findings of fact.[582] The obligation to issue a reasoned opinion derives from Article 30 §2 of the Constitution for all judicial organs; the fact that the IDT is not bound by rules of evidence, adopts speedy procedures and its decisions are not subject to appeal with respect to the determination of the facts, does not diminish the obligation of the IDT to provide a reasoned opinion. Reasoning is required not only for appeal purposes, but also because the parties and the public at large have an autonomous right to know the grounds on the basis of which the IDT reached a specific decision.[583]

488. A judgment delivered without a sufficiently reasoned opinion shall be set aside on appeal.[584] The extent of the analysis and evaluation required depends on the circumstances of the case and the issue at hand. In *Argyrides* the Supreme Court reversed the first instance judgment, noting that it was not reasoned; whereas, there were conflicting testimonies and evidence presented before the IDT, it did not analyse and justify its findings, or explain how it evaluated the evidence before it in order to reach its decision. Accordingly, it could not be determined whether the findings of the IDT were correct, since a reasoned opinion had not been issued.[585] In *Kyriakides* the Supreme Court held that the first instance District Court judge had failed to evaluate the evidence before it and explain adequately why it had accepted the evidence of the witnesses for the applicant and not the evidence of the witnesses for the company. The Supreme Court ordered a re-hearing of the case by a different judge.[586]

489. It should be noted that section 30 §3 of Law 24/67 used to provide that the President of the IDT has jurisdiction in his absolute discretion to retry any case or review any judgment on any payment made by the Fund at any time, if the President considers this fair and just. In *Filippou* the IDT had given judgment in favour

---

580. *G & K Exclusive Fashions Ltd* [1993] 1 CLR 979 (in Greek).
581. *Agathocleous* v. *Christodoulou* [1992] 1 CLR 176 (in Greek).
582. *Glykis* v. *Municipal Committee of Nicosia* [1985] 1 CLR 206.
583. *Loutsi* v. *Kemtaxi Ltd* [1995] 1 CLR 704 (in Greek), *Argyrides* v. *Fetokaki* [2001] 1 CLR 328 (in Greek), *JA Cabras & Bros Ltd* v. *Charalampous* [1992] 1 CLR 302 (in Greek), *Christou* v. *Fairways Larnaca Ltd* [2005] 1 CLR 300 (in Greek).
584. *Colocassides Co Ltd* v. *Kimoni* [1989] 1CLR 132 (in Greek), *Drousiotis* v. *Ieronymides* [1990] 1 CLR 1026, *Vasiliou and others* v. *Menelaou and another* [1990] 1 CLR 1125 (in Greek), *Aristidou* v. *Loizides* [1991] 1 CLR 297 (in Greek).
585. *Argyrides* v. *Fetokaki* [2001] 1 CLR 328 (in Greek).
586. *Hellenic Bank Ltd* v. *Kyriakides*, Civil Appeal 209/2010, dated 9 September 2015 (in Greek).

of the employee. However, at a subsequent stage, following an *ex parte* application by the employer, the President of the IDT, who was not the judge presiding over the specific case, ordered that the judgment should be set aside and that the case should be retried. The Supreme Court held that when section 30 §3 of Law 24/67 refers to the President of the IDT, it means the presiding judge of the section trying the specific case, irrespective of whether he has the rank of a President or a judge; a different judge unrelated to the specific section which has tried the case, even if he has the rank of President of the IDT, may not exercise the powers granted under section 30 §3 of Law 24/67. Accordingly, the President of the IDT had exceeded his authority. Moreover, the fact that the decision to set aside the judgment and retry the case had been taken without first informing the employee and giving him the opportunity to be heard, amounted to a violation of the rules of natural justice.[587] Section 30 §3 of Law 24/67 was eventually abolished by Law 159(I)/2002.

D. *Statute of Limitations*

490. Any application before the IDT has to be filed within a period of 12 months from the date when the alleged rights of the claimant arose (section 12 (10A) of Law 8/67). In *Pantelidou* v. *Bank of Cyprus* the applicant alleged that its employer had not revealed to her the true facts regarding her rights following retirement and that her employers and the employers' provident fund had conspired in order to maliciously deprive her of her rights. It was undisputed that the application before the IDT was filed more than seven years after her retirement which was the date when her alleged rights arose. The IDT considered, however, with an interim decision, that the allegations of the employee that the employer had committed fraud and deception might potentially extent the prescription period on the basis of the common law doctrine of equity;[588] the jurisdictional question was left open to be determined at the hearing of the dispute, once all the facts had been determined.

491. The employer filed an application for grant of leave of *certiorari*, which, however, was rejected by a single judge of the Supreme Court sitting at first instance; it was held that the right to appeal was available for the employer and there were no exceptional circumstances justifying the determination of the jurisdictional question by means of *certiorari*. Moreover, the application for *certiorari* was premature as the IDT had not yet finally considered the jurisdictional issue, but only postponed its decision for a later stage.[589] The employer appealed against the decision not to grant leave for *certiorari*. A five-member bench of the Supreme Court, acting as an appellate court, unanimously reversed the first instance judgment and held that the fact that there are alternative means of redress available does not by

587. *Filippou* [1993] 1 CLR 857 (in Greek).
588. L. Loucaides, 'The Dependence of Cypriot Law from Common Law', *Subjects of Cypriot Law*, (Nicosia, 1982, in Greek): 36–77, G. Pikis, T*he English Common Law: The Rules of Equity and their Application in Cyprus* (Larnaca, 1981, in Greek).
589. *Bank of Cyprus and another* [2008] 1 CLR 1352 (in Greek).

itself imply that leave for *certiorari* cannot be granted, if exceptional circumstances are proven.

492. It was held that since the employee had retired and had signed a written contract which discharged the employer's provident fund from any obligations and in consideration collected the agreed sum, the employment relationship between the parties had ended and the only existing relationship was a contractual one. The IDT does not have, however, jurisdiction to adjudicate contractual relations, but only employment relations and accordingly had no jurisdiction; the leave for *certiorari* was granted.[590] It should be noted that there are two stages in an application for *certiorari*; during the first stage the applicant appears *ex parte* and it is determined whether leave should be granted, whereas during the second stage, once leave has been granted, all parties appear and a final decision is made. Following the decision of the five member appellate bench to grant leave, an application for *certiorari* was filed and was adjudicated by the single judge of the Supreme Court sitting at first instance whose decision had been reversed by the appellate court; he determined that he was bound by the findings of the appellate court and granted the *certiorari*.[591]

493. This time it was the employee who appealed; his appeal was heard by the Full Bench of the Supreme Court, which surprisingly included also the judge whose judgment was under appeal. The Full Bench, which included the five members of the appellate court,[592] unanimously held that the five member bench of the appellate court had exceeded their jurisdiction as they had determined the substance of the dispute at the stage where they should have simply decided whether to grant leave for *certiorari* or not; since the application to grant leave is heard *ex parte*, the determination of the substance of the dispute without hearing the employee amounted to a violation of the principles of natural justice; the Full Bench thus set aside both the decision of the five member appellate court to grant leave for *certiorari* and the decision of the single judge to grant *certiorari* and ordered a re-hearing of the appeal against the decision not to grant leave for *certiorari*.[593]

494. A new five-member bench of the Supreme Court subsequently decided by majority[594] to affirm the first instance judgment not to grant leave for *certiorari* on the grounds that there were no exceptional circumstances and that the application was premature, since the IDT had not yet reached a definite conclusion on the issue

590. *Bank of Cyprus and another* [2009] 1 CLR 1114 (in Greek).
591. *Bank of Cyprus and another* [2009] 1 CLR 1642 (in Greek).
592. With the exception of one of them who surprisingly recused himself due to potential conflict of interest, although if such possibility for conflict of interest existed he should have recused himself also during the hearing of the first appeal against the decision not to grant a *certiorari*.
593. *Bank of Cyprus and another* [2011] 1 CLR 1506 (in Greek).
594. Even more astonishingly one of the members of the original appellate court's composition was the author of the new appellate court's decision, which essentially reversed the original decision which he had co-signed.

of its jurisdiction.[595] The *Pantelidou* v. *Bank of Cyprus* cases are a solid example of the peculiarities of the Cypriot legal system and the difficulties and inconsistencies associated with the construction of legal provisions. The outcome is hardly satisfactory as the legal question that gave rise to the dispute, namely whether the doctrine of equity could potentially extend the prescription periods prescribed in Law 8/67, remains unresolved; it should be mentioned that even the judgment of the original five member bench of the Supreme Court did not determine this question, but rather considered that the dispute had become a contractual one due to the conclusion of a contract between the former employee and the employer's provident fund, a finding which in any event seems correct.

495. With respect to the original question, it is submitted that once the legislator has clearly established a prescription period, it is not possible to extend that period by reference to the common law doctrine of equity, as the doctrine may not apply in such a manner so as to contravene existing legislation. Section 29 §1(c) of the Courts of Justice Law (14/60) provides that the principles of equity may apply in Cyprus only to the extent that there is no contrary provision in any law,[596] such as is the case with section 12 (10A) of Law 8/67. A more difficult question is whether the 12-month limitation period begins from the time the employee has left his employer, or from the time the employer refuses to pay him the compensation due, especially where the employer previously represented to the employee that he would proceed to the payment; it is suggested that in the latter circumstances, the doctrine of promissory estoppel might apply and the limitation period ought properly commence from the time when the employer explicitly refused to pay the compensation due to the employee.

496. In *Georgiou* the IDT had concluded that the limitation period for a substantial part of the claims had expired; More than 12 months had elapsed from the time when such rights had arisen and the collective agreements governing the employment relationship provided that the benefits of the employees could not be accumulated and claimed after the end of the employment relationship. The employee appealed before the Supreme Court alleging that section 12(10) of Law 8/67, providing that the application should be filed within a period of 12 months from the date when the right arose, does not apply with respect to claims which were accrued before the termination of the employment relationship; the limitation period should begin from the date when the employment relationship was terminated. The Supreme Court affirmed the IDT's assessment and held that the terms of the collective agreement did not allow for the accumulation of benefits and that accordingly, the employee should have claimed such accrued benefits before the end of the year when they arose.[597]

595. *Bank of Cyprus and another*, Civil App. 2/2009, dated 14 May 2012 (in Greek).
596. See also A. Emilianides, *Family and Succession Law in Cyprus* (Kluwer, 2012): 151ff.
597. *Georgiou* v. *Ironhold Estates Ltd* [2007] 1 CLR 1051 (in Greek).

§3. ARBITRATION

497. The IRC provides that, where both parties so agree, they may refer all or any of the issues of a dispute over interests to arbitration instead of mediation, at any point in time either before or after the submission of the dispute to the Ministry. By doing so, they both accept that the decision of the arbitration shall be binding for the parties. A dispute about grievances may be referred to arbitration, instead of mediation, if the parties so wish; if a dispute over grievances has been submitted for mediation, and no settlement of the dispute by mediation has been achieved, the dispute is submitted to binding arbitration.

498. If a dispute is submitted to arbitration, the Ministry ensures that a mutually accepted arbitrator is appointed within a week of receiving a request to this effect by either side and assists him to carry out his task speedily by providing such facilities as may be requested by him e.g. a conference room, clerical staff and necessary information. The Ministry further ensures that the arbitrator's award is issued within 15 days of the last arbitration session; however, in cases concerning dismissals, the award should be issued within three days of the last session. The machinery of the arbitration is the same as the one provided for collective grievances.[598] The parties may further submit a dispute to arbitration under the Arbitration Law, Cap. 4, provided that they have both signed a valid arbitration agreement.[599]

598. See Part II, Ch. 6 below.

599. For Cap. 4 see A. Georghiades, 'The Institution of Arbitration in Cyprus' [2010] 2 *Cyprus Law Tribune*: 21–38 (in Greek).

Part II. Collective Labour Relations

Chapter 1. Trade Union Freedom

§1. Freedom to Establish and Join Unions

I. Positive Freedom

499. Article 21 of the Constitution corresponds to Article 11 of the ECHR, and safeguards the right of every person to freedom of peaceful assembly and association. The right to freedom of association with others specifically includes the right to form and to join trade unions for the protection of one's interests.[600] This right entails a positive obligation that multiple trade unions could be formed where the employees would so wish (*pluralisme syndical*) and accordingly the imposition of a single mandatory trade union is prohibited.[601] It applies both against the state and third parties.[602] In the IRC both the employer and employee organizations have recognized the right of employers and employees to organise freely and to belong to organizations of their own choice without any interference or victimization from either side.

500. The Supreme Court has held that the constitutional protection of a right to form and to join a trade union properly entails the safeguarding of the generally recognized activities of trade unionism, including the right to be heard[603] and the right of negotiation and conclusion of collective agreements as a means of achieving the aims of the trade union. Collective bargaining by trade unions should thus be considered as an integral part of the right to form a trade union, as in the absence of

600. A. Emilianides, 'The Freedom of the Worker to Organize in Cyprus', in *Die Koalitionsfreiheit des Arbeitnehmers/The Freedom of the Worker to Organize*, Berlin, New York, 1980: 1057–1069, L. Loucaides, 'Legal Protection of the Freedom of Trade Unionism in Cyprus' (1986) 15 Cyprus Law Review: 2346–2359, A. Eftychiou, 'The Law of Freedom of Trade Unionism' (1988) 22 Cyprus Law Review: 3455–3463 (in Greek), R. Prentzas, *Freedom of Trade Unionism* (Nicosia: Ermogenis, 1997, in Greek).

601. *Pancyprian Trade Union of Nurses* v. *Ministry of Health* [1994] 4 CLR 174 (in Greek).

602. *Pancyprian Trade Union of Nurses* v. *Ministry of Health* [1994] 4 CLR 174 (in Greek), *Yiallouros* v. *Nicolaou* [2001] 1 CLR 558 (in Greek).

603. *Pancyprian Trade Union of Nurses* v. *Ministry of Health* [1994] 4 CLR 174 (in Greek). See also *National Union of Belgian Police* v. *Belgium*, judgment of 22 October 1975.

collective bargaining trade unions would not be in a position to promote and safeguard the financial and social interests of their members.[604]

501. In a recourse brought by the *Cypriot Shipowners Union* against the Registrar of Trade Unions, the Supreme Court held that the meaning and scope of the notion of freedom of association in relation to trade unions should be interpreted in accordance with international labour law, as found, *inter alia*, in the relevant ILO conventions; thus, international conventions and covenants should serve as a guide to the interpretation of the relevant constitutional provisions.[605] The Republic of Cyprus has, *inter alia*, ratified the Freedom of Association and Protection of the Right to Organize Convention 87/1948 by Law 17/1966, the Right to Organize and Collective Bargaining Convention 98/1949 by Law 18/1966, the Collective Bargaining Convention 154/1981 by Law 241/1988 and the Labour Relations (Public Service) Convention 151/1978 by Law 65/1980; the Conventions have superior effect to any municipal legislation.

502. By virtue of Article 3 of Law 17/66 workers and employers shall have the right to establish and, subject only to the rules of the organization concerned, join organizations of their own choosing, whose object is to further and defend the interests of workers or of employers (Article 10), without previous authorization; such organizations shall have the right to draft their constitutions and rules, to elect their representatives in full freedom, to organise their administration and activities and to formulate their programmes. The public authorities shall refrain from any interference which may restrict this right or impede the lawful exercise thereof. Furthermore, by virtue of Article 4 such trade unions shall not be liable to be dissolved or suspended by administrative authority and shall have the right to establish and join federations and confederations and affiliate with international organizations of workers and employers (Article 5).

503. Law 18/66 provides that workers shall enjoy adequate protection against acts of anti-union discrimination in respect of their employment, in respect of acts calculated to make the employment of a worker subject to the condition that he shall not join a union or shall relinquish trade union membership, or which cause the dismissal of or otherwise prejudice a worker by reason of union membership or because of participation in union activities outside working hours or, with the consent of the employer, within working hours (Article 1). Both workers and employers' organizations should enjoy adequate protection against any acts of interference by each other or each other's agents or members in their establishment, functioning or administration; acts of interference include acts which are designed to promote the establishment of workers' organizations under the domination of employers or employers' organizations, or to support workers' organizations by financial or other

604. *Pancyprian Trade Union of Nurses* v. *Ministry of Health* [1994] 4 CLR 174 (in Greek). See also *Demir and Baykara* v. *Turkey*, judgment of 12 November 2008, *Wilson and the National Union of Journalists and others* v. *UK*, judgment of 2 July 2002.

605. *Cypriot Shipowners Union and another* v. *The Registrar of Trade Unions and others* [1988] 3 CLR 457, affirmed on appeal on the interpretative approach *Registrar of Companies and others* v. *Cypriot Shipowners Union* [1991] 3 CLR 93 (in Greek).

means, with the object of placing such organizations under the control of employers or employers' organizations (Article 2). Respect for the right to organize (Article 3) and collective bargaining (Article 4) should be fully guaranteed.

504. Law 241/88 provides that measures should be taken to promote collective bargaining; collective bargaining is defined as extending to all negotiations which take place between an employer, a group of employers or one or more employers' organizations, on the one hand, and one or more workers' organizations, on the other, for determining working conditions and terms of employment, and/or regulating relations between employers and workers and/or regulating relations between employers or their organizations and a workers' organization or workers' organizations (Article 2). Collective bargaining should be made possible for all employers and groups of workers in all branches of economic activity and bodies and procedures for the settlement of labour disputes should be conceived so as to contribute to the promotion of collective bargaining (Article 5). The measures should be the subject of prior consultation and potential agreement between public authorities, employers' and workers organizations (Article 7); this has occurred with the adoption of the IRC.

505. Cyprus has further ratified the European Social Charter with Law 64/1967, as amended with Laws 5/1975, 31/1988, 203/1991 and 10(III)/1993. Article 5 of Law 64/67 guarantees the freedom of workers and employers to organize and form or join local, national or international organizations for the protection of their economic and social interests, whereas Article 6 safeguards the right to bargain collectively; in order to safeguard the effective application of the right to collective bargain, the Republic has undertaken to promote joint consultation between workers and employers, machinery for voluntary negotiations between employers or employers' organizations and workers' organizations, with a view to the regulation of the terms and conditions of employment by means of collective agreements, the establishment of conciliation and voluntary arbitration for the settlement of labour disputes.

506. In *Pasyno*, the Ministry of Health refused to recognize the right of the Trade Union of Nurses to negotiate the application of the five-day week for nurses, arguing that it was not acceptable for the government to negotiate with any trade union other than the Pancyprian Trade Union of Public Servants (PASYDY). Eventually, the Ministry of Health revoked its decision following the legal opinion of the Deputy Attorney-General;[606] despite this, the Supreme Court had no problem in declaring that the government violated the right of the petitioners to be heard and to enter into collective bargaining and effectively coerced them to join PASYDY instead of their own trade union.[607]

606. See L. Loucaides, 'Legal Protection of the Freedom of Trade Unionism in Cyprus' (1986) 15 *Cyprus Law Review*: 2346–2359.
607. *Pancyprian Trade Union of Nurses* v. *Ministry of Health* [1994] 4 CLR 174 (in Greek).

507. A similar issue arose with respect to the efforts of the Democratic Labour Federation of Cyprus (DEOK), a relatively new and small in membership trade union, to safeguard its rights to be recognized as a trade union.[608] An industrial dispute arose when eight out of a total of 130 employees of a local furniture-making factory requested to be represented in their relations with their employer by DEOK; they also requested that their deductions from contributions on their wages be paid to the funds of DEOK and not to the funds of the Pancyprian Federation of Labour (PEO) or the Cyprus Workers' Federation (SEK), with both of which the employer had concluded a collective agreement. Both the PEO and SEK disagreed. Then Deputy Attorney-General Loukis Loucaides opined that the employer was liable under the Constitution to respect the right of its members to belong to DEOK and to not discriminate against them *vis-à-vis* members of the other trade unions.[609] Since the employees had opted to join DEOK, they should also be free to choose that their trade union dues would be paid to DEOK and not to the other trade unions.

508. Loucaides further opined that the employer should recognize the right of DEOK to fight for the interests of its members and to pursue their protection through collective bargaining. The employer had an obligation to offer the trade union the opportunity to be heard and to also apply the collective agreement to DEOK so as not to discriminate against, or alienate the employee-members of DEOK. The state further had a positive obligation to protect the employees and their unions from such interventions. In a subsequent opinion Loucaides emphasized the distinction between the right of recognition of a trade union, irrespective of the number of its penetration in the workforce and the conclusion on the part of employers of collective agreements with any trade union; whereas the employer was obligated to recognize and hear the trade union and to give the union the opportunity to defend the interests of its members, there was no obligation on behalf of the employer to actually conclude a collective agreement with DEOK; the employer remained free to conclude a collective agreement with PEO and SEK and not with DEOK.

509. In *ETYK* employees of the National Bank of Greece (Cyprus) disagreed with the position of the Cyprus Union of Bank Employees (ETYK) in a labour dispute that had arisen between the Bank and ETYK and applied for the registration of a new trade union which would consist only of employees of the National Bank of Greece (Cyprus). ETYK argued before the Registrar of Trade Unions that the new union was instigated by the Bank itself which would ultimately control the new union, so that it would essentially amount to a puppet of the Bank. The Registrar dismissed the objections of ETYK and registered the new trade union. ETYK filed a recourse before the Supreme Court. The Supreme Court, however, rejected the recourse; it was held that ETYK had no legitimate interest to retain its monopoly and maintain its members contrary to their own will. Since everyone has a right to

608. See in detail C. Christodoulou, *A Study of Labour Law in Cyprus* (PhD Wales, 1992): 110–128.
609. See the opinion in L. Loucaides, 'Legal Protection of the Freedom of Trade Unionism in Cyprus' (1986) 15 *Cyprus Law Review*: 2346–2359.

form and join a union, the employees could do so and ETYK had no right to regulate the rights of its former members or claim that it was in a better position to safeguard their interests.[610]

510. The Republic of Cyprus has further ratified Convention No. 135 concerning Protection and Facilities to be afforded to Workers' Representatives in the Undertaking, also known as the Workers' Representatives Convention by Law 30(III)/1995. It is therefore provided that employee representatives in the undertaking shall enjoy effective protection against any act prejudicial to them, including dismissal, based on their status or activities as a representative or on union membership or participation in union activities, insofar as they act in conformity with existing laws or collective agreements or other jointly agreed arrangements (Article 1). Such facilities in the undertaking shall be afforded to workers' representatives as may be appropriate in order to enable them to carry out their functions promptly and efficiently, provided that the granting of such facilities shall not impair the efficient operation of the undertaking concerned (Article 2). Any violation of the provisions of Law 30(III)/95 amounts to a criminal offence punishable by a fine of approximately 3,400 euro (section 6 of Law 30(III)/95). The competent court for the settlement of any dispute of civil nature in accordance with Law 30(III)/95 is the IDT.

511. In *Iordanou* the Supreme Court annulled the decision of the Public Service Commission to transfer the petitioner, who was an active member of PASYDY; the Court held that participation in a trade union is safeguarded by Article 21 of the Constitution and accordingly an official of a trade union should not be transferred from the seat of the union, unless there are important grounds, otherwise their active participation in the trade union and accordingly the exercise of the freedom to trade unionism might be unjustifiably hindered.[611] This does not imply that a trade unionist should not be transferred, but rather that the administration should carefully examine any difficulties to be caused for the trade union and give sufficient reasons for its decision to transfer; the aim is to achieve a balance between the exercise of the constitutional right safeguarded under Article 21 and the needs of the administration.[612]

II. Limitations

512. Article 21 of the Constitution enumerates exhaustively the causes in respect of which freedom of trade unionism may be limited. Restrictions may be placed on the exercise of the right to form or join a trade union, if such restrictions are prescribed by law and are absolutely necessary in the interests of the security of the

610. *Union of Bank Employees* v. *Republic* [2009] 4 CLR 469 (in Greek).
611. *Iordanou* v. *Republic* [1967] 3 CLR 245, *Mikellides* v. *Educational Service Committee* [1983] 3 CLR 487.
612. *Papas* v. *Cyprus Grain Commission* [1974] 3 CLR 143, *Mavrommatis* v. *Educational Service Committee* [1974] 3 CLR 226, *Sophocleous* v. *Republic* [1981] 3 CLR 360.

Republic or the constitutional order or the public safety or the public order or the public health or the public morals or for the protection of the rights and liberties guaranteed by the Constitution to any person, whether or not such person is a member of such trade union. It is explicitly provided that any trade union the object or activities of which are contrary to the constitutional order is prohibited. Any other limitations of freedom of trade unionism should be accordingly declared unconstitutional. For a norm to be regarded as a 'law' it should be formulated with sufficient precision so as to enable the citizen to foresee to a reasonable degree the consequences that a given action may entail in order to regulate his conduct.

513. The Supreme Court should further consider whether the interference with the right to trade unionism is necessary in a democratic society. In doing so the Supreme Court should assess whether the interference corresponded to a pressing social need; whether it was proportionate to the legitimate aim pursued; and whether the reasons given by the authorities to justify it are relevant and sufficient. Legislation which purports to limit fundamental rights is *ipso facto* of a temporary character. Therefore, even if the limitation was permissible at the time it was introduced by legislation in light of national or social realities prevailing at the time of enactment, it may still be declared unconstitutional if the grounds justifying its enactment have in the meantime disappeared. In order to declare whether a legislative measure was 'necessary' for the purposes of Article 21, paragraph 3 of the Constitution, there should be a serious, though not inevitable, risk that one or more of the causes defined therein would be imperilled. Limitations must be interpreted restrictively so as to safeguard the practical and effective protection of the constitutional right.[613]

514. It is further provided that a law may provide for the imposition of restrictions on the exercise of these rights by members of the armed forces, the police or gendarmerie. This restriction is consistent with paragraph 2 of Article 11 of the ECHR, but should be interpreted restrictively.[614] Legislation providing for the imposition of such restrictions should be accessible, certain and devoid of arbitrariness.[615] The Police Law, Cap. 285 provided that it is not lawful for any member, other than a special constable, to be or to become a member of any trade union the objects of which are to control or influence pay, pensions or conditions of service of the force; however, the formation of two police associations, one by senior officers and the other by all other ranks was allowed, to bring such matters to the notice of the Chief of the Police. This restriction has since been repealed.

515. Section 55 of the current Police Law 73(I)/2004 provides that a member of the police may be a member of any trade union, association or body affiliated to a trade union, or of any association or body the objects of which are to control or influence the conditions of employment in any trade or profession, or the pay, pensions or terms of service of the force. The only restriction set by section 55 is that

613. *Demir and Baykara* v. *Turkey*, judgment of 12 November 2008.
614. *Ibid.*
615. *Rekvenyi* v. *Hungary*, judgment of 20 May 1999.

members of the force may not protest in public, while in police uniform, for matters pertaining to their pay, pensions or conditions of service, a restriction which seems fully consistent with the principles set by the ECtHR.

516. With regard to members of the armed forces, section 28A of the Army Law 33/1990, as amended by Law 55(I)/2005, provides for a restriction similar to the one applicable to members of the police force under the pre-existing Police Law, Cap. 285. It is thus provided that no member of the armed forces may become or remain a member of any trade union, association or body affiliated to a trade union, or of any association or body the objects of which are to control or influence the conditions of employment in any trade or profession, or the pay, pensions or terms of service of the force. However, the formation of two professional associations by army officers is allowed, one by army officers and the other by non-commissioned officers, to study and bring such matters to the notice of the Minister, through the Commander-in-Chief of the National Guard; only members of the military may be members of such associations. It is further provided that no member of the armed forces may be a member of any union, association, foundation, club or other organized entity, unless following a written approval by the Minister.

517. There is no similar restriction for civil servants or other members of the administration. Section 59 of the Public Service Law 33/67 used to provide that a civil servant is allowed to be a member of a trade union, only if the members of such a trade union are exclusively civil servants. Despite recommendations by the ILO to amend the abovementioned provision, due to opposition by the PASYDY the relevant provision remained unchanged[616] until the adoption of Law 65/80, which ratified in the domestic legal order Convention No. 151 for labour relations in the Public Service. Article 4 of Law 65/80 safeguards that public employees should enjoy adequate protection against acts of anti-union discrimination in respect of their employment, particularly in respect of acts calculated to make the employment of public employees subject to the condition that they shall not join or shall relinquish membership of a public employees' organization, or cause the dismissal of or otherwise prejudice a public employee by reason of membership of a public employees' organization or because of participation in the normal activities of such an organization. This clarifies that the same rights enjoyed by Law 18/66 extend to public servants.

518. Article 5 of Law 65/80 further provides that public employees' organizations shall enjoy complete independence from public authorities and shall enjoy adequate protection against any acts of interference by a public authority in their establishment, functioning or administration; acts of interference are defined as any acts which are designed to promote the establishment of public employees' organizations under the domination of a public authority, or to support public

616. A. Emilianides, 'The Freedom of the Worker to Organize in Cyprus', in *Die Koalitionsfreiheit des Arbeitnehmers/ The Freedom of the Worker to Organize*, Berlin, New York, 1980: 1057.

employees' organizations by financial or other means, with the object of placing such organizations under the control of a public authority. Facilities should be afforded to public employees' organizations in order to exercise their rights (Article 6) and measures promoting collective bargaining should be applied (Article 7). Consistent with Law 65/80, the new Public Service 1/1990, section 63 of Law 1/90 explicitly provides that freedom to trade unionism and the unhindered exercise of all relevant rights is safeguarded for public servants. Thus, civil servants are free to join any union in or outside the civil service.

§2. Freedom Not to Join, Including Security Clauses

519. Whereas Article 11 of ECHR does not explicitly provide for the recognition of the freedom not to join a trade union, Article 21 of the Constitution explicitly provides that no person shall be compelled to join any association or to continue to be a member thereof. It follows that Article 21 explicitly guarantees, subject to the limitations discussed above, both the positive freedom of every person to form and join an association or trade union, and the negative freedom not to join or continue to be a member of a trade union and that compulsory trade unionism is not accepted under Cypriot law.[617] Thus, the Constitution prohibits both closed shop provisions requiring the employer to exclusively hire employees who are members of the bargaining union and union shop agreements permitting the employer to recruit employees provided they join the bargaining union within a specified period of time; accordingly general organization clauses to the effect that the employer shall employ workers belonging to a specific trade union and restricted organizational clauses which provide that the employer shall employ workers who belong to the trade union with which the collective labour agreement was signed, shall be void and have no effect.[618] Employees should be able to freely abstain from joining a trade union, or withdraw from it and form another trade union, if they so wish.

520. The constitutional provisions are further supplemented by section 50 of the Trade Union Law 71/65, which provides that it is illegal to make the employment of an employee subject to the condition that he shall not join, or shall relinquish trade union membership, or to cause the dismissal or otherwise discriminate against an employee on the ground that the latter is a member, or participates in the activities, of a trade union. The aim of the legislation is to prohibit discrimination on the basis of trade union membership and restriction of the right of an employee to participate in a trade union. On the other hand, the right of the employer to employ a person of his choice, irrespective of whether that person is a member of a trade union or not, remains unrestricted.

617. A. Loizou, *Constitution of the Republic of Cyprus* (Nicosia, 2001, in Greek): 135, C. Tornaritis, *The State Law of the Republic of Cyprus* (Nicosia: Cyprus Research Centre, 1982, in Greek).

618. C. Tornaritis, *The Human Rights as Recognized and Protected by the Law of the Republic of Cyprus* (Nicosia: 1974, reprint from (1974) 4–6 *Cyprus Law Tribune*): 22. See also *Sørensen and Rasmussen* v. *Denmark*, judgment of 11 January 2006, *Sigurjohnsson* v. *Iceland*, judgment of 30 June 1993, *Young, James and Webster* v. *UK*, judgment of 13 August 1981. See, however, *Sibson* v. *UK*, judgment of 20 April 1993, *Gustaffson* v. *Sweden*, judgment of 25 April 1996.

521. An interesting issue arose with regard to the Cyprus Telecommunications Authority (CYTA), a semi-public organization. A Regulation of the CYTA General Regulations provided that each trade union of CYTA has the right to indicate, proportionally to its size, half of the members of the staff committee of CYTA. It was raised that the participation of members of three trade unions in the staff committee violated the rights of the applicant, who was not a member of any of these trade unions. The argument was rejected by the Supreme Court which held that the members indicated by the trade unions are appointed by the Director General of CYTA and should not necessarily belong to a given trade union. Furthermore, they should always exercise their duties without bias and by choosing the best candidates for promotion.[619] Whereas this is an aspirational statement of principles, it seems rather unconvincing to state that the members of the committee indicated by the trade union should not belong to the trade union which had proposed them, or that there is no actual danger of bias in such a case; it would seem rather plausible that an employee might be indirectly pressed to become a member of a specific trade union in order to improve his chances for promotion.

619. *Kolokasidou* v. *CYTA* [1992] 4 CLR 4801 (in Greek), *Elia* v. *CYTA*, cases 1670/2010 *et al.*, dated 19 July 2013 (in Greek).

Chapter 2. Trade Unions and Employers' Associations

§1. DESCRIPTION

I. Employee Trade Unions

522. In 1932, during the British Rule of Cyprus, the first Trade Union Law was introduced. Under this law, trade unions would no longer be considered as illegal and as an impediment to trade and membership to a trade union would not be considered as a criminal offence. Trade unions were overseen by a Registrar, appointed by the colonial government.[620] Even though initially there seemed to be no interest on the part of workers to join together under a trade union, by 1939, 46 trade unions had been registered with a total membership of 2,544. Nonetheless, this was far from a structured, coordinated activity, as these unions – which had tiny memberships – were all independent from each other, and there was no higher body to which they could belong in order to better organize themselves collectively.

523. The World War II period proved to be particularly favourable to the growth of the trade union movement in Cyprus. The unemployment that struck the economy in the first years of the War, made unorganized workers seek unity. By the end of the War, four trade union groups had been registered in Cyprus. These were the Pancyprian Trade Union Committee (PTUC), with 12,863 members, the Pancyprian Workers' Confederation, with 1,190 members, the Confederation of Turkish Trade Unions, with 843 members, and eight Independent Trade Unions, with 584 members. So, by 1945, trade union membership totalled 15,480. The apparently dominant position of PTUC owed to affiliations with the strong and influential – at the time – Communist Party of Cyprus, AKEL.[621] In other words, no form of unity between the different trade unions existed. They were seriously split, owing to deep political ideological differences. This was especially evident between the two largest unions, PTUC and the Pancyprian Workers' Confederation, as the former was openly supportive of AKEL, whereas the latter was thought to promote the interests of employers. As a result of such differences, continuous attempts to unite the various trade unions under one body, failed.

524. In the decade following the end of the War, and more precisely between 1946 and 1956, the trade union movement grew considerably. Even though in 1946 the movement started to noticeably decline in membership, from 1952 onwards trade union membership started to increase steadily. By 1956 there were six trade union groups in Cyprus. These were namely, PEO with 27,143 members, SEK with 5,129 members, the Cyprus Federation of Independent Trade Unions with 2,954 members, the Cyprus Federation of Turkish Unions with 1,813 members, the Cyprus Civil Service Association with 3,935 members, and trade unions which were

620. Apart from this Registrar, there was no provision for any special government department, which would be responsible for industrial issues.

621. See T. W. Adams, *AKEL: The Communist Party of Cyprus* (Stanford: Hoover Institution Press: 1971).

not affiliated to any federation group with 1,954 members. Hence, by 1956 trade union membership totalled 42,928.[622]

525. The trade union movement became better organised after independence, despite some fluctuations in the membership patterns. In 1960, membership totalled 65,380. Even though there was no significant increase in the figure until 1969, owing to the inter-communal troubles of 1963 and 1967 (where a loss in membership was even recorded), after 1969 the figure started to rise once again. By 1970, it was, in fact, at 73,500. This momentous boost was due partly to the fact that this period was marked by increased economic activity, as a result of the growth of industry, trade and services. This precipitated an increase in white- and blue-collar workers, who also sought to get organized. They even sought to create splinter groups and split off from the original bigger trade unions, mainly PEO and SEK. The growing number of white-collar and professional trade unions was a clear trend in the late 1960s and early 1970s. One example of this new type of union was ETYK, formed in 1969.

II. Employer Associations and Trade Unions

526. Unlike the employee trade union movement, organization of employers does not have such a long history. It was not until after independence that one could actually speak of a full-scale employers' movement. Up until the eve of independence and, more specifically, until 1956, there was but one association to represent employers and this only represented building constructors. Outside the construction sector, there was an association representing hotel owners, and the Cyprus Chamber of Commerce and Industry (KEBE), which still exists today. Yet these had no specialisation on matters of collective negotiations at the time. This ran contrary to the experience of the trade union movement, which, as already noted, was, by the time of independence, well established and well organized. It had already gained considerable expertise in the field of industrial relations, through its continuous struggles for furthering the claims of the working classes. The imbalance of power was therefore evident, and this caused a great deal of concern to the then colonial Department of Labour.

527. In view of these fears, the Department of Labour took the initiative to attempt to promote the employers' movement, by seeking the establishment of one single pancyprian association of employers, which would represent the entire industry of Cyprus. Despite intensive efforts, however, the colonial Department of Labour failed to accomplish this in the period preceding independence. This was mainly due to the fact that a great degree of mistrust existed in the island at the time, between Greek Cypriots and the colonial authorities, which was further exacerbated by the fact that the former eagerly sought, in their vast majority, the restoration of the

622. A. Avraamides, 'A Brief History of Labour Relations in Cyprus: The Colonial Period – Labour Relations in Cyprus 1931–1956', in J. H. Slocum (ed.), *The Development of Labour Relations in Cyprus* (Nicosia: Proodos, 1972): 22.

island's peace and their national identity. Resulting from this, under the revolutionary conditions that prevailed, any initiative on the part of the colonial government was seen with suspicion, and was considered to be a potential 'political trap'.[623]

528. An association open for all employers was officially established in 1960, immediately after the island gained its independence. Founded by 19 businessmen, it started with 28 direct members and 4 trade associations covering 167 firms. Originally, it operated under the name of 'Employers' Advisory Association of Cyprus', but in 1970 it was renamed 'Cyprus Employers and Industrialists Federation' (OEB) – the name that it still has today. This name change was very important, as it reflected changes, both at the organizational level and also in connection with the aims and competencies of the Federation. The OEB today constitutes a serious player in decision-making procedures on industrial issues. As the most representative employers' association, it controls, to a great extent, nominations of employers' representatives to official institutions. Among its chief objectives are to safeguard and promote the interests of its members, to defend the system of private enterprise, promote economic development and achieve social progress. Finally, it seeks to endorse and maintain a balance of power between the business community and trade unions. OEB has undertaken the role of a coordinating body in the field of employers' organizations.[624]

529. Similar to the experience of the trade union movement, the development of the Employers' Federation was temporarily negatively affected in the aftermath of the 1974 invasion. Membership was reduced at the time, as owing to the economic catastrophe, many enterprises – members of the OEB – had to close down. This however, was only a temporary effect, as membership levels rose again following the economic recovery of the late 1970s. The 1990s saw a great boost in the membership levels of OEB, owing to the rapid economic expansion of the services sector. More specifically, during this period, 15 professional associations from the service sector joined the Federation. This upward trend continued in the next decade, as in the first few years, from 2000–2003, seven service sector organizations joined OEB. This raised membership levels from 19 to 26 professional associations.[625]

§2. Role

530. The trade union movement in Cyprus still enjoys a great degree of recognition and status. Changes in the structure of the Cypriot workforce means, however, that most of the labour force is no longer manual or found in high-density

623. M. Sparsis, *The Cypriot System of Industrial Relations* (Nicosia: Cyprus, 1993): 5.
624. M. Yannakourou and E. Soumeli, *The Evolving Structure of Collective Bargaining in Europe 1990–2004*, Research Project co-financed by the European Commission and the University of Florence, VS/2003/0219-S12.359910, 2004: 32.
625. *Ibid*: 33.

workplaces, but rather consists of white-collar employees, a factor which has limited the ability of employee trade unions to mobilize their members. It is estimated that more than 50 per cent of Cyprus' working population is organized today in trade unions, even though this figure has dropped in the last 30 years from over 80 per cent, owing mainly to a shrinking of the industrial sector, and the rapid development of the tertiary sector. Whereas this shrinking of trade union density levels might indicate a continuous dilution of trade union power,[626] nonetheless, trade unions remain, today, a very important actor in the formulation of industrial matters. Total trade union membership is currently estimated at more than 200,000, whereas there are nearly 187 registered employee trade unions according to the official data of the Registrar of Trade Unions.[627]

531. The two largest and most important employee trade union confederations are PEO and SEK. The two main confederations also include federations of trade unions organized along industry lines with PEO having eight federations as members and SEK seven. The difference between the two unions is mainly an ideological one; PEO, has always been considered as the left-wing trade union, as its policies have always been deemed to be influenced by AKEL, whereas SEK has always been regarded as the right-wing trade union. PEO regularly supports the candidates of AKEL, whereas SEK those of the right-wing party DISY. Nonetheless, the unions have avoided any rifts between them, as their demands have largely been similar over the years. Throughout the post-independence period, employee trade unions have sought to establish grounds for mutual cooperation. The trade union movement had common demands, common struggles and common claims, both on bread-and-butter issues, as well as on more important industrial matters. This is still the case today, as the trade unions act more as partners, rather than competitors in the achievement of their goals.

532. The main competition that exists amongst them, is the attraction of members to their ranks, even though it can generally be noted that the left-wing trade union PEO attracts more white collar workers, whereas the right-wing trade union SEK attracts more blue collar workers. This, is not however, the rule, as political party affiliations play a crucial role, mainly in attracting supporters of the left-wing party, AKEL (regardless of class) to the ranks of PEO. PEO currently has 83,000 members, whereas SEK 73,000. The much smaller DEOK has approximately 9,500 members and is aligned with the socialist party EDEK. Another smaller trade union is the Pancyprian Federation of Independent Trade Unions (POAS).

533. In practice, relations between trade unions and political parties remain at a high level.[628] It should not be considered, however, that all trade unions are related

626. See G. Ioannou and S. Sonan, *Trade Unions in Cyprus: History of Division, Common Challenges ahead* (Berlin: Friedrich Ebert Stiftung, 2014).

627. A thousand trade unions, either of employees, or employers, have been registered since the creation of the registry. See http://www.mlsi.gov.cy/mlsi/dlr/dlr.nsf/page26_gr/page26_gr?OpenDocument.

628. See Y. Katsourides, *Political Parties and Trade Unions in Cyprus* (Hellenic Observatory Papers on Greece and Southeast Europe, LSE, 2013), G. Ioannou, *Labour Relations in Cyprus: Employment, Trade Unionism and Class Composition* (PhD thesis, University of Warwick, 2011).

to political parties; there are important autonomous unions that are not part of either PEO or SEK and who are not directly controlled by any political party; examples include PASYDY, which represents nearly all public servants, with approximately 19,000 members, ETYK, which represents nearly all bank employees, with 10,000 members and the organizations of secondary and primary education teachers, Organization of Greek Secondary Education Teachers (OELMEK) and the Pancyprian Organization of Greek Teachers (POED) respectively, with approximately 5,000–6,000 members each.

534. The OEB and KEBE are the major confederations of the business community of Cyprus. OEB comprises overall, more than 50 professional associations and more than 4,500 major individual enterprises in the services sector, as well as the manufacturing, construction and agricultural sectors of the economy. These enterprises are, in their majority, small and medium sized enterprises (SMEs),[629] and together they employ about 60 per cent of the total workforce of Cyprus – a percentage that corresponds to about 171,000 employees.[630] KEBE has over 12,000 companies and 144 professional associations as affiliate members that are estimated as employing 75 per cent of the private sector workforce. However, many of its members are also members of OEB and are represented by OEB for the purposes of collective bargaining; thus, for the purposes of collective bargaining KEBE members employ less than 35 per cent of the private sector workforce.[631]

535. Major sectoral employer federations have also gained prominence over the years and are registered members of OEB or KEBE; these include the Pancyprian Association of Hoteliers (PASYXE) which is a member of KEBE and the Cyprus Federation of the Association of Building Constructors (OSEOK) which is a member of OEB. There are currently 44 registered employer trade unions according to the official data of the Registrar of Trade Unions.[632] There are also organizations with mixed representations of interests, such as the Pancyprian Professional Small Shopkeepers' Federation (POVEK) with approximately 8,000 members.

§3. Structure

I. Registration

536. The Trade Union Law 71/1965 came into force on 1 January 1966, when the Trade Union Law, Cap. 117 was abolished; it remains into force since, as amended by Laws 22/1970, 48/1991 and 97(I)/1996. The Trade Unions Regulations

629. In the Cypriot economy, enterprise size is determined as follows: small enterprises are those that employ 1–15 employees, medium enterprises are those that employ 16–250 employees, and large enterprises are those that employ over 250 employees.
630. Cyprus Employers and Industrialists Federation (OEB), *Aims and Objectives*. Available at: http://www.kypros.org/CIO/oeb/index.html.
631. E. Soumeli, 'Cyprus: Industrial Relations Profile', available at http://www.eurofound.europa.eu/sites/default/files/ef_files/eiro/country/cyprus.pdf.
632. See http://www.mlsi.gov.cy/mlsi/dlr/dlr.nsf/page26_gr/page26_gr?OpenDocument.

were approved in 1968 as secondary legislation.[633] The Permanent Secretary of the Ministry of Labour, Welfare and Social Insurance acts as the Registrar of Trade Unions and keeps a registry of all registered trade unions. The registry includes both employer and employee trade unions; section 2 of Law 71/65 provides that the objectives of the trade union may refer to the regulation of the relations between employees and employers, or between employers, or between employees.

537. No other formal recognition is required, other than registration; registered trade unions enjoy all rights and privileges provided for under the Law (section 36 of Law 71/65). The certificate of registration of the trade union is indisputable proof that the trade union is a registered one (section 10 of Law 71/65). A registered trade union is a legal person under private law and may accordingly own and possess property, conclude contracts (section 37 of Law 71/65), sue and be sued in its respective name and be represented by its officials, or advocates (section 46 of Law 71/65). A trade union may not be registered as a company and the company law does not apply with regard to trade unions (section 61 of Law 71/65).

538. A trade union must submit an application in order to be registered within 30 days from its establishment (section 71 of Law 7/65). By virtue of section 8 of Law 71/65, for a trade union to be registered in any trade or profession where more than 20 persons are employed, the trade union should have at least 20 members. The application should bear the signatures of at least seven members of the trade union, who may act as its officials; if, however, the total number of employees in the specialized profession of the trade union does not exceed seven persons, the trade union may bear the signatures of only three members of the trade union. The application must be accompanied by two copies of the constitution of the trade union duly signed by the applicants.

539. If the Registrar is satisfied that the formalities have been complied with and that the objectives of the trade union are not illegal,[634] he may proceed with the registration of the trade union by virtue of section 9 of Law 71/65. However, the Registrar may request additional information, or conduct inquiries in order to ascertain that the trade union fulfils the requirements of the Law (section 11 of Law 71/65). Furthermore, the Registrar may request the change of the name of the trade union, if this might lead to confusion or deceit of the public, or the members of any trade union, or if it is identical or similar to the name of an already registered trade union (section 12 of Law 71/65). The Registrar may further refuse to register a trade union if it represents multiple classes of workers, without safeguarding in its constitution that the interests of each class shall be adequately protected and promoted (section 13 of Law 71/65). The decision of the Registrar to refuse the registration of a trade union is subject to administrative review by the Council of Ministers within 15 days (section 14 of Law 71/65); recourse against the decision of the Council of

633. Since amended in 1992, 1996, 1999, 2000 and 2002.

634. The objectives of the trade union are not illegal, simply because they are restrictive of trade in such a manner that any contract or trust is void (section 39 of Law 71/65), or that any of its members may be liable for a criminal offence (section 38 of Law 71/65).

Ministers may be filed by the applicants before the Supreme Court (section 15 of Law 71/65).

540. The Registrar may apply before the District Court in order to revoke or cancel the certificate of registration, if it is proven that this was issued by mistake, or if the members of the trade union have been reduced below the minimum number, or that the provisions of Law 71/65 have been violated on purpose and despite the warning of the Registrar, or if the trade union, or its funds, are used for illegal purposes or for objectives which are not permitted by the trade union's constitution. Before applying to the District Court, the Registrar should give written notice of at least one month to the trade union (section 16 of Law 71/65). If a trade union fails to apply for registration, or if it fails to be registered, or its registration is revoked or cancelled, the trade union does not enjoy any rights under the Law,[635] it is dissolved and no person may participate in its administration or represent it[636] (section 17 of Law 71/65).

541. By virtue of section 18 of Law 71/65, the constitution of the trade union should provide for all major issues related to the trade union, which are enumerated in the First Schedule of Law 71/65. Any amendments to the constitution should be sent to the Registrar within 14 days from the date of the amendment. The trade union should also have a registered seat to which all notifications and announcements should be sent (section 19 of Law 71/65). Changes to the registered seat, officials (section 22 of Law 71/65), or name of the trade union should be registered with the Registrar; a change of name can only come into force following its registration and if the secretary of the trade union signs an affidavit before the District Court that at least two-thirds of the total number of members of the trade union voted in favour of the change (section 23 and 24 of Law 71/65). The dissolution of the trade union should also be sent to the Registrar within 14 days of the decision and only has effect following its registration; if the Registrar refuses to register it, claiming that it was made contrary to the trade union's constitution, the trade union may apply before the District Court (section 27 of Law 71/65).

542. Two, or more, trade unions may also opt to merge into a single trade union pursuant to separate majority positive vote of at least two-thirds of the total number of members of each trade union (section 25 of Law 71/65); the Registrar approves and registers the merge following the submission of an application which is accompanied by two copies of the new constitution (section 26 of Law 71/65). The Registrar may further register a confederation of trade unions, whose members are not natural persons, but registered trade unions, in accordance with sections 53–56 of Law 71/65; all trade union members of the confederation should be registered. The application for the registration of a confederation must be submitted by the secretary and another official of each trade union which shall become a member of the

635. However, this does not affect any obligations undertaken by the trade union which may be executed against the property of the trade union, if any.

636. Unless to the extent that representation refers to judicial measures taken against it, or with the purpose of dissolving the trade union.

confederation; it should also be accompanied by a declaration that the majority of the members of the registered trade union so decided in a general assembly by secret vote.

543. In *Komodromos* the Registrar refused the registration of the results of the elections of various bodies and organs of POED and further directed the holding of new elections. The Supreme Court first held in an interim decision that the Registrar had no authority to direct the holding of elections by a trade union and there was no legal base for him exercising such a power; his decision to direct the holding of new elections was therefore flagrantly illegal.[637] The Supreme Court then considered the substance of the matter. It was argued on behalf of the respondents that the Registrar should enjoy a discretion enabling him to carry out his duties as the watchdog of legality in the trade unions.

544. The Supreme Court rejected this submission and held that the registration of the change of officers of the trade union was mandatory for the Registrar under section 22 of Law 71/65 and that he had no discretion on the matter, not even to consider whether such a change had been effected in accordance with the constitution of the trade union.[638] This seems an odd conclusion; while the Registrar should not enjoy any, ambiguous and potentially arbitrary, discretion on whether to register, confirming that legality has been complied with does not properly amount to the exercise of discretion on behalf of the Registrar. The Registrar should be expected to safeguard that the acts of the trade unions are consistent with the applicable legislation and that formalities have been accordingly complied with.

545. An interesting case considering the limits of the powers of the Registrar was the case of the *Cyprus Shipowners Union*.[639] The applicant trade union took a resolution for partial amendment of their rules; some of the amendments were refused by the Registrar, whereas for other proposed amendments, the Registrar invited discussions with the applicants. The Supreme Court annulled the decision of the Registrar and held that the duty of the Registrar under section 18 of Law 71/65 is restricted to ascertaining whether the altered rules have made provision in respect of the several matters contained in the First Schedule and if they have, then the Registrar has no discretion to refuse their registration. The decision was appealed.

546. The Full Bench of the Supreme Court did not consider that it was necessary to finally decide on the question of the extent of the powers of the Registrar under section 18 of Law 71/65. A majority of four Supreme Court justices held that the amendments adopted by the trade union did not violate any of the provisions of Law 71/65 and that accordingly the decision of the Registrar to reject them was not

637. *Pagkiprios Organosis Ellinon Didaskalon Limassol Branch and others* v. *Registrar of Trade Unions* [1982] 3 CLR 177.
638. *Komodromos and others* v.*The Registrar of Trade Unions* [1983] 3 CLR 495.
639. *Cypriot Shipowners Union and another* v.*The Registrar of Trade Unions and others* [1988] 3 CLR 457.

a proper one. However, a dissenting opinion supported by three judges held that the powers of the Registrar are not limited to a mere mandatory registration of the amendments approved by the trade union, but on the contrary had to ascertain that such amendments were in accordance with the law; the minority held that the Registrar's decision to reject the proposed amendments should be affirmed.[640] It is submitted that irrespective of the substance of the dispute, the dissenting opinion is correct in holding that the Registrar may consider whether the amendments are made in accordance with the law.

II. Administration

547. Any person over 16 years of age may join a trade union. No other restrictions of race, sex, political or religious grounds may be applied to the admission of membership, unless there are special grounds which might justify such restriction and which refer to the objectives of the trade union. In any event, only a person who is actually engaged in, or working at, a trade or calling to which the trade union relates, may become a member; incapacity of an official of the trade union to engage in his trade or profession because of the exercise of his duties as official, or temporary unemployment, does not deprive a member from membership status. It is further noted that, unless the constitution provides otherwise, members who leave the profession or trade may retain their membership status and shall not be deprived of any of their rights so long as they continue to renew their membership and pay any fees due to the trade union (section 20 of Law 71/65).

548. An interesting question arose in the *Cyprus Shipowners Union* case, with regard to the right of members of a trade union to vote. A proposed amendment to the rules of the trade union provided that members of the trade union could have multiple votes, under the rule that each member would have one vote for every 500 cubic volume capacity of their ships. A majority of four judges of the Supreme Court held that the trade union had the right to provide for criteria for the exercise of the right to vote; the Shipowners Union was a peculiar one, having companies as members and its proposed amendment was not unlawful.

549. A minority of three judges disagreed and held that no quantitative or qualitative criteria could be adopted for the weight of a vote of a member of a trade union; both the objective of establishing a trade union and the principle of equality under Article 28 of the Constitution direct that all members of a trade union should have the right to one vote. Otherwise, one could adopt criteria for determining the exercise of the right to vote on the basis of wages, salaries, property value or similar considerations. The minority held that the freedom to participate in a trade union would be hindered, if members of the trade union enjoyed different rights with regard to the right to vote; this would undermine the democratic principles. It is submitted that the dissenting judgment of the Supreme Court seems more convincing.

640. *Registrar of Companies and others* v. *Cypriot Shipowners Union* [1991] 3 CLR 93 (in Greek).

550. Only members over 21 years of age may act as members of the administration of the trade union (section 21 of Law 71/65).[641] Furthermore, any persons who have been convicted for an offence which entails dishonesty or fraud may not act as members of the administration of the trade union, or manage or collect its funds, for a period of five years from the time of conviction. The Registrar, or any member of the trade union, may apply before the District Court for an injunction prohibiting any person from acting as an official of the trade union pending his prosecution for an offence which entails dishonesty or fraud, so long as the prosecution commenced with the consent of the Attorney-General of the Republic (section 31 of Law 71/65). The District Court may further grant an injunction, following an application by the Registrar or any member of the trade union, which prohibits any unauthorized or incompetent person from acting as an official, or to collect funds of the trade union, or which prohibits any illegal or unauthorized payment by the funds of the trade union.

551. A trade union may utilize its funds in order to fulfil its objectives (section 28 of Law 71/65). The income of a trade union is normally provided by its members; unions collect a percentage of their members' wages, usually 1 per cent, which is normally deducted by the employer and paid directly to the trade union. Whether the employer would deduct, however, the percentage from the employees' wages and pay it to the trade union is a matter of collective agreement and is not provided for by any existing legislation.[642] There is no state funding of trade unions, nor is funding from political parties affiliated with the trade union allowed. The Registrar has the power to inspect the accounts, list of members and other documents of the trade union at any time (section 35 of Law 71/65) and to request detailed accounts (section 34 of Law 71/65). An annual report of the accounts of the trade union is submitted to the Registrar by 15 February of each year (section 33 of Law 71/65).

552. The use of the funds of the trade union for the promotion of political aims is expressly prohibited under section 29 of Law 71/65, unless this has been approved by a resolution adopted in secret voting by the trade union members; the Registrar should secure that all members had an equal and effective right to vote. Political aims which may be approved by a resolution refer to the support of a candidate, or potential candidate for election to a public post, or to the registration of voters for such purposes, or to the reimbursement of a member of the trade union for loss of income owing to election or appointment to a public post, or even for political assemblies or distribution of political announcements or press releases. Payments for the promotion of such political aims should be paid by a separate fund of the trade union, called the 'political fund'. No property of the trade union, other

641. The latter provision may violate the right of non-discrimination safeguarded under Art. 28 of the Constitution. For similar considerations in another context see A. Emilianides, 'Do Minimum Age Requirements Violate the Right to Stand for Election under the European Convention on Human Rights?' [2009] 5 *European Human Rights Law Review*: 670–683.

642. See *Trade Union of Hourly-Paid Staff of the Ministry of Defence* v. *Republic* [2001] 3 CLR 139 (in Greek).

than funds collected specifically for the political fund, may be used, either directly or indirectly for the promotion of political aims (section 30 of Law 71/65).

553. Members of the trade union are not obligated to contribute to the political fund and they shall only contribute if they so wish, in which case they should serve a notice to the registered seat of the trade union of their intention to do so. Members who have not served, or have revoked, such a notice, have no obligation to pay any contribution to the political fund and should not be discriminated against, or lose any benefits, due to the fact that they do not contribute to the political fund. Contribution to the political fund shall not be a requirement for the admission of new members to the trade union under any circumstances (sections 29 and 30 of Law 71/65). The intention of the legislator was to enable trade unions to participate in elections, or support candidates if the majority of their members so wishes, but not to coerce members who do not wish to do so to contribute to the support of such political aims; this is achieved by the setting up of a separate political fund and the introduction of strict provisions for contribution to this fund.

III. Civil and Criminal Aspects

554. An agreement, or collaboration, by two or more persons to conduct any act in order to promote an industrial dispute, shall not give rise to civil or criminal responsibility, unless such act would amount to a criminal offence, or give rise to a civil action even without agreement or collaboration (section 40 of Law 71/65). Accordingly, members of a trade union would be liable under criminal or civil law, only for acts which would give rise to such liability if they had performed them on their own, without any collaboration with other trade union members. The aim of this provision is to specify that participation in a trade union and acts performed by a trade union neither reduce, nor establish increased liability.

555. Intimidation, bullying and harassment against trade union members in order for them not to exercise their rights, either by the employer, or by other trade union members, or by anyone else, amounts to a criminal offence (section 45 of Law 71/65). Law 71/65 further provides for various other criminal offences, such as the failure to provide the notifications stipulated by the Law (section 49 of Law 71/65), providing false information to any member of a registered trade union, or a person wishing to become member of a registered trade union with the intention to defraud (section 48 of Law 71/65) and malicious possession or improper use of any property of the trade union (section 47 of Law 71/65). A criminal prosecution for offences pursuant to Law 71/65 may take place only by, or with the written consent of the Attorney-General (section 52 of Law 71/65).

556. However, there shall be no civil liability of a person for the mere reason that he induces another to violate a contract of employment, or interferes with the profession, trade or occupation of another person, or the right of such other person to freely dispose his funds or work, so long as such an act was made for the purpose of promoting an industrial dispute (section 41 of Law 71/65). Otherwise, trade unionists might not properly exercise their rights out of fear of civil liability towards the employer.

557. Certain agreements which are concluded between trade unions, or trade union members, while legal, are not enforceable by courts and their violation does not give rise to damages (section 42 of Law 71/65). These include: (i) agreements between members of a trade union, concluded under their capacity as trade union members, regarding the terms under which they shall sell their goods, or exercise their profession, (ii) agreements for the payment of any subscription or fine to any trade union, (iii) agreements referring to the use of the funds of the trade union to provide benefits for its members, or to pay a fine imposed by a court to any person, or to make payments to any employer or employee who is not a member of the trade union in order for the latter to comply with the constitution or the decisions of the trade union, (iv) agreements between two trade unions and (v) bonds securing the execution of any of the agreements under (i) – (iv) above. This is because such agreements are considered of a voluntary nature and accordingly it was thought that judicial enforcement, or award of damages in case of violation of such agreements, would effectively undermine their voluntary character and the voluntary nature of participation in trade unions. In light of the growing importance and power of trade unions, the non-enforceability provided in section 42 of Law 71/65 should probably be reconsidered.

558. Section 43 of Law 71/65 is a very ambiguous and poorly drafted provision. Section 43, paragraph 1 stipulates that 'no court has jurisdiction to adjudicate a lawsuit against a registered trade union or any of its members or officials, which is filed against both the defendants and the remaining members of the trade union, for a tort which is claimed to have been committed by or on behalf of the trade union'. Paragraph 2 of section 43 provides that: 'nothing contained in this section should be construed as depriving any court of its jurisdiction to adjudicate actions against trade unions or any of its officials, which refer to the property or rights of the trade union, other than in relation to torts committed by or on behalf of the trade union for the promotion of an industrial dispute'.

559. The abovementioned provision was considered by the District Court of Limassol.[643] The court concluded that paragraph 1 of section 43 provides for a general blanket immunity from tortious liability for all registered trade unions, their officials and members,[644] where paragraph 2 of section 43 provides, as a way of exception that no such blanket immunity applies in torts against trade unions or their officials which refer to the trade unions rights or property; even in the latter case, however, the Court has no jurisdiction to adjudicate torts which were committed for

643. *Spyrou and another* v. *Union of Employees of Ports Authority of Cyprus*, Action 5624/10, decision of 26 October 2012 (in Greek).

644. A. Emilianides, 'The Freedom of the Worker to Organize in Cyprus' in *Die Koalitionsfreiheit des Arbeitnehmers/ The Freedom of the Worker to Organize*, Berlin – New York, 1980: 1057 argued that s. 43 should be interpreted as providing for immunity of trade unions, their officials and members, from tortious liability in the case of tortious acts committed against their own members which refer to the promotion of an industrial dispute.

the promotion of an industrial dispute. The court subsequently considered whether the blanket immunity provided for in paragraph 1 of section 43 could be justified. It was held that there was no reasonable justification on why trade unions, or their officials, or members, should enjoy blanket immunity from tortious liability; paragraph 1 of section 43 was therefore unconstitutional as being contrary to the principle of non-discrimination safeguarded under Article 28 of the Constitution.

Chapter 3. Institutionalized Relations between Employers and Employees

§1. Introduction

560. There are few institutionalized relations between employers and employees in Cyprus in light of the voluntary character of the system of cooperation between the social partners; neither the legislator, nor social partners have opted to institutionalize the process of participation of employees at either the enterprise, or industry level. The trade union representatives essentially act as the institutionalized representatives of the employees and this has also remained the case with regard to the implementation of the European Works Council Directive 2009/38/EC with Law 106(I)/2011. Workplace representation is therefore exercised through the trade unions and their representatives, with the exception of the establishment of health and safety committees in establishments with more than 10 employees.

561. Employees have no statutory rights to be represented at management level, or enjoy any other form or representation in the workings of the company other than those referred to above; however, collective agreements may provide for additional employee representation. Trade union representatives therefore deal with the various issues that may arise in the workplace and consult with the management of the employer. In order to exercise their rights, trade union representatives generally enjoy some facilities by the employer and limited time-off in order to meet; however, the main trade union representative of major trade unions, such as ETYK or PASYDY, might be released from other working duties altogether.

§2. Works Councils

562. Since Cypriot accession to the EU on 1 May 2004, Law 68(I)/2002, as amended by Laws 143(I)/2003 and 167(I)/2007, came into effect and harmonized Cypriot law with the European Works Councils Directives 94/45/EC, 97/74/EC and 2006/109/EC.[645] Law 68(I)/2002 was eventually repealed by Law 106(I)/2011 which incorporates Directive 2009/38/EC into the Cypriot legal order.[646] Law 106(I)/2011 largely reproduces the content of the Directive and aims at improving the right to information and to consultation[647] of employees in Community-scale undertakings which are situated in the Republic of Cyprus and Community-scale groups of undertakings whose controlling undertaking is situated in the Republic of

645. See E. Soumeli, 'European Works Councils Law and Practice' (2004), available in http://www.eurofound.europa.eu/observatories/eurwork/articles/european-works-councils-law-and-practice.
646. Of the European Parliament and of the Council of 6 May 2009 on the establishment of a European Works Council on a Procedure in Community-scale undertakings and Community-scale groups of undertakings for the purposes of informing and consulting employees.
647. Information and consultation are defined in section 2 of Law 106(I)/11 which essentially reproduces Article 2 of Directive 2009/38/EC.

Cyprus.[648] European Works Councils (EWC) are bodies representing the European employees of a company. Through them, workers are informed and consulted by management on the progress of the business and any significant decision at European level that could affect their employment or working conditions. Cyprus has opted to exclude from the ambit of the directive merchant navy crews.[649]

563. The thresholds for defining Community-scale undertakings and Community-scale groups of undertakings are, by virtue of section 2 of Law 106(I)/11, at least 1000 employees within the EU[650] and at least 150 employees in each of at least two Member States. The thresholds shall be based, by virtue of section 6 of Law 106(I)/11, on the average number of employees, under any status, including part-time employees, employed during the previous two years; expired fixed-term or part-time employment contracts shall be converted into full-time annual employment according to what constitutes full-time employment in the undertaking or sector of economic activity.[651] All enterprises situated in the Republic of Cyprus have to inform in writing the Ministry of Labour, Welfare and Social Insurance about the number of their employees. Failure to comply with any of the provisions of Law 106(I)/11 would amount to a criminal offence punishable by two year imprisonment and/or fine of 34,000 euro.[652]

564. Law 106(I)/11 does not therefore apply to local Cypriot companies, irrespective of their size, but applies only to fairly large multinational companies, either based in Cyprus or in another country but with operations in Cyprus, which employ a significant number of employees in at least two Member States. Furthermore, the competence of the EWC and the scope of the information and consultation procedure for employees governed by Law 106(I)/11 is limited to transnational issues.[653] In light of the above, the application of Law 106(I)/11 and pre-existing Law 68(I)/02 in the Cypriot legal order, has thus so far been rather negligible to virtually non-existent, as the number of undertakings actually falling under the provisions of Law 106(I)/11 are relatively few and the rights provided in the directive had generally been safeguarded by the system of tripartite cooperation; accordingly, there has been little interest from social partners or the Ministry of Labour, Welfare and Social Insurance to actively promote the practical implementation of the legislation.[654]

565. The central management of the Community-scale undertaking or group of undertakings shall, by virtue of section 7 of Law 106(I)/11, be responsible for

---

648. 'Controlling undertaking' is defined in section 5 of Law 106(I)/11 which essentially reproduces Article 3 of Directive 2009/38/EC.
649. As allowed to do under Article 1(7) of Directive 2009/38/EC.
650. Or the EEA countries, and in particular Iceland, Norway, Liechtenstein and Switzerland.
651. Thereby implementing the relevant provisions of Article 2 of Directive 2009/38/EC.
652. Thereby implementing the relevant provisions of Article 11 of Directive 2009/38/EC.
653. Defined in section 3(4) of Law 106(I)/11 which essentially reproduces Article 1(4) of Directive 2009/38/EC.
654. See also E. Soumeli, 'Cyprus: Industrial Relations Profile' (2011) available at http://www.eurofound.europa.eu/sites/default/files/ef_files/eiro/country/cyprus.pdf.

creating the conditions and means necessary for the setting up of an EWC or an information and consultation procedure. Where the central management is not situated in a Member State, the central management's representative agent in a Member State, shall be responsible; in the absence of such a representative, the management of the establishment or group undertaking employing the greatest number of employees in any one Member State shall take on the responsibility. The central management shall be responsible for obtaining and transmitting to the parties concerned the information required for commencing negotiations, and in particular the information concerning the structure of the undertaking or the group and its workforce.

566. The central management shall initiate negotiations for the establishment of an EWC or an information and consultation procedure on its own initiative, or at the written request of at least 100 employees or their representatives in at least two undertakings or establishments in at least two different Member States. For this purpose, a Special Negotiating Body (SNB) shall be established, in accordance with section 8 of Law 106(I)/11; representatives of employees on the SNB and their substitutes, are elected from the existing employee trade unions and where no union exists, directly from the employees by direct elections. Employees in undertakings, or establishments, where there are no representatives of the employees for grounds beyond their control, have the right to elect or appoint the members of the special negotiating body. The Republic has therefore opted to give priority to trade union representatives with regard to representation in the EWC. By virtue of section 13 of Law 106(I)/11, the same rules apply to the election of Cypriot members of the EWC if the directive's subsidiary requirements apply.

567. By virtue of section 9 of Law 106(I)/11, the members of the SNB shall be elected or appointed in proportion to the number of employees employed in each Member State by the Community-scale undertaking or group of undertakings, by allocating in respect of each Member State one seat per portion of employees employed in that Member State amounting to 10 per cent, or a fraction thereof, of the number of persons employed in all the Member States taken together; it has been provided that the central management and the EWC may agree on the participation of workers who are third country nationals as observers. The central management and local management and the competent European workers' and employers' organizations shall be informed of the composition of the SNB and of the start of the negotiations.

568. The SNB shall, by virtue of section 10 of Law 106(I)/11, have the task of determining, with the central management, by written agreement, the scope, composition, functions, and term of office of the EWC, or the arrangements for implementing a procedure for the information and consultation of employees. With a view to the conclusion of an agreement, the central management shall convene a meeting with the SNB and inform the local managements accordingly. Before and after any meeting with the central management, the SNB shall be entitled to meet without representatives of the central management being present, using any necessary means for communication. For the purpose of the negotiations, the SNB may request assistance from experts of its choice which can include representatives of competent recognised Community-level trade union organizations; such experts and such trade union representatives may be present at negotiation meetings in an advisory capacity at the request of the special negotiating body.

569. It is further provided that the SNB may decide, by at least two-thirds of the votes, not to open negotiations, or to terminate the negotiations already opened; such a decision shall stop the procedure to conclude the agreement. A new request to convene the SNB may be made at the earliest two years after the decision unless the parties concerned agree on a shorter period. Any expenses relating to the negotiations shall be borne by the central management so as to enable the SNB to carry out its task in an appropriate manner; in particular the central management shall undertake the expenses of election or appointment of the SNB, the organization of the meetings of the SNB including expenses of translation, accommodation, travel expenses, printing and cost of living, as well as the expenses of an expert who shall assist the SNB in carrying out its task.[655]

570. The central management and the SNB must negotiate in a spirit of cooperation, by virtue of section 11 of Law 106(I)/11, with a view to reaching an agreement on the detailed arrangements for implementing the information and consultation of employees. The agreement shall determine the undertakings covered, the composition of the EWC, the number of members, allocation of seats,[656] term of office, functions and procedure for information and consultation of the EWC and arrangements for linking information and consultation; it shall also determine the venue, frequency and duration of meetings of the EWC, financial and material resources to be allocated to the EWC, the duration of the agreement and procedure for renegotiation. Alternatively, the central management and the SNB may decide, in writing, to establish one or more information and consultation procedures instead of an EWC; the agreement must stipulate by what method the employees' representatives shall have the right to meet to discuss the information conveyed to them. This information shall relate in particular to transnational questions which significantly affect workers' interests. For the purposes of concluding the agreements, the SNB shall act by a majority of its members.

571. Law 106(I)/11 provides for subsidiary requirements which may apply if so decided by the central management and the SNB, or where the central management refuses to commence negotiations within six months of the request, or where after three years from the request, the parties are unable to conclude an agreement (sections 12–16 of Law 106(I)/11). These satisfy the provisions of Annex I of Directive/38/EC. The confidentiality of information given to members of the SNB and their experts is also safeguarded by section 17 of Law 106(I)/11; the obligations continue to apply even after the expiry of their term of office. Section 17(2) of Law 106(I)/11 has provided that the central management is not obligated to transmit information

655. Thereby implementing Article 5(6) of Directive 2009/38/EC.

656. Taking into account the need for balanced representation of employees.

when its nature is such that, according to objective criteria, it would seriously harm the functioning of the undertakings concerned or would be prejudicial to them, or if the information is characterized as confidential by the legislation in force; confidential information may, however, be revealed to the EWC following a court order. No particular provisions have been laid down to pursue the aim of ideological guidance with respect to information and the expression of opinions.[657]

572. It is further provided under section 18 of Law 106(I)/11 that the central management and the EWC should work in a spirit of cooperation with due regard to their reciprocal rights and obligations; the same should apply to cooperation between the central management and employees' representatives in the framework of an information and consultation procedure for workers. Members of the EWC should have all the means required to apply their rights arising and to represent collectively the interests of the employees of the Community-scale undertaking or group of undertakings (section 19 of Law 106(I)/11). Members of the SNB, the EWC and employees' representatives shall, in the exercise of their functions, enjoy all the protection and guarantees provided by the national legislation to employees' representatives and insofar as this is necessary for the exercise of their representative duties in an international environment, the members of the SNB and of the EWC shall be provided with training without loss of wages.

§3. Safety Committees

573. In every workplace, establishment, enterprise or undertaking with more than two employees with the same employer, there is a safety representative who represents the employees on matters relevant to safety at work.[658] Section 8 of the Health and Safety at Work Law 89(I)/1996 further provides for the establishment of a safety committee with an advisory role in workplaces with 10 or more employees. Whereas the employers remain responsible for the health and safety of their employees, they should consult with the employee representatives in workplaces with fewer than 10 employees and with the safety committee in workplaces with more than 10 employees.

574. In workplaces with 10–19 employees, the safety committee consists of 2 members, with 20–49 employees of three members and one additional member is added for every 50 additional employees. Thus, in a workplace with 200 employees, the safety committee should consist of six members; there is no ceiling on the number of potential members of the committee, although if the employer employs more than 200 employees, then section 10 of Law 89(I)/96 provides for the appointment of a safety officer. The safety officer should be employed full-time on issues relating to safety and health at work and should control and administer any issue

657. As would be possible in accordance with Article 8(3) of Directive 2009/38/EC.
658. See also OEB, *Handbook of Officer of Labour Relations: Health and Safety at the Workplace* (Nicosia, 2015, in Greek): 24–28.

relevant to health and safety at the workplace, conduct inspections, prepare reports and recommendations and organize training sessions.

575. Safety representatives are elected by the employees for a period of three years; the election should be organized by the employer in cooperation with any existing safety representatives, 15 days prior to the end of term of any existing safety representatives. A person may be elected as a representative if he has been employed for more than two years; a person may be re-elected for unlimited terms. If the representative's employment is terminated, or if he resigns from his duties, a substitute is elected for the remaining term within 15 days (Regulations for Safety Commission at Work 134/97). The role of the safety representative or committee is primarily consultative and advisory; employers are required to consult with the representatives of the employees in order to achieve a safe and healthy workplace (section 13 of Law 89(I)/96). The employer or his representative chairs the safety committee.

576. By virtue of the Regulations for Safety at Work 134/1997 the safety representative or committee should generally represent the employees for all issues relevant to health and safety at the workplace, make recommendations to the employer, accompany during inspections and inform about potential hazards in the workplace the inspectors appointed by the Minister of Labour, Welfare and Social Insurance and carry out their own inspections, promote training in health and safety and encourage co-operation on health and safety issues, consult with other employees and discuss in committee any problems relevant to health and safety at the workplace. Safety committees should meet once every three months and keep minutes of such meetings; special meetings may be convened if there are urgent issues that need to be discussed. The employer should provide the committee members with all necessary information and facilitate them in the carrying out of their duties, including training and time to undertake their duties without loss of pay.

Chapter 4. Collective Bargaining

§1. Levels of Bargaining

I. Industry/Company Level Bargaining

577. Existing legislation does not differentiate between levels of bargaining; for instance, a 'bargaining unit' is defined in the Recognition of Unions and the Right to Provide Facilities for the Aim of their Recognition Law 55(I)/2012 as the enterprise in which the recognition of the trade union for the purposes of negotiation of the collective agreement is sought, without any further differentiation between levels. Collective bargaining is considered as mostly decentralized, in view of the non-legally binding character of collective agreements; accordingly, the norm would be to conduct bargaining at sectoral-industry[659] or company level. However, some major inter-industry agreements have been agreed over the years, the most important of which is the IRC, whereas others include the 1992 Agreement between PEO, SEK and OEB on the gradual reduction of working hours, which was signed in 1992, the 1995 National Plan for Productivity and Health and Safety between OEB, KEBE, PEO, SEK, DEOK, POAS and PASYDY, and the 2004 Agreement on the Procedure for Labour Disputes in Essential Services between OEB, KEBE, PEO, SEK, DEOK and the Ministry of Labour, Welfare and Social Insurance.

578. Recent years have seen an increase in company level collective bargaining; it is estimated that more than 400 company level agreements are currently in force. However, industry level collective bargaining maintains its significance and major sectoral level collective agreements are in force, As noted, however: 'given that a level is defined as dominant with regard to the percentages of workers whose pay is set on that particular level, it is difficult to say which level predominates … despite the numerical preponderance of the enterprise level, the sectoral level is regarded as just as important, if not more important as far as coverage is concerned'.[660] Industry level collective agreements cover for instance, approximately 25,000 employees in the construction industry, 16,000 employees in the hotel industry and nearly 10,000 employees in the banking industry. The overall coverage of collective bargaining is estimated at 50–55 per cent.

579. At industry-sectoral level, bargaining is carried out between the relevant employer associations and the relevant employee trade union confederations, either between PEO and SEK on the one hand and OEB on the other, or between the relevant federation of employees on the one hand and the relevant federation of employers on the other [such as between ETYK and the Cyprus Bank Employers' Association (KEST)]. At company level collective bargaining is conducted between the employer on the one hand and the local employee trade union typically with the

659. As Christofides argues, owing to the country's small size, the terms 'sectoral' and 'national' are sometimes considered as synonymous, Christofides 2003: 11.

660. E. Soumeli, 'Cyprus: Industrial Relations Profile' (2011) available at http://www.eurofound.europa.eu/sites/default/files/ef_files/eiro/country/cyprus.pdf.

aid of representatives of the major trade union confederations, i.e. PEO or SEK. As far as the public sector is concerned, collective bargaining is carried out by special joint mechanisms and predominantly following negotiations with PASYDY. Sectoral collective bargaining might in some cases, such as hotels or construction, be also considered as a yardstick for enterprise level negotiations, so that minimum wages agreed at the industry level result in higher payments being negotiated at the enterprise level.[661]

§2. Content of Bargaining

I. Normative/Obligatory

A. *The Cypriot Corporatist Model*

580. As already identified, the industrial relations structure of Cyprus is defined by cooperation between three parties: the trade unions, the employers' representatives and the government. Organized interests – in the form of organised employers and organized labour – play a central role in this structure, as they are actively incorporated into the policy-making process. This system of interest intermediation is often recognised to be the central core of the notion of corporatism[662] and this is why the Cypriot industrial relations structure has been labelled as the 'Cypriot corporatist model'.[663] Workers are represented through their trade unions, ranging from national, multisectoral bodies, to smaller ones that stand for independent sectoral interests.[664] The two main multisectoral trade union confederations, PEO and SEK, control, to a large extent, the process. Employers are represented through either or both of the two main organizations: OEB and KEBE, which represent their members on a number of tripartite bodies, both across the island, as well as internationally. Finally, the government is represented through the Ministry of Labour, Welfare and Social Insurance (as well as the Ministry of Finance and the Planning Bureau, which are responsible for the economic aspects of the system).

581. The Ministry of Labour, Welfare and Social Insurance is mainly responsible for controlling and supervising the overall running of the labour market, and more specifically, it is the body in charge of the system of industrial relations. Specifically, the Industrial Relations Service monitors the collective bargaining process.

661. Soumeli characterizes these sectors as 'pace making sectors'.
662. P. Schmitter, 'Still the Century of Corporatism?', in Philippe Schmitter and Gerhard Lehmbruch (eds.), *Trends Towards Corporatism Intermediation*, London: Sage, 1979, 7–49 (first published in *Review of Politics* 36, 1974).
663. See in detail C. Ioannou, 'The Development of the 'Cypriot Corporatist Model': The Emergence of a 'Corporatist Culture' and its Impact on the Process of Europeanisation' (2009)10 *Cyprus and European Law Review*: 700–736, C. Ioannou and G. Kentas, 'The Mediating Impact of Corporatism on the Europeanisation of the Cypriot Labour Sector' (2009) 21(2) *The Cyprus Review*: 115–135.
664. L. Christofides, *National Study for the Republic of Cyprus*, RILSA-ILO Research Project: Nicosia, 2003, p. 8.

Tripartite bodies – including representatives from all three aforementioned parties – determine policy on all issues relating to the labour market. At the national level, the Labour Advisory Board exists, which is chaired by the Minister of Labour, Welfare and Social Insurance, and consists of three representatives from each of OEB and KEBE on the employers side, three representatives from each of PEO and SEK, and one representative from DEOK on the trade unions' side; representatives from POAS and PASYDY may attend as observers, whereas representatives from other employees' and employers' movements that have interest in the specific subject matter being discussed may express their views.

582. The function of the Labour Advisory Board is to advise the Minister of Labour, Welfare and Social Insurance on all national labour matters, while it also acts as an important vehicle for the development of labour policy. Every proposed piece of labour legislation, social programme, and every labour market policy more generally, is discussed in the Labour Advisory Board before being presented to the House of Representatives. The latter is rarely expected to overturn a unanimous recommendation from the Labour Advisory Board.[665] The Board further has ad hoc sub-committees which deal with particular issues. As far as the local level is concerned, problems are dealt with by the District Labour Advisory Committees. There exist currently a large number of permanent tripartite bodies of social dialogue which function at the Ministry of Labour, Welfare and Social Insurance.[666]

583. All tripartite bodies operate on the basis of formal, written constitutions and rules, which have previously been discussed and agreed by the parties concerned, and adherence to the constitutions and rules is strict. There can be no deviation from the rules except in exceptional cases, which have previously been discussed and agreed upon by the parties concerned.[667] It should be underlined that these constitutions and rules provide for a permanent secretariat, whose function is to prepare the agenda for the meetings, to keep and circulate the minutes of the meetings, to follow the implementation of the decisions taken at the meetings, and to provide the data, documents, statistics and information to the members. In addition to the constitutions and rules, the terms of reference of the tripartite bodies are also clearly defined, so as to enable their members to concentrate on the issues that they are authorised to handle, and prevent them from side-tracking into irrelevancies.

584. As far as the frequency of the meetings of the tripartite bodies is concerned, there is no fixed or predetermined time interval. These are held, however, at regular intervals, in accordance with the rules and regulations of the tripartite body concerned. Ad hoc meetings may also be held, as the rules and regulations also provide for these. Regularity of meetings is, in fact, considered to be important, in order to maintain the continuity of the system. It must be noted, however, that both the frequency and the regularity of meetings that are officially reported, do not record the informal contacts that take place between the members. Owing to the

665. *Ibid.*, 14.
666. See a list at http://www.mlsi.gov.cy/mlsi/mlsi.nsf/mlsi26_gr/mlsi26_gr?OpenDocument.
667. M. Sparsis, *Tripartism and Industrial Relations: The Cyprus Experience*, Nicosia, 1998: 16.

small size of Cypriot society and the kind of contacts that exist among people, but owing also to the Cypriot mentality that favours informal links and relations, a community is inevitably formed between the members of these bodies. Even though these 'informal community contacts' are not officially documented, it is worth taking them into account as an important addition to the frequency of tripartite member meeting. In fact, informality constitutes an important parameter of Cypriot industrial relations.

585. It has been an important part of the official philosophy of the Republic of Cyprus that, in the realm of labour policy, cooperation between the parties involved and affected, is an essential element of the success of the system. How this has been put into practice, however, can be seen through the 'Basic Agreement', which was the first social contract signed between the social partners in 1962, shortly after independence. This secured the right to organise, negotiate, sign collective agreements, and the right to strike, and also provided for a procedural framework dealing with industrial disputes. In 1977 this Agreement was replaced by the IRC, which was designed to safeguard the interests of both sides of the negotiation.[668] The latter adopted the main conventions of the ILO and is, as already indicated, essentially a gentlemen's agreement that regulates the collective bargaining process. One of the most defining characteristics of the 'Cypriot corporatist model' is its reliance on collective bargaining agreements, which involve negotiations between the parties concerned.

586. Almost all major issues proposed by the Ministry of Labour, Welfare and Social Insurance follow tripartite discussions between the parties. The policies and programmes of the Ministry are only prepared after consultation and with the full support of the employers' and workers' organizations of Cyprus; in this respect, 'tripartite cooperation is the cornerstone of the policies of the Ministry of Labour and Social Insurance of the Republic'.[669] It should be noted, however, that sectoral social dialogue differs somewhat from social dialogue at the national level, as social dialogue at the sectoral level should properly be more of a bilateral dialogue. However, in practice, sectoral social dialogue often ends up being discussed at a national level in the tripartite bodies. This has led major single-sector trade unions, such as ETYK, to argue that they are essentially excluded from the official bodies of tripartite representation. Finally, social dialogue at a company level typically takes place in accordance with the provisions of the IRC.

587. Collective bargaining, based on the principle of tripartite cooperation, has traditionally played a chief role in regulating industrial relations in the country. At the same time, legislation has largely constituted a secondary tool for regulation.[670]

668. O. Messios, *Social Dialogue and Conflict Resolution in Cyprus,* Report financed by the European Foundation for the Improvement of Living and Working Conditions, EF/04/46/EN, Dublin, 2004, p. 2, M. Spanos, 'Preamble to the Industrial Relations Code', in Republic of Cyprus, Ministry of Labour and Social Insurance, *Industrial Relations Code,* Nicosia: Press and Information Office, 1977: 4.

669. Sparsis, see above: 10.

670. Yannakourou and Soumeli, see above: 29.

This limited role of statutory regulation in the Cypriot labour market is one of the key features of the 'Cypriot corporatist model'. The system is largely based on voluntarism. The system of collective bargaining thus clearly involves continuous social dialogue and compromises between employers, employees and the government. In light of its voluntary nature, there is no mandatory content of the collective agreement; the parties may freely choose what to include and what not to include in a collective agreement.

B. Recognition by the Employer for Bargaining Purposes

588. Law 55(I)/2012 established the procedure for registered trade unions to be recognized by employers, so as to enable collective bargaining between the employer and the trade union. Law 55(I)/12 was adopted in order to address the refusal by certain employees to recognize registered trade unions and engage into collective bargaining with them. It should be noted, however, that the Law does not oblige an employer to actually conclude a collective agreement, but only to recognize and negotiate with a trade union for the purposes of concluding a collective agreement. If the negotiations fail, then the provisions of the IRC should be followed.[671] The competent court for any disputes of a civil nature under Law 55(I)/12 is the IDT (section 20 of Law 55(I)/12).

589. It is accordingly provided that if an employer refuses to recognize a registered trade union for the purposes of negotiation for the conclusion of a collective agreement, the trade union may apply to the Registrar for the issuance of an order of recognition (section 3 of Law 55(I)/12). In case of multiple applications by different trade unions within the same bargaining unit, the Registrar shall liaise with the trade unions so that their applications are joined, in which case they shall be considered as a single application. If the trade unions do not consent to the joinder of their applications, the Registrar shall examine them in turn in the order in which they were submitted (section 4 of Law 55(I)/12).

590. By virtue of section 5 of Law 55(I)/12, the Registrar should preliminarily examine within five working days, whether the criteria for the acceptance of the application are satisfied and inform the trade union accordingly; if the criteria are satisfied, the Registrar shall address the application to the employer. The criteria for acceptance of an application are stipulated under section 7 of Law 55(I)/12 and are the following: (i) the application should specifically define the bargaining unit, (ii) the employer should have employed an average of at least 30 employees in the bargaining unit, during the last six months prior to the submission of the application,[672] (iii) at least 25 per cent of employees of the bargaining unit should be

671. See also OEB, *Handbook of Officer of Labour Relations: Basic Labour Legislation* (Nicosia, 2015, in Greek): 94.

672. This includes employees of either definite, or indefinite duration, as well as part-time employees, or other persons who are engaged in circumstances which amount to an employer–employee relationship.

members of the applicant trade union[673] and (iv) no procedure for mediation is pending before the Department of Labour Relations with regard to the recognition or organization of the trade union.

591. Once he receives the application by the Registrar, the employer must send within five working days a list of all employees employed during the last six months under any employment status (section 6 of Law 55(I)/12). Within 10 working days from receipt of the application, the employer may object in writing before the Registrar (section 8 of Law 55(I)/12); in this case the Registrar may hold either joint or private meetings with the employer and the trade union. The Registrar should decide, within 15 working days from the notification of the application to the employer, whether the application is approved. If the application is not approved, then the applicant trade union may not submit another application for the same bargaining unit for a period of six months (section 9 of Law 55(I)12).

592. If the application is approved, then the Registrar organizes a secret vote in the bargaining unit within ten working days, in order to establish whether the employees wish to be represented by the trade union for the purpose of collective bargaining. However, if more than 50 per cent of the employees are already members of the trade union, then the Registrar issues an order of recognition without holding a secret vote (section 10 of Law 55(I)/12). If there is a dispute about the list of employees who have a right to vote, the Registrar may request any data he considers necessary from any trade union, public service, or authority. During the secret vote, the employer and his representatives have no right to attend (section 11 of Law 55(I)/12). In anticipation of the voting, the trade union may organize assemblies within the bargaining unit as agreed with the employer, or as determined by the Registrar; the employer shall facilitate such assemblies, but the assemblies should not impede the proper functioning of the business (section 13 of Law 55(I)/12).

593. If more than 50 per cent of actual votes, representing at least 40 per cent of all employees who had a right to vote, are in favour, then the Registrar issues an order of recognition (section 11 of Law 55(I)/12). However, if the necessary votes are not secured, no new application for recognition of the trade union for the specific bargaining unit may be accepted for a period of two years, unless the Registrar becomes convinced that the trade union has already organized more than 50 per cent of those who are employed in the bargaining unit; if the Registrar holds that the trade union has not organized at least 50 per cent of the employees, then the application shall be rejected and no new application may be accepted for a period of two years under any circumstances (section 12 of Law 55(I)/12).

594. A question could be raised whether the requirements set out in Law 55(I)/12 are consistent with the content of the right as safeguarded by Article 21 of the Constitution. Since collective bargaining should be considered as an integral part of

673. 24.51 per cent is rounded to 25 per cent for the purposes of this section.

the right to form and join a trade union,[674] the requirement that an application for recognition for the purposes of collective bargaining should be accepted only if at least 25 per cent of the employees of the bargaining unit are members of the applicant trade union and if the applicant trade union enjoys the support of the majority of the employees of the bargaining unit following a secret vote, might be considered as inconsistent with the right safeguarded under Article 21 of the Constitution. If only the major trade union in a bargaining unit enjoys recognition for the purposes of collective bargaining, then this may lead to a violation of the right of numerically smaller trade unions who may effectively be indirectly coerced into joining the numerically larger trade union instead of their own, in order to have the right to be heard and to engage into collective bargaining.[675] It should be noted, however, that recognition criteria applicable for collective bargaining purposes are hardly considered as unreasonable under the ILO convention, as 'the employer cannot reasonably be expected to conclude an agreement with a union which is not representative'.[676]

595. In order to exercise his powers under the Law, the Registrar may, by virtue of section 15 of Law 55(I)/12, be accompanied by any other person, including members of the police force if he has reasonable grounds to believe that he shall be prevented from performing his duties. The Registrar shall inform the employer in advance for his presence, unless he considers that this might adversely affect the performance of his duties. The Registrar may further conduct inquiries, investigations, audits or inspections as needed for the application of Law 55(I)/12, including requesting from any person in the workplace to facilitate or assist him in the exercise of his powers, and to request any person to provide information or clarification and to further sign a declaration that he has provided such information or clarification truthfully.

596. By virtue of section 17 of Law 55(I)/12, the employer and his representatives and employees, as well as any representative of the trade union, must provide any documents and information in their possession relevant to the exercise of his powers under the Law, and facilitate the exercise of his powers. The Registrar may further receive and examine complaints with regard to disputes arising under Law 55(I)/12, pursuant to section 17 of the Law. Any information that the Registrar received while exercising his duties shall be treated as confidential and shall not be disclosed or disseminated (section 18 of Law 55(I)/12).

597. If an employer refuses to negotiate, or negotiate in good faith, or recognize or meet with the representatives of the trade union, even after the issuance of a recognition order by the Registrar, then the trade union may file a complaint to the Registrar, or file an application to the Department of Labour Relations for mediation in

674. See in detail L. Loucaides, 'Legal Protection of the Freedom of Trade Unionism in Cyprus' (1986) 15 *Cyprus Law Review*: 2346–2359.
675. See in this respect *Pancyprian Trade Union of Nurses* v. *Ministry of Health* [1994] 4 CLR 174 (in Greek).
676. S. de Silva, Collective Bargaining Negotiations, (ILO Publications, 1996): 11, available at http://www.ilo.org/public/english/dialogue/actemp/downloads/publications/srscbarg.pdf.

an industrial dispute. It is a criminal offence punishable by fine, for any employer to refuse to recognize, or negotiate with the trade union following the issuance of a recognition order, or to impede the representatives of the trade union from exercising their duties and have access to the employees for the purposes of the issuance of a recognition order, or to intimidate or influence the free will of the employees in a procedure for recognition, or to unilaterally amend the terms of employment of the employees of the bargaining unit. It is further a criminal offence punishable by fine, for any person to impede the Registrar in the exercise of his powers under the Law (section 21 of Law 55(I)/12). The court may further order any person to comply with the provisions of Law 55(I)/12 within a set period of time (section 23 of Law 55(I)/12).

C. *Collective Bargaining under the IRC*

598. In section B of the IRC it is accepted by both employers and employee organizations that collective bargaining constitutes the basic way for the determination of conditions of employment and remuneration. Therefore, both sides undertake: (i) to promote collective bargaining and joint consultation and (ii) to negotiate in a spirit of good faith and mutual understanding, bearing in mind the prevailing industrial relations principles and practices, the public interest, the usual criteria on which the determination of wages and conditions of employment is based, as well as such criteria as might be agreed upon by the government and the two sides in industry with regard to a prices and incomes policy. Both parties have agreed to follow the procedure specified in the IRC for the negotiation or renewal of collective agreements.

599. Section C of the IRC recognizes the existence of issues considered as bargainable, in accordance with the generally accepted principles and practices of industrial relations, of issues which are considered as consultative and of issues considered as prerogatives of the management, i.e. the employer. The IRC does not attempt to define each category of issues, leaving them to be specified in the particular collective agreements to be agreed between the parties. In general, however, issues pertaining to salaries and benefits of employees, working time, annual leave and similar issues are always considered as bargainable, whereas issues pertaining to discipline of employees, working hours of the enterprise, distribution of annual leave amongst employees, job description and similar issues are normally considered as consultative.[677] With regard to management decisions, however, such as pricing, production, collaborations, or wider strategy of the company, the employer is expected to act without consulting with either the union or the employees as these are considered as prerogatives of the management.

600. Even if no reference has been made in a specific collective agreement to an issue as being consultative, i.e. proper for joint consultation, the employer should

677. See OEB, *Handbook of Officer of Labour Relations: Settlement of Industrial Disputes, Code of Industrial Relations, Essential Services, Arbitration* (Nicosia, 2015, in Greek): 14.

nevertheless engage in joint consultation with the union of employees so long as the union or the employees contend that a decision on the issue adversely affects them or may have repercussions on their relations with their employer. As regards consultative issues, the final decision rests with the employer. It is recognised, however, that the employer is bound to pay due regard to the union's or the employees' views on such issues and to give reasons for any negative answer. Furthermore, both sides may, in case of disagreement, ask for the advice and assistance of the Ministry of Labour, Welfare and Social Insurance.

601. In practice, the content of collective agreements may normally cover the following areas: working time, overtime and payment of overtime, salaries, wages, allowances, increases, COLA and other benefits, annual leave, sick leave and benefits, holidays, pregnancy leave, medical care, provident fund, welfare fund, travel expenses, termination of employment, payments to employees' trade unions, grievances and settlement of disputes normally by adopting the provisions of the IRC, employee representation, employment exclusivity clauses, discipline, force, renewal and amendment of the collective agreement.[678] A collective agreement is usually in force for at least two years and may be renewed, either automatically, or by the conclusion of a new agreement.

602. In general, the IRC provides for the following procedure for the conclusion of a new collective agreement: the recognized union(s) representing the employees of the undertaking concerned may submit to the employer claims in writing, with a view to concluding a collective agreement, covering the class of employees whom they represent, comprising the submitted claims as well as other conditions of employment which may already exist within the undertaking. The employer is obliged to commence direct negotiations with the union(s) concerned on the submitted claims not later than three weeks from the day of receiving the claims or, in the case of organizations operating on an island-wide basis, not later than one month (provided the union has in the meantime explained its claims in writing), after giving the unions reasonable notice of his intention to commence such negotiations.

603. In case of an existing collective agreement, the party seeking to amend it, should give the other party at least two months' notice prior to the expiration of such agreement, of its intention to do so, accompanied by a list of claims and/or modifications, except where, in the case of small-sized undertakings, it is otherwise stipulated in the collective agreement. If both parties agree, however, it is not necessary to submit claims two months in advance for renewal of existing agreements, provided notification is given in writing of the intention to do so and provided the claims are submitted at any time before the expiration of the agreement. In such cases the existing collective agreement will continue to be in force for a period equal to the length of the delay in the submission of the claims, unless such delay does not exceed 15 days. Where the party seeking the modification of an existing

678. See also C. Christodoulou, *Handbook of Cypriot Labour Law* (Nicosia: Epifaniou, 2009, in Greek): 105ff.

agreement has failed to give notice of its intention to the other side before commencement of the two-month period prior to the expiration of the agreement, the collective agreement shall remain in force for another year.

D. Collective Bargaining in the Public Sector

604. Special rules govern collective bargaining in the public sector. Collective bargaining in the public service is carried out within the framework of the Joint Staff Committee (JSC).[679] The JSC was set up in 1962[680] and aims to secure co-operation between the government, in its capacity as employer, and the representative trade union of the public servants; it constitutes the official consultative body in the public service, discusses the terms of employment of public servants and submits suggestions to the government for examination and approval. The functions of the JSC include appointments and promotions, working hours, leave, medical treatment, discipline, remuneration, retirement, welfare benefits, training and in general legislation affecting the terms of employment of public servants.

605. The JSC is chaired by the Permanent Secretary of the Ministry of Finance and its members include the Director of the Department of Public Administration and Personnel and two representatives of PASYDY. A number of sub-committees function within the framework of the JSC. Decisions of the JSC which are reached unanimously are submitted in the form of a proposal to the Council of Ministers by the Minister of Finance; when it is not possible to reach a unanimous decision, the differing views are submitted to the Council of Ministers. If the Council of Ministers has a different view on any decision of the JSC, it informs it accordingly and if the JSC disagrees, the matter is resubmitted to the Council of Ministers for a final decision to be reached; a committee of Ministers composed of the Minister of Finance, the Minister of Labour, Welfare and Social Insurance and a third Minister who is appointed by the Council of Ministers, acts as the liaison between the JSC and the Council of Ministers.

606. In practice the JSC acts as a negotiating body, for the purpose of collective bargaining between the government and PASYDY. In 1987, joint departmental staff committees were established within each Ministry; these committees negotiate on special issues and their decisions are subsequently submitted to the JSC. A procedure for the examination of personal grievances submitted by public servants in connection with their service has also been introduced. Furthermore, the Board for the examination of disputes arising at the JSC was established; the Board effectively provides for the reference of a dispute to compulsory arbitration when all procedures provided at the JSC level have been exhausted and discussions have resulted in deadlock. A dispute is submitted to the Board accompanied by a joint report prepared by the two sides

679. See C. Christodoulou, *A Study of Labour Law in Cyprus* (PhD Wales, 1992): 202–215, *idem, Handbook of Cypriot Labour Law* (Nicosia: Epifaniou, 2009, in Greek): 150–162.

680. During British rule, from 1947 onwards, a similar committee called the Joint Consultative Committee was in force, modelled after the British National Whitley Council.

which details the background to the issue, the negotiations held and the matters of dispute. To date no disputes have been referred to compulsory arbitration of this kind, which indicates that the parties, and especially the government, do not consider arbitration as a viable method for the settlement of disputes over rights in the public sector.

607. Additional committees have been established in other parts of the public sector. The Joint Labour Committee (JLC) is the respective competent organ for collective bargaining for the hourly paid staff of the government; the JLC is the organ responsible for submitting recommendations to the Council of Ministers with regard to the terms of employment of the hourly paid staff of the government, in a similar manner as the JSC is for public servants. The JLC is chaired by the Permanent Secretary of the Ministry of Finance and its members include the Permanent Secretaries of the Ministry of Agriculture, Natural Resources and Environment and of the Ministry of Communications and Works, as well as two representatives from each of SEK and PEO. A similar mechanism is also provided in the educational service of the Republic, through the Joint Staff Committee of the Educational Service.

608. The system of collective bargaining in the public sector differs substantially from the system introduced under the IRC for the private and semi-public sector. Decisions taken between the executive and PASYDY at the level of collective bargaining in the JSC always need the approval of the Council of Ministers and constitute a state act and not simply a private collective agreement; accordingly, if consensus cannot be reached, the Council of Ministers may always take a final decision on the matter and approve legislative proposals irrespective of the views of PASYDY. Whereas the bargaining power of PASYDY has always been a major obstacle for the government to exercise its executive prerogative, the government has the power to act unilaterally and has exercised this power over the years.

609. The Council of Ministers may accordingly draft bills to be introduced to the House of Representatives by a particular Minister in accordance with Articles 54(f) and 80 of the Constitution and such power is not restricted by the existence of an agreement with the trade union concerned. Furthermore, the House of Representatives could always reject legislative proposals, even if these had been the outcome of collective bargaining between the Council of Ministers and PASYDY; the House of Representatives may undeniably restrict the power of the executive by amending or rejecting the bills introduced by the executive.[681] This power of the House of Representatives may be exercised irrespective of whether the trade unions supported, or had agreed to such bills and accordingly there is nothing in the Constitution prohibiting the House of Representatives from unilaterally amending the content of collective agreements signed by the Government and PASYDY.[682]

681. For the powers of the Council of Ministers and the House of Representatives under Cypriot constitutional law see A. Emilianides, *Constitutional Law in Cyprus* (The Hague: Kluwer, 2013).

682. See, however, the views of C. Christodoulou, *Handbook of Cypriot Labour Law* (Nicosia: Epifaniou, 2009, in Greek): 43–55 and C. Christodoulou, *The Decision of the House to Amend the Agreement for Principled Restructuring of certain Positions in the Public Service* (Nicosia, 1984, in

II. Binding Effect

610. In view of the non-binding nature of collective agreements in Cyprus, collective agreements have no binding effect, unless they are incorporated in individual employment contracts. However, both employer and employee associations have agreed in the IRC to faithfully observe the provisions of collective agreements resulting from collective bargaining. It has further been provided that any action by an employer which violates a valid collective agreement is condemned and that the employers' association concerned will take all measures deemed necessary for the observance of the agreement. The parties have generally opted to respect the provisions of the IRC, which has contributed over the years to the success of the 'Cypriot corporatist model'.

611. The state has traditionally considered that both the employers' associations and the employee trade unions have showed willingness to cooperate and to show good faith, a factor which accordingly did not necessitate the introduction of legislative measures for the regulation of collective agreements. Thus, while the IRC does not have legally binding effect, it is still considered as an agreement with substantial weight and which both employers and employees have undertaken an obligation to respect.[683]

612. Following the recent economic crisis and increase in unemployment, however, and the signing of the MoU with the Troika, there has been a gradual marginalization of trade unions and subsequent partial deregulation of labour relations. In most cases the employee trade unions and the employer associations in all sectors, public, semi-public, or private, agreed for a transient suspension, or modification of the provisions of collective agreements in order to address the adverse effects of the economic crisis by restricting the rights of the employees. However, there have also been many cases where employers have unilaterally violated, or disregarded provisions of collective agreements in response to the economic crisis; accelerated unemployment led employees, and even trade unions, to be extremely reluctant to file complaints over the violation of collective agreements in fear of retributions, which led to the partial destabilization of the system.[684]

§3. Extension

613. Collective agreements cover both organized and unorganized employees, i.e. irrespective of whether the employees are members of the trade union(s) who engaged into collective bargaining or not. No mechanism exists, however, under

---

Greek) who argues that the House of Representatives may not amend the collective agreement between PASYDY and the Council of Ministers.

683. See, however, C. Christodoulou, *Handbook of Cypriot Labour Law* (Nicosia: Epifaniou, 2009, in Greek): 133–138 who argues that the provisions of the IRC are legally binding.

684. See, *inter alia*, O. Christou O, C. Ioannou and A. Shekeris, 'The Cypriot Welfare State in a Time of Crisis', in K. Schubert (ed.), *Challenges to European Welfare Systems*, (Berlin: Springer, 2015), G. Ioannou, 'Employment in Crisis: Cyprus 2010–2013 (2014) 26(1) *Cyprus Review*: 107–126.

Cypriot law for the extension of collective agreements to cover employers and employees not parties to, or covered by such agreements.[685] Parties may be considered to be bound by a collective agreement only if they voluntarily become parties to such a collective agreement.

§4. INTERPRETATION

614. There are no special rules for interpreting the terms of a collective agreement under Cypriot law and accordingly normal rules of interpretation under contract law apply.[686] A collective agreement is a reflection of the consensus between the employee trade union and the employer, which has been achieved following collective bargaining; accordingly, the intention of the parties should be identified. Words should be given their ordinary meaning and be read in the context of the agreement, so that the intention of the parties is ascertained; the criterion is what a reasonable person would understand by the language in which the parties have expressed their agreement.

685. Eurofound, *Extension of Collective Bargaining Agreements in the EU*, 2009, available in http://www.eurofound.europa.eu/sites/default/files/ef_files/pubdocs/2011/54/en/1/EF1154EN.pdf.
686. For which see P. Polyviou, *Law of Contract*, v. II (Nicosia: Chryssafinis and Polyviou, 2014, in Greek): 455ff.

Chapter 5. Strikes, Lock-outs and Other Legal Forms of Industrial Action

§1. The Content of the Right to Strike

I. The Positive Aspects of the Right to Strike

615. The right to strike is safeguarded by virtue of Article 27 of the Constitution.[687] There is no definition of a strike in the Constitution; however, this is generally regarded as referring to a collective stoppage of work of economic character; political strikes are not guaranteed under Article 27 of the Constitution.[688] The right to strike is therefore exercised collectively and not individually; a single employee cannot go on strike. The individual employee shall therefore be a bearer of the right to strike, but only if this right is exercised collectively with other employees and typically, if it is carried out by a recognized trade union, or by a legally formed labour organization; it should be noted, however, that there is no explicit obligation under Article 27 of the Constitution for the strike to be exercised through a trade union so far as it is exercised in an appropriate collective manner by the employees.

616. A strike further presupposes the existence of an employer–employee relationship. Abstention from work which is unrelated to employer–employee relationship, or abstention from work of self-employed persons, such as advocates,[689] does not therefore fall under the ambit of Article 27 of the Constitution, although it may well fall under the negative aspects of the right to work, which is safeguarded under Article 25 of the Constitution.[690] In the *Quarry Rock and Sand Splitters* case the members of the association of quarry rock and sand splitters indefinitely suspended their sales, an act which was held to violate competition law rules by the Committee for the Protection of Competition. The members of the association filed a recourse before the Supreme Court arguing that their actions fell under the constitutionally protected right to strike, claiming that Article 27 extends to any kind of abstention from work.

617. The Supreme Court held that both the right to strike and the notion of a lock-out presuppose a conflict between the employer and his employees and

---

687. See C. Christodoulou, *A Study of Labour Law in Cyprus* (PhD Wales, 1992): 216–258, C. Christodoulou, *Handbook of Cypriot Labour Law* (Nicosia: Epifaniou, 2009, in Greek): 76–92, T. Eliades, 'The Right to Strike' [1970] 2 *Cyprus Law Tribune*: 28–30. See also Case C-341/05, *Laval un Partneri Ltd* v. *Svenska Byggnadsarbetareförbundet* [2007] ECR I-11767, C-438/05, Case C-438/05, *International Transport Workers' Federation and Finnish Seamen's Union* v. *Viking Line ABP* and another [2007] ECR I-10779.

688. C. Tornaritis, *The Human Rights as Recognized and Protected by the Law of the Republic of Cyprus* (Nicosia: 1974, reprint from (1974) 4–6 *Cyprus Law Tribune*): 23.

689. In *Rousos* v. *Republic* [1984] 3 CLR 1437 the abstention of advocates from work is poorly characterized as 'strike' and there is discussion about the application of Article 27 of the Constitution to such strike.

690. See in detail A. Emilianides, *Professional Law of Advocates* (Nicosia: Dikaionomia, 2007, in Greek): 68–70.

accordingly a lock-out would consist of the refusal of the employer to accept the services of his employees. However, in this case, the suspension of sales by the members of the association was not related to their employees. Accordingly, the Supreme Court held that the right to strike is a social phenomenon which historically and logically presupposes an employer-employee relationship and refers to the collective abstention of employees from their work in order to promote their collective rights; it is therefore typically applied by the legally constituted trade unions for the safeguard of the interests of employees. The recourse was rejected.[691]

618. In *Panayia Myrtidiotissa* the appellants argued that the employment agreements signed with their employees were void due to economic duress and coercion by the employees. The Supreme Court noted that the employees had exercised their collective right to strike in order to promote their interests; the right to strike aims at the improvement of the working conditions and the terms of payment and cannot by itself be characterized as coercion, or economic duress, nor can it invalidate a lawfully concluded agreement between the parties. A different interpretation would unjustifiably restrict the right to strike.[692]

619. Whereas Article 27 of the Constitution does not expressly provide for lock-outs, it could be argued that the right to strike includes a right to lock out by the employers; if the aim of the constitutional legislator was to restrict such right it would have been expected to do so expressly.[693] This view is also consistent with Article 6 of the European Social Charter, which has been ratified by Law 64/67, which refers to the right of both workers and employers to strike. The right of the employers to lock out has also been impliedly recognized by the employee trade unions in the IRC which refers to the option of strike, or lock-outs in case of deadlock; in practice the right of employers to lock out has never been questioned by employee trade unions.

620. It is questioned whether Article 27 also covers sympathy strikes, i.e. strikes which relate to the employment or non-employment or terms of employment of persons who are employed by another employer and whose aim is to show solidarity or sympathy towards the employees who have a dispute with their employer in connection with their employment. Former Attorney-General Criton Tornaritis expressed the view that there is no legal protection of sympathy strike in Cyprus, noting that in order to enjoy constitutional protection the strike must be related to

691. *Association of Industrialists of Quarry Rock and Sand Splitters and others* v. *Commission for the Protection of Competition* [1992] 4 CLR 711 (in Greek).

692. *Ship Panayia Myrtidiotissa* v. *Sidiropoulou and another* [1998] 1 CLR 1000 (in Greek).

693. This view is supported by C. Christodoulou, *A Study of Labour Law in Cyprus* (PhD Wales, 1992): 229–230. The question was left open in *Association of Industrialists of Quarry Rock and Sand Splitters and others* v. *Commission for the Protection of Competition* [1992] 4 CLR 711 (in Greek). See C. Tornaritis, 'The Right of Employers to Lock Out' [1972] 1–2 Cyprus Law Tribune: 18-21 (in Greek).

the promotion of an existing or imminent labour dispute. He further observed that it is doubtful whether this right is safeguarded under Cypriot law;[694]

621. Former Deputy Attorney-General and former ECtHR judge Loukis Loucaides, however, disagreed with this view and argued that there is nothing in Article 27 of the Constitution excluding sympathy strikes from its ambit; trade unionism depends on the solidarity of employees and a sympathy strike aims at safeguarding the wider interests of employees against their employers. Loucaides further argued that the existing legislation defines an industrial dispute as any dispute between employers and employees which is related to the employment of any person or his terms of employment or work, a definition which is wide enough to also cover the case of sympathy strike.[695] It is submitted that this latter view is the correct one. In any event sympathy strikes occur rarely in the Cypriot legal order.

II. Restriction of the Right

622. Exercise of the right to strike may be regulated by law only for the purposes of safeguarding the security of the Republic, or the constitutional order, or the public order, or the public safety, or the maintenance of supplies and services essential to the life of the inhabitants or the protection of the rights and liberties guaranteed by the Constitution to any person.[696] A law cannot render the right to strike meaningless and accordingly regulation of the right to strike should be in accordance with constitutional provisions; the right may be restricted only if it is absolutely necessary. Accordingly, an employer may not fire employees because they exercise their right to strike, as the right does not amount to a termination of the employment agreement and a dismissal in such a case would be unlawful;[697] as soon as the strike is over, the employee has a right to demand the continuation of the existing employment agreement. According to the prevailing opinion, however, the employer may refrain from paying the employee for the period during which he participated in a strike.[698]

623. The members of the armed forces, of the police and of the gendarmerie do not enjoy the right to strike by virtue of Article 27 of the Constitution. It is further provided that a law may extend such prohibition to the members of the public service. No such prohibition has been extended to members of the public service, however; on the contrary, section 63 of the Public Service Law 1/90 safeguards the unhindered exercise of the freedom of association (and any related rights) of public

694. C. Tornaritis, 'Sympathy Strike in accordance with the Existing Law in Cyprus' [1969] 4 *Cyprus Law Tribune*: 3–8 (in Greek).
695. L. Loucaides, 'The Right of Strike and Sympathy or Solidarity Strike' (1984) 5 *Cyprus Law Review*: 831–838 (in Greek). See also C. Christodoulou, *A Study of Labour Law in Cyprus* (PhD Wales, 1992): 235.
696. A. Loizou, 'Restriction of the Right to Strike under the Constitution of Cyprus and International Conventions' [1995] 11 *Lysias*: 23–30 (in Greek).
697. A. Loizou, *Constitution of the Republic of Cyprus* (Nicosia, 2001, in Greek): 170.
698. See the obiter comments in *Artemiou* v. *Republic* [1990] 3 CLR 1327 (in Greek).

servants. Indeed, Cypriot civil servants have enjoyed the right to strike since Independence and this has never been questioned by the state. The prohibition of the right to strike for members of the armed forces and the police is rooted in the belief that the exercise of such a right would be incompatible with the fundamental role of members of the armed forces and the police and would endanger the rights and interests of citizens as a whole.

624. It should be noted, however, that Article 8 of the International Covenant on Economic, Social and Cultural Rights of the UN, which has been ratified in the Republic of Cyprus by law 14/1969, provides that 'lawful restrictions' may be imposed on the right to strike for members of the armed forces or the police. Former Attorney-General Criton Tornaritis has argued that restriction does not exclude the notion of prohibition and that accordingly there is no inconsistency between Article 27(2) of the Constitution and Article 8 of the Convention.[699] This view does not seem convincing, however, as lawful restrictions presuppose the existence of a right, which under Article 27(2) of the Constitution is denied for members of the armed forces and the police; a right cannot be restricted, if it is inexistent.[700]

625. Section 44 of Law 71/65 provides that members of a trade union engaged in an industrial dispute may lawfully attend the premises of an enterprise in order to peacefully receive or provide information, or to encourage employees to work or abstain from their employment. Protestations and picketing are thus lawful, but they should not extend beyond the area where the industrial dispute is situated. The requirement that members of the trade union should not extend the picketing beyond the area where the industrial dispute is situated seems a rather arbitrary one; in practice the right to strike would normally include picketing outside the premises of the enterprise, since the objective is to make the strike known 'to the public and attract its sympathy and support'.[701]

626. The CJEU held that collective action in the exercise of the right to strike constitutes a restriction on freedom of establishment of nationals of a Member State in the territory of another Member State, as guaranteed by the TFEU. The CJEU acknowledged that the right to strike is a fundamental right, that the right to take collective action for the protection of workers is a legitimate interest which, in principle, justifies a restriction of one of the fundamental freedoms guaranteed by the Treaty and that the protection of workers is an overriding reason of public interest.[702]

699. C. Tornaritis, *The State Law of the Republic of Cyprus* (Nicosia: Cyprus Research Center, 1982, in Greek): 471–472, C. Tornaritis, *The Human Rights as Recognized and Protected by the Law of the Republic of Cyprus* (Nicosia: 1974, reprint from (1974) 4–6 *Cyprus Law Tribune*): 24–25.
700. See also C. Christodoulou, *A Study of Labour Law in Cyprus* (PhD Wales, 1992): 225.
701. *Ibid.*: 227.
702. Case C-341/05, *Laval un Partneri Ltd* v. *Svenska Byggnadsarbetareförbundet* [2007] ECR I-11767, C-438/05, Case C-438/05, *International Transport Workers' Federation and Finnish Seamen's Union* v. *Viking Line ABP* and another [2007] ECR I-10779.

627. However, the CJEU added that the objective of protecting workers would no longer be tenable if it were established that the conditions of employment at issue were not jeopardized or under serious threat; the restriction should thus be suitable for ensuring the attainment of the legitimate objective pursued and does not go beyond what is necessary to achieve that objective.[703] In a controversial judgment, it was held that a trade union is precluded from attempting by means of collective action in the form of a blockade of sites, to force a provider of services established in another Member State to enter into negotiations with it on the rates of pay for posted workers and to sign a collective agreement, the terms of which prescribe more favourable conditions that those resulting from the relevant legislative provisions.[704]

III. Strikes in Essential Services

628. The right to strike in essential services is partly covered by the Supplies and Services (Transitional Powers Continuation) Law, Cap. 175A, a law which was enacted in Britain at the end of World War II and maintains in force the Defence Regulations 79A and 79B and the Essential Services Order 1943. Section 3 of Cap. 175A authorizes the Government to direct any person to perform services for the purpose of maintaining, controlling and regulating supplies and services and in particular to secure their equitable distribution and to ensure that all resources of the community are available for use and are used in a manner calculated to serve the interests of the community. It further authorizes the government to require persons employed in undertakings engaged in work essential for any such purpose, not to terminate their employment or abstain from work and to issue regulations to prohibit strikes and lock-outs. Furthermore, the Council of Ministers may, by virtue of Regulation 79B, prohibit any strike, declare an industry or undertaking or the work performed by a group of workers to be essential and make requisition orders.[705]

629. The Committee of Independent Experts of the ILO has since 1962 been demanding the abolition of Cap. 195A as being contrary to both the ILO Convention for the Abolition of Forced Labour 105/1957, which has been ratified by the Republic of Cyprus, as well as Convention 87/1948 on freedom of association and protection of the right to organize. The Republic of Cyprus, however, following advice by the Attorney-General, observed that Article 10 of the Constitution prohibits compulsory labour except in case of emergency threatening the life or well-being of the inhabitants. Since the provisions of the Essential Works Order of 1943 and the Defence Regulations 79A and 79B can only be applied to the extent that they are not inconsistent with the constitutional provisions, it was opined that there was no need to amend the existing legislation, as conformity with the ILO

703. *International Transport Workers' Federation and Finnish Seamen's Union* v. *Viking Line ABP* and another [2007] ECR I-10779.

704. Case C-341/05, *Laval un Partneri Ltd* v. *Svenska Byggnadsarbetareförbundet* [2007] ECR I-11767, C-438/05, Case C-438/05.

705. See C. Tornaritis, 'The Nature of the Legislation on Essential Services and Works' [1975] 3 *Cyprus Law Tribune*: 9–12 (in Greek).

conventions was effected automatically. The Republic further argued that the only occasion when recourse was made to the Regulations 79A and 79B was in connection with a threatened strike by the employees of the Electricity Authority of Cyprus (EAC) which would have resulted in the discontinuation of the supply of electricity on the island and accordingly the restriction would be consistent with Article 27 of the Constitution.[706]

630. Since 1981 OEB has been suggesting an amendment of the IRC with regard to strikes in essential services so as to provide for mandatory arbitration. The position of the employee trade unions has been that no amendment of the IRC is needed, since in any case dynamic measures in the organizations offering essential services is rare.[707] The right-wing Clerides government had proposed in 1995 the introduction of legislative measures so that strikes in the area of essential services are discouraged; however, the proposal was not accepted by the social partners.[708] Following intense and lengthy debate between the Government, OEB, PEO and SEK, the parties adopted the Agreement on the Procedure for Settlement of Labour Disputes in Essential Services in 2004 which contains provisions relating to the right to strike in essential services.

631. Part IV of the Agreement which refers to the 'minimum service' in essential services is binding on all parties. Both the employers' associations and the employees' trade unions adopt the interpretation given by the ILO to the term of minimum service; accordingly provision may be made for a minimum service with a view to ensuring that the basic needs of the population are met during a strike in essential services. The parties have further agreed that the system of negotiated minimum service shall apply.

632. The parties have agreed to determine by direct negotiations a minimum service in all determined essential services; such minimum service is restricted to services which are strictly necessary to meet the basic needs of the population or the minimum requirements of the service, while maintaining the effectiveness of the pressure exerted by the strike. Determined essential services are defined as all services, works, projects or activities which are necessary for the continuous supply of electricity, supply of water for drinking purposes, supply of telecommunications, safe air control, air transport and port traffic, function of ports, hospitals and prisons, maintenance and reparation of equipment and electrical installations in the National Guard, police and the fire department.

633. In case the parties fail to agree on the determination of the content of minimum service, the dispute is compulsorily referred to a three member arbitration

706. See in detail C. Christodoulou, *A Study of Labour Law in Cyprus* (PhD Wales, 1992): 235–248.
707. See for the exchange of correspondence C. Christodoulou, *A Study of Labour Law in Cyprus* (PhD Wales, 1992): 244–248.
708. See C. Christodoulou, *Handbook of Cypriot Labour Law* (Nicosia: Epifaniou, 2009, in Greek): 139.

committee established by the Minister of Labour, Welfare and Social Insurance following consultation with the parties and from a pre-determined list of 15–30 persons decided by the interested parties. The members of the arbitration committee should be of recognized competence, integrity and prestige and should have a high sense of objectivity and responsibility, as well as wide knowledge and experience in the settlement of industrial disputes, knowledge of the matters pertaining to the dispute and should not have a conflict of interest.

634. The decision of the arbitration committee is mandatory for both parties. Following the determination of the minimum service, the parties set out special committees which are composed of an equal number of representatives from the employers' associations and employees' unions respectively which shall be responsible for monitoring and applying the minimum service and which shall deal with any urgent issues that might arise during a strike or lock-out. However, the adoption of the Agreement has not settled the question of strike in essential services.

635. In 2012 the Civil Aviation Law 213(I)/2002 was amended by Law 12(I)/2012; paragraph 6 of Law 213(I)/02, as amended, prohibits to any Section 4 person, who in accordance with his terms of employment, has an obligation to provide management services of the air traffic flow, to refuse to provide such services, if requested by the Director of the Civil Aviation Department, by invoking the right to strike; the prohibition of the right to refuse to provide services applies, if such refusal would lead to the downgrading of such services below the minimum service limit for the management of air traffic, or might adversely influence public safety. The amendment to Law 213(I)/02 was surprisingly introduced by the leftist Christofias government and was a deviation from the tradition of voluntary regulation of collective labour relations with soft law provisions.

636. The discussion over the introduction of specific legislation to regulate issues which had been the object of agreement between the parties in 2004, in a manner similar to the enactment of Law 12(I)/12, was intensified during the current Anastasiades government; the leader of the governing right-wing party DISY Averof Neophytou has openly supported the introduction of legislation for restricting the right to strike in essential services. In May 2015, the OEB submitted a draft bill to the government for the legislative regulation of strikes in essential services; the OEB argued that the employee trade unions have violated the Agreement by refusing to engage in mandatory arbitrations and as a result the legislative regulation of the issue so that there are binding rules governing it is now deemed necessary.[709] The employee trade unions reacted very negatively to both the OEB and DISY proposals, on the grounds that they deviate from the system of voluntary regulation of labour relations and effectively aim at imposing a new model which is no longer

709. See 'The proposal of OEB about the essential services', OEB 25 May 2015, available at http://www.oeb.org.cy/anakoinoseis/eprotasetesoebgiatisousiodeisyperesies.

based on the goodwill of the parties, but rather amounts to criminalization through the introduction of mandatory provisions.[710]

§2. Statistics

637. The IRC provides that unofficial strikes during a valid collective agreement are discouraged and that, in such a case, the trade union concerned should take all measures necessary to end the strike. In general, the aim of voluntary corporatism prevailing in Cyprus is to limit strikes to an absolute minimum. This has proved to be the case over time, as the number of strikes in Cyprus remains at relatively low levels, although the recent financial crisis has led to a significant increase in strikes in comparison to previous years. This changed a continuous trend of steady decrease in the number of strikes, from 32 in 1994 to between 13–25 strikes per year from 1995 to 2005 (with the glaring exception of 2000 when there were only six strikes), to 10 in 2006, eight strikes in 2007 and 2008 and only four strikes involving no more than 200 workers in 2010. Since then, and as a result of the financial crisis and measures limiting the rights of workers, there has been an escalation of strikes, reaching the highest point in 20 years, with 42 strikes in 2011, 56 in 2012, 31 in 2013 and 43 in 2014. Table 1 presents the statistics during the past 10 years.

Table 1 Strikes

Year	*Work stoppages*	*Workers involved*	*Workdays lost*
2005	25	14,637	15,339
2006	10	25,955	26,898
2007	8	3,396	10,289
2008	8	743	1,034
2009	6	573	1,743
2010	4	200	200
2011	42	26,007	25,305
2012	56	37,542	48,294
2013	31	44,089	60,564
2014	43	23,741	29,653

710. See 'Disagreements about the right to strike' *Phileleftheros* 22 September 2015, available at http://www.oeb.org.cy/anakoinoseis/eprotasetesoebgiatisousiodeisyperesies.

Chapter 6. Settlement of Industrial Disputes and Protection of Vital Needs

§1. Mediation

A. Introduction

638. Contrary to prevailing practice in other fields of law, the Republic of Cyprus has a long tradition of mediation mechanisms in labour law disputes.[711] Industrial relations are a field where the social partners have voluntarily agreed upon dispute resolution mechanisms which are often used in practice. The Labour Relations Service of the Ministry of Labour, Welfare and Social Insurance is responsible for providing mediation assistance by intervening in a dispute after negotiations have reached a deadlock and the two sides (employers-trade unions) have formally requested for the mediation of the Ministry. The Industrial Relations Service mediates approximately 250v300 such cases annually and has succeeded in resolving more than 90 per cent of cases without a strike; the low number of strikes registered in Cyprus confirms that the existing conflict resolution mechanisms enjoy a high degree of effectiveness.[712] Table 2 presents the number of labour disputes to which mediation was provided in the past 10 years:

Table 2 Labour disputes submitted for mediation

Year	*Labour disputes*	*Workers involved*
2005	219	44,665
2006	251	65,564
2007	212	57,858
2008	185	38,174
2009	229	41,871
2010	255	31,677
2011	299	73,495
2012	316	30,962
2013	280	46,191
2014	229	19,197

711. A. Emilianides and X. Xenofontos, 'Mediation in Cyprus', in C. Esplugues, J.L. Iglesias, G. Palao (eds), *Civil and Commercial Mediation in Europe: National Mediation Rules and Procedures* (Cambridge: Intersentia, 2012): 87–95.

712. European Foundation for the Improvement of Living and Working Conditions, *Social Dialogue and Conflict Resolution in Cyprus* (2004), available at http://www.eurofound.europa.eu/pubdocs/2004/46/en/1/ef0446en.pdf.

639. The mediation process is governed by the procedures of the IRC, which provides detailed procedures for dispute resolution in the private and semi-public sectors, with the public sector adhering to a different set of rules. The mediation process governed by the Code is not a mandatory procedure and is not governed by legislation; however, a collective agreement between employers and their employees may expressly provide that any labour law dispute is to be subject to mediation. The aim of such mediation is to assist employers and employees in reaching a mutually acceptable solution, mediation being defined as essentially a structured process whereby the parties to the dispute attempt by themselves, on a voluntary basis, to reach an agreement on the settlement of their dispute with the assistance of the Ministry of Labour, Welfare and Social Insurance acting as mediator.

640. The process of mediation is carried out free of charge by qualified government officials; the process is not in principle confidential and is never carried out at a distance, but rather in the presence of the parties; the parties may request legal advice if they so wish. Mediation takes place in the district offices of the Ministry. Both parties have the opportunity to express their positions and the mediator may at any time request further clarifications, or he may comment on the position of the parties and express his own views on the issue. The mediator may further have private meetings with each party in order to find common ground and a number of meetings may be needed in order to reach consensus. When the mediator submits his proposal to the parties, then either party may accept it, or reject it. The mediator may under no circumstances impose a proposal on the parties.[713]

641. In order to safeguard the non-contentious nature of collective bargaining, section D of the IRC stipulates that before any announcement is made in the press, this will be agreed upon, if possible by both sides, during the process of collective bargaining or the discussion of a dispute. However, the two sides may make public statements which aim at popularizing their claims or official position, insofar as such statements do not refer to the proceedings at specific negotiation meetings. The Ministry of Labour, Welfare and Social Insurance may make a public announcement regarding a dispute in which it mediates, if such a dispute attracts the interest of the public, so long as an announcement is objective and of an informative nature and, where possible, prepared in consultation with the two sides. If, however, the dispute affects public interest, the Minister of Labour, Welfare and Social Insurance may make a public statement without consulting either side.

642. There are two types of industrial relations disputes which the Ministry mediates; these are industrial disputes over interests (concerning the conclusion of a collective agreement, or the renewal of an existing one) and industrial disputes over rights which refer to the interpretation of a collective agreement (grievances). If mediation fails to produce results in disputes over interests, then the unions may

713. See also OEB, *Handbook of Officer of Labour Relations: Settlement of Industrial Disputes, Code of Industrial Relations, Essential Services, Arbitration* (Nicosia, 2015, in Greek): 17–18.

go on strike or employers may lock out their employees. In the case of grievances, however, this is not an option as both parties have agreed not to proceed to strikes, or lock-out for disputes over grievances; in this case, the mediator shall refer the matters to binding arbitration.

B. Mediation over Interests

643. The Code provides that in the case of negotiations for the conclusion of a collective agreement for the first time and where it is established that all possibilities of direct negotiations have been exhausted, both sides, either jointly or separately, may, after the lapse of a reasonable period from the commencement of the negotiations, submit the dispute to the Senior Industrial Relations Officer or the District Labour Officer, as the case may be, for mediation. Such reasonable period should not be shorter than six weeks from the date of receipt of the claims by the employer, and not longer than three months, except where direct negotiations have been carried out in good faith during that period. As regards negotiations for the renewal of a collective agreement, a dispute shall not be submitted to the Ministry for mediation earlier than 21 days from the date of expiration of the existing collective agreement. No dispute over the renewal of an existing collective agreement shall be submitted to the Ministry later than two months from the date of the expiration of the agreement unless negotiations started without delay and have been carried out in good faith beyond that period.

644. Submission of a dispute to mediation by one side implies an obligation of the other side to accept the mediation. The Ministry offers to mediate in a dispute, even where such mediation has not been requested, if it considers it expedient to do so. In such a case acceptance of the offer for mediation by one side implies a similar obligation of the other side. During mediation, the mediator shall assist the parties in reaching a mutually acceptable agreement to their dispute by holding joint and separate meetings with them. The mediator may propose a formulated proposal to the parties, which may then opt to either accept or reject the proposal. The Ministry will make every effort to deal promptly with the disputes and to see that they are settled the soonest possible.

645. If the Ministry cannot achieve a mutually accepted solution to a dispute it shall, at the request of either side, declare the dispute as having reached a deadlock and either side will be free to take any lawful measures in furtherance or support of their claims or interests. Before such measures are taken, 10-days notice should be given to the other side and communicated to the Ministry. The Ministry may not, however, declare a dispute over interests as having reached deadlock before the lapse of at least six weeks from the date of submitting the dispute to the Ministry, unless, in the opinion of the Ministry, no useful purpose is served by further mediation.

C. Mediation over Grievances

646. In grievances over the interpretation or implementation of an existing collective agreement, the grievance should be presented to the employer by the union, in writing, provided that if machinery for the settlement of grievances exists in the undertaking concerned, the procedure envisaged by such machinery should be followed. The representatives of the trade union and employers' association concerned (and/or of OEB) may participate in the discussion of a grievance. The procedure for examining a grievance should be completed within a month at most. Neither party to an industrial dispute shall resort to a strike or lock-out in disputes about grievances It is noted, however, that if an employer or employee, flagrantly violates the provisions of an existing collective agreement, against a recommendation by the Ministry of Labour, Welfare and Social Insurance, the aggrieved party may directly resort to any lawful action, including a strike or lock-out in defence of its interests.

647. Discussion of a grievance between the employer and the trade union may also occur with regard to personal grievances which affect the interpretation and/or implementation of an existing collective agreement. A grievance not settled at the stage of direct negotiations may be submitted for mediation to the Ministry of Labour, Welfare and Social Insurance, in which case the Ministry undertakes to deal with it within a reasonable time and in any case not later than 15 days from the date of submission. If no settlement of the dispute is achieved by the Ministry within 15 days of the date it began dealing with it, the dispute should be submitted to binding arbitration. Grievances over dismissals should be dealt with as expeditiously as possible and the time limits should be halved.

§2. ARBITRATION

648. The IRC provides that where both parties so agree, they may refer all or any of the issues of a dispute over interests to arbitration instead of mediation, at any point in time either before, or after the submission of the dispute to the Ministry. By so doing, they both accept that the decision of the arbitration shall be binding on the parties. A dispute about grievances may be referred to arbitration, instead of mediation if the parties so wish; if a dispute over grievances has been submitted for mediation, and no settlement of the dispute by mediation has been achieved, the dispute is submitted to binding arbitration.

649. If a dispute is submitted to arbitration, the Ministry ensures that a mutually accepted arbitrator is appointed within one week of receiving a request by either side to this effect and assists him in carrying out his task speedily by providing such facilities as may be requested by him, e.g. a conference room, clerical staff and any information deemed necessary. The Ministry further ensures that the arbitrator's award is issued within 15 days of the last arbitration session; in cases concerning dismissals, however, the award should be issued within three days of the last session. Arbitration costs should be shared equally by the two sides; however, the arbitrator may, in consultation with the Ministry, issue special directions on this matter.

650. Whereas arbitration is generally governed in the Republic by the Arbitration Law, Cap. 4, procedures under the Trade Disputes (Conciliation, Arbitration and Inquiry) Law, Cap. 187 are excluded from its ambit under section 33 of Cap. 4. It has been questioned whether the arbitration provided by the IRC is governed by Cap. 4. In an interesting decision, Polys Polyviou who acted as an arbitrator in a dispute over grievances between ETYK and the National Bank of Greece (Cyprus) noted that a dispute over grievances under the IRC was referred to arbitration by the Minister of Labour, Welfare and Social Insurance with specific terms of service for the arbitrator; the 'binding' character of the arbitration does not arise from a legal provision, but rather from the fact that the parties have accepted that a decision in an arbitration under the IRC shall be binding on them. Accordingly, the arbitration procedure under the IRC is governed by its own rules and not by the provisions of Cap. 4.[714]

651. The above view seems convincing, also in light of the fact that the IRC provides that model arbitration rules shall be specified by the Ministry of Labour, Welfare and Social Insurance in cooperation with the parties; the Ministry has not yet specified any such rules. It would therefore seem that whenever a dispute over grievances is referred to arbitration by the Ministry in accordance with the provisions of the IRC, this is not governed by Cap. 4; Cap. 4 anyway provides for arbitration on the basis of an agreement by the parties, whereas arbitration in a dispute over grievances is referred to by the Ministry which appoints the arbitrator, typically with the agreement of the parties, and not by the parties themselves. Thus, in disputes over grievances where the dispute is referred to arbitration by the Ministry, the provisions of Cap. 4 do not apply. However, in disputes over rights where the parties themselves agree voluntarily to refer the dispute to arbitration, the parties may opt for the application of the provisions of Cap. 4 to the arbitration.

652. Whereas however, Cap. 4 does not apply in disputes over grievances under the IRC, it could be argued that Cap. 187 might govern the arbitration in such cases. Cap. 187 provides that the Council of Ministers may refer any labour dispute to arbitration before an arbitration tribunal, following a submission before it by either party to the dispute. A labour dispute is defined in section 2 of Cap. 187 as any dispute between employers and employees, or between employees themselves, which refers to the employment and terms or conditions of employment of any person. Cap. 187 applies with respect to any labour disputes with the exception of persons employed in the military, naval or air services of the Republic, or the police force.

653. The arbitration tribunal is composed of a single arbitrator appointed by the Council of Ministers, who could be assisted by auditors indicated by the parties and appointed by the Council of Ministers. However, the Council of Ministers may also appoint an equal number of arbitrators indicated by the parties, as long as a neutral referee who shall decide in case of disagreement is also appointed. The Council of

---

714. *Industrial dispute between the National Bank of Greece (Cyprus) and ETYK concerning the dismissals of Charis Economides and Renos Stylianou*, decision of 5 December 2008 (in Greek), available at http://www.etyk.org.cy/dnn5/trapezikos/2008/6/04-23.pdf.

Ministers pays the fees of the arbitrator(s). If any negotiation, or mediation procedures are pending, the Council of Ministers shall not refer the dispute to arbitration, unless the mediation or negotiations have failed and unless both parties to the dispute so agree.

654. The decision of the arbitration tribunal should be consistent with existing legislation and is submitted to the Council of Ministers, which may publish such decision. If any questions are raised with regard to the proper interpretation of the decision, the Council of Ministers, as well as either party to the dispute, may apply before the arbitration tribunal for a supplementary decision, which is considered as an integral part of the initial procedure. If no procedural regulations have been enacted, as is the case, the arbitration tribunal may set its own procedure.

655. In disputes over grievances, the Minister refers the dispute to arbitration in a manner which is similar to the machinery provided for in Cap. 187. It could therefore be argued that Cap. 187 may provide the legal basis for the power of the Minister of Labour, Welfare and Social Insurance to refer to arbitration disputes over grievances, as effectively exercising by delegation the powers of the Council of Ministers in accordance with the provisions of the Delegation of the exercise of Powers arising from legislation, Law 23/1962.

656. It would further seem that the Council of Ministers and by delegation the Minister of Labour, Welfare and Social Insurance may refer a dispute to arbitration under Cap. 187, even in disputes over rights, whenever the mediation procedure has failed to produce results; however, the Minister has so far refrained from using this procedure in such cases, as this might be interpreted as being inconsistent with the IRC.[715] The adoption of the Agreement on the Procedure for Settlement of Labour Disputes in Essential Services in 2004 would further imply that the Ministry is unwilling to use the mechanism of arbitration provided in Cap. 187 in cases of deadlock in disputes over rights and opts to extend voluntary agreements in those cases. In principle the Minister should attempt to refer a dispute over rights to arbitration only in exceptional circumstances, where it is clear that all attempts for mediation have been exhausted and preferably with the agreement of both parties.

§3. Public Inquiry

657. The IRC provides that, if both parties agree, any dispute over interests may be referred to a Board of Inquiry. Neither side shall take industrial action during the course of the inquiry and where either side has taken industrial action prior to the reference of the dispute to a Board of Inquiry, every effort will be made to suspend such action; however, this action may not provide grounds for not conducting the inquiry. Cap. 187 further provides for the power of the Council of Ministers, and by delegation the Minister of Labour, Welfare and Social Insurance, to appoint a Board

715. See also C. Christodoulou, *Handbook of Labour Law* (Nicosia: Epifaniou, 2009, in Greek): 123–124.

of Inquiry for labour disputes, in order to determine the cause of the dispute and promote its settlement. The Board of Inquiry is not bound by rules of evidence; it has full power to require any person to furnish documents, to attend the board and give evidence, to issue interim reports and may set its own procedure.

658. This procedure aims at conducting an objective inquiry of the dispute, inform public opinion and avoid further confrontation between the parties by making particular suggestions as to the causes of the dispute. The procedure of inquiry is rarely used for labour disputes. It was, however, used in 2007 in a highly publicized dispute between ETYK and the National Bank of Greece (Cyprus); a three-member board of inquiry was appointed[716] following the suggestion of the Minister, which was called upon to determine the causes of the dispute and make suggestions for the settlement of the dispute. The board of inquiry met numerous times over a period of five months and heard several witnesses; the unanimous report of the board of inquiry was presented to the Council of Ministers and to the parties concerned.[717]

§4. Protection of Vital Needs

659. An Agreement on the Procedure for Settlement of Labour Disputes in Essential Services was signed on 16/5/2004 between the Ministry of Labour, Welfare and Social Insurance and social partners, i.e. OEB, KEBE, SEK, PEO and DEOK. The Agreement extends the procedures provided for by the IRC. By a decision of the Council of Ministers of 2 November 2005, the Agreement, which originally covered the private and semi-public sectors, was extended so as to also apply to essential services in the public sector. The procedure provided in the Agreement applies in case of deadlock in essential services under the procedures provided by the IRC and refers only to disputes over rights, as in the case of disputes over grievances the IRC provides for mandatory arbitration.

660. Essential services are defined in the Agreement as all services whose interruption would endanger the life, personal safety or health of the whole, or part, of the population. Term 3 of the Agreement provides that in case of negotiations, either for the conclusion of a collective agreement for the first time, or for a renewal of a collective agreement, and if it is ascertained that all possibility for negotiation under the existing procedures for each sector has been exhausted and deadlock is declared, the parties are required to refer, either jointly or separately, their dispute to a three-member arbitration committee by notifying the Minister of Labour, Welfare and Social Insurance.

716. Members of the board of inquiry were: George Stavrinakis appointed by the Minister, Christodoulos Chistodoulou proposed by ETYK and Ioannis Koukiades proposed by the Bank.

717. See e.g. ETYK, 'Unanimous decision, there are agreements which bind the banks, the Directive does not abolish the agreements, there was vindictiveness by the Bank', 21 December 2007, available at http://www.etyk.org.cy/dnn5/egkyklioi/2007/21_12_2007.pdf.

661. Within 15 days from the notification of deadlock, the Minister, following consultation with the parties, appoints suitable persons as members of the committee, out of a predetermined list of 15–30 members which is prepared by the parties; the predetermined list of members shall be valid for a period of two years. The members of the arbitration committee should be of recognized competence, integrity and prestige and should have a high sense of objectivity and responsibility, as well as wide knowledge and experience in the settlement of industrial disputes, knowledge of the matters pertaining to the dispute and not have a conflict of interest.

662. The arbitration committee fully examines the matters of the dispute and may request documents, information and other evidence from the parties and use any means it considers necessary or useful in order to carry out its work. The decision should be issued and notified to the parties within six weeks from the reference of the dispute and published. The decision is not, however, binding for the parties; accordingly, the parties may reply in writing to the Minister within seven days whether they accept the decision and if not, they should provide reasons for their rejection. If the decision is not accepted by either party to the dispute, then any party may proceed to measures (i.e. strike or lock-out), following a written notice of 25 days. Either party may also proceed to measures if the arbitration committee fails to issue a decision within the six-week period. Undeniably, the stipulation that the arbitral award shall not be binding on the parties is a very odd one and defeats the purpose of the Agreement.[718]

718. See also C. Christodoulou, *Handbook of Cypriot Labour Law* (Nicosia: Epifaniou, 2009, in Greek): 148–149.

Selected Bibliography

In Greek

Antoniou, M., *The Law of Termination of Employment in Cyprus* (Nicosia: OEB, 2000).

Antoniou, M., *Social Policy and Occupation: Harmonization of the Cypriot Legislation with the Acquis Communautaire* (Nicosia: OEB, 2002).

Christodoulou, C., *Handbook of Cypriot Labour Law* (Nicosia: Epifaniou, 2009).

Eftychiou, A., 'The Law of Freedom of Trade Unionism' (1988) 22 Cyprus Law Review: 3455–3463

Loizou, A., 'Restriction of the Right to Strike under the Constitution of Cyprus and International Conventions' [1995] 11 *Lysias*: 23–30.

Loizou, A., 'The Working Woman, her Rights to Equality and the Protection of Maternity' (1983) 4 *Cyprus Law Review*: 697–707.

Loucaides, L., 'The Right of Strike and Sympathy or Solidarity Strike' (1984) 5 *Cyprus Law Review*: 831–838.

Nicolaou, E., 'Sexual Harassment in the Workplace', in G. Serghides (ed.), *Property Relations between Spouses and Various Legal Issues* (Nicosia, 2010): 646–655.

Papamiltiades, T., 'Labour Law' *Corpus de Jure Cyprii*, v. II (Nicosia: Cyprus Bar Council, 1988): 265–308.

Prentzas, R., *Freedom of Trade Unionism* (Nicosia: Ermogenis, 1997).

Synodinou, T., *Cypriot Private Law* (Thessaloniki: Sakkoulas, 2014).

Tornaritis, C., 'Sympathy Strike in accordance with the Existing Law in Cyprus' [1969] 4 *Cyprus Law Tribune*: 3–8.

Tornaritis, C., 'Collective Employment Agreement' [1972] 1–2 *Cyprus Law Tribune*: 14–17.

Tornaritis, C., 'The Right of Employers to Lock-Out' [1972] 1–2 *Cyprus Law Tribune*: 18–21.

Tornaritis, C., 'Women and Law, especially in the Republic of Cyprus' [1973] *Cyprus Law Tribune*: 3–8.

Tornaritis, C., 'The Nature of the Legislation on Essential Services and Works' [1975] 3 *Cyprus Law Tribune*: 9–12.

Tornaritis, C., *Gender Equality under the Law* (Nicosia, 1980).

Selected Bibliography

In English

Christodoulou, C., *A Study of Labour Law in Cyprus* (PhD Wales, 1992).

Cronin, J.B., 'International Labour Organization Recommendation 119: Job Security in Cyprus' (1968) 17 ICLQ: 760–772

Ioannou, C., *The Eager Europeanisation of Cypriot Social Policy: When Accession becomes a National Goal* (PhD thesis, Manchester, 2007).

Eliades, T., 'The Termination of Employment Law: A Halting Point over Wrongful Dismissals' [1972] 1–2 *Cyprus Law Tribune*: 25–28

Eliades, T., 'The Right to Strike' [1970] 2 *Cyprus Law Tribune*: 28–30.

Emilianides, A., 'The Freedom of the Worker to Organize in Cyprus', *Die Koalitionsfreiheit des Arbeitnehmers/ The Freedom of the Worker to Organize* (Berlin, New York, 1980): 1057–1069.

Emilianides, A., 'Age Discrimination Law in Cyprus', N. Bokum *et al.* (eds.), *Age Discrimination Law in Europe* (The Hague: Kluwer, 2009): 55–65

Emilianides, A., 'Redundancy Law in Cyprus', M. van Kempen *et al.* (eds.), *Redundancy Law in Europe* (The Hague: Kluwer, 2008) 29–37.

Flourentzos, S., 'Cyprus', in Anders Etgen Reitz (ed.), *Labor and Employment Law in the New EU Member and Candidate States* (American Bar Association, 2007): 85–106.

Georgiou, G., 'Cyprus', *Individual Dismissals across Europe* (Brussels: Ius Laboris, 2008): 51–58.

Georgiou, G., A. Praxitelous and N. Aplikiotou, 'Cyprus', *The Employment Law Review* (2nd edn, Business Research, London, 2011): 99–112.

Hadjiprodromou, Y., and G. Georgiou, 'Cyprus', *Collective Redundancies Guide* (Brussels: Ius Laboris, 2009): 35–44.

Ioannou, N., 'Social Policy and Employment', in C. Stefanou (ed.), *Cyprus and the EU: The Road to Accession* (Aldershot: Ashgate, 2005): 199–219.

Ktenas, N., 'Employment', *Introduction to Cyprus Law* (3rd edn, Andreas Neocleous & Co LLC, Limassol, 2010): 991–1016.

Ktenas, N., 'Cyprus', in E. Clifton-Day *et al.* (eds.), *Employment Law in Europe* (London: Bloomsbury, 2009).

Loucaides, L. 'Legal Protection of the Freedom of Trade Unionism in Cyprus' (1986) 15 *Cyprus Law Review*: 2346–2359.

Nedjati, Z., 'Collective Bargaining and Collective Agreements' [1973] 2-3 *Κυπριακό Νομικό Βήμα* : 35–38.

Slocum, John H., *The Development of Labour Relations in Cyprus* (PIO, Nicosia, 1972).

Tornaritis, C., 'The Social and Economic Rights under the Law of the Republic of Cyprus', *Mélanges Bridel* (Lausanne, 1968): 533–556.

Index

The numbers given are paragraph numbers

Index

www.ingramcontent.com/pod-product-compliance
Lightning Source LLC
Chambersburg PA
CBHW071435230926
51846CB00001B/240
* 9 7 8 9 0 4 1 1 8 6 6 0 7 *